Diagnostic Literacy Assessments and Instructional Strategies

A Literacy Specialist's Resource

Stephanie L. McAndrews

INTERNATIONAL
Reading Association
800 BARKSDALE ROAD, PO BOX 8139
NEWARK, DE 19714-8139, USA
www.reading.org

The International Reading Association attempts, through its publications, to provide a forum for a wide spectrum of opinions on reading. This policy permits divergent viewpoints without implying the endorsement of the Association.

Executive Editor, Books   Corinne M. Mooney
Developmental Editor   Charlene M. Nichols
Developmental Editor   Tori Mello Bachman
Developmental Editor   Stacey Lynn Reid
Editorial Production Manager   Shannon T. Fortner
Design and Composition Manager   Anette Schuetz
Project Editors   Tori Mello Bachman and Christina Lambert
Cover   Lise Holliker Dykes; Art, PhotoDisc and iStockPhoto

The publisher would appreciate notification where errors occur so that they may be corrected in subsequent printings and/or editions.

Library of Congress Cataloging-in-Publication Data
McAndrews, Stephanie L.
   Diagnostic literacy assessments and instructional strategies : a literacy specialists resource / Stephanie L. McAndrews.
      p. cm.
   Includes bibliographical references and index.
   ISBN 978-0-87207-608-2
   1. Language arts--Ability testing. 2. Literacy--Evaluation. 3. Lesson planning. I. Title.
   LB1576.M39713 2008
   372.6'044--dc22
                                                                                                2008019084

I dedicate this book to my loving husband, Peter, and my daughters, Laura and Katherine, for their enduring patience and encouragement.

This book is written in fond memory of my friend and University of Arizona advisor John Michael Bradley. As a result of his guidance and support throughout my college career, I was able to carry on his passion for reading by designing my own literacy program and clinic. Now I can empower literacy specialist candidates to make informed decisions that have a positive impact on the lives of the children and teachers they touch.

CONTENTS

CHAPTER 4

Oral Reading and Fluency

CHAPTER 5

Reading and Listening Comprehension

ABOUT THE AUTHOR

Stephanie L. McAndrews is an associate professor and the literacy program director at Southern Illinois University Edwardsville. She teaches graduate and undergraduate courses in literacy, including Diagnostic and Assessment of Literacy; Emergent, Middle Level, and Content Area Literacy; and Organization and Administration of Literacy Programs. She has developed the Master of Science in Literacy Education degree, the Post-Master's Literacy Specialist Program, and the Cougar Literacy Clinic, where graduate students assess, analyze, and tutor students in grades 1–12 in reading and writing. Stephanie earned her BS degree in Elementary Education as well as her MA and PhD degrees in Language, Reading, and Culture from the University of Arizona. In addition, she is an experienced classroom teacher, reading specialist, and Reading Recovery teacher.

Stephanie is actively involved in the field of literacy. She is the president of the College Instructors of Reading Professionals Special Interest Group, the past president of the Lewis and Clark Reading Council, on the board of the Illinois Reading Council, and an active member of the International Reading Association and the National Reading Conference. She has published a book chapter and articles in the *Illinois Reading Council Journal* and the *Missouri Reader*. She has presented at local, state, national, and international conferences throughout the United States as well as in England and Costa Rica. She helped develop the *Early Reading Support Kit and Handbook* for the Illinois State Board of Education that was distributed to reading specialists throughout the state, evaluated primary-grade literacy assessments, and piloted the statewide Illinois Snapshot of Early Literacy Assessment. In addition, she is a literacy consultant to school districts in Illinois and Missouri. Her primary goal is to enhance the literacy development of prekindergarten through grade 12 students by cultivating literacy leaders who are knowledgeable about the literacy processes and who can make informed instructional and programmatic decisions.

Author Information for Correspondence
Please feel free to contact the author with comments and questions about this book. Stephanie's e-mail address is smcandr@siue.edu.

PREFACE

*D*iagnostic Literacy Assessments and Instructional Strategies: A Literacy Specialist's Resource has been written for the literacy specialist or reading coach who works with educators and students to support students' language, reading, and writing development. Attaining such a position is generally a result of advanced education and certification as either a literacy specialist or a reading specialist. Because the person in this position often supports development in reading, language, and writing, throughout this book the position will be referred to as a *literacy specialist.*

A position statement from the International Reading Association (IRA; 2000) recommends that the roles of the literacy specialist include instruction, assessment, and leadership. This is echoed by Bean (2004), who contends that the role of the specialist is not only teaching students to read but also providing leadership for the classroom, school, and community. Bean defines these roles as follows:

- Instruction: The reading specialist supports classroom teaching and works collaboratively to implement a quality reading program.

- Assessment: The reading specialist evaluates the literacy program in general and can assess the reading strengths and needs of students and communicate these to classroom teachers, parents, and specialized personnel such as psychologists, special educators, or speech-language pathologists.

- Leadership: The reading specialist is a resource to other educators, parents, and the community.

This expanded role includes the collaboration of the literacy specialist, classroom teachers, special education teachers, and speech-language pathologists to enhance each student's literacy development. Therefore, the assessments and strategies included in this book are not just for the literacy specialist to use with students—they can be modeled or used as a resource for all professionals who work with students, including classroom teachers. After the data from the initial and ongoing assessments are analyzed and evaluated, instruction can be planned that addresses the strengths and needs of each student by using specific strategies to help the student learn more about the reading and writing process.

How Was This Resource Developed?

This resource is based on current research of effective literacy practices, my years of piloting these practices, and my experiences as a classroom teacher, reading specialist, Reading Recovery teacher, literacy consultant, and university literacy professor. These experiences have provided ongoing insight on the complex decision-making process involved in supporting a student's language, reading, and writing development. As a reflective practitioner, I have analyzed, adapted, and created numerous literacy assessments and instructional strategies. The initial assessments and strategies were part of a six-year longitudinal study of the effectiveness of my instruction and student learning while I was a reading specialist and doctoral student in the literacy clinic at the University of Arizona (McAndrews, 1999). As a literacy professor, I began organizing language, reading, and writing assessments and strategies into annually adapted course packets. Each of the assessments and strategies have been researched, piloted, and adapted by me and my graduate students in the Literacy Specialist Program. To expand, adapt, or delete each assessment and strategy according to its usefulness in assessing and enhancing students' literacy learning, I also used feedback from literacy specialist candidates who used these assessments and strategies with students in classrooms and in the university literacy clinic. That course packet grew into what is now this book.

How Is This Resource Organized?

Diagnostic Literacy Assessments and Instructional Strategies incorporates multiple literacy processes that meet the *Standards for Reading Professionals* (IRA, 2003), the IRA and National Council of Teachers of English (NCTE) *Standards for the English Language Arts* (1996), and the findings from the National Reading Panel report (National Institute of Child Health and Human Development [NICHD], 2000). The literacy processes identified as central to reading achievement according to the National Reading Panel are phonemic awareness, phonics, fluency, vocabulary, and comprehension. In addition, IRA has identified that language and writing composition are also important. Although not a literacy process, motivation and attitude significantly affect a student's literacy development, especially in regards to text and material selection, so this topic is also addressed.

Each chapter begins with a section designed to help the reader understand the topic identified in the chapter title. To guide the reader, important words that are defined throughout the text are boldfaced.

Chapter 1 provides a definition of literacy and introduces the literacy processes, then explains the purpose and types of assessment. Diagnostic teaching—using assessment and literacy knowledge to inform the planning, implementation, and evaluation of learning and teaching—is fully explained.

Chapters 2 through 6 each address a different literacy process: Language and Vocabulary Development; Phonological Awareness, Phonics, Word Identification, and Emergent Text Concepts; Oral Reading and Fluency; Reading and Listening Comprehension; and Emergent Writing and Writing Composition. These processes are not discrete concepts but rather each is related, and they are often dependent on one's knowledge of the others.

Each of these chapters is divided into the following subsections: Understanding, Objectives, Assessments, and Strategies. The first section in each chapter provides background information for understanding the specific literacy process. Next is a listing of the objectives for student learning for each literacy process, followed by selected literacy assessments to identify a student's literacy strengths and needs. For most assessments, the purpose, procedure and analysis, a full or partial example to help you understand the assessment and instructional implications more fully, and example with analysis are included. Occasionally, suggestions for adaptions are provided. The assessment data can then be used by the literacy specialist to develop instructional objectives and by the student to develop personal literacy goals.

The final section of each of these chapters provides specific literacy strategies that literacy specialists and classroom teachers can model and students can use to develop literacy, independent problem-solving abilities, and desire for lifelong learning. According to *The Literacy Dictionary: The Vocabulary of Reading and Writing* (Harris & Hodges, 1995), strategies are plans to improve one's performance in learning. These literacy strategies can be used for self-assessment as well as ongoing assessment of a student's learning.

Although some of the strategies were developed or adapted by me, the majority came from conferences, professional development resources, published texts, and my interactions with practicing professionals. Every effort was made to credit the source for each strategy. The assessments and instructional strategies have been selected on the basis of my piloting them during instruction in literacy clinics, resource rooms, classrooms, and tutoring sessions, beginning in 1990, as well as current teachers and literacy specialists using them and providing me with feedback. These strategies were found to be beneficial not only for students who had reading and writing difficulties but also for the typically developing students as well.

It should be noted that the assessments and strategies are organized in each chapter in the order in which you most likely would want to administer or teach them. This is not meant to be a prescriptive order; the order in which you administer the assessments or teach the strategies depends on the needs of your students. Not all students will get all assessments, but if you are unsure of the student's skills or needs, give the first assessment first. Also, although the assessments are intended to be administered individually you can teach the strategies to students individually, in small groups, or as a class. Also, the grade levels listed with each strategy indicate developmental levels. Therefore, students who are at a higher grade level but lower developmental level should use strategies at the developmental level.

Chapter 7 focuses on helping students to develop positive attitudes and motivation toward literacy. This chapter is important because literacy specialists and teachers can provide students with a variety of strategies for reading and writing, but if the students are not motivated and have a poor attitude toward learning, any literacy strategy will have a limited effect. This chapter provides a variety of assessments, such as interviews and surveys, and strategies designed to identify a student's attitude and motivation toward reading and writing, as well as strategies to enhance the student's attitude and motivation.

Reproducible copies of the assessments and strategy tools are available in the Appendix. It is important to note that not all assessments or all strategies are appropriate for every student. The decisions should be made on the basis of the literacy specialist having foundational knowledge of literacy theory and development, the background knowledge and interests of the learner, and the complexity of the text or literacy task. It is the goal of *Diagnostic Literacy Assessments and Instructional Strategies* to provide the literacy specialist or other educator with a range of assessments and instructional strategies that can be carefully selected to meet the literacy needs of individual students to help them become lifelong readers, writers, and learners. As a literacy leader, the literacy specialist can use this book to support teachers and paraprofessionals in selecting and analyzing appropriate assessments and instructional strategies.

Acknowledgments

This book is a result of my collaboration with many colleagues and teaching professionals. I especially appreciate my sister-in-law and colleague Cindy L. McAndrews for providing graphic organizers, feedback, and support. I want to thank all the teachers and university students at Southern Illinois University Edwardsville who piloted the assessments, taught reading and writing lessons, collected student samples, and gave helpful feedback. I also want to thank my friends and colleagues from the University of Arizona: John Bradley, Ken Goodman, Patty Anders, and Carolyn Carter. Their support, wisdom, and love of literacy continue to inspire me to this day.

LIST OF ASSESSMENTS AND STRATEGIES

Chapter 4

Chapter 5

An Introduction to Literacy Assessment and Instruction

Understanding Literacy

Literacy, as organized in this text, includes multiple integrated processes such as language and vocabulary development; phonological awareness, phonics, word identification, and emergent text concepts; oral reading and fluency; reading and listening comprehension; and emergent writing and writing composition (see Figure 1.1). While the assessment and development of each of these processes is described in separate chapters, it is important to note that these are not discrete processes but are interrelated and dependent on the knowledge of the other processes. Language development, both in and out of school, plays an important role in the comprehension of reading as well as the composition of writing, and therefore language and vocabulary are the first processes that are addressed. According to Goodman (1968), **reading** is an interaction between the reader and written language, through which the reader attempts to reconstruct the writer's message; Routman (1992) adds that the reader also connects the writer's message with his or her background knowledge. The reading and writing processes integrate graphophonics (letter-sound relationships), syntax (grammar and structure of sentences), semantics (meaning of the text), and background knowledge and experience in order to comprehend or compose a text. Throughout this book, the term *text* refers to any written communication form including books, brochures, magazines, newspapers, environmental print, electronic information, and so forth. One of the goals of this book is to help students develop their metacognition, or awareness and knowledge of their mental processes, in order to monitor, regulate, and direct them while communicating, comprehending, and composing text.

As a literacy specialist, it is your responsibility to support the literacy development of all students in the school, either directly or by working with classroom teachers and other professionals. Some students are able to develop their language, reading, and writing processes with minimum modifications of materials, strategies, or extended time. Other students, however, need additional support from you, special education teachers, or speech-language pathologists. Whether a student has been diagnosed with a learning disability, it is important to use appropriate assessments to understand how the student processes information and then to select specific strategies to enhance the student's literacy processes.

Understanding Learning Differences and Disabilities

Students who have learning differences or who have been identified as having learning disabilities have increased difficulties in processing information. **Learning disabilities** are

Figure 1.1   Literacy Processes

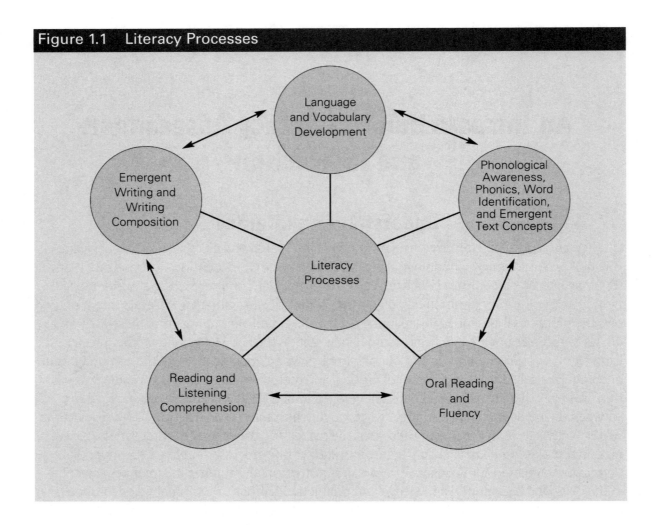

neurologically based conditions that interfere with the acquisition, storage, organization, and use of skills and knowledge. They are identified by deficits in academic functioning and in processing memory, auditory, visual, and linguistic information. Students with a learning disability have normal to above-normal intelligence, and the disability is not caused by emotional disturbance; social or cultural conditions; or a primary visual, hearing, or motor disability. Students should receive comprehensive vision, hearing, and overall physical exams to rule out or make adaptations for physical disabilities.

According to the National Dissemination Center for Children With Disabilities (NICHCY; 2004), there are four stages of information processing used in learning:

1. **Input** is the process of recording in the brain the information that comes from the senses; for literacy, these are predominantly visual and auditory processes.

2. **Integration** is the process of interpreting the input such as sequencing, abstraction, and organization. Students with a sequencing disability might retell a story in an incorrect order, reverse words, or have to start from the beginning of a sequence to determine what comes next, such as the days of the week or the alphabet. Students

who have an abstraction disability have difficulty in inferring meaning. They may read a story yet not be able to generalize from it. They find it difficult to understand homophones, jokes, puns, or idioms. Students with an organization disability find it difficult to make bits of information cohere to concepts and relate to what has been learned previously. They may learn a series of facts without being able to answer general questions that require the application of these facts.

3. **Memory** is the brain's storage for retrieval. Short-term memory retains information briefly while we attend to it or concentrate upon it, such as remembering a phone number long enough to dial it. When information is repeated often enough, it enters long-term memory, where it is stored and can be retrieved later. Students with memory disabilities need many more repetitions than usual to retain information.

4. **Output** of information is achieved through language or motor (muscular) activity. Language disabilities almost always involve what is called *demand* or *responsive language* rather than *spontaneous* or *assertive language*. Motor disabilities can be poor coordination of large muscle groups, called gross motor disabilities, or poor coordination of small muscles, called fine motor disabilities. Students with motor disabilities often write slowly, or their handwriting is unreadable. They may also make frequent spelling, grammar, and punctuation errors.

Learning disabilities can be classified by their effects at one or more of these stages. It is important to remember that all students have individual strengths as well as weaknesses at each stage. Students who have difficulties in literacy may have a diagnosed or undiagnosed learning disability. Traditionally, these students have been identified by having a discrepancy between their IQ score (potential for learning) and their achievement score (the level at which they are performing) using standardized tests; following identification and qualification, an individualized education program is developed. There are several classifications of learning disabilities. Some students are diagnosed with general learning disabilities or nonverbal learning disabilities, while others have specific disabilities. A learning disability cannot be legally identified until students have received specific instruction in each of the processes over a prolonged period of time.

A **visual processing disorder** involves the ability to process visual information, such as the identification and discrimination of letters and words, spatial awareness, and visual memory. Some students have difficulty recognizing the position and shape of what they see. Letters may seem reversed or rotated. These students may skip words, read the same line twice, or skip lines. Those diagnosed with an **auditory processing disorder** may have difficulties with auditory discrimination (distinguishing between similar sounds and words), auditory figure-ground (distinguishing between relevant speech and background sounds), or auditory memory (recalling what words were heard).

More recently, however, the educational focus has been less on labeling students and more on documenting students' specific strengths and needs during authentic reading and writing tasks and providing different levels of instructional intervention for students who have difficulties in literacy processing. As a literacy specialist, you should be an integral member of the literacy team who can provide support to all students, especially those who have literacy processing problems. One of your roles is to directly assess and evaluate students' strengths and needs or to support others in this process.

Understanding Assessment and Evaluation

Assessment is the process of gathering both qualitative and quantitative data about attributes of student learning through tests, observations, work samples and other means. **Evaluation** is the process of interpreting the results of the assessments to judge student learning and the effectiveness of teacher instruction and the school program, as well as to determine the consistency between curriculum and lesson planning, instructional materials and activities, and assessment. Therefore, evaluation is used to make instructional decisions in terms of specified objectives to improve student learning. The student, classroom teacher, literacy specialist, or other professional can do the evaluation, and it should result in some sort of action (Gunning, 2004). For this book, I prefer using a more general definition used by Black and Wiliam (1998) in which assessment refers to all those activities undertaken by teachers and by students, which provide information to be used as feedback to modify the teaching and learning activities in which they are engaged. It is important to understand and communicate to others the purposes of assessment, the frames of reference of assessments, ways to analyze the assessment data, and the implications for instruction based on this data. There are three purposes for assessment: (1) assessment for learning, (2) assessment as learning, and (3) assessment of learning (Cooper, 2006).

Assessment for learning is used to provide verbal or written feedback to students and to inform instruction. It comprises two phases, the diagnostic assessment or preliminary assessment and the formative assessment. **Diagnostic assessments** provide an in-depth analysis of students' specific strengths and needs. The predominantly qualitative data is then used to identify specific objectives to be taught. They are given before and during instruction. An informal reading inventory and a running record with a comprehension assessment are examples of a diagnostic assessment, along with most of the assessments in this book. **Preliminary assessments** are designed to identify students' prior knowledge on a given topic to be taught. These assessments are often developed by the teacher and given to the students prior to instruction. **Formative assessments** occur throughout the learning process during group instruction or independent activities to monitor student learning and are typically informal in nature. Students are usually aware of what they are expected to learn and the criteria for the assessment. Formative assessment can be based on a variety of sources such as objective checklists, portfolios, works in progress, teacher observation, and conversation. Often these assessments examine the students' process of learning, not just product. Assessment used during the process of learning shows the students their strengths and needs and their amount of change or development during the completion of a task. Another form of assessment that really does not fit any category because it does not inform instruction is a **screening assessment**, a quick assessment designed to see if students are basically at, above, or below grade level; however, diagnostic assessments would need to be given to plan for instruction. In the Response to Intervention model, the frequent assessments for progress monitoring are of this type. These tests are easy to give and it is easy to report their scores to the public, yet generally these tests do not provide any qualitative data for specific analysis of students' strengths and needs, which would be required to plan appropriate instruction.

Assessment as learning occurs throughout the learning process and emphasizes self-evaluation, which is the ability of students to observe, analyze, and judge their performance on the basis of criteria and determine how to improve performance (Abromeit, 2001). Students self-assess their learning and take responsibility for moving their thinking forward as in metacognition. In order to support self-evaluation, Ross (1998) suggests that educators involve students in defining the criteria to judge their performance, teach students how to apply the criteria to their own work, give students feedback on their self-evaluations, and help students develop productive goals and action plans. Several of the assessments in this book are specifically designed for peer- and self-evaluation.

Assessment of learning is exemplified by a **summative assessment**, which is given at the conclusion of instruction or at the end of a learning unit to assess the product of what students have learned, evaluating student learning based on standards. Assessment of the product becomes more meaningful for students when they are not only aware of the steps of the process to complete the task, but also when they are aware of evaluation criteria ahead of time.

Standardized Assessments

Standardized assessments are secure tests that are administered to groups for the purposes of measuring academic achievement and comparing students with one another. They are developed, administered, and scored using strict established procedures and guidelines. The tests reveal little about the test takers' thought processes, as the format tends to have more traditional question structures such as multiple choice, and only numeric or quantitative data is reported. Standardized tests can be norm referenced or criterion referenced (see Figure 1.2). They should be evaluated to make sure they are both reliable and valid. **Reliability** is a measure of the consistency and dependability of results if students repeat the test. **Validity** is the degree that test scores appropriately reflect the level of knowledge and skills that a test is designed to measure. Effective tests must also have **content validity**, meaning that they measure skills and strategies in the same way in which they were taught.

Norm-referenced assessments are ones in which students are compared with a representative sample of students who are the same age or same grade. Norm-referenced reporting includes a variety of scores. **Raw scores** are the number correct on each subtest. **Percentile ranks** identify the percentage of students in their peer group (age or grade level) who took the assessment that the student's score surpassed. A **stanine** is a standard score representing a range of scores within an interval in a 9-point scale with a mean of 5 and a standard deviation of 2. **Grade- and age-equivalent scores** provide an estimate of the performance that an average student at a grade or age level is assumed to demonstrate. However, these can be misleading because the scores are not stable and the standard changes by grade or age. For instance, students could be one to two grade levels below their actual grade level and still be in the average range. A **scaled score** is a conversion of students' raw score on a test to a common scale that allows a numerical comparison between students.

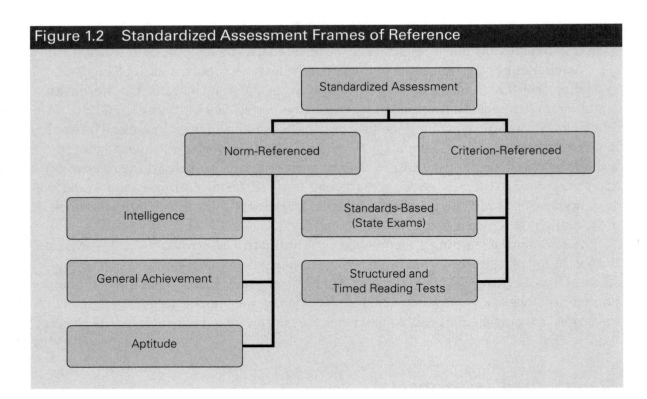

Figure 1.2 Standardized Assessment Frames of Reference

Achievement tests are often used as institutional assessments to provide the school board, school administration, and the general public with evidence of the effectiveness of the school program at the curricular and programmatic levels. Results are measured against the stated missions of a school or specific program (Gunning, 2004). In the past, the primary identification for placement in special education was comparing the results of an intelligence test with a standardized achievement test. Now teachers must demonstrate that a significant amount of intervention was provided prior to testing for or placing a child in special education. The data from these norm-referenced tests can complement other forms of assessment; however, they often only provide general information such as approximate achievement level or expected level of achievement. The data often do not measure reading the way it is taught or used, nor do they assess writing; therefore, this book does not include the administration of norm-referenced tests.

Criterion-referenced assessments are designed to measure student performance against a defined set of learning requirements or expectations. Most criterion-referenced tests measure the knowledge, skills, and abilities as defined in learning standards or curricula developed by state educational agencies or school districts. The test results are reported in terms of what students know or are able to do as compared with the defined criterion and therefore are more useful for making instructional decisions than norm-referenced tests. A weakness of some criterion-referenced tests is that they may have arbitrary criterion for passing or cut-off scores. Another weakness, which is also present in norm-referenced tests, is that criterion-referenced tests may not assess reading skills or strategies in an authentic manner. Some tests use brief passages and multiple-choice questions such as those found in many basal reader tests or technology-based assessments (Gunning, 2004).

Informal Assessments

An **informal assessment** does not adhere to such strict administration guidelines. It often assesses students individually and evaluates students' typical behavior while performing real-world tasks. Although some quantitative data is reported, its usefulness to inform instruction comes from the qualitative and behavioral data. Informal assessments can also be criterion-referenced, growth-referenced, or authentic (see Figure 1.3).

One type of informal criterion-referenced test is an Informal Reading Inventory in which students read complete passages and are evaluated based on analysis of their word accuracy, miscue analysis, retelling, and free response to comprehension questions. This analysis can provide placement levels for reading instruction as well as identify strengths and needs to inform instruction.

Growth-referenced assessments can be any informal assessments that are used to evaluate what students can do in comparison with their prior performance. Examples include portfolios of student work as well as pretests and posttests used to identify the student growth throughout the year and over time.

Authentic assessments, which could also be criterion-referenced if they are measured against a criterion such as a rubric, include tasks that are typical of the kinds of reading or writing that students perform in and out of school (Hiebert, Valencia, & Afflerbach, 1994). They are the least formal method of assessment and emphasize the process of how students learn, rather than just the product of what students learned (Gunning, 2004). Running records (Clay, 1993a), miscue analysis (Goodman, 1987), oral and written retellings, think-aloud protocols, writing composition analysis, observations, anecdotal records, checklists,

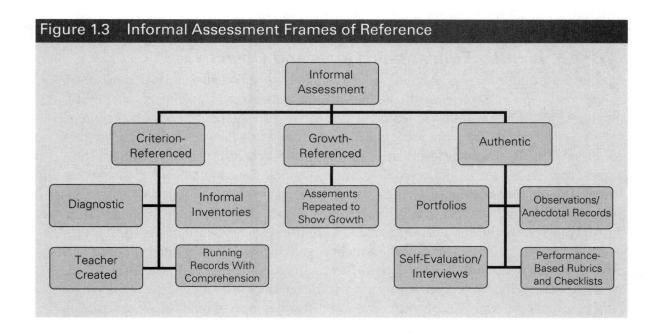

Figure 1.3   Informal Assessment Frames of Reference

rating scales, and rubrics are often used to evaluate learning in authentic assessments. To determine student interests, attitudes, and beliefs, you can use questionnaires and interviews. Self-evaluation, a form of authentic assessment, is critically important because students reflect on their own learning, put together portfolios of their own work, and make goals and plans for future learning. These self-evaluations can include the students using checklists, rubrics, logs, journals, conferences, and portfolios to evaluate their own learning. This book includes a variety of informal assessments because they provide not only ongoing quantitative data, such as reading levels, but also qualitative data on how students process language, reading, and writing. Student self-evaluations can be used to help them develop self-improving strategies to enhance their literacy learning.

Understanding the Cycle of Decision Making for Assessment and Instruction

There are many important decisions that you need to make in order to enhance students' literacy and lifelong learning. Paris et al. (1992) develops phases of decision making for authentic literacy assessments that include identifying dimensions of literacy, identifying attributes of literacy, identifying methods for collecting evidence of literacy proficiency, scoring student work samples, and interpreting and using the data. In a different model, Walker (2004) identifies five roles of diagnostic teachers: reflecting, planning, mediating, enabling, and responding. Expanding upon phases of decision making (Paris et al., 1992) along with the Decision-Making Cycle of Diagnostic Teaching (Walker, 2004), the Reading Recovery lesson framework (Clay, 1993), and the Scaffolded Reading Experience (Graves & Graves, 1994), I developed the cycle of decision making for literacy assessment and instruction (see Figure 1.4). Each phase of the cycle is important so that instruction can be based on assessment of specific objectives and not based on a predetermined sequence in a program.

Phase 1: Identify Educational Goals and Objectives

As educators, our primary goal is to develop our students' knowledge and problem-solving abilities by providing experiences that enhance their higher order thinking. Bloom (1956) developed Bloom's Taxonomy, a method of classification for thinking behaviors that were believed to be important in the processes of learning, with six hierarchical levels of cognitive complexity. The lowest three levels are knowledge, comprehension, and application. The highest three levels are analysis, synthesis, and evaluation. Educational objectives and strategies have been developed on the basis of this taxonomy.

According to Forehand (2005), although this Bloom's Taxonomy has been used over the past 50 years by teachers to encourage students to use higher order thinking, Lorin Anderson, a former student of Bloom, led a new group of cognitive psychologists, curriculum theorists, and instructional researchers to update the taxonomy because the original taxonomy reflected only the type of cognitive process, not the depth of knowledge. The revision by Anderson and Krathwohl (2001) includes several changes in terminology and structure, as

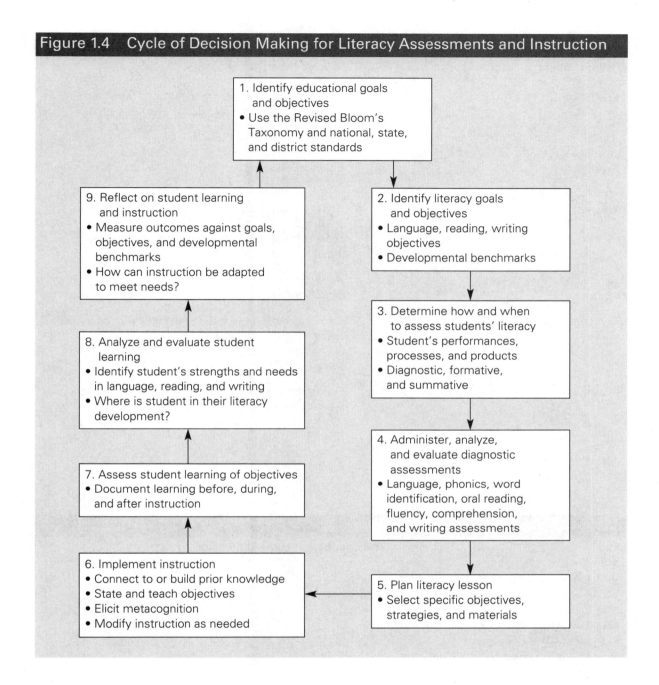

Figure 1.4   Cycle of Decision Making for Literacy Assessments and Instruction

1. Identify educational goals and objectives
   • Use the Revised Bloom's Taxonomy and national, state, and district standards

9. Reflect on student learning and instruction
   • Measure outcomes against goals, objectives, and developmental benchmarks
   • How can instruction be adapted to meet needs?

2. Identify literacy goals and objectives
   • Language, reading, writing objectives
   • Developmental benchmarks

8. Analyze and evaluate student learning
   • Identify student's strengths and needs in language, reading, and writing
   • Where is student in their literacy development?

3. Determine how and when to assess students' literacy
   • Student's performances, processes, and products
   • Diagnostic, formative, and summative

7. Assess student learning of objectives
   • Document learning before, during, and after instruction

4. Administer, analyze, and evaluate diagnostic assessments
   • Language, phonics, word identification, oral reading, fluency, comprehension, and writing assessments

6. Implement instruction
   • Connect to or build prior knowledge
   • State and teach objectives
   • Elicit metacognition
   • Modify instruction as needed

5. Plan literacy lesson
   • Select specific objectives, strategies, and materials

well as a broader use as a tool for planning, instruction, and assessment. The terminology of the six categories was changed from nouns to verbs, the top two levels were switched, and the bottom level was renamed. Table 1.1 shows a comparison of the original and the revised taxonomies along with the new definitions described by Anderson and Krathwohl (2001, pp. 67–68).

Forehand (2005) describes the structural changes, from the original one-dimensional form to the revised two-dimensional form (see Table 1.2). The knowledge dimension examines the kind of knowledge to be learned, while the cognitive process dimension

Table 1.1 Original and Revised Bloom's Taxonomy

Original Bloom's Taxonomy	Revised Bloom's Taxonomy
Evaluation	*Creating*: Putting elements together to form a coherent or functional whole; reorganizing elements into a new pattern or structure through generating, planning, or producing
Synthesis	*Evaluating*: Making judgments on the basis of criteria and standards through checking and critiquing
Analyses	*Analyzing*: Breaking material into constituent parts; determining how the parts relate to each other and to an overall structure or purpose through differentiating, organizing, and attributing
Application	*Applying*: Carrying out or using a procedure through executing, or implementing
Comprehension	*Understanding*: Constructing meaning from oral, written, and graphic messages through interpreting, exemplifying, classifying, summarizing, inferring, comparing, and explaining
Knowledge	*Remembering*: Retrieving, recognizing, and recalling relevant knowledge from long-term memory

Table 1.2 Revised Bloom's Taxonomy

The Knowledge Dimension	The Cognitive Process Dimension					
	Remember	Understand	Apply	Analyze	Evaluate	Create
Factual Knowledge	List	Summarize	Classify	Order	Rank	Combine
Conceptual Knowledge	Describe	Interpret	Experiment	Explain	Assess	Plan
Procedural Knowledge	Tabulate	Predict	Calculate	Differentiate	Conclude	Compose
Metacognitive Knowledge	Appropriate use	Execute	Construct	Achieve	Action	Actualize

Fisher, D. (2007). *Instructional design—The taxonomy table.* Corvallis: Oregon State University Extended Campus. Retrieved March 17, 2007, from oregonstate.edu/instruct/coursedev/models/id/taxonomy/#table (Reprinted with permission).

examines the process used to learn. The knowledge dimension has four levels: factual, conceptual, procedural, and metacognitive. The cognitive process dimension has six levels: remember, understand, apply, analyze, evaluate, and create. In addition, each of the four levels in the knowledge dimension is subdivided into either three or four categories; for example, the factual level is divided into factual knowledge, knowledge of terminology, and knowledge of specific details and elements. The levels in the cognitive process dimension are also subdivided into three to eight categories; for example, the remember level is subdivided into the three categories of remembering, recognizing, and recalling, while the understanding level is divided into eight separate categories. Forehand (2005) explains that the grid containing 24 subcategories is most helpful to teachers in both writing objectives and aligning standards with the curriculum. According to Forehand (2005), the Revised Bloom's Taxonomy table clarifies the fit of each lesson plan's goal or objective. Therefore, using the Revised Bloom's Taxonomy can help you move students through a learning process.

Phase 2: Identify Literacy Goals and Objectives

Prior to planning for instruction, you and the other school professionals need to work together to determine which literacy goals and objectives will be taught and assessed for oral language, reading, and writing. These objectives should be based on predictable patterns of growth, development, and learning and should be written in terms of the cognitive process and knowledge dimensions of the Revised Bloom's Taxonomy (Anderson & Krathwohl, 2001).

The following program goals for oral language, reading, and writing are based on the dimensions of literacy along with their attributes as identified by Paris et al. (1992):

- Engagement with language by orally sharing ideas and responding to ideas of others
- Engagement with text through reading by connecting ideas in text with background knowledge
- Engagement with text through writing by constructive expression of ideas through writing on a variety of topics with different genres and styles
- Knowledge about literacy by understanding purposes and structures of genres and knowing how to use reading and writing strategies
- Orientation to literacy by demonstrating motivation to read, write, and learn independently
- Ownership of literacy by developing independent reading and writing habits and monitoring their own progress
- Collaboration by negotiating the meaning through discussion and cooperation
- Connectedness of the curriculum by providing reading and writing activities that are embedded throughout the school curriculum.
- Connection to literacy made between school and home

In developing literacy goals and objectives, it is important to know and understand the *Standards for the English Language Arts* (IRA & NCTE, 1996). The state or school district standards, which can often be found on state or school district webpages, are also important and may be required by administrators to be included on the teachers' lesson plans. Paris et al. (1992) recommend that you consider these questions: What do students need to know about literacy based on your knowledge of literacy development and expectations at a given grade level? How can students demonstrate the literacy processes? Then, what are the dispositions of a literacy learner?

Next, you and other members of the school literacy team should collaborate and map out the expected goals and objectives for each grade level. As a group, determine the specific objectives for language, vocabulary, phonemic awareness, phonics, word identification, oral reading, fluency, listening and reading comprehension, and writing composition that are appropriate to assess student development. Refer to the Revised Bloom's Taxonomy (Anderson & Krathwohl, 2001) to develop knowledge and cognitive process objectives to evaluate literacy learning. As defined by Paris et al. (1992), these learning objectives for assessment and instruction contain three main parts: (1) the student action, (2) the content, and (3) the standard of performance required to meet the objective. The criteria for the assessment relates to the third part of the objective, the standard of performance. Criteria are developed by analyzing the learning outcomes and identifying the specific characteristics that contribute to the overall assignment; these are the standards by which learning is judged. The student outcomes are measured against the stated purposes and goals, the developmental benchmarks, and the stated learning objectives. (In each of the literacy process chapters in this book, there is a list of general literacy objectives.)

Phase 3: Determine How and When to Assess Students' Literacy

You can obtain evidence of literacy development through multiple criterion-referenced and growth-referenced assessments of the students' performances, processes, and products; examples include diagnostic inventories, observations, anecdotal records, oral reading records, checklists, rating scales, rubrics, work samples, audiotaped and videotaped performances, and self-assessments, such as those in this book. Information on students' literacy proficiency can be obtained through individual or group assessments as well as through information from the students, their family, classroom teachers, classroom assistants, and other professionals.

Evidence of a students' learning should be collected throughout the year and should be organized in the students' literacy learning portfolio. This data could include diagnostic assessments, performance-based checklists and rubrics, self-evaluations, interviews, and observation notes. At the end of each grading period or semester, specific literacy assessments can be readministered in order to evaluate and identify new literacy strengths, improvements, and ongoing needs.

The specific assessment should be selected on the basis of its relation to the stated goals and objectives. When possible, assessments should use authentic oral language, reading, and writing tasks. The assessment should provide evidence of specific literacy strengths and needs and not just general levels and scores. You should use discretion when selecting assessments or literacy experiences so that the most information is gained from the fewest tasks. This allows more time for learning and less time assessing. These tasks should be within or close to the students' zone of proximal development (ZPD), explained later in this chapter. You should have the expectation that the students will be able to complete at least part of the task correctly but that students may not have the prior knowledge necessary to complete the task with 100% accuracy. If the students become too frustrated or can complete the task too easily, the literacy task may need to be stopped and another more appropriate assessment given.

The assessments are organized in the Appendix in the order in which they appear throughout the book. The Assessments and the Related Literacy Processes chart provides a list of the assessments and the Purposes for Assessments chart lists each assessment's purpose and which students would benefit from it. Within each chapter there are directions for how to administer each assessment. Some include cut-off scores that indicate where to stop the assessment and directions for continuing to higher levels.

Phase 4: Administer, Analyze, and Evaluate Diagnostic Assessments

The following general assessment procedures should be used for administering the literacy assessments in this book; for specific instructions see the directions for the individual assessment. First, obtain background information about the student's language and literacy development from the parents, classroom teachers, and all other involved professionals to help guide the selection of assessments. Determine if your students with visual, auditory, or other physical differences need any accommodations. Next, select those assessments that provide the information needed to guide your instruction. Obviously not all assessments need to be administered to every student; the decisions are made on the basis of developmental benchmarks, prior knowledge of your student's literacy development, and an analysis of each assessment after it is administered.

Prepare the environment for assessment. If possible the assessments should be administered individually in a quiet, separate room in order to reduce distractions. You should sit next to and slightly behind the student and hold a clipboard containing all record sheets. In this arrangement your interactions are more conversational, you can more easily observe the student's behaviors, and the student remains focused on the task rather than what you are writing. The student should be able to sit comfortably at the table with his or her feet on the floor; if the table is too tall, a block may be used on which the student can rest his or her feet.

To have more accurate documentation, equip the room with discrete audiovisual equipment. At the minimum, you should have equipment for audiotaping the student's oral responses. Record with a pencil the student's responses and behaviors during assessment, then review the audiotape for additions or corrections. Only the materials needed for the assessments should be placed on the table, including at least two sharpened pencils. If necessary, you could administer some of the silent reading or writing assessments in groups; however, more useful information is obtained if the student is observed individually. In a group situation, it is sometimes beneficial to provide personal workspace dividers to help the students stay focused on their own papers.

You should not attempt to administer all of the assessments during a single session. It is important to watch for and keep anecdotal notes on the behavior of the student and to notice signs of inattentiveness, restlessness, or stress. Allow the student to have water, restroom, or stretch breaks as needed. The length of the assessment periods will vary depending on the particular assessment and the attention span of the student. For elementary students, it is usually best to keep the assessment time to no more than 30–60 minutes per day with breaks. Older students may be able to attend for up to two hours per day with breaks. However, use the student's behavior to guide your decision.

Although there is no specific order in which the assessments must be given, it is recommended that you to start with one of the interest or literacy inventories if you do not know the student well. In doing so, you establish rapport and help the student feel more relaxed in the assessment process. It is beneficial to administer the reading word lists prior to text reading, because the results can help determine which level to begin the text reading. If the assessment session is longer than 30 minutes, you might consider providing a break and interspersing reading and writing assessments to help keep the student more engaged.

After administering each assessment, quickly review the student's responses to determine which assessment to give next. At the end of each assessment session, analyze and evaluate the student's literacy development according to the assessment protocol. For assessments with multiple levels, continue to the next level until the highest instructional level has been reached. Identify the student's strengths and needs for each assessed area of literacy by integrating information within or between assessments. This diagnostic data will be used to make instructional decisions.

Phase 5: Plan Literacy Lessons

In planning literacy lessons, it is necessary to understand **diagnostic teaching**, which is defined as "the process of using assessment and instruction at the same time to identify the instructional modifications that enable readers (and writers) to become independent learners" (Walker, 2004, p. 5). During planning, focus on the whole act of language, reading, and writing. If individual skills and strategies are to be taught, start with a text that contains examples of the element to be taught, read the text or portions of the text, teach the skill or strategy, and then return to the text to use it in context. Then provide opportunities to apply the skill or strategy in new contexts. Get to know your students' background knowledge and coordinate the students' strengths with suitable literacy experiences.

Vygotsky's Zone of Proximal Development. After analyzing the language and literacy assessments and previous instruction, you can make tentative decisions about the selection of appropriate objectives, instructional strategies, and materials at the leading edge of the

Table 1.3 Zone of Proximal Development Chart		
Below the Zone of Proximal Development	**Within the Zone of Proximal Development**	**Above the Zone of Proximal Development**
Independent level: Easy	Instructional level: Just right	Frustration level: Too hard
Student reads or writes on his or her own	Teacher reads or writes with student	Teacher reads to or writes for student

students' ZPD. The ZPD as defined by Vygotsky (1978) is "the distance between the actual developmental level as determined by independent problem solving and the level of potential development as determined through problem solving under adult guidance or in collaboration with more capable peers" (p. 86). In other words, your instruction should be at the level at which the students would be able to do the task with some scaffolding. See the Zone of Proximal Development Chart in Table 1.3 to understand the ZPD.

Cambourne's Model of Literacy Development. One effective model of literacy learning, developed by Cambourne (1988), demonstrates how literacy development occurs. Students are engaged in literacy when they have been immersed in it and have had numerous demonstrations of how texts are constructed and used. Teachers should maintain high but achievable expectations; however, the responsibility of learning remains with the students. Students need numerous opportunities to use their developing literacy processes. You should expect and allow approximations because this is how learning occurs. Finally, students need to receive specific, timely, and constructive feedback. When all of these elements are in place, learners are likely to continue to engage in literacy activities for their own purposes. With Cambourne's (1988) model in mind, there emerge several steps in planning instruction.

First, identify the instructional objectives for student learning on the basis of strengths and needs identified in the assessments and prior instruction, as well as knowledge of literacy development. Literacy objectives should be written in observable and measurable ways and connected to the IRA and NCTE *Standards for the English Language Arts* (1996), state or district standards. The Revised Bloom's Taxonomy (Anderson & Krathwohl, 2001), as shown in Table 1.2 on page 10, is beneficial in identifying verbs for objectives that move students along the continuum of higher order thinking. Although specific objectives are made on the basis of students' needs, it is important to integrate several literacy processes within a lesson.

Second, determine how the objectives will be achieved using carefully selected strategies and instructional materials within the students' ZPD that focus on authentic reading and writing experiences. Your primary goal is to move students toward new levels of independence while comprehending and composing texts that are increasingly complex. One way of accomplishing this goal is through explicit teaching of strategies using the gradual release of responsibility instructional model developed by Fielding and Pearson (1994). There are four steps to this model:

1. Demonstration—The teacher explains and models the strategy.

2. Guided practice—The teacher gradually gives the students more responsibility for completing the task.

3. Independent practice—The teacher provides opportunities for independent practice with specific feedback.

4. Application—The students apply the strategy in real reading (or writing) situations.

Another way of accomplishing this goal is through implicit instruction such as modeling thinking aloud for your students as you read and write text, thereby providing them with the opportunity to become aware of the many strategies and monitoring behaviors that effective readers and writers use. Have the students keep a list of the different types of things you do to help you understand or compose the text, then discuss and post the strategies in the students' own words. Once you model the think-aloud process, guide students in their own think-aloud process.

Whatever strategy and instructional model you choose, you should anticipate your students' responses and preplan adaptations for different learning styles and interests. However, you also need to adapt your lessons during teaching to meet the needs of individuals. These modifications should be recorded for future use.

In addition, select appropriate reading and writing materials on the basis of students' instructional level and interest so that with scaffolded instruction, students will be successful. Although the students should also be allowed to provide input on text selection, to extend their learning they should read and write texts from a variety of genres, including fiction, nonfiction, classic, and contemporary. You should consider incorporating technology to better equip them in using other media. The texts can also be correlated with content area learning standards. You should analyze text characteristics prior to assigning reading and plan how you are going to introduce the text, provide background knowledge, and connect the text with your students' prior knowledge. (See Chapter 7 for strategies for selecting and analyzing texts.)

Next, determine the context of instruction, such as where and in what format your instruction will take place. What part of the instruction is individual, paired, small group, or whole group? It is suggested that you provide individual instruction or flexible grouping on the basis of the instructional objectives for each student.

Finally, decide how to assess the students' learning for each of the objectives. You should record details on student performance and document the evaluation of each area. You and the students should discuss and reflect on specific strengths and needs. Not all areas of literacy need to be included in every lesson; however, it is beneficial for each lesson to include authentic reading and writing experiences.

Fountas and Pinnell's Literacy Frameworks. Effective instruction comes from careful planning of the entire literacy program. Fountas and Pinnell developed literacy frameworks for grades K–2 and for grades 3–6 as tools for designing and managing the instructional program. For the primary grades, Fountas and Pinnell (1996) developed reading and writing workshops. The reading workshop consists of four elements: reading aloud, shared reading, guided reading and independent reading. The elements in the writing workshop include shared writing, interactive writing, guided writing or writing workshop, and independent writing. It should be noted that "the elements are not fixed and separate, and the activity in the classroom moves smoothly around them" (Fountas & Pinnell, 1996, p. 25).

For grades 3–6, Fountas and Pinnell (2001) developed a three-block framework: language and word study, reading workshop, and writing workshop. Language and word study includes shared language or literacy, interactive edit, handwriting, word study, modeled or shared reading and writing, and interactive read-aloud. The elements of the reading workshop are independent reading, guided reading, and literature study. The writing workshop includes independent writing, guided writing, and investigations.

The Example Literacy Lesson Plan Format (see Appendix) provides a guide for planning specific lessons and documenting student learning. You can use this lesson plan to teach students or to support classroom teachers in their teaching of either individual or group instruction. The elements in the lesson plan include the objectives, materials, procedures, assessment, evaluation, and reflection. Although not every element may be present in every lesson, you need to make informed decisions about what you are going to teach and why you are going to teach it. This comprehensive lesson plan is very detailed in order to guide you in your thinking process to make informed instructional decisions. Initially, it is important to write down everything; eventually, you will make decisions about what essential elements are needed and what needs to be written down. However, the objectives and the evaluation of student learning should always be documented.

Phase 6: Implement Instruction

When implementing instruction, you should reflect on your teaching before, during, and after the reading event. You should identify why you teach as you do. You should consider and select instructional alternatives while anticipating the consequences of your decisions. Provide instruction that is meaningful and that emphasizes success. Focus on what students can do rather than looking for causes of disabilities.

Mediate students' learning by scaffolding your instruction. **Scaffolding**, provided within students' ZPD, is "a process that enables a student or novice to solve a problem, carry out a task, or achieve a goal which would be beyond his (or her) unassisted efforts" (Wood, Bruner, & Ross, 1976, p. 90). Adjustments should be made in the type and amount of support or scaffolding that you provide in order for students to be successful. Encourage active reading and problem solving. Assess during instruction because assessment is continuous as students learn. Adjust instruction while teaching to ensure successful learning, and do not wait until the lesson is over. Make instructional decisions on the basis of students' ability to construct meaning or compose writing by using information from texts and information that the students already know. According to Clay (1993b), this challenging, scaffolded instruction enables students to develop a self-extending system, whereby they use multiple techniques and strategies while problem solving.

You enable your students to be independent learners by providing them with the resources to understand themselves as readers, thinkers, and problem solvers. Elicit metacognition by first verbalizing your own thinking during the reading and writing process and then guiding your students in doing the same. Select strategies that will facilitate learning in the most efficient way for the students. Build your students' independence by developing their concepts as oral communicators, readers, and writers. Respond to the needs of the individual. Observe the literacy behaviors of each student. Accept individual differences yet expect all students to communicate orally, read, and write.

Phase 7: Assess Student Learning of Objectives

It is important to provide students with clear explanations of what to do, and whenever appropriate, explain the criteria for judging their behavior to enhance their learning. Without this explanation, students may be confused and use time inefficiently when trying to figure out what they are supposed to learn. Both during and at the end of a lesson, it is essential to bring closure to students' learning by using your own assessment or students' self-assessments of learning. Oral, written, or observation assessments can be used, such as oral reading records, retellings, or written reflections. Again, be sure to document students' responses and behaviors.

Phase 8: Analyze and Evaluate Student Learning

Once the assessments have been administered, both the quantitative and qualitative data can be analyzed to provide specific information about the students' strengths and needs in their language, reading, and writing processing. Many of the assessments can help identify the independent, instructional, and frustration levels of students' reading and writing. Because there are many factors, including background knowledge, which affect students' functioning level, grade levels can only be approximate. In addition, an analysis can identify strategies that students use or neglect while problem solving. This information is often even more important when planning which strategies or concepts to teach. Other assessments, such as observations, work samples, checklists, or rubrics, provide additional information about how students perform during authentic oral language, reading, and writing tasks. Narrative comments and quantitative scores based on the objectives of literacy can be documented and evaluated. The following are examples of literacy questions adapted from Gunning (2004) that you could ask of your teaching or others' teaching to help plan, revise, and improve the literacy programs and instruction:

- Where are the students in their language, reading, and writing development?
- At what grade level are the students reading and writing?
- Is the reading or writing at the independent, instructional, or frustration level?
- How adequate are the students' listening, reading, and writing vocabularies?
- What comprehension and word analysis strategies do the students use?
- Do the students know how to study?
- What are students' interests and attitudes toward reading or writing?
- Do students enjoy reading or writing a variety of genres?
- Do students read and write on their own?
- What kinds of writing tasks have students attempted?
- Are students' reading and writing improving?
- What strengths and needs do the students have in language, reading, and writing?

Phase 9: Reflect on Student Learning and Instruction

Finally, you and the students reflect on the students' learning, the students' affect, and your teaching. You could ask the students questions such as What did you learn? What did I do that helped you learn? What did you like about the lesson? What was difficult for you?

What might help you learn better? If the students omit any of the objectives, talk about them and ask the students to explain what was learned. Reflecting on their own learning helps solidify the students' learning. To increase active engagement during group lessons, have the students share their responses with a partner before selecting a few students to respond to the whole class. It is hoped that when your students go home after school and a family member asks about what they learned in school today, the students will have a specific response. Remind families periodically that this is an important dialogue to have with their child.

For your own reflection of the lesson, answer the following questions: What went well and why? What didn't go well and why? What did I learn about my teaching? How can instruction be adapted to meet the students' needs in the future? Finally, what do the students need to be instructed on next to move along in their literacy development? For additional ideas or to share your concerns, talk with your colleagues and other professionals.

Finally, return to Phase 1 to measure student outcomes against goals, objectives, and developmental benchmarks. The data of student responses should be interpreted and used to show individual growth over time. This data can also be used to compare student, classroom, or program data. In order for this information to be useful to you, Paris et al. (1992) suggest that careful consideration should be made in the selection of methods for recording, organizing, and accessing assessment data. These methods include a process portfolio, in which ongoing assessment documents and data are kept; an archival portfolio, in which a summary of previous assessment data are kept and passed to the next teacher; aggregated records, which are a collection of assessment data from different sources; and electronic storage/retrieval where student data are recorded in an electronic file.

These nine integrated phases in the cycle of literacy assessment and instruction support you in using assessment to inform instruction. The assessment results should then be used to improve opportunities for student learning by connecting assessment data with new instructional goals and objectives, to inform families of students' growth, and to help students monitor and evaluate their own work. Cycling back to Phase 1 allows for the development of new program goals and learning objectives.

Looking Ahead

This introduction to literacy assessment and instruction provided background information on literacy, assessment, and diagnostic instruction, which will serve as a useful foundation as you use this book. It is important to remember that *literacy* is a broad term that encompasses the processes of language, vocabulary, phonemic awareness, phonics, word identification, fluency, reading and listening comprehension, and writing composition. Diagnostic literacy instruction is using assessment to inform instruction. In other words, assessment is not separate from instruction but occurs before, during, and after instruction. When planning for instruction, you must make numerous decisions on the basis of your knowledge of literacy development, strategies, materials, and students' strengths and needs.

CHAPTER

Language and Vocabulary Development

Understanding Language Development

Not only is language learning a social function, it is essential to becoming an effective thinker, reader, and writer. Halliday (1975) notes that one function of language is to help discover meaning from the world around us. This is essential for emergent readers and writers as well as for the continued development of literacy through adulthood. The important relationship between language development and emergent reading is documented by Morrow (2005). Students need an adequate language foundation to begin learning to read, therefore teachers and parents need to talk and read with children in order to help expand their language. Research has shown that early readers come from homes where rich language and a great deal of oral language are used (Dickinson & Tabors, 2001). In addition, early readers demonstrate an awareness of story language and can retell stories using literary conventions such as "Once upon a time" and "They lived happily ever after." When telling stories, early readers also tend to use the delivery and intonation like those of an adult reading aloud (Morrow, 2005), which is related to fluent oral reading. Although language plays an important role in reading comprehension, it is crucial to communicating in general (Johnson, 2001). In reference to teaching intermediate and older students, Fountas and Pinnell (2001) explain that using language orally to discuss, share opinions, question, criticize, describe, and perform is the precursor to sharing thinking in writing.

There are two types of language: (1) **receptive language** is the language that the students understand and (2) **expressive language** is the language that the students produce. Although a speech-language pathologist generally assesses language difficulties, it is often the classroom teacher or literacy specialist who refers students for further evaluation and supports the speech-language pathologist in language instruction. Therefore it is important that the literacy specialist have a foundation in language development. There are three aspects of language: form, content, and use or pragmatics.

Language Form

Language form describes the structure of language and is also concerned with rules for segmenting and combining linguistic symbols in order to produce meaningful utterances. These symbols are typically expressed orally (phonemes), graphically (letters), or manually (signs). The categories of language form are phonology, morphology, and syntax.

Phonology. Phonology involves the study of the **phonemes** of a language (the smallest unit of sound that can change meaning, such as changing /p/ in *pat* to /b/ in *bat*) and the combination of phonemes to build larger units such as syllables and words. Phonology encompasses articulation, pronunciation, and intonation. **Articulation** is the process of producing speech sounds in the mouth and throat and is classified by manner, place, and voice. There are seven places of articulation for English consonants: bilabial (made with both lips in contact), labio-dental (made with contact between the lower lip and upper teeth); lingual-dental (tongue and teeth), lingua-alveolar (tongue against the ridge behind the teeth), lingua-palatal (tongue against the palate or hard roof of the mouth); velar (base of the tongue and the soft back of the mouth), and glottal (unrestricted airflow through the larynx or vocal cords). These places of articulation are cross-referenced with the manner in which the sounds are produced.

The manner of articulation describes how the tongue, lips, vocal chords, and other speech organs are involved in making a sound, primarily consonant sounds. Voicing in articulation refers to whether the sound produced in the vocal chords vibrates or not: /th/ in *then* is voiced, while /th/ in *thin* is voiceless. In English, there are eight manners of articulation, ranging from the greatest amount of constricted airflow to the least amount. There are **stop consonants** in which the airflow is stopped abruptly: /p/, /t/, and /k/ (voiceless) and /b/, /d/, and /g/ (voiced). **Fricative consonants** are partially blocked with turbulent airflow: /f/, /th/ in *thin*, /s/, /sh/, and /h/ (voiceless) and /v/, /th/, /z/, and /zh/ (voiced). **Affricate consonants** start like stops and end like fricatives: /ch/ (voiceless) and /j/ (voiced). Manners with very little obstruction and voiced are approximates and they include **nasals**, as in /m/, /n/, and /ng/, when air flows through the nose, not the mouth; **liquid lateral**, as in /l/, when the tongue touches the teeth and air flows from the side of the tongue, and **liquid rhotic**, as in /r/, where sound is made with the blade of the tongue and air flows from the sides is a vowel-like consonant; and **glides**, as in /w/ and /y/ (voiced) and /hw/ (voiceless), which are also vowel-like consonants with the tongue closer to the roof of the mouth with slight turbulence. The last part of diphthongs, /ow/ and /oi/, are also glides. **Vowels**, on the other hand, have unrestricted airflow, and the lips are retracted. Vowels are categorized by tongue height, tongue advancement, and whether the tongue is tense or lax. Vowels also differ in how much the mouth is open: /ĭ/ (closed), /ĕ/ (half-closed), /ŭ/ (half-open), /aw/ (half open), /ŏ/ (mostly open), and /ă/ (open).

The International Phonetic Alphabet (IPA) is a standardized set of graphic symbols including Latin and Greek symbols for transcribing speech sounds in any language. A speech therapist would use the IPA to transcribe and then classify students' articulation of phonemes. The consonant chart shown in Table 2.1 has been adapted from the International Phonetic Association (2005) to include speech sounds written with the English phonetic spelling so that it is more understandable to professionals other than speech-language pathologists. In this chart you will see the manner, voice, and place of articulation for English consonants. Understanding these elements of articulation is important to the literacy specialist in interpreting students' speech or spelling and when planning subsequent instruction. Developmental spelling assessments give credit for substituting letters that have the same place and manner but differ in voice. For example, students may write *budado* for *potato*. This spelling is not random; rather it represents substituting /b/ for /p/ and /d/ for /t/, which are similar sounding phonemes but should be voiceless, not voiced. You can help students say the

Table 2.1 Consonant Sounds of English

	Manner	Voicing	Place of Articulation						
			Bilabial	Labio-dental	Lingual-dental	Lingua-alveolar	Lingua-palatal	Velar	Glottal
Obstruents	Stop	Voiceless	p			t		k	
		Voiced	b			d		g	
	Fricative	Voiceless		f	th (thin)	s	sh		h
		Voiced		v	th (then)	z	zh		
	Affricate	Voiceless					ch		
		Voiced					j		
Approximates or Sonorants	Nasal	Voiced	m			n		ng	
	Liquid Lateral	Voiced				l			
	Liquid Rhotic	Voiced				r			
	Glide	Voiced	w			y			
		Voiceless					hw		

International Phonetic Association (2005). *The international phonetic alphabet* (Revised). Retrieved March 26, 2008, from www.arts.gla.ac.uk/ipa/ipachart.html

correct sound, feel the vibration difference by putting their hand to their throat as they say these two words, and then write the correct letter.

The vowel sound chart pictured in Table 2.2, also adapted from the IPA categorizes the English vowel sounds, by tongue height, tongue advancement, and whether the tongue is tense or lax. Keywords are provided for each of the vowel phonemes. This chart is important to understand how different vowels are produced. In some regions of the country, /ĕ/ and /ĭ/ often sound similar, such as in *pen* and *pin*. Students who confuse these sounds need to be taught that the difference is in the tongue height and how wide the mouth is open.

Phonology also includes examining the pronunciation of words and intonation. **Pronunciation** is the ability to pronounce words. Students may mispronounce words such as *libary* for *library*, or *pŭskĕtē* for *spaghetti*, and listeners may still understand the word; however if students say *affect* when *effect* is meant, it does have an impact on meaning. **Intonation**, conversely, is the patterns of pitch, stress, and juncture that affect the meaning of words, phrases, and sentences. Pitch is the rise and fall of the voice, such as the difference in the voice for a statement, command, or question. **Stress** is putting more emphasis on a syllable, such as the differences in the word *dessert* and *desert*, or on a word, such as "*I* wouldn't say that" versus

Table 2.2	Vowel Sounds of English				
Vowel Phoneme	Keyword	Tongue Height	Tongue Advancement	Tense/ Lax	Lip Rounding
/ē/	key	high	front	tense	retracted
/ĭ/	win	high-mid	front	lax	retracted
/ā/	rebate	mid	front	tense	retracted
/ĕ/	red	low-mid	front	lax	retracted
/ă/	had	low	front	lax	retracted
/ōō/	moon	high	back	tense	retracted
/ŏŏ/	wood	high-mid	back	lax	retracted
/ō/	okay	mid	back	tense	retracted
/aw/	law	low-mid	back	tense	retracted
/ŏ/	cod	low	back	tense	retracted
ə	about	mid	central	lax	retracted
ŭ	bud	low-mid	central	lax	retracted
/er/	butter	mid	central	lax	retracted
/ir/	bird	mid	central	lax	retracted

Note. Some consonant and vowel phonemes have been adapted from the Latin symbols in the International Phonetic Alphabet (IPA) to help relate sounds to known English graphemes.

"I wouldn't say *that*." **Juncture** is the flow and pauses between the sounds within and between words. This includes appropriately blending sounds or pausing within a word such as *a note* or *an oat*. Juncture also includes taking appropriate pauses between words, for example, "My dad coaches soccer" and "Peter, my dad, coaches soccer."

Once the incorrect speech has been identified, you can assist the students in properly articulating the sounds or pronouncing the words. You can reinforce the correct articulation, pronunciation, or intonation by demonstrating and verbalizing how to make the sound or pause. The students can be given a mirror to practice the correct articulation and use an audiotape to practice the pronunciation or intonation. It is beneficial to place these sounds in the context of words and sentences in the students' vocabulary.

Morphology. **Morphology** of a language is based on minimal units of meaning called **morphemes**. **Free morphemes** may be nouns, pronouns, verbs, adjectives, or prepositions, which are the words that make up our vocabulary. **Bound morphemes** often involve affixes (prefixes, infixes, suffixes) that are attached to free morphemes. Brown's 14 grammatical morphemes (Brown, 1973) are important in understanding and supporting students' language acquisition and vocabulary development. Morphological awareness is related to students' reading of derived words and more generally to their decoding skills. The relations of sounds, spelling, and meaning of morphemes in words is complex, and it influences word reading. Carlisle and Stone (2005) agree with other morphological studies (Nunes, Bryant, & Bindman, 1997; Rubin, Patterson, & Kantor, 1991; Treiman & Cassar, 1996) that explicit instruction be provided in word reading and spelling that links phonological, orthographic (spelling), syntactic, and morphemic elements. Instruction on linking base words and affixes to their meanings helps students analyze unfamiliar words that contain familiar morphemes,

Table 2.3 Examples of Brown's 14 Morphemes

Morpheme	Example
Present progressive (-*ing* with no auxiliary verb)	Mommy driving
In	Ball in cup
On	Doggie on sofa
Regular plural (-*s*)	Kitties eat my ice cream. (forms: /s/, /z/, /ez/)
Irregular past	Came, fell, broke, sat, went
Possessives	Mommy's balloon broke.
Uncontractible copula (verb *to be*)	He is. (response to "Who's sick?")
Articles	I see a kitty. I throw the ball.
Regular past (-*ed*)	Daddy pulled the wagon. (all three sounds: /ed/, /d/, /t/)
Regular third person (-*s*)	Kathy hits. (forms: /s/, /z/, /ez/)
Irregular third person	Does, has
Uncontractible auxiliary	He is. (response to "Who's going home?")
Contractible copula	Man's big. (for "Man is big.")
Contractible auxiliary	Daddy's drinking juice. (for "Daddy is drinking juice.")

therefore expanding their vocabulary. The chart in Table 2.3 shows examples of Brown's 14 morphemes and can be used to identify the presence or absence of these morphemes in students' speech and to plan instruction to support the students' use of these morphemes. Brown (1973) reports that these morphemes are mastered between 19 and 50 months of age, although I have found that some school-age children receiving reading support, including English-language learners (ELL), need specific instruction in using these morphemes correctly.

Syntax. The third aspect of language form is **syntax**, which is based on the grammatical structure of a sentence and describes the rules for combining words into phrases and phrases into meaningful sentences. Syntax includes sentence patterns (noun phrases, verb phrases), sentence transformations (question, negative, passive versus active voice), and embeddings (adding modifiers, compounding, conjoined or embedded clauses). By supporting students in their understanding of the syntax of Standard English, they will be able to use this knowledge to make predictions and comprehend while reading and they will be able to write coherent and complete sentences.

Language Content

Language content is often analyzed by content categories (Bloom & Lahey, 1989). The semantics of a language deals with the vocabulary or meaning of words and the use of content and function words. Table 2.4 identifies, defines, and gives an example of each of the content categories. Bloom and Lahey (1978) report that children are able to communicate these content categories between 10 and 40 months of age, although I have found that many school-age children still have difficulties with them. Table 2.4 also gives an approximate age of when students are able to communicate these categories. Because all of the age ranges are before school age, students who are unable to demonstrate these categories will need support in developing these content categories. This chart can be used to identify the content categories students use or do not use in speech.

Table 2.4 Language Content Categories

Content Category	Age (in Months)	Briefly Defined	Example
Existence	10–18	Object in environment	"Doggie."
Nonexistence	14–30	Object no longer present	"All gone."
Recurrence	20–40	Reference to reappearance	"More milk."
Rejection	24–48	Opposing action or refusal	"No!" "I don't want that."
Denial	24–48	Negates identity, state, or event	"Not a kitty."
Attribution	34–38	Often includes the use of adjective	"Big man."
Possession	34–38	Object is associated with a person	"Mommy's car."
Action	34–38	Refers to movement but not change of location	"Eat cookie."
Locative action	38–40	Movement with change of location	"Come here."
Locative state	38–40	Spatial relationships	"Doggie outside."
State	38–40	Refers to state of affairs: Internal state External state Attributive state Possessive state	"He's tired." "It's cold." "It's broken." "That's mine."
Quantity	38–40	Number or plural	"Two baby." "Birdies."
Notice	40+	Attention to person, object, or event	"I see Mommy."
Dative	40+	Use of indirect object	"Give cookie to me."
Additive	40+	Joining objects, events, or states, often by *and*	"I got a truck and a bear."
Temporal	40+	Reference to time	"It broke yesterday." "I'm gonna get it."
Causal	40+	Cause and effect	"I go 'cuz I got shoes on."
Adversative	40+	Two events/states are in contrast	"I want to go but I can't."
Epistemic	40+	Mental states of affairs (with verbs such as *know, think, remember, wonder*)	"What does this mean?' "I don't know."
Specification	40+	Distinguishing one from another and later involves joining two dependent clauses	"I want that one." "It looks like a fishing thing, and you fish with it."
Communication	40+	Contains communication verbs	"Tell Mommy I want this." "Mommy said not to do this."

Language Use and Pragmatics

Language use and pragmatics examine how people use language to communicate. **Language use** categories are function categories that have been developed to describe the basic intentions a language user has for making an utterance. For example, people may want to make a request, make a statement, comment on information being discussed, regulate their environment, or just maintain communication (Fey, 1986; Halliday, 1975; Lahey & Bloom, 1988). Language use categories can be divided into assertive functions in which a person expresses a request or an assertion and responsive functions in which a person responds to a request or assertion (Fey, 1986). **Spontaneous language** occurs when we initiate speaking, such as selecting the subject, organizing our thoughts, and finding the correct words before opening our mouths. **Demand language** occurs when someone else creates the circumstances in which communication is required. For instance, when a question is asked we must simultaneously organize our thoughts, find the right words, and answer. A child with a language disability may speak normally when initiating conversation but respond hesitantly in demand situations—pausing, asking for the question to be repeated, giving a confused answer, or failing to find the right words.

Pragmatics is examining the language choices people make in social interactions and the effects of these choices on others (Crystal, 1987). This variety in language is called a **register**, which is determined by the social circumstances. Most people use several registers. For example, the way in which students talk with their teachers or principal should be a more formal register in comparison with the way they talk to their friends. This formal register should be taught and reinforced in school so that students will be comfortable using it when talking with employers, business people, and professionals, because the language people choose to use could positively or negatively affect the way they are perceived by others.

Understanding language form, content, and use helps the literacy specialist to be a better observer of language development and be able to adapt instruction to meet the needs of students who have difficulties with their receptive or expressive language. The major aspects of form, content, and use can be added to Tompkins's (2002) four language systems, shown in Table 2.5, which summarizes the phonological, syntactic, semantic, and pragmatic language systems; defines basic terms; and explains how those terms are used in school.

A Note on English-Language Learners

Although this book focuses on native speakers of English, an increasing number of ELLs are entering the U.S. school system. A basic understanding of language acquisition can help teachers to better serve ELLs. According to Young and Hadaway (2006), there are several factors that affect English-language acquisition, including the age at which the child enters the school system; the child's level of first-language literacy; and the similarities of the first language to English in terms of type of script, directionality of text, syntax, phonology, and punctuation.

Young and Hadaway (2006), citing Collier (1995), offer the following suggestions to enhance English-language acquisition:

Table 2.5 Overview of the Four Language Systems

System	Description	Terms	Uses in Grades K–8
Phonological System (Form)	The sound system of English with approximately 44 sounds and 70 graphemes	Phoneme: the smallest unit of sound Grapheme: the written representation of a phoneme using one or more letters	Pronouncing words Detecting regional and other dialects Decoding words when reading Using invented spelling Reading and writing alliterations and onomatopoeia
Syntactic System (Form)	The structural system of English that governs how words are combined into sentences	Syntax: the structure or grammar of a sentence Morpheme: the smallest meaningful unit of language Free Morpheme: a morpheme that can stand alone as a word Bound Morpheme: a morpheme that must be attached to a free morpheme	Word order Adding inflectional endings to words Adding prefixes and suffixes to root words Combining words to form compound words Saying/writing simple, compound, and complex sentences Combining sentences Using capitalization and punctuation to indicate beginnings and ends of sentences
Semantic System (Content)	The meaning system of English that focuses on vocabulary	Semantics: meaning	Learning the meanings of words Learning multiple meanings of words Studying synonyms, antonyms, and homonyms Using a dictionary and thesaurus Reading and writing comparisons (metaphors and similes) and idioms
Pragmatic System (Use)	The system of English that varies language according to social and cultural uses	Function: the purpose for which a person uses language. Standard English: the form used in textbooks and by television newscasters. Nonstandard English: other forms of English	Varying language to fit specific purposes Reading and writing dialogue in dialects Comparing standard and nonstandard forms of English

- Model academic language and make connections between language and content concepts;

- Focus on strategic thinking, problem solving, and comprehension techniques that students can use;

- Emphasize activation of students' prior knowledge, respect for their native language and culture, and ongoing assessment using multiple measures.

Once teachers have a better understanding of their learners in terms of family, cultural, and language background, they can focus their attention on selecting and implementing the most effective instructional strategies. (p. 13)

Objectives for Language Development

Although most objectives are written in terms of what students are able to do, receptive language objectives are difficult to observe, and therefore those objectives are written in terms of what the literacy specialist provides to help students develop receptive language.

To develop receptive language students will do the following:

- Be surrounded with rich language and quality literature

- Associate language with pleasure and enjoyment

- Have opportunities to classify sounds, such as phonemic awareness activities

- Hear a rich supply of new words in context

- Have opportunities to listen and respond

- Have opportunities for following directions

- Be provided Standard English and family language models

To develop expressive language students will do the following:

- Pronounce words correctly

- Articulate speech sounds correctly

- Speak fluently without repetitions, revisions, unusual pauses, or fillers

- Use a variety of long, complex, and compound sentences

- Use formal or Standard English grammar

- Use a wide variety of vocabulary words in the correct context

- Produce statements and questions that are clearly understood

- Respond to request for information, action, and clarification

- Communicate appropriately in a variety of settings and situations

Language Development Assessments

Literacy specialists are valuable in identifying students who may have potential language difficulties, monitoring the progress of those students already identified, and continuing to support their language development. Two oral language assessments are included in this book: the Language Observation Scale (see Appendix) and the Oral Presentation Assessment (see Appendix). The speech-language pathologist can use this information to determine if additional assessments are needed. Transcribed language samples and standardized language assessments are needed to analyze specific elements in a student's expressive or receptive language to plan intervention that develops the student's language proficiency. The Peabody Picture Vocabulary Test-III (PPVT-III) is a test of receptive vocabulary for Standard English and a screening test of verbal ability for 2-year-olds through adults (Williams & Wang, 1997). Literacy specialists can better support a student's language learning if they have a better understanding of student's language form, content, and use. The literacy specialist, the speech-language pathologist, and the classroom teacher work together to assess the student's language development and identify appropriate strategies.

Language Observation Scale

Purpose: This expressive language observation scale was developed using some of the ideas from the Language Development Checklists (Allen & Marotz, 1994) for 3- to 5-year-olds and the Loban Oral Language Scale (Loban, 1961) for elementary-grade children. It is designed to evaluate the language development of students who may exhibit a language delay or language processing disorder (all grades).

Procedure and Analysis: After observing the student over time, circle the number on each of the scales in the following example that best describes the student's communicative behavior. Using a scale of 1–4, *1* indicates almost no evidence of this behavior and communication is significantly interrupted and *4* indicates the student predominantly exhibits the correct behavior with almost no interference with communication. Write down specific examples for areas of need.

Identify the strengths and needs in language areas such as articulation, pronunciation, fluency, sentence complexity, grammar, vocabulary, and assertive and responsive communication. If the student scores a 1 or 2 in any language area or scores a 3 in several areas, the child should be referred to a speech-language pathologist for further language or speech evaluation. Explicit or implicit instruction and modeling should be provided for these areas of need.

Example and Analysis: Language Observation Scale, grade 2

Articulation, Pronunciation, and Fluency	Score			
1. Articulation: Correctly produces speech sounds	1	②	3	4

2. Pronunciation: Correctly pronounces words and does   1   2   ③   4
   not add or delete sounds

3. Linguistic fluency: Speech is fluent and not disrupted   1   ②   3   4
   by repetitions, revisions, unusual pauses, and fillers
   such as *um* or *like*

The student correctly articulates most sounds, except he says the /d/ sound for /th/, (*dis* for *this*) and deletes /s/ with blends such as *tar* for *star*. The deletion of /s/ does affect communication. The student does not pronounce the past tense -*ed*. It should be noted that he also does not spell words with past tense -*ed*. He is generally fluent but sometimes pauses and says *um* when he's figuring out what to say, not only in pressure-induced situations such as talking in front of the class but in casual conversations as well.

Instructional Implications: Refer to speech-language evaluation for the /th/ and /s/ sounds because the student is now in grade 2. The child can work on the /th/ sound by sticking his tongue out between his teeth and the /s/ sound by closing teeth and rapidly putting his tongue to the front of his teeth. Then practice words with /s/ blends (/st/, /sp/). Use kinesthetic strategies such as placing a finger on the wrist and sliding the finger up the arm as the student says each sound, /s-s-t/, stopping at the shoulder for /t/. Read and write words and sentences with /th/ sounds and /s/ blends. Also read and write words with past tense -*ed*. Discuss language fluency concerns with the hesitations and the filler *um* and provide opportunities for the student to plan out what to say prior to being asked to speak out in class. Continue classroom support in these areas.

Oral Presentation Assessment

Purpose: This assessment evaluates oral presentations in terms of language, organization, content, visual media, manner, and audience participation. It can be used by the teacher, by peers, or by the student as a self-assessment (grade 3 and above).

Procedure and Analysis: Provide the assessment in the following example to the student before planning her presentation. Model both positive and negative examples of each element. During the presentation, write down specific observations under each heading and score it. After the presentation, the student completes a self-evaluation and then you give the student specific feedback on the effective elements of the presentation and suggestions for improvement. After the initial assessment, provide constructive feedback and a group discussion can follow. Then, for future presentations, this assessment can be used by peers or for self-assessment.

During the presentation, evaluate each element with a plus sign (+) if all of the descriptors were clearly observed, a checkmark (✓) if most of them were, or a minus sign (−) if they were rarely or never observed.

Example and Analysis: Oral Presentation Assessment, grade 6

Presentation Topic: Country Reports—Cuba

Score	Did the presenter...
	Language:
✓	Use appropriate language for the audience?
+	Convey the information clearly to the audience?
✓	Use appropriate and specific vocabulary?
+	Pronounce words correctly?
+	Use grammatically correct sentences?
−	Use complex and compound sentences with adjectives, adverbs, prepositions, and conjunctions?

The student's language was generally appropriate, grammatically correct, and clearly communicated. However, she referred to the people as *Spanish*, not *Cuban*. She started many of her sentences with the word *Cuba* and used a limited number of different sentence structures.

Instructional Implications: Provide instruction on varying sentence structures. Have the student watch and listen to her videotaped presentation. She or you can write each sentence on a separate line and examine the first word and the sentence structures. Rewrite to vary the structure of the sentences. Discuss the difference in vocabulary between language, ethnicity, and national origin.

Language Development Strategies

Although specific articulation; pronunciation; and syntactic, pragmatic, and semantic language strategies can enhance both the receptive and expressive language of students, language can often be developed through more general strategies or activities. Because language is used to communicate ideas, work on those objectives that significantly interfere with communication first. Do not wait until language objectives are met before working on reading and writing objectives and vice versa. These processes are interrelated and may be enhanced by using them in the context of another process. Students' language is often a reflection of the language they hear in their home and their community. However, school plays an essential role in language development and learning a more formal language register. Johnson (2001) asserts that teachers should provide opportunities for children to engage in many kinds of talking, intentionally plan for oral language development, and provide a classroom context and environment that is conducive to oral development because "oral

language is not only a means to gain understanding but is also a way to display [students']
competence" (Johnson, 2001, pp. 20).

General language development strategies begin by being a good listener during
conversations with students. Respond and show interest in what the students are saying. Ask
the students questions to learn more information or to clarify information. Encourage the
students to speak in complete sentences and to use language to express feelings and needs.
Frequently use and explain the meaning of words with which the students are not familiar in
order to expand their vocabulary. Finally, encourage the students to participate in appropriate
adult and formal English conversations.

Education must be viewed as a social activity in which students are engaged in sharing
ideas with and learning from others, not an individual activity in which teachers attempt to
transmit knowledge and students simply regurgitate that knowledge. Talking and reading with
students are the two most important activities teachers can do to enhance students' language
development. Because talking requires no materials, it can be done not only in the classroom
but also anywhere—in the hall, at lunch, or during activities off school grounds. Students who
have many conversations with adults and peers learn the words and ideas they need to
understand when reading and writing. Reading to students of all ages builds the desire to
read, gives an educational advantage, and develops vocabulary and reading strategies. This
can be an enjoyable experience for both the listener and the reader. Reading aloud to students
develops lifelong readers and learners. (For specific strategies for reading to students refer to
Chapter 5, Reading and Listening Comprehension.) Language can be promoted through
conversations in a variety of situations: structured question-and-answer periods, the use of
aesthetic talk (an emotional response), efferent talk (to inform and persuade), and dramatic
talk (telling stories). The following are more specific strategies for articulation, pronunciation,
syntax, pragmatics, and semantics.

Articulation Strategies

Purpose: To improve the articulation of specific sounds (all grades).

Procedure: Identify the sounds to be worked on and use the consonant and vowel articulation
charts in Tables 2.1 and 2.2 on pages 22 and 23 to determine the manner, place, and voice of
articulation. Using modeling, demonstrate and describe how to articulate the sound or
phoneme. Give students a mirror so they can practice. Provide a picture of a known object that
preferably begins with or contains that sound. Provide examples of the phoneme in the initial
placement in a word, then in the final and medial placements. Whenever possible, have
students practice the articulation of sounds in sentences. It is not necessary for students to be
able to correctly articulate a sound before they are able to differentiate it, so continue
instruction on phonics in context. For more specific strategies, see the speech-language
pathologist.

Pronunciation Strategies

Purpose: To improve the pronunciation of words including word endings (all grades).

Procedure: Identify the words students have difficulties pronouncing. Ask for clarification of the word and model the Standard English pronunciation of each word. When students mispronounce a word, simply say the word correctly in a new or rephrased sentence using a friendly tone. Remember, do not expect perfection! Some pronunciation differences are caused by dialects; therefore, you must first determine if it is important to change the students' pronunciation to Standard English. If the students' pronunciation greatly affects communication, model the pronunciation and ask the students to repeat it in isolation and then in context of a sentence. If the students do not correctly repeat your pronunciation, you can break the word into syllables or phonemes or write the students' phonetic pronunciation above the correct pronunciation. Point out the similarities and differences in the two pronunciations. Then have the students practice saying the word in the context of a sentence.

Syntactic Language Strategies

Purpose: To improve the students' sentence structure in regards to missing parts of speech, incorrect word order, or incorrect inflection such as verb tenses, plurality, possession, or suffixes added to adjectives and adverbs (all grades).

Procedure: Identify the syntactic elements with which the students are having difficulties. When students' natural speech is nonstandard, restate the content of what the students said using standard sentence grammar. Evaluate the students' syntax to determine if it is a repeated pattern and if it is important to correct. Help students by writing down what they said in context and rewriting it using standard formal English. Then have students create a new sentence verbally or in writing using the formal syntactic structure. In the future, point out examples of this structure in text.

Pragmatic Language Strategies

Purpose: To improve the language choices students make during social interaction and the effects of these choices on others (all grades).

Procedure: The teacher demonstrates a formal register and helps students to identify when they are not using a formal register. Explain to the students that there are many different registers in the English language. How students speak at home may be different from how they speak to their grandmother and how they speak with their friends. Students should be taught in school to use a formal register, also referred to as Standard English, so they can be clearly understood by people from a variety of communities. Because students may not be aware of the differences in syntax between their natural speech and Standard English speech, it is important for you to teach it explicitly. Also, because writing is usually a formal form of communication, it is beneficial to use writing to point out differences between Standard English and students' natural English. Write common statements that students say and then help students rewrite it using Standard English.

Semantic Language Strategies

Purpose: To provide opportunities for students to have meaningful communication with others by connecting ideas to themselves, their environment, literature, and media (all grades).

Procedure for Connecting Ideas to Themselves: Ask students to talk about themselves—their family, friends, feelings, likes, and dislikes—during sharing time or show-and-tell. Provide opportunities for make believe or role playing, including pretending about home living, jobs, and travel. Providing puppets, stuffed animals, action figures, and dolls to talk with often encourages reluctant speakers.

Procedure for Connecting Ideas to Their Environment: Ask students to talk about their experiences inside and outside of the school environment. Take students on field trips to the supermarket, post office, bank, zoo, park, museum, library, or hospital, and discuss what they learned. While there, ask for or give explanations of what is happening and what might happen next. Play games such as "I spy with my little eye something _____" (describe it and see if they can find it); or play the alphabet game, in that the students need to come up with adjectives or adverbs for each letter. Ask students questions about the world around them. How, why, and "tell me" questions encourage students to think more deeply and answer with more than one word. Plan experiments, art, music, and food preparation activities that encourage discussion and vocabulary development.

Procedure for Connecting to Literature and Media: Share and discuss ideas and themes from a variety of fiction and nonfiction literature and media. Plan thematic units and provide numerous opportunities for discussion and language development. Gradually increase the complexity of ideas and vocabulary in the texts. Talk about the content, graphics, and connection to other texts. Ask a variety of questions beginning with *who*, *what*, *when*, *how*, and *why*. Ask students what the most important message was. Have students retell the story or text by looking at the pictures or from memory using the language from the text. Students can even make up stories together based on common story structures such as "Once upon a time I met..." or older students can write limericks such as "There once was an old man from...." Provide opportunities for students to express themselves orally through retelling stories, puppetry, drama, songs, finger plays, nursery rhymes, jokes, riddles, or poetry readings. It is also beneficial for students to share a summary of what they learned each day or after each lesson. (For more specific directions for using puppets and giving oral presentations see the following sections.)

Oral Language and Retelling Strategies Using Puppets

Purpose: To enhance oral language development of all ages and connect the development of oral language to reading books; to develop creative expression of characterization, voice inflection, storyline, and so forth; to enhance language development; to improve comprehension skills of main idea, details, sequence, setting, plot, and so forth; to promote cooperative learning strategies; to develop the performance or audience connection; to integrate social studies, science, health, and math with language arts; to involve parents with the learning process through project-based lessons; and to apply art concepts and skills in the student creation of puppets and props (grades K–3).

Procedure for Creating Puppets: There is a variety of puppets and stages available for purchase. Better yet, students can create puppets and stages. Teachers can have puppets that go with specific characters in books or children can use more generic puppets and create their own original dialogue. Puppets can be many sizes and forms: stick puppets, finger and hand puppets, puppets in a cup, big-mouth puppets, sock puppets, and glove puppets. Stuffed animals can even be made into puppets by removing stuffing from their hind ends and sewing in a glove or mitten. Stages can be created using a variety of materials, such as by pinning a sheet across a doorway, making a hedge with green paper scrolled between two dowels, or creating a television stage from a cardboard box.

Procedure for Retelling: Puppets can be used to retell a written or oral story or to act out a favorite part. When you demonstrate reading with a puppet, read the story with expression, pretending that the puppet is talking. Familiar stories could be revised or students could create their own story and act it out with puppets.

Procedure for Using a Story Map: Fill in Characters, Setting, Problem, Event 1, Event 2, Event 3, and Solution on a story map. Make puppets (finger, hand, or stick) of the main characters then ask students to act out the story with puppets. Adaptations include creating a new story with the same characters and acting out the new story for the class or families.

Language Development Through Oral Presentations

Purpose: To develop an effective oral presentation with the six major elements of language, organization, content, manner, visual media, and audience participation in order to share information with their peers (grade 3 and above).

Procedure: Provide opportunities for students to express themselves through oral presentations on a topic they are familiar with or have researched. A familiar topic would include family stories, a favorite book, or a favorite activity. Students could also research science, social studies, math, literature, arts, or sports topics. Discuss each of the following elements with the students: language, organization, content, manner, visual media, and audience participation using the Oral Presentation Assessment (see Appendix). Provide students with both appropriate and inappropriate examples of each element of language, such as the following:

Language—Use appropriate language for the audience. Convey information clearly to the audience. Use formal grammar structures. Questions to consider include Who is my target audience? and What do they already know about the subject?

Organization—It is important to have a clear structure so that your audience can understand the information easily. Include an introduction that captures the interest of the audience and tells why they would want to know about your topic. Tell the audience exactly what you want to say, say it, and then summarize the main ideas of what you said. Leave enough time for questions.

Content—In a 10-minute presentation you should keep to approximately three main ideas; for example, The background of the family and the historical period; the key events; and the effects, memories, and reflections of the events.

Manner—Practice the presentation in front of a mirror until you are comfortable with the material and are able to speak clearly, audibly, and at an understandable pace. Practice correctly pronouncing difficult words. Use notes with major headings, keywords, and a few choice sentences. Try to maintain eye contact with the audience, looking throughout the room, not just at one or two people. Also be aware of and avoid nervous gestures.

Visual media—It is helpful to present visual material that is relevant and enhances the content. Consider showing a computer presentation, web links, transparencies, video, photographs, slides, charts, or objects such as clothing or family treasures. Be sure to present the visuals at the appropriate time when you talk about them.

Audience participation—Provide an opportunity for the audience to interact. This can be done by asking or answering questions during or after the presentation. It is important to allow time at the end for the audience to ask you questions.

Feedback is important to enhancing oral presentation skills. Use the five major elements to give feedback using a peer group evaluation such in as the Oral Presentation Assessment detailed earlier in this chapter.

Strategies for articulation, pronunciation, syntax, pragmatics, and semantics enhance language development. Additional strategies for using text to enhance language and comprehension are described in Chapter 5, Reading and Listening Comprehension. Strategies for developing vocabulary, which are closely related to semantic strategies, are described in the next section.

Understanding Vocabulary Development

One aspect of language is vocabulary development. Learning vocabulary is a generative process going from the known to the unknown, from simple to complex, and from the literal to the metaphorical. According to Blachowicz and Fisher (2006), there are two dimensions of vocabulary knowledge: depth and breadth. **Vocabulary depth** is how much you know about the word, such as whether you recognize the word, can use the word, and can define the word. **Vocabulary breadth** is how the word is connected to other words, for example: heart, lungs, and stomach are all organs in the body.

Nilsen and Nilsen (2004) describe two kinds of words: limited (closed) and infinite (ever-expanding). **Limited words** are the most common function words such as conjunctions, auxiliary and linking verbs, and pronouns. These closed sets of words are among the words that most 5-year-olds know and that have stayed basically the same for thousands of years. **Infinite words** include nouns, verbs, adjectives, and adverbs. These types of words are ever-expanding because they change and grow and combine with other words to create new meanings. Infinite words are the vocabulary words that we want students to continue to learn. Many English words were borrowed long ago from Latin, Greek, French, and more recently, Spanish. Helping students see the connections between words helps them expand their knowledge of words.

Vocabulary needs to be taught, not just tested (Nilsen & Nilsen, 2004). Because language is a social activity it is important that students work together to negotiate multiple meanings, rather than copy or recite dictionary definitions. Help students understand vocabulary by presenting sets of words that have similar root words. Discuss similarities and differences in words. Help students make predictions about word meanings by comparing phonological (sound) similarities, orthographical (spelling) similarities, semantic (meaning) similarities, and pragmatics (common sense and knowledge about historical connections between the users of both words).

The students' concept knowledge needs to be developed in addition to vocabulary. A **concept** is the category or class into which events, ideas, and objects are grouped. It may be further clarified by examples and characteristics common to members that belong to the same class (Crank & Bulgren, 1993). Identifying examples and nonexamples enhance students' understanding and remembering of concepts (Bos & Anders, 1990).

Objectives for Vocabulary Development

To expand their vocabulary development, students will do the following:

- Use context and sentence structure to figure out the meaning of words
- Figure out words by their prefixes, suffixes, and root words
- Use Latin roots and affixes to expand their knowledge of new vocabulary words
- Identify how English is enriched by words from other languages
- Define multiple meanings of basic words
- Demonstrate how words follow regular patterns as they acquire new meanings

- Expand knowledge of word meanings through identifying synonyms, antonyms, and examples
- Group and organize vocabulary words to learn their meanings
- Provide examples of how the meanings of words move from literal to figurative
- Interpret figurative language
- Identify characteristics, examples, and nonexamples of concepts

Vocabulary Development Assessments

Because it is impossible to assess the full extent of a person's vocabulary knowledge, vocabulary tests are difficult to construct. However, being able to identify synonyms or antonyms of a word can be indicators of basic language understanding. The synonym and antonym vocabulary assessments measure students' vocabulary knowledge by determining if students can identify the synonym or antonym of words on graded word lists. These tests can be administered by reading the words to the students, thereby measuring their listening vocabulary, or the tests can be administered by students reading the words on their own, thereby measuring their reading vocabulary. These assessments were developed by Laster and McAndrews (2004); the original idea for this type of assessment came from an unpublished manuscript by Gutkoska in 1982.

In a study conducted by Laster and McAndrews (2004), it was found that there was a significant correlation between the grade level on reading the antonym test and the highest instructional grade level for comprehension on the Qualitative Reading Inventory-3 (QRI-3; Leslie & Caldwell, 2001). Because some students are successful at reading words in isolation yet have poor passage comprehension, the beginning passage level based on the QRI word lists is often too low, resulting in one or more additional passage readings. This synonym and antonym screening tool could be used to determine the starting grade level for administering the QRI. In addition, if students were found to be a grade level or more below their actual grade level then intervention with vocabulary building strategies would be needed.

Synonym and Antonym Vocabulary Assessments

Purpose: To screen for reading or listening vocabulary (Laster & McAndrews, 2004). These tests are used to identify the students' reading or listening vocabulary level (all grades).

Procedure and Analysis: The Synonym Vocabulary Assessment and the Antonym Vocabulary Assessment (see Appendix) can be administered to groups or individuals as a listening vocabulary test in kindergarten and higher and as a reading vocabulary test for grade 1 and higher. Administer the tests separately. Students reading at or below third-grade level will read orally and begin on level 1, which equates to grade 1. Students reading above the third-grade level can read silently if you do not want to assess word recognition. To minimize assessment time for older students, you can begin testing three grade levels below their actual grade level. Go to a lower level if they score less than 60% or at the frustration level.

Write the examples listed on the assessment form on the board first, and do the examples together. Tell the students to read each line of words and circle the word that means the same or almost the same as the first word in each line. (For the antonym test, instruct students to read each line of words and circle a word that means the opposite as the first word in each line.) Students can use a blank bookmark to help keep their place. Throughout the assessment, in front of each line number put a plus sign (+) if correct and a minus sign (–) if incorrect. Write the total correct and calculate the percentage to determine the student's functioning level: Independent (90%–100%), Instructional (70%–80%), Frustration (60% and below).

Continue until students reach the frustration level or become frustrated and then repeat that grade level by having students listen as you read the words. To determine students' listening vocabulary level, begin testing at the students' frustration level. Instruct the students to follow along as you read the words in each line and have them circle the word that means the same or almost the same as the first word in each line. (For an antonym test, give the same directions, but replace "a word that means the same," with "a word that means the opposite.") Use a different colored pen to mark and score listening responses. Continue the listening vocabulary testing until the students score 60% or below, their frustration level.

The highest grade level at which students score 70% or above is the students' reading or listening vocabulary level. Identify whether the students' reading vocabulary is below, at, or above their current grade level. If their reading vocabulary is below their current grade level, assess their listening level. Students who score below their grade level may require more attention to vocabulary development before and during reading a new text.

Example and Analysis: Synonym Vocabulary Assessment: Reading

LEVEL 1 Functioning Level: Instructional   Score: 8/10 = 80%

+/_		A	B	C	D
+	1. see	run	more	look	us
+	2. little	come	long	away	small
+	3. say	talk	goes	like	just
+	4. mom	dog	mother	many	with
–	5. start	begin	last	round	slow
+	6. big	door	right	fun	large
–	7. hop	hard	ball	dark	jump
+	8. alike	grew	pot	same	most
+	9. glad	happy	sail	rope	hold
+	10. street	time	thin	very	road

LEVEL 2 Functioning Level: Frustration   Score: 5/10 = 50%

+/_		A	B	C	D
–	1. go	anything	leave	(rest)	summer
+	2. pair	read	should	(two)	middle
–	3. cut	last	(round)	slow	slice
+	4. thin	shout	(skinny)	live	under
+	5. hear	kind	magic	help	(listen)
+	6. car	secret	chew	(automobile)	juice
+	7. fear	(afraid)	lunch	yellow	welcome
–	8. stir	hospital	(stood)	mix	know
–	9. below	live	(place)	under	took
–	10. all	this	every	(find)	lunch

This second-grade student was instructional at the first-grade level and reached frustration at the second-grade level for identifying synonyms while reading. There was no particular pattern to the incorrect responses. The Level 2 test should be readministered as a listening test to see if the student knows the synonyms orally.

Instructional Implications: Provide word card pairs to match synonyms, cloze sentences that can be completed with several synonyms, and a thesaurus to find other words during writing.

Vocabulary Development Strategies

Verbal interaction and vocabulary instruction result in an increase in word knowledge, concept knowledge, and reading comprehension. According to Nagy (1988), the most effective methods of vocabulary instruction include providing information about word meanings and etymology (the history of the words), showing vocabulary in a variety of contexts, and exposing students multiple times to the new word. Learning words in context of reading, experiences, and discussion have been found to be most effective, but memorizing long lists of isolated words has been found to be relatively ineffective (Nagy, 1988). In general, when introducing students to new vocabulary words, it is beneficial to use visual, auditory, and kinesthetic methods of instruction. Specifically point out individual word parts such as affixes and roots. Have students read or use the word in context, practice pronouncing it, and then provide their own definition or examples. The vocabulary strategies are divided between those that are appropriate for younger and older students and those that are more applicable for upper elementary and above students. In addition, there is a section on concept strategies that examines the categories into which events, ideas, or objects are grouped.

Personal Dictionaries

Purpose: To place newly learned words in a dictionary to be used for future reference (grade 1 and above).

Procedure: After learning new vocabulary words, students can write the word, definition, and an example or picture clue under each letter of the alphabet.

Example: On the "A" page, write the word *Antonym*, its definition ("A word that means the opposite") and an example (stop and go).

Adaptation: Make a class vocabulary chart with the same information.

Act Out, Visualize, or Draw

Purpose: To demonstrate the meaning of vocabulary words (all grades).

Procedure: Make up rules similar to games such as charades or an adaptation of Milton Bradley's board game Pictionary, in that others have to guess the word you act out or draw. For instance, on a card write the sentence(s) that the vocabulary word came from and underline it. Then act out that word and have students try to guess what it is.

Example: *Holes* (Sachar, 1998): "The warden got a <u>pitchfork</u> out of the back of the pick-up. She poked it through X-Ray's dirt pile, to see if anything else might have been buried in there as well" (p. 69). A student will act out poking a pile with a pitchfork. The other students will then try to guess the word.

Cloze Procedure

Source: Taylor, 1953; Walker, 2004

Purpose: Originally used to measure readability and comprehension of a passage, this strategy can be used to help develop students' vocabulary development (grade 2 and above).

Procedure: Words are omitted or covered in the text and students supply the missing words. This modified cloze technique uses semantic and syntactic clues to determine the missing or covered vocabulary word. Graphophonic cues can be provided, such as the beginning letter or letters, to enhance the students' prediction of the word.

Example: *The Mitten* (Brett, 1989):

1. He wanted mittens made from _____ as white as snow. (wool)

2. "If you drop one in the snow," she _____, "you'll never find it." (warned)

3. Baba did not want to _____ white mittens. (knit)

4. A hedgehog came _____ along. (snuffling)

5. A big owl, _____ by all of the _____, swooped down. (attracted; commotion)

6. They saw the owl's _____ _____. (glinty talons)

7. Just the sight of the ____ mitten made him ____. (cozy; drowsy)

8. A great bear ____ by. (lumbered)

9. The bear gave an _____ sneeze. (enormous)

10. It was the mitten _____ against the blue sky. (silhouetted)

Compare and Contrast Vocabulary Words

Purpose: To identify the similarities and differences between two words (grade 2 and above).

Procedure: Select and write two words, and then write how they are different, how they are similar, and a summary statement comparing the two words.

Example: *Excited* versus *nervous*

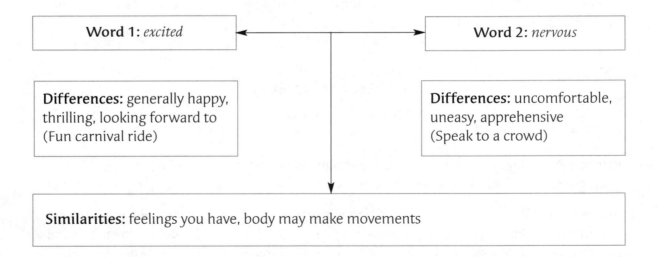

Word 1: *excited*	Word 2: *nervous*
Differences: generally happy, thrilling, looking forward to (Fun carnival ride)	**Differences:** uncomfortable, uneasy, apprehensive (Speak to a crowd)

Similarities: feelings you have, body may make movements

Summary of comparison: They are both feelings you have, but when you are excited you are happy and when you are nervous you are uncomfortable.

Contextual Processing

Source: Walker, 2004

Purpose: To learn how to identify word meanings by the context (grade 1 and above).

Procedure: Select a paragraph from the text in which the meaning of new vocabulary is apparent from the surrounding context and write it on an overhead or type it on a computer. Ask students what the paragraph tells them. After the students reply, ask "Why did you think that?" The students write down what they think the word means. Then the students think of how the word can be used and identify words with similar meanings.

Adaptation: For individual learning, the students copy the sentence and page number in which the word is used. They predict what the word means and then check with a dictionary or discuss meaning with the teacher. Finally, they write their own meaning.

Homonym Vocabulary

Purpose: To identify words with the same spelling and different meanings, or different spellings and different meanings (grade 1 and above).

Procedure: Select and write two words that are homonyms, write their definitions, draw the words, and then use them in a sentence.

Example:

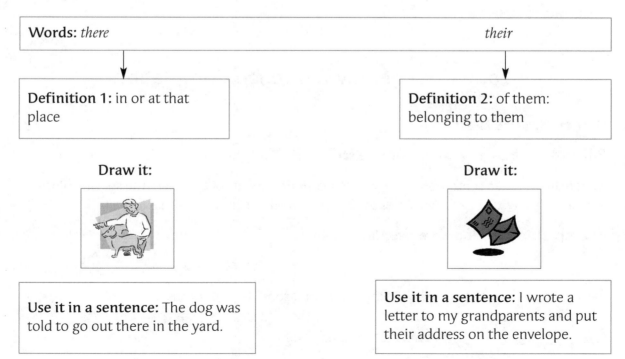

Words: *there*   *their*

Definition 1: in or at that place

Definition 2: of them: belonging to them

Draw it:

Draw it:

Use it in a sentence: The dog was told to go out there in the yard.

Use it in a sentence: I wrote a letter to my grandparents and put their address on the envelope.

Identifying Affixes

Purpose: To identify word meanings by defining affixes (grade 2 and above).

Procedure: The students or teacher writes prefixes, suffixes, and root words on separate index cards. Help students make, pronounce, and define the parts of the words.

Example: Add the prefixes *re-* or *pre-* or suffixes *-ing*, *-er*, or *-ed* to root words. In the students' personal dictionary, make a page for common definitions of affixes and Latin roots. Practice covering up parts of words in text to read unknown multisyllabic words.

Illustrating Compare and Contrast Affixes

Source: Nilsen & Nilsen, 2004

Purpose: To learn the difference between affix meanings (grade 6 and above).

Procedure: The teacher or the students select prefixes that are opposite. Students then fold an 11" × 17" sheet of paper in half and on the left side illustrate words that have one prefix and on the right side illustrate words for the opposite prefix.

Example: Nilsen and Nilsen (2004): super—Superman, superscript, supercilious, superior; sub—submit, subdivision, subservient, subliminal, submerge. Other examples of comparing only two words are maximum–minimum, inductive–deductive, and accelerate–decelerate.

Latin Root Family Sentence Completion

Source: Nilsen & Nilsen, 2004

Purpose: To learn new words with the same or similar Latin roots (grade 3 and above).

Procedure: Make sentences for words that contain similar roots. Delete the specific word and provide a word box for students to choose a word to complete the sentences.

Example: *Sonus*—Latin word referring to sound

Word box: | resonates　resounding　sonata　sonnets　sonorous |

1. A _____ is a musical composition.

2. If an idea _____ with you, it "sounds right."

3. A person who speaks in _____ tones has an imposing and effective voice.

4. _____ are poems that sound almost like music because of their rhythm.

5. All speakers long for their ideas to be met with _____ applause.

Latin Root Lessons

Purpose: To identify meanings of words with similar Latin roots (grade 3 and above).

Procedure: Select a Latin root that is used in multiple words. Write the words and the definition.

Example:

Root: *fin*   **Meaning:** *end*

Word	Definition
definite	clear or exact, not vague, having settled limits
confine	keep within limits, restrict, keep in, shut in, boundary, border, limit
finale	the concluding part of a piece of music or a play, the last part, end

Morphology of Words

Source: Ogle & Correa, 2007

Purpose: To use as a pre- and a posttest to assess and learn vocabulary by chunking words into parts, which students can then use to figure out word meanings (grade 2 and above).

Procedure: Select vocabulary words from a text or from concepts in an instructional unit. Provide students with a box for each word part. As a pretest, ask students to divide the word into word parts and write what each part probably means and what the word probably means. Afterward have students revise the first part if needed, write the definition, write a quote from the text, and write related words.

Example: *Entomologist* from the text *Buzz* (Bingham, Morgan, & Robertson, 2007).

Entomologist

word parts	entom	olog	ist
part meaning	insect	study	person

Probably means: A person who studies insects

Dictionary definition: A scientist who studies insects. Some study the classification, life cycle, distribution, physiology, behavior, ecology, or population dynamics of insects (Dunn, 2007).

Quote from text: "Forensic entomologists may be called to the scene of a crime to gather evidence, or may be sent samples by a police forensic scientist" (Bingham et al., 2007, p. 131).

Related words: entomology: the study of insects; biologist: a person who studies life

Vocabulary Building

Purpose: To define and use vocabulary words (grade 1 and above).

Procedure: Write a vocabulary word, predict its definition, write the dictionary definition, and draw it. Predict synonyms and antonyms, and then use the thesaurus to write the actual synonyms and antonyms. Write three sentences for the word, and then replace the vocabulary word with the synonyms to see if the sentences still make sense.

Example: *Reveal*

Word: *reveal*   **Guess the definition:** to show something
Use it in a sentence: Her smile revealed her white teeth.

Dictionary definition: To make known; to display or to show	**Draw it:**

Predict synonym: to show **Actual synonyms:** to show, display	**Predict antonym:** to hide **Actual antonyms:** to hide, to cover up

---

Use the word in three different sentences to show the meaning:
1. The magician revealed the rabbit to the crowd.
2. She took off her hat and revealed her new haircut.
3. He asked his friend to never reveal his secret to anyone.

> **Write one of the sentences with a synonym and another with an antonym.**
> 1. The magician showed the rabbit to the crowd.
> 2. The magician hid the rabbit from the crowd.
> **Did it change the meaning of any of the sentences?** Yes

Vocabulary Grid or Four-Block Vocabulary

Purpose: To expand word meanings (grade 1 and above).

Procedure: For individual words, divide the paper into four quadrants. Put the word in a circle in the center. In the four rectangles, write the definition, the sentence where it was found, a new sentence demonstrating an understanding of the word, and draw a picture or a memory clue.

Adaptation: For multiple words, fold the paper in five columns and put headings on each column such as Vocabulary word; Definition; Word that makes you think of it; Sentence you can use it in; and Antonym, synonym, or example of it.

Vocabulary Jeopardy

Purpose: To identify the parts of speech, spelling, or meaning of vocabulary words (grade 3 and above).

Procedure: This group participation game is similar to the U.S. game show *Jeopardy*. Use the following categories: Part of speech (identify what part of speech a word is after hearing it used in a sentence); Spelling (spell the word correctly); Use it (use the word in an original sentence); Synonyms (name the vocabulary word after hearing synonyms for it); and Antonyms (name the vocabulary word after hearing antonyms for it). Place answers in each of the boxes and have the students ask the correct questions.

Example:

Title: *Hitler's Daughter*   **Author:** Jackie French (2003)

Part of speech	Spelling	Use it	Synonyms	Antonyms
verb (scrunched)	s-q-u-e-l-c-h-e-d	Her face was animated when she talked. (animated)	continued (persisted)	fact (opinion)

noun (parka)	p-e-r-m-i-t-t-e-d	Anna is enthusiastic when she tells exciting stories. (enthusiastic)	sad (mournfully)	minimum (maximum)
adverb (obligingly)	g-e-s-t-u-r-i-n-g	She put ointment on the wound. (ointment)	gloomily (dismally)	agreed (objected)
adjective (mournful)	n-e-g-o-t-i-a-t-e-d	Mark acted defensively when he thought that Hitler really had a daughter. (defensively)	pasture (paddock)	purposefully (offhandedly)

Vocabulary Knowledge Rating

Source: Blachowicz & Fisher, 1996

Purpose: To rate understanding of a word (grade 3 and above).

Procedure: List each vocabulary word from the reading on the chart. The students rate their knowledge for each of the words by placing a checkmark (✓) under the correct category: Can define it, Think I know it, Have heard or seen it, or Have no clue. Read the text and then discuss the word meanings. Once the students learn the word's meaning, they can write each word in a sentence to show the word meaning.

Example:

Title: *Wanted…Mud Blossom*   **Author:** Betsy Byars (1991)

Word	Can define it	Think I know it	Have heard or seen it	Have no clue
accusation				✓
excavation		✓		

Sentences:

1. They made an accusation that the girl took the cookie because there were crumbs on her face.

2. After they dug the hole to the gold, the excavation was done.

Vocabulary Self-Collection Strategy

Purpose: To identify unknown words in text and then define them (grade 1 and above).

Procedure: While reading, students write down words that they cannot pronounce or understand or that are particularly interesting, along with the page number where the words can be found. This can be done on sticky notes. The class or group discusses the words in the context of the story until its meaning is understood.

Example: *terns and noddies* in *The Tale of Rabbit Island* (Ching, 2002). Have the students read the sentence: "Every chance he got Hapa would spend time with the birds and help them with their chores. He gathered twigs for the sooty terns and noddies to build their nests" (p. 3). Terns and noddies are birds.

Vocabulary Wheel

Purpose: To expand word meanings (all grades).

Procedure: Write a vocabulary word and the part of speech in the center of a sheet of paper. In circles around it write synonyms, antonyms, examples, and other forms of the word. Also write the word in a sentence and illustrate the word.

Example: *Liquid*

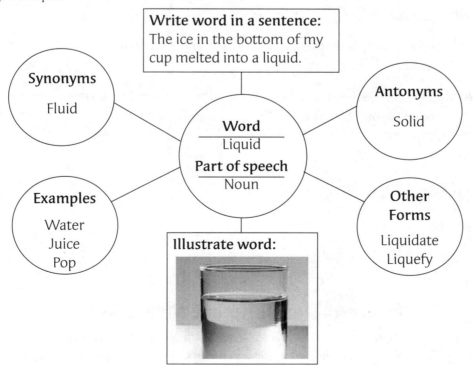

Word Hunt

Purpose: To find and define vocabulary words in context (grade 2 and above).

Procedure: On index cards write the following headings for each word: Vocabulary word, Where I found it, Sentence where the word was used, My definition, and Dictionary definition. Students then fill in the information on each card. Students could also identify words with affixes or Latin roots in the text.

Example:

Vocabulary word: *Palfrey*

Where I found it: *Crispin* (Avi, 2002, p. 162)

Sentence where the word was used: It was there I saw a woman riding sidesaddle astride a great black palfrey whose saddle and harness were trimmed with gleaming silver.

My definition: A horse.

Dictionary definition: A small saddle horse, especially for a lady.

Word Sort by Meaning

Source: Walker, 2004

Purpose: To categorize words on the basis of similar letter patterns, word meanings, or grammatical functions (all grades).

Procedure: Students or teacher identifies keywords from a text and writes them on index cards. Then the students sort the words by the aforementioned patterns. For higher order development the students provide the reason that the words are grouped together.

Example:

Word cards: run, dog, cat, walk, hop, jump, girl, boy

Sort: dog, cat, girl, boy = nouns

run, walk, hop, jump = verbs or things they can do

Concept Development Strategies

A concept is a mental representation, image or idea of tangible and concrete objects and intangible ideas and feelings. Visual and auditory information facilitates the development of concepts. The following strategies not only help develop a broader sense of a concept, but also develop important mental processes by identifying associated objects or ideas, analyzing and discriminating between ideas, grouping and regrouping them based on their similarities and relationships, and synthesizing information by summarizing and forming generalizations.

Concept of Definition

Source: Schwartz & Raphael, 1985

Purpose: To identify word meanings on the basis of categories, properties, and illustrations (grade 2 and above).

Procedure: Write the word to be defined in the center of the map. Using context and a dictionary fill in the three main parts of the map, including What is it? (category), What is it like? (properties), and What are some examples? (illustrations). You could also fill in some comparison words.

Example: *Gas*

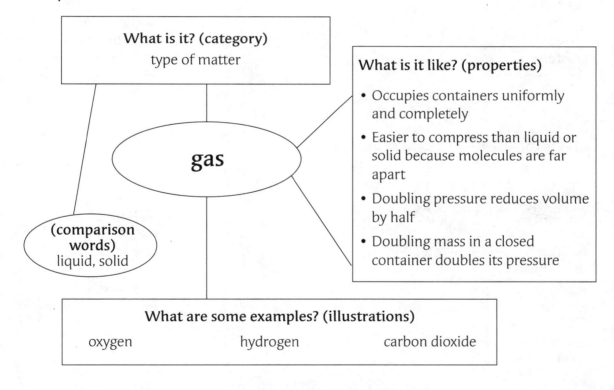

Idea Web

Source: Ogle and Correa, 2007

Purpose: To gauge students' prior knowledge when used as a pretest, or to determine knowledge learned when used as a posttest (all grades).

Procedure: Students choose words from a list of terms to be learned and place them under the appropriate category or concept. They can use as many words as they know, and they can use each word only once. Some categories will have blank spaces even though you used all of the words.

Example: *Arthropods*

antennae	exoskeleton	mantises	entomologist	arachnid	molting
thorax	cephalothorax	crayfish	abdomen	wasps	myriapod
entomology	scorpion	crustacean	migration	metamorphosis	invertebrate
beetles	insecta	pollination	centipedes	compound eye	

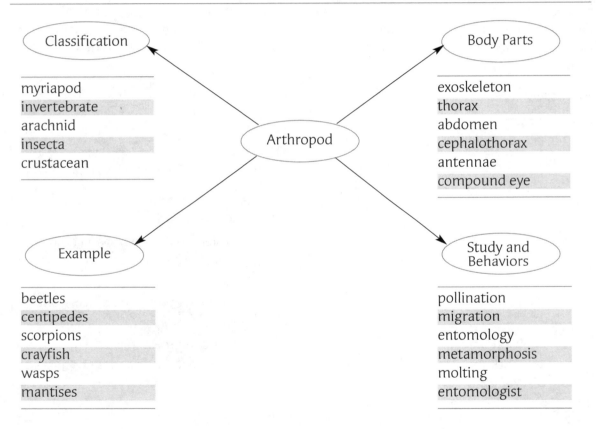

Concept Ladder

Source: Gillet & Temple, 1994

Purpose: To identify hierarchical concept relationships (grade 3 and above).

Procedure: Using context, background knowledge, a dictionary, and the Internet, complete each step of the concept ladder by answering the questions about the concept to show how it is related to other concepts.

Example: *Guitar*

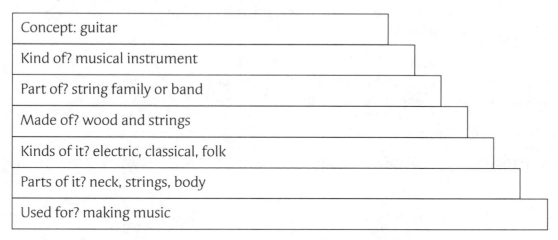

| Concept: guitar |
| Kind of? musical instrument |
| Part of? string family or band |
| Made of? wood and strings |
| Kinds of it? electric, classical, folk |
| Parts of it? neck, strings, body |
| Used for? making music |

Label Diagrams

Purpose: To use diagrams to identify word meanings (all grades).

Procedure: Add vocabulary labels to drawings.

Example: The skeletal system of the human body, the water cycle, or the life cycle of a butterfly.

Linear Array

Source: Nagy, 1988

Purpose: To show linear relationships of degrees of variation in words (grade 3 and above).

Procedure: Draw an array in a line with points marked with words in sequence.

Example: *Water temperatures*

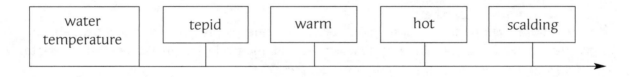

| water temperature | tepid | warm | hot | scalding |

List-Group-Label

Source: Taba, 1967, in Tierney & Readence, 2000

Purpose: To organize words on the basis of their relationship to one another and to label the relationship (grade 2 and above).

Procedure: Students or teacher identifies keywords from a text and writes them on index cards, and then the students group the words by their relationship to one another. For higher order development, the students provide the label.

Example: *Body systems*

Digestive system	Circulatory system	Respiratory system
esophagus	heart	trachea
stomach	blood vessels	lungs
intestines	arteries	alveoli

Mnemonic Devices

Purpose: To assist students in remembering concepts or the order of concepts (grade 3 and above).

Procedure: Identify the topic with several subtopics that the students need to remember in order. Identify the first letter of each word. Create a sentence or a phrase using these first letters.

Example: Classification of living things: kingdom, phylum, class, order, family, genus, and species. The mnemonic sentence: "*K*athy *p*lays *c*hess *o*n *f*ather's *g*reen *s*hirt."

Schematic Word Map

Source: Tierney & Readence, 2000

Purpose: To identify key concepts using lines to show how words are hierarchically related (grade 3 and above).

Procedure: Develop the target concept. Define the concept, present the concept, and begin constructing the hierarchy. Guide students to relevant and irrelevant attributes, and complete the map with additional examples and nonexamples.

Example: *Reptiles.* The supraordinate concepts would be cold-blooded, vertebrate, and animal at the top of the hierarchy. A coordinate concept at the same level would be amphibians, while subordinate concepts would be examples such as alligators, snakes, and lizards.

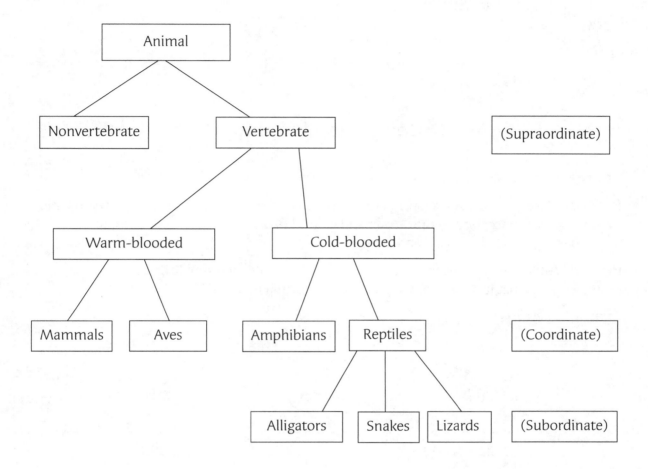

Semantic Feature Analysis Matrix

Source: Johnson & Pearson, 1984, in Walker, 2004

Purpose: To sort out the similarities and differences among a group of events, people, objects, or ideas (all grades).

Procedure: Identify items to be classified and attributes that make them similar and different. Classify each animal by the attribute, by putting a plus sign (+) or a minus sign (−) in each box indicating the presence of each feature.

Adaptation: Use a schematic word map.

Example: *Animals*

	Lives in water	Breathes air	Lays eggs	Has fur
Whales	+	+	−	−
Seals	+ sometimes	+	−	+
Sharks	+	−	+	−
Fish	+	−	+	−
Bears	−	+	−	+

Semantic Mapping

Source: Johnson & Pearson, 1984, in Walker, 2004

Purpose: To expand and develop a definition of a word by using a graphic organizer in which ovals represent concepts, and the arrows and words boxes represent the relationships or properties of the word (grade 2 and above).

Procedure: Write the concept in the center oval. Students then supply descriptors, examples, and what it is used for with arrows connecting them.

Example: *Conifers*

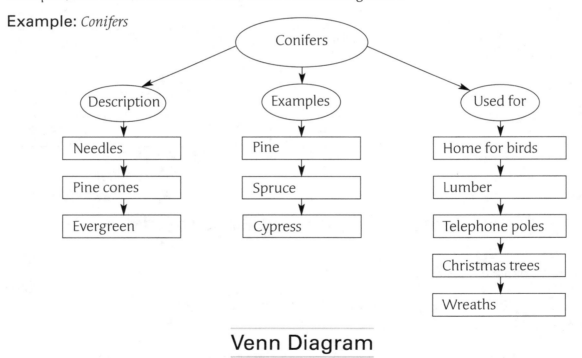

Venn Diagram

Purpose: Comparing and contrasting two or three concepts (all grades).

Procedure: Draw two or three interlocking circles. Label each with the concepts. In the center write the attributes they have in common.

Adaptation: H-Diagram. Attributes of one concept are written in the left and attributes of the other concept on the right side of the H. Similarities are in the crossbar of the H.

Example: Ferrous and Nonferrous Metals

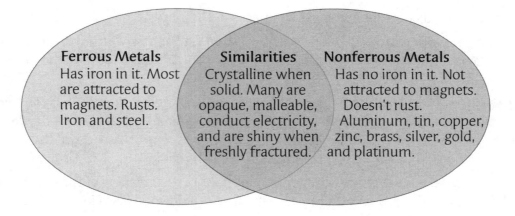

Ferrous Metals
Has iron in it. Most are attracted to magnets. Rusts. Iron and steel.

Similarities
Crystalline when solid. Many are opaque, malleable, conduct electricity, and are shiny when freshly fractured.

Nonferrous Metals
Has no iron in it. Not attracted to magnets. Doesn't rust. Aluminum, tin, copper, zinc, brass, silver, gold, and platinum.

Figurative Language Strategy

Purpose: To identify and describe the meaning of figurative language such as simile, metaphor, and irony as it is used in text (grade 3 and above).

Procedure: Discuss the meaning of figurative language. Then draw a picture of the literal meaning and a picture of the implied meaning.

Example: In *Amelia Bedelia Helps Out* (Parish, 1963) Amelia Bedelia takes everything literally. For example: Miss Emma says, "'Now I want you to stake the beans. Here is the string to tie them. You can use this saw to cut the stakes.' She took the saw and cut the steak into fifteen pieces. 'Now hold the steak while I tie it.'" Amelia Bedelia and Effie Lou steaked those beans. The students can draw two pictures: one depicting a woman tying steak to the beans and one depicting tying the beans to a stake. Students should then label each picture with a sentence and underline the homophone or figurative language. Other examples of literal and figurative language in *Amelia Bedelia Helps Out* include Amelia stealing—or taking—all of the bases and then literally running home to her house when she was playing baseball and putting money in the river bank, not in the bank building.

Vocabulary Strategies on Your Own

Purpose: To figure out the meanings of unknown words, when the student is reading and no one is around to help (all grades).

Procedure: Instruct students to select one or more of the following strategies to help predict the word meaning:

- Read or reread the sentence or paragraph to see if the meaning of the word can be figured out by the context.

- Make a prediction about the part of speech of the word.

- Break the word into word parts: prefix, root, and suffix. Ask yourself if you know the meaning of the word parts or if you know the meaning of words with the same or similar word parts.

- Determine if the word is important to your understanding of the text. If you think it is important, look the word up in the glossary or dictionary. After reading the definition or definitions, reread the sentence to see if it makes sense. Write down the word, the definition, a sentence, or a drawing to help you remember it.

- If you determine that the word is not important to the meaning of the text, make a prediction and read on. You might write the word down to learn its meaning later.

CHAPTER

Phonological Awareness, Phonics, Word Identification, and Emergent Text Concepts

Understanding Phonological Awareness

An understanding of phonological awareness, phonics, word identification, and emergent text concepts are necessary processes in reading and writing text. When teaching these processes, think about a whole–part–whole model. Start with a text or idea, teach specific skills or strategies as needed to read or write that text, and then apply the skills and strategies to reading or writing the text. Although these processes are interrelated, their definitions, objectives, assessments, and strategies will be addressed separately, so that they can be more clearly understood. However, an integration of these processes is needed to identify and write words in context.

Terms such as *phonological awareness*, *phonemic awareness*, and *phonics* are frequently confused with one another. **Phonological awareness** is the ability to recognize that speech is made up of sentences that can be broken into sentences or phrases, sentences that can be divided into words, and words that can be further divided into smaller units of sound, such as syllables, onsets, and rimes, and individual sounds or phonemes (Johnson & Roseman, 2003). The term **onset** corresponds to the consonant or consonant cluster, also called a consonant blend, before the initial vowel sound, such as /st/ in the word *stop*. The term **rime** corresponds to the vowel-consonant cluster at the end of the word such as /op/ in *stop*. Rimes also can consist of only vowels, such as in the word *see* where /s/ is the onset and /ee/ is the rime. Some words, such as the word *at*, have a rime but no onset.

Phonemic awareness, the final stage in phonological awareness, is the ability to recognize that a spoken word consists of a sequence of individual sounds or phonemes, to distinguish between different phonemes, and to manipulate phonemes in words to change their meaning (Yopp, 1992; Yopp & Yopp, 2000b). A **phoneme** is the smallest unit of speech that distinguishes one word from another in a language or dialect. For example, the word *cat* is made up of three distinct English phonemes: /k/, /ă/, and /t/. If you change the initial phoneme from /k/ to /s/, you get the word *sat*, which is a new word with a different meaning. Some phonemes sound very similar and are sometimes difficult to distinguish, such as the final phoneme in the words *half* and *have*. ELLs may have difficulties distinguishing between English phonemes that are not in their native language. According to a meta-analysis of evidence from the National Reading Panel report, phonemic awareness instruction helps children learn to read (Ehri et al., 2001). However, learning phonemes in context of hearing words and stories makes them more meaningful and easier to learn.

Some phonemic sounds correspond to individual letters such as /a/ in *apple*, while other phonemes are made up of combinations of letters such as /th/ in *that* or /oy/ in *boy*. The correlation of sounds or phonemes to letters or graphemes is called **phonics**. Although these terms are related, phonological awareness and phonemic awareness are auditory processes, whereas phonics is both an auditory and a visual process. Phonics will be described in more detail later in this chapter.

Objectives for Phonological Awareness

To develop phonological awareness, students will do the following:

- Identify and demonstrate that spoken language is divided into words
- Identify and demonstrate that spoken words are divided into smaller units of sound, such as syllables
- Identify and demonstrate that spoken words can be divided or segmented into individual sounds or phonemes
- Aurally differentiate between English speech sounds
- Identify and demonstrate that spoken sounds can be blended to make words
- Aurally differentiate between English words
- Identify and demonstrate that orally substituting phonemes results in creating new words
- Identify and produce the initial, final, and then medial phonemes within words they hear
- Identify and produce words that have the same initial, final, or medial phoneme
- Identify and demonstrate that rhyming words can be orally made by substituting the initial sound prior to the vowel sound
- Identify and demonstrate that oral words can be put together to make sentences
- Identify and demonstrate that sentences can be put together to communicate with other people

Phonological Awareness Assessments

These assessments are to determine if a student can blend, segment, and differentiate English speech sounds. Although all students should be given a hearing test, if a student does not score at least 70% on these assessments further assessment by a speech-language pathologist or an audiologist may be needed to determine if the student has an auditory processing disorder or other hearing impairment. These assessments are most appropriate for a student at the emergent reading and writing level unless there is an indication of difficulties in discriminating, blending, or segmenting sounds.

Auditory Discrimination Assessments

Purpose: The following section describes three auditory discrimination tests: the Consonant Auditory Discrimination Assessment (see Appendix), Short and Long Vowel Auditory Discrimination Assessment (see Appendix), and the Diphthong and Controlled Vowel Auditory Discrimination Assessment (see Appendix). Each of these assessments is designed to determine a student's ability to recognize the fine differences between English phonemes in words, and each is generally administered to primary-grade students unless a discrimination issue is observed. These tests use a similar format to the Wepman Auditory Discrimination Test (Wepman, 1958, revised in 1973). Each test consists of word pairs that differ by a single phoneme or are the same; the examiner says the word pair, and the student has to say whether the words are the same or different. The Consonant Auditory Discrimination Assessment compares words that differ by auditorially similar initial or final consonant sounds. The Short and Long Vowel Auditory Discrimination Assessment compares the five short-vowel sounds with one another, compares the five long-vowel sounds with one another, and compares the short and long sound of each vowel. The Diphthong and Controlled Vowel Auditory Discrimination Assessment compares diphthongs (/ay/, /uy/, /oy/, /ow/) and controlled vowels (/er/, /ar/, /or/, /al/, /aw/, /ew/) to long and short vowels.

Procedure and Analysis: Sitting shoulder to shoulder with the student, but facing opposite directions so that the student cannot see the words pronounced, say "I am going to say two words, and I want you to tell me if they are the same or different." Record the student's response as *S* for same and *D* for different. Score with a plus sign (+) for correct and minus sign (−) for incorrect. Functioning levels are Independent (90%–100%), Instructional (70%–89%), Frustration (69% and below). Identify those phonemes that the student does not distinguish between. Correlate these phonemes with those in other assessments.

Example and Analysis: Short and Long Vowel Auditory Discrimination Assessment

Functioning Level: Instructional   Score: 35/40 = 88%

	Response/Score		Response/Score
1. get-get	S +	21. cake-cake	S +
2. hat-hot	D +	22. jean-June	D +
3. pet-pat	S −	23. high-hay	D +
4. had-had	S +	24. bite-beat	D +
5. nut-not	S −	25. home-home	S +

This second-grade student was able to identify all of the sounds that were the same and distinguish between each of the long-vowel sounds. The short-vowel sounds that the student was unable to distinguish were between /ĕ/ and /ă/, /ŭ/ and /ŏ/, /ĭ/ and /ĕ/, /ĕ/ and /ĭ/, and /ă/ and /ĕ/.

Instructional Implications: Provide instruction on short-vowel sounds using strategies such as a picture sort (described later in this chapter).

Phoneme Blending Assessment

Purpose: The Phoneme Blending Assessment (see Appendix) is used to identify a student's phonic knowledge of blending sounds into words. It was developed using the general format of the Yopp-Singer Test of Phoneme Segmentation (Yopp, 1995). Blending or synthesizing the sounds to form words are strategies used when decoding unfamiliar words (Walker, 2004). This assessment is generally given if a student scores at or below 70% on the first-grade reading word list or there is evidence that the student has difficulties blending sounds into words.

Procedure and Analysis: Tell the student, "Today we're going to play a word game. I'm going to say separate sounds and I want you to say the word. For example, if I say '/o/-/l/-/d/', you should say 'old.'" Practice items include /r/-/i/-/de/, /g/-/o/, /m/-/a/-/n/. While administering the assessment, put a plus sign (+) next to items the student blends correctly, mark a minus sign (−) next to items the student blends incorrectly, and record incorrect responses on the blank line. Identify those phonetic elements that the student is unable to correctly blend. Make a note if the student is unable to say a real word.

Example and Analysis:

	+ or − and response		+ or − and response
1. c/a/t	+	12. d/ay	+
2. s/ee/d	− see	13. p/l/a/ce	− play
3. m/i/ne	− my	14. t/o	+
4. g/o	+	15. th/r/ee	− voiced thē
5. h/e	+	16. j/o/b	− j/ŏ/, jŏg

This second-grade student was able to blend about half of the words correctly, including all of the words with only two sounds. The incorrect blended responses were real words except for two. The remaining were real words, yet the final sound of the target word was generally deleted or was substituted with another sound. The student substituted *b* for *g*.

Instructional Implications: Because the final sound was deleted or changed, you could try a strategy such as having the student listen to a segmented word, identify the picture card that represents it, and then say the complete word. Based on the student's needs, these words should have different word endings. The student could also sort pictures based on the final *b* and *g* sounds, such as *bag, crab, pig,* and *tub.* To extend this into a phonics strategy, use magnetic letters to make these words. Another example would be to change consonant-vowel words into consonant-vowel-consonant (CVC) words such as changing *see* to *seed.*

Phoneme Segmentation Assessment

Purpose: The Yopp–Singer Test of Phoneme Segmentation (Yopp, 1995; see Appendix) is used to identify a student's phonic knowledge by the rime patterns recognized in words. Segmenting words into their single-letter sounds, or analytic phonics, is a strategy used while spelling words. This assessment is generally given if a student scores at or below 70% on the first-grade writing word list or there is evidence that the student has difficulties segmenting sounds in words to write them.

Procedure and Analysis: Tell the student, "Today we're going to play a word game. I'm going to say a word and I want you to break the word apart. You are going to tell me each sound in the word in order. For example, if I say 'old,' you should say '/o/-/l/-/d/.'" Record the student's responses. Practice with the words *ride, go,* and *man.* As you administer the assessment, put a plus sign (+) next to items the student correctly segments and record incorrect responses on the blank line.

Identify those phonetic elements that the student is unable to correctly segment. Make a special note if the student is able to separate blends but is not able to separate consonant digraphs.

Phonological Awareness Strategies

Although all these strategies are auditory, they can be changed to phonics activities by having students read or write the letters or words. These activities also help develop vocabulary, so it is important to discuss the meanings of the words during instruction.

Auditory Discrimination

Purpose: To identify the initial, final, and then medial phonemes (grades K–2).

Procedure: Ask students to identify the initial, final, and then medial phonemes within words they hear in conversations or in books; for example, listen for initial /s/ or later identify the initial sound in *sat*, *sit*, *sip*, and *sad*. Use strategies that make phonemes prominent in students' attention and perception.

Example: Model specific sounds, such as /s/ in the word *sat*, and ask students to produce each sound in isolation and in many different words until they are comfortable with the sound and understand its nature.

Blending Phonemes

Purpose: To blend phonemes into words (grades K–2).

Procedure: Begin by identifying just one phoneme, such as /m/-ilk or /s/-at, working gradually toward blending all the phonemes in words. Ask students to orally blend phonemes into words. This helps students eventually decode or sound out words.

Example: /s/-/ă/-/t/ makes what word?

Adaptation: Put your left hand on your right shoulder and say the initial sound, then put your hand on the inside of your elbow for the medial sound, and then put your hand on your right palm and say the final sound. Now run your hand from shoulder to palm to blend the sounds.

Segmenting Phonemes

Purpose: To identify the initial and final phonemes and then each phoneme within words (grades K–2).

Procedure: Ask questions such as What is the first sound in *soup*? and What is the last sound in *kiss*? Beginning phonemes are easier to identify than final phonemes. Once students are comfortable listening for individual phonemes, ask students to orally break words into component sounds. This helps students eventually write words.

Example: goat = /g/-/ō/-/t/

Pushing Pennies

Purpose: To identify and separate each phoneme in a word (grades K–2).

Procedure: Along the short side of a sheet of construction paper, make three 1" × 1" boxes for words with three phonemes. Flip the paper over and on the long side of the paper make four 1" × 1" boxes for words with three or four phonemes. Make picture cards for words with three and four phonemes. Select a picture card to put on the paper and give the students a penny to put under each phoneme box. Model the activity by pronouncing the word slowly and pushing one penny up into each box on the paper as each sound is pronounced. Students repeat this process, making sure that there is a one-to-one match between the pronunciation of each phoneme and the pushing of each penny.

Example:

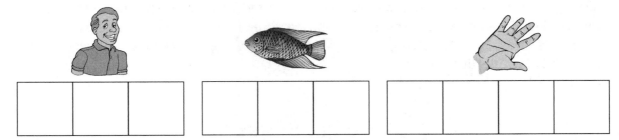

man = /m/ box 1, /ǎ/ box 2, /n/ box 3

fish = /f/ box 1, /ǐ/ box 2, /sh/ box 3

hand = /h/ box 1, /ǎ/ box 2, /n/ box 3, /d/ box 4

Adaptation: To change this into a phonics activity, ask students to write the letters that represent each sound. Start with phonemes represented by only one letter.

Oral Rhyming Words

Purpose: To identify and generate rhymes (grades K–4).

Procedure: Teach rhymes in context first by reading a rhyming couplet, leaving off the last word and having the students complete the rhyme. Have students say as many words as they can that rhyme with one of the words in the couplet.

Example: *Green Eggs and Ham* by Dr. Seuss: "Would you could you in a boat? Would you could you with a _____ (goat)?"

Seven-Step Activity

Purpose: To rhyme, blend, segment, isolate sounds, and substitute phonemes (grades K–2).

Procedure: Say to students, "I have a secret word. Can you guess what I'm saying?" Rather than saying the letters of the word, say each sound separately, such as /s/-/a/-/t/ (*sat*). Now ask students to think of words that rhyme with *sat* (*mat, rat*). Make up several sets of words to use as the secret word of the day. Ask students, "What is the first sound you hear in *sat*? We spell that sound with what letter? What is the last sound you hear in *sat*? We spell that sound with what letter?" Ask students to say all the sounds apart as you did initially: /s/-/a/-/t/. Use two fingers to clap the sounds in *sat*, then do the same with some of the rhyming words. Ask, "If we say *sat* without the /s/, what is left?" then substitute new beginning sounds, such as /b/ for *bat*. Say, "If I put a /b/ in front, what is my new word?"

Extension: Use wipe-off boards and write words that rhyme with the word of the day, or use magnetic letters on a cookie tray. Words can be sorted by common spelling patterns or word families. If some words rhyme but are spelled differently, put them in a separate column. As students' skills improve, emphasize substituting beginning sounds and segmenting each word into individual sounds.

Picture Sorts

Purpose: To hear the difference in the sounds of phonemes by sorting pictures by their initial, final, or medial sound(s) (grades K–2).

Procedure: Identify one or two initial, final, or medial sounds for students to identify or differentiate on the basis of assessment data. For closed picture sorts, ask students to find and name all of the pictures of words that contain a particular phoneme. For example, have students find all the pictures of words that begin with the /p/ sound (*pig, pencil, paper, pan, purse, penguin*). For an open sort, ask students to tell you what all the picture names have in common. For example, they all have the *-ar* sound in them (*car, star, arm, card, jar*). Students could also sort the pictures by two different sounds.

Understanding Phonics

Phonics is a way of teaching the relationships between the sounds of a language and the letters used to represent those sounds. A **phoneme** is the smallest unit of speech sound that affects the meaning of a word. A **grapheme**, also known as a phonogram, is a written symbol of a phoneme, which in English may be a letter or a group of letters. For example, the word *knows* has three phonemes (/n/, /ō/, and /z/) which are represented by three graphemes (*kn, ow, s*). Phonics begins with letter and sound identification. Phonics is then used during the decoding process to read words and during the encoding process to write or spell words. Although phonics is essential for learning to read, it must be coupled with other word identification and comprehension strategies that include using syntax and semantics in order to make reading meaningful.

English is a semiphonetic language, which means that letters or combinations of letters can represent more than one sound, such as the -ough in *though* and *cough*, and the same sound can be represented by one or more different combinations of letters, such as in *ate* and *eight*. Therefore, phonics alone cannot be used to identify all words.

There are several types of phonemes or sounds in the English language, and it is important for you to be familiar with the following definitions, which were adapted from *The Literacy Dictionary* (Harris & Hodges, 1995). A **consonant** is a speech sound made by partially or completely closing part of the vocal tract, while a **vowel** is a voiced speech without stoppage to or restriction of the airflow as it passes through the vocal tract. The **long vowel** sounds have a relatively long duration of time in which the sound is stressed, and the vocal cords are tense. In English, they are also the names of the alphabet letters. They are phonetically represented with a **macron**, or bar, over them: /ā/, /ē/, /ī/, /ō/, and /ū/. The **short vowel** sounds have a relatively short duration or a weak stress of the vowel sound, and the vocal cords are relaxed. They are phonetically represented with a **breve**, similar to a *u*, over them: /ă/, /ĕ/, /ĭ/, /ŏ/, and /ŭ/. The **schwa** is a midcentral vowel in an unaccented or unstressed syllable such as the initial vowel in the word *alone* or the final vowel in the word *table*. It is represented with an upside down *e*, written /ə/. A **diphthong** is a vowel sound produced when the tongue moves or glides from one vowel sound to another vowel or semivowel sound in the same syllable, such as in the words *boy* and *bough*. **Vowel digraphs** and **trigraphs** are two or more letters that represent a single vowel sound. Examples include ai, ea, ee, ei, eigh, ey, ie, igh, oa, oo, ou (/ŭ/), and ow (/ŏ/). Controlled vowels are those vowels that change their sound because they are followed by an /r/, /l/ or /w/ sound. The vocalic -r or /er/ sound can be written with ar, er, ir, ur, or, and ear, as seen in the mnemonic sentence *Her* (er) *first* (ir) *nurse* (ur) *works* (or) *early* (ear) *on grammar* (ar). **Consonant diagraphs** are two letters, generally consonants, which represent one sound. This combination of letters can create a new sound such as the following:

th = voiced /th/ in *this* and voiceless /th/ in *thin*

ch = /ch/ in *chair*, /k/ in *chorus*, /sh/ in *chef*

wh = /hw/ in *what*

sh, ti, ci, si = /sh/ in *shoe, nation, special, session*

si = /zh/ in *vision*

ph = /f/ in *phone*

ng = nasal /n/ sound in *sing*

One of the letters can be silent, such as the following:

gh = /g/ in *ghost*

rh = /r/ in *rhyme*

gn, kn, pn = /n/ in *gnat, know,* and *pneumonia*

dge = /j/ in *edge*

wr = /r/ in *write*

mb = /m/ in *thumb*

A *consonant blend* is a sequence of two or more distinguishable consonant sounds before or after a vowel sound, such as /str/ in *street*. And finally, there are **hard** and **soft** *c* and *g* sounds.

The hard *c* in *cat* is represented by /k/ and the soft *c* in *city* is represented by /s/. The hard *g* in *goat* is represented by /g/ and the soft *g* in *giant* is represented by /j/. The Individual Phonics Summary (see Appendix) provides a chart with these phonetic elements.

Understanding Word Identification

The terms *word identification* and *word recognition*, although similar, differ slightly in their definitions. Harris & Hodges (1995) define both **word recognition** and **word identification** as "the process of determining the pronunciation and some degree of meaning of an unknown word" (p. 282). However, word recognition is further defined as the "quick and easy identification of the form, pronunciation, and the appropriate meaning of a word previously met in print or writing" (p. 283). For words that are in a reader's meaning vocabulary, unlocking the pronunciation leads to the word's meaning. During assessment, word recognition is determined by those words that students are able to read automatically, while word identification is demonstrated by the processes students use in their attempts to read or self-correct an unknown word. Word identification processes include phonic analysis and using context clues of syntax and semantics.

Phonic analysis is the identification of words by their sounds, which involves the association of speech sounds with letters and the blending of these sounds into syllables and words. Structural and analogy clues support phonic analysis. **Structural analysis** includes the identification of roots, affixes, compounds, hyphenated forms, inflected and derived endings, contractions, and, in some cases, syllabication. Readers also employ analogy clues by using the words they know to help them recognize words that are unfamiliar. Students can learn to manipulate the onsets (consonants before the vowel) and rimes (the vowel and consonants following it within a syllable). For example, a student who is able to read *cat* can change the onset to /s/ when reading the new word *sat*. Being able to associate sounds with a cluster of letters, such as the rime /at/, leads to more rapid, efficient word identification.

Using **context clues** for word identification involves drawing on information from syntactic and semantic clues in the surrounding words, phrases, or sentences as well as drawing on clues from pictures and typography. **Syntactic clues** help the reader to predict the unknown word's part of speech on the basis of the word order. **Semantic clues** help the reader by associating words with the topic of the text or sentences. For example, when reading a story about dogs, the expectation is that the text may also contain words such as *bark*, *woof*, and *wagging*. Picture clues or illustrations can often help with the identification of a word if there is strong picture support for the unknown word. Typography such as boldfaced, capitalized, or italicized words also provides a context clue students can use to identify words that may be particularly important. (Typography is addressed further in Chapter 5, Reading and Listening Comprehension.)

Context clues allow readers to cross-check their identification of words. For example, a reader encountering the word *scratch* for the first time should look carefully at the letters of the word, apply what he or she knows about phonics and word parts, and ensure that an attempted pronunciation matches the letter clues. The reader should always cross-check to be sure that the word makes sense in terms of syntactic and semantic cues. Cunningham (1995) offers examples of activities that build and extend students' cross-checking activities.

Beginning readers recognize very few words instantly. Through repeated exposure to the same words, instant-recognition vocabulary grows. It is particularly important that developing readers learn to recognize those words that occur very frequently in print. A mere 100 words make up a full 50% of the words read, even by adults. *The, and, to, you, he, it,* and *said* are examples of these high-frequency words. Developing readers also need to learn to recognize high-frequency words instantly because many of those words are not phonically regular (Pikulski, 1997). Based on phonics generalizations, *to* should rhyme with *go, said* should rhyme with *paid,* and so on. Students' ability to recognize words can be developed by teachers' pointing out the words, by a variety of game-like activities, and by writing those words. However, it appears that instant recognition of words, especially high-frequency words, develops best when students read large amounts of text, particularly text that is relatively easy for the reader (Cunningham, 1995).

Objectives for Phonics and Word Identification

To develop phonics and word identification skills the students will do the following:

- Identify the names of the consonant letters and the sounds they represent, including the soft and hard *c* and *g*
- Identify the names of the vowels and the long and short sounds they represent
- Identify the sounds of consonant digraphs and the letters that represent them
- Identify the sounds of vowel digraphs and the letters that represent them
- Identify the sounds of diphthongs and the letters that represent them
- Blend sounds to decode phonetically regular words
- Use phonics and word knowledge to decode phonetically irregular words
- Recognize high-frequency words automatically
- Identify words by cross-checking the graphophonic, syntactic, and semantic cues in the context of reading texts
- Segment words into phonemes to represent the word using inventive spelling
- Segment words into phonemes to write the word using conventional spelling
- Write specified high-frequency words using conventional spelling
- Write irregularly spelled words and homophones correctly
- Identify words that are spelled incorrectly
- During writing, circle words that are believed to be misspelled and later use resources to correct the spelling

Understanding Emergent Text Concepts

One aspect of emergent literacy is having a basic understanding of how the English written language works and of the concepts needed for reading and writing text. Although some of these concepts include basic phonics, they are broader concepts that are developed through the interaction with books and other texts. Clay (1997) coined the term *concepts about print* to assess and teach emergent readers basic concepts such as print contains a message, directionality and the return sweep when reading, one-to-one matching, letter and word identification, identification of punctuation, and concepts of letters and words. Students are able to demonstrate many of these concepts even before they can read.

Objectives for Emergent Text Concepts

To develop emergent text concepts using a book the students will do the following:

- Demonstrate that print contains the message by pointing to the text rather than the picture when asked where to begin reading
- Demonstrate directionality and return sweep by pointing left to right and returning to the left side on the next line as the teacher reads
- Demonstrate one-to-one matching by pointing to each word written in the sentence as the teacher reads it
- Demonstrate letter and word identification by pointing to a given uppercase and lowercase letter and word after a sentence is read
- Demonstrate knowledge of punctuation marks by pointing to each type and telling its purpose
- Demonstrate the concept of a letter by identifying only one letter, two letters, first letter, and last letter
- Demonstrate the concept of a word by identifying only one word, two words, first word, and last word

Phonics and Emergent Text Concepts Assessments

Letter and Sound Identification Assessment

Purpose: The Letter and Sound Identification Assessment (see Appendix) is an individual assessment that provides information about a student's ability to identify all uppercase and lowercase letters and the sounds they represent out of sequence; it can be used for all grades K–2 students and those who are unsure of letter names and sounds. The letters *a* and *g* are presented by two different but commonly used fonts. This assessment is modeled after Clay's (1993) Letter Identification Test.

Procedure and Analysis: Give the student a copy of the letter chart and place an index card under the first row. Say, "I want you to tell me the names of each letter and the sound or sounds it makes." Point to the first letter and ask, "What letter is this?" Write the student's response on your record sheet. Ask, "Do you know what sound it makes?" If the letter is marked with an asterisk (*) there are multiple sounds, so ask, "Do you know what other sound that makes?" If the student does not know the sound ask, "Do you know a word that starts with that letter?" Prompt the student for the short and long sounds of vowels and hard and soft *c* and *g* and the consonant and vowel sounds of *y*. Write a plus sign (+) for each correct letter and correct sound; write a minus sign (–) for incorrect and write out all incorrect responses. If a student says, "I don't know," write "IDK" and pause to see if they try something. Although students are not scored on knowing a word, this assessment provides a connection between known words and initial sounds during instruction.

Identify the known and unknown uppercase letters, lowercase letters, and sounds. Separate the consonants and the vowels. If the student does not know the sound of a letter but knows a word beginning with that sound, list the word the student knows. These would be the first sounds to teach using this word as a keyword. Identify substitutions of similar-looking letters or substitutions of similar-sounding phonemes.

Example and Analysis: Letter and Sound Identification Assessment, grade 1

	Letter	Sound	Word		Letter	Sound	Word
B	+	+		b	d, s-c +	+	
O*	+	/ŭ/, IDK –	IDK	o*	+	/ŭ/, /ō/–	OK +
S	+	+		s	+	+	
A*	+	/ă/, IDK –	apple +	a*	IDK, s-c +	/ă/, /ā/ +	
W	+	/dŭ/–	IDK	w	+	/dŭ/–	done –
Z	+	/zē/–	zebra +	z	t, s-c +	/t/, s-c +	zebra +
F	+	/ĕ/–	fish +	f	+	/ĕf/–	fish +
H	+	/ă/–	IDK	h	+	/āch/–	IDK
K	+	/kŭ/ +	Katelyn	k	+	/kŭ/ +	
J	G	/jŭ/ +	IDK	j	g	/gŭ/–	go –
U*	+	/yŭ/–	you –	u*	+	/yŭ/–	you –
				a*	+	/ă/, /ā/ +	
C*	+	/k/, IDK –	cat +	c*	+	/k/, IDK –	me, Cindy +
Y*	IDK	/wŭ/, IDK –	no	y*	+	/wŭ/, IDK –	IDK
L	+	/lŭ/–	Laura +	l	1–	/wŭ/, IDK –	IDK
Q	+	/kŭ –	IDK	q	p	/p/	IDK
M	+	+		m	+	+	
D	+	/dŭ/ +		d	b	/b/	bear
N	+	+		n	+	+	
X	+	/ĕ/–	x-ray	x	+	/ĕ/–	x-ray
I*	+	/ă/, /ĕ/ –	no	i*	+	–	IDK

	Letter	Sound	Word		Letter	Sound	Word
P	+	+	Peter	p	+	+	
E*	+	/ĭ/, IDK –	Elizabeth	e*	+	/ĭ/, IDK –	IDK
G*	+	/g/ +, –	go	g*	+	/g/ +, –	go
R	+ speech?	/w/ speech?	wabbit	r	+ speech?	/w/speech?	wabbit
V	w, s-c +	IDK –	IDK	v	+	IDK –	IDK
T	+	+		t	f	/f/	fish
				g*	IDK, 8 –	ā –	IDK
Total	24/26			Total	22/28	both 6 /26	

- Letters: This student knew most of the uppercase letters, except *J* and *Y*. She thought *l* and *g* were numbers. She substituted *g* for *j*, *p* for *q*, *b* for *d*, and *f* for *t*. The student self-corrected *b*, *a*, and *z*. She was able to identify both fonts of *a*.
- Sounds: The student knew the uppercase and lowercase sounds for six letters.
- Unknown consonant sounds: /c/ and /g/ (soft sounds), /w/, /z/, /f/, /h/, /j/, /y/, and /l/. The student often began with the sound of the letter name, sometimes adding a /ŭ/, elongating the sound. I only marked it incorrect for /l/ because it does not make that sound at all.
- Unknown vowel sounds: /e/, /i/, /o/, /u/, and /y/. The student was able to identify both sounds of a for the lowercase, but not the uppercase.
- Known words for unknown letters: *a*, *z*, *f*, *c*, *l*, *e*, *x-ray* uses the letter but not the sound.

Instructional Implications: Begin by teaching the sounds for *a*, *z*, *f*, *c* and *l* because the student has known words representing the sounds. Then explain that letter names, except for the long-vowel sounds, do not always start with the sound of the letter names. Be sure to teach the sounds in context and help create keywords for each sound.

Phonics Skills for Grades K–3

Purpose: The Phonics Skills for Grades K–3 (see Appendix) checklist was developed to be introduced and mastered at each primary-grade level.

Procedure and Analysis: This can be used as an ongoing record sheet to document the teacher's instruction or the student's learning of the specific phonemes based on grade level. Simply check each phonetic element as it is taught or learned.

Analyze the phonetic elements that can be reinforced and those that need to be taught in context of reading and writing texts. Students can be grouped based on the type of phonetic element they need to work on: consonants, long vowels with a silent *e*, short vowels, consonant digraphs, vowel digraphs, inflectional endings, and so forth.

Individual Phonics Summary

Purpose: When all the assessments are completed, the Individual Phonics Summary (see Appendix) can be used to document missed phonetic elements from all the reading and writing assessments. It is important to note, however, that these phonemes should be taught in the context of reading and writing and not in isolation.

Procedure and Analysis: After literacy assessments have been complete, highlight in yellow the missed phonemes while reading. Highlight in blue the missed graphemes while writing. Highlight in green the missed elements in both reading and writing. Circle elements once the student is able to read and write them correctly.

Identify the phonic elements the student can read or write. For miscues identify if there are any visual or auditory similarities. Finally identify any similarities between missed elements between reading and writing. Select phonic strategies to support the learning of these elements, and when possible, make connections to texts.

Emergent Text Concepts Assessment

Purpose: This 25-question Emergent Text Concepts Assessment (see Appendix) provides information about emergent text concepts, such as directionality; one-to-one matching of words to print; and concepts of letters, words, and punctuation in the context of a storybook. This assessment is based on Clay's (1993a) Concepts About Print observation task. Unlike Clay's assessment, however, this one does not require a specific published text. This assessment is appropriate for a student who reads at or below first-grade reading level.

Procedure and Analysis: Select a picture book with a picture and two to three lines of print on each page. For questions 1–7, first ask the questions then read the page. For questions 8–25, read each page and then ask the questions. Fill in the blanks on questions 15–17. Write the student's responses and a plus sign (+) if correct and a minus sign (−) if incorrect. If any of the concepts are absent write "N/A" and change the denominator of the fraction for the total number of questions.

Answer the following questions to evaluate the student's understanding of emergent text concepts: Does the student understand directionality, including one-to-one matching and the return sweep (going to the next line) (Questions 1, 3–10)? Does the student know the purpose of the punctuation marks (Questions 11–14)? Can the student identify and know the difference between words and letters in context (Questions

15–24)? Does the student understand that reading is a comprehension process (Questions 1 and 25)? For instruction, identify known text concepts to reinforce and unknown text concepts to teach.

Example and Analysis: Emergent Text Concepts Assessment

Title: *Five Little Ducks*   Author: Raffi (1989)

What You Do	What You Say	Response
Hold book with the spine to the student.	1. Where is the front of the book?	1. pointed +
Show the cover and read the title and author of the book. Ask the question. Read the statement.	2. What do you think this book is going to be about? I'll read this story and you can help me.	2. ducks +
Find the first page with a picture and print. (Read any text on preceding pages without pictures and then stop.)	3. Where do I begin reading? Read the page.	3. pointed to words +
On the next page that has at least two lines of text, ask questions and then read the page.	4. Show me where to start? 5. Which way do I go? 6. Where do I go next? 7. Point to each word as I read.	4. pointed to first word + 5. moved left to right + 6. turned page – 7. not one-to-one match –
On the next page, read the following prompts:	8. Point to the first word on the page. 9. Point to the last word on the page. 10. Show me the bottom of the picture.	8. pointed to first word + 9. last word in line 1 – 10. pointed +
Read along until you come to a period, question mark, comma, and quotation marks, and then stop, point, and ask questions.	11. What's this for (.)? 12. What's this for (?)? 13. What's this for (,)? 14. What are these for ("")?	11. the end + 12. questions + 13. a word – 14. 2 words –
Find two letters that have both a uppercase and lowercase on that page. Point to the uppercase letter and ask...	15. Can you find a lowercase letter like this? (point to uppercase B) 16. Can you find a capital or uppercase letter like this? (point to lowercase f)	15. pointed to d – 16. pointed to F +

Read until you find a page with two words that start with the same lowercase letter. Select the second.	17. Can you find the word *one*?	17. pointed to *out* –
Find a page with preferably one line of text or cover one line of text. Read the page. Hand the student two index cards and demonstrate how to close them like a curtain.	18. I want you to close the cards like this until all you can see is one letter. 19. Now show me two letters. 20. Show me just one word. 21. Now show me two words. 22. Show me the first letter of a word. 23. Show me the last letter of a word. 24. Show me an uppercase letter.	18. d + 19. du + 20. duck + 21. duck said + 22. Q + 23. k + 24. M +
Read to the end of book.	25. What was this story about?	25. Five little ducks went away. + Score: 17/25

The student knew most of the emergent text concepts. He did not know the return sweep and was not accurate with one-to-one matching. He pointed to the last word in the line, not the last word on the page. He did not know what the comma and quotation marks were for. He could not discriminate between *out* and *one*, but they had the same first letter.

Instructional Implications: Reinforce the known concepts and directly teach the specific unknown concepts while reading texts together.

Word Identification Assessments

Fry's Instant Sight Words for Reading and Graded Reading Words

Purpose: Fry's Instant Sight Words (Fry, Kress, & Fountoukidis, 1993) includes 10 lists of 100 words each that are the most common words in English ranked in frequency order. The first 100 words make up half of all written material. The Graded Reading Words Assessment (see Appendix) includes a selected sample of the first 300 words from Fry's Instant Sight Words (see Appendix) and other high-frequency, phonetically regular and irregular words. There are

9 leveled lists based on frequency of use and difficulty of decoding, beginning with preprimer list and ending with the grades 9–12 list.

These lists are used to identify known sight words, decoding strategies, miscue patterns, as well as knowledge of phoneme–grapheme relationships. Fry's Instant Sight Words are predominantly administered to a student who is reading at or below the third-grade level to determine the student's knowledge of all of the high-frequency words. It can also be used as an instructional check sheet for known and unknown words identified during authentic reading. The Graded Reading Words contain only a representative sample of the Fry's Instant Sight Words; therefore, it is a quicker screening instrument and provides an approximate grade level for the student's reading of words.

Procedure and Analysis: You will need two copies of the words—one for the students to read from and the other on which to document the student's responses. The Graded Reading Words Assessment has a separate word list from which students can read. For Fry's Instant Sight Words lists begin with the very first word. For the Graded Reading Words Assessment, select the list that is at least two grade levels below the student's current grade, unless you have evidence to show that the student would be lower. It is often beneficial to provide a bookmark or index card for the student to keep his or her place. For emergent readers write or type the words on index cards and present them one at a time. Say to the student, "Read each word in the column, and then move the card down. I cannot help you; if you don't know the word, try to figure it out. I am going to write down everything you say." On the assessment sheet, above each word write a plus sign (+) for a correct response and a minus sign (−) for incorrect and write down all incorrect responses phonetically, with vowels marked. Mark a slash for every two seconds the student pauses between decoded word parts. This helps to differentiate between an automatic word (sight word) and a decoded word or self-corrected word. If the word is self-corrected, record all attempts and mark "s-c." Try to finish all the words within one grade level. Continue until the frustration level is reached.

For recording guidelines, refer to Coding and Scoring Oral Reading Behaviors Guide (see Appendix). If the student scores at or above 70% on a given list or column, go to next list; if not, go to the previous list if it was not already assessed.

These reading word assessments identify the high-frequency words the student can read automatically (sight words), as well as those that the student can identify using phonics and knowledge of words. In addition, patterns of strategies used during decoding or miscues can be identified. The student's knowledge of phoneme–grapheme relationships can also be documented on the Individual Phonics Summary (see Appendix). There are three scores obtained for reading words: the automatic score, the identified score, and the total score. The **automatic score** is the percentage of words the student was able to read immediately within one second; these are often called the student's sight words. The **identified score** is the percentage of the words the student was able to correctly read after one second. These included the correct reading of the word after hesitations, decoded sounds, or incorrect words. The **total score** is the total percentage of correctly read words. For the functioning level use the number of correctly read words: Independent (18–20), Instructional (14–17), and Frustration (13 and below). An analysis would include known words, the strategies the student used when problem solving, and known grapheme–phoneme relationships. In addition, the patterns between phonetic elements in known and unknown words should be identified.

Example and Analysis: Graded Reading Words Assessment, grade 6

Grade 4 Reading Words
Automatic Score: 14/20 = 70%

Functioning Level: Instructional
Total Score: 15/20 words = 75%

+	+	they've, −	+	+
been	**difference**	**they're**	**beautiful**	**piece**
+	know, s-c +	+	+	+
pretty	**knew**	**sign**	**brought**	**finally**
+	+	unusual, −	exit, −	when, −
trouble	**learned**	**usually**	**excited**	**whether**
+	eight, −	+	+	+
half	**weight**	**whole**	**through**	**tomorrow**

Grade 5 Reading Words
Automatic Score: 10/20 = 50%

Functioning Level: Frustration
Total Score: 11/20 words = 55%

+	+	confused, −	+	+
heard	**couldn't**	**conclusion**	**library**	**environment**
+	+	+	trouble, s-c +	/exkit/, −
watched	**sure**	**laughed**	**terrible**	**excellent**
/nōedge/, −	+	+	/acfused/, −	different, −
knowledge	**experience**	**certain**	**athletic**	**difference**
spread, −	high, −	problem, −	onion, −	+
separate	**height**	**probably**	**opinion**	**picture**

On the third-grade reading word list, this student was at an independent level, so the example started with the grade 4 list. On the grade 4 list, he attempted each word he was shown, and when he did not know the word, he substituted a different word with the same beginning sound as the word that he was shown. There were only two instances in which he did not correctly identify the beginning sounds but correctly read the ending word sounds (*his/this* and *weight/eight*). There were two instances in which he went back to try a word again, and in both instances, he successfully decoded the word (*know/knew* and *trouble/terrible*).

As the word lists grew more difficult, the student began substituting more words. In two words he substituted the end of the contraction (*we've/we're, they've/they're*). In the grade 5 list, he began substituting nonwords (*acfused/athletic, exkit/excellent, nōedge/knowledge*). Occasionally, he left out or substituted medial word sounds *(onion/opinion)*. These results suggest that he usually attends well to beginning word sounds, although he does not consistently attend to medial and final word sounds. In addition, he successfully decodes words when he reattempts them; however, this strategy was not used very often.

Instructional Implications: The primary focus will be on attempting the sounds beyond the initial letter and predicting real words. If first attempts are not real words, the student should attempt the word again.

Fry's Instant Sight Words for Writing and Graded Writing Words

Purpose: Fry's Instant Sight Words (see Appendix) or the Graded Writing Words Assessment (see Appendix) can be used to identify a student's known writing words, writing strategies, miscue patterns, and knowledge of phoneme–grapheme relationships; this assessment is also used to evaluate the student's handwriting. Fry's Instant Sight Words are predominantly administered to a student who spells at or below the third-grade level to determine the student's knowledge of writing all of the high-frequency words. It can also be used as an instructional check sheet for known and unknown words identified during authentic writing. The Graded Writing Words Assessment contain only a representative sample of the Fry's Instant Sight Words lists, so this is a quicker screening instrument and provides an approximate grade level for student's writing of words.

Procedure and Analysis: Select appropriate paper (lined or unlined depending on the student's ability) for the student to write on. Have the student fold the paper in half to make two columns. For the Fry's Instant Sight Words assessment, begin with the very first word. For the Graded Writing Words Assessment, select the list that is at least two grade levels below the student's current grade, unless you have evidence to show that the student would be at an even lower level. For emergent writers, begin at the preprimer list, and before reading the words, ask the student to write his or her first and last name and any words they know. Read each word one at a time. Remind the student to write letters for the sounds in the word, even if they are not sure how to spell the word. If the word is a common homophone, as indicated by an asterisk, provide a sentence for the student to understand the context of the word. After you dictate each word, write a plus sign (+) above each correctly spelled word. For all incorrect responses write what the student wrote above each word; be sure to indicate reversals and capital letters. Write a comma between each attempt and "s-c" if the student self-corrected the spelling. If the student scores at or above 70% on a given list or column, go to next list; if not, go to the previous list if it was not already assessed.

To determine the student's functioning level, use the number of words correctly spelled: Independent (18–20 words), Instructional (14–17), and Frustration (13 and below). For the developmental spelling stage, evaluate each word based on Table 3.1. These writing word assessments identify the high-frequency words the student can write automatically as well as those that the student can spell using phonics and knowledge of words. In addition, patterns of strategies and miscues can be identified. The student's knowledge of phoneme–grapheme

Table 3.1 Developmental Spelling Stage Rubric

Conventional	Transitional	Phonetic	Semiphonetic	Prephonetic
The word is spelled correctly, or in writing composition at least 90% of words are spelled correctly.	Overgeneralizes when applying simple spelling rules. All sounds are represented graphically	Use of a vowel; at least half of the sounds are represented graphically.	Some sound-symbol relationships, one to two letters could represent a word.	Letters or shapes are written but do not represent the sounds.

relationships can also be documented on the Individual Phonics Summary (see Appendix). Use the Handwriting Rubric Assessment (see Chapter 6) to compare the student with the expected standard and identify areas of strength and need such as letter formation, spacing, directionality, reversals, and capitalization. Data can also be correlated with reading words, dictation, and the writing sample. During instruction help the student make connections between known and unknown words in the context of authentic reading and writing.

Example and Analysis: Graded Writing Word Assessment, grade 3

Grade 2 Writing Words: 15/20 words = 75%   Functioning Level: Instructional
Developmental Stage: Transitional

+	+	+	+	+
very	before	right	goes	always
arond	wercs	+	there	+
around	works	great	their	don't
+	yous	wood	+	+
where	use	would	who	your
+	+	+	+	+
wanted	first	please	talked	long

This student was at the independent level for the grade 1 writing words and instructional at the grade 2 words, misspelling only five of them. She is at the transitional spelling stage for grade 2 because her incorrect spelling words can be sounded out, and she generally included letters representing all of the sounds in the words. Two of the words were homophones so I gave her a sentence, yet she was unable to spell the correct one (*wood/would, there/their*). One sounded similar (*yous/use*). For the other two words she had the beginning and ending sounds correct, but the middle sounds were wrong (*wercs/works, arond/around*). However, on the third-grade list she was at the frustration level and between the phonetic and transitional developmental spelling stage. She had most of the letters, some were just out of order (*faivorite/favorite*), (*frenid/friend*), (*dosn't/doesn't*), and (*realy/really*). These are words she should be familiar with, and we will work on learning to write them correctly. She generally writes all of the sounds, just not the correct letters.

Instructional Implications: Praise this student for being able to include letters for almost all of the sounds. Focus on vowels, the hard and soft /c/ and /g/, and homophones. Provide opportunities in her writing to circle words that do not look correct to her. Practice the read, cover, and write technique with these words.

Sentence Dictation Assessment

Purpose: The Sentence Dictation Assessment (see Appendix) is used to identify known writing vocabulary, as well as a student's abilities to divide words he or she hears into their sounds (phonemic segmentation), to write the letter or letters that represent these sounds, and to use a word analogy for known words to help the student spell new words. These sentences were created based on incorporating as many phonograms as possible in the fewest words in the context of a story. The first dictation sentence came from Clay (1993a) and evaluates 27 phoneme–grapheme relationships. I developed the next two, which evaluate 50 and 153 phonemes–graphemes, respectively.

Procedure and Analysis: It can be administered to older students if the student is below grade 5 on the writing words assessment. Select paper with line widths appropriate for the student's age. There are three different dictation sentences: one for emergent writers, one for students in grades 1 and 2, and the other for students in grades 3–5.

Give the student lined paper. Say, "I am going to read you a story, and then I will go back and read one word at a time. Write down each word I say. If you do not know how to write a word, say the word to yourself, and write down the letters for the sounds you hear." The student is to write these words as sentences, not as a list.

Score the dictation sentences by assigning one point for each correct phoneme–grapheme correlation. Mark a checkmark (✓) above all the correct words and a minus sign (–) for deleted words. For misspelled words write the student's response above the word. Count each correct underlined phoneme–grapheme correlation and put the total in the score. Determine the functioning level by the percentage of correct graphemes written: Independent (90%–100%), Instructional (70%–89%), Frustration (69% and below). If the student scores at or above the instructional level on a given dictation test, go to the next level test. Continue until the frustration level is reached. To analyze the sentence dictation, identify the correct and incorrect graphemes or patterns of spelling in order to plan instruction. Write additional information about use of punctuation and capitalization, as well as handwriting and spacing. The Individual Phonics Summary (see Appendix) can be used to indicate the phonetic elements that the student needs to work on.

Example A and Analysis: Kindergarten and Primer Sentence Dictation, Grade 1
Functioning Level: Frustration   Score: 16/41 graphemes = 39%

✓ --f ✓b-- D-G e t   –   t - - -   ✓ M GO- - 2- t - -   - -m t- s-   - L

<u>I</u> <u>h a v e</u> <u>a</u> <u>b i g</u> <u>d o g</u> <u>a t</u> <u>h o m e</u>. <u>T o d a y</u> <u>I</u> <u>a m</u> <u>g o i n g</u> <u>t o</u> <u>t a k e</u> <u>h i m</u> <u>t o</u> <u>s ch oo l</u>.

This student attempted to write all of the words except *home* and was able to write at least one sound with most of them, representing the correct letter for each word. She correctly wrote the letters *l, b, t, m, a,* and *s*. She wrote the correct sound but used capitals for *D, G* (twice), *M, O,* and *L*. She substituted the letter *f* for *v*, and the number *2* for the word *to*.

Instructional Implications A: The student is beginning to correlate letters and sounds, and therefore she should be encouraged to write words with at least two sounds in her daily journal.

Example B and Analysis: First-and Second-Grade Sentence Dictation, Grade 3
Functioning Level: Instructional   Score: 44/50 graphemes = 88%

✓ ✓   ✓   ✓   ✓   ✓   ✓   ✓   ✓   ✓   ✓   ✓   wather
<u>Th e</u> <u>f ar m er</u> <u>s aw</u> the <u>b l a ck</u> <u>a n d</u> <u>wh i te</u> <u>t oy</u> b <u>oa</u> t <u>ou</u> t <u>o</u> n the <u>w a t</u> er.

✓ flotid   ✓   ✓   shine   stile   birgh   ✓ ✓ ✓   ✓
<u>I</u> t <u>f l oa t ed</u> <u>u n d</u> er the <u>sh i n y</u> <u>s t ee l</u> b <u>r i dge</u> <u>t o</u> <u>a</u> <u>s m a ll</u> b <u>ea</u> ch.

This student was able to correctly write most of the correct sounds. He understands that for every spoken word or sound there is a written word or letter. He used capital letters correctly and remembered all the punctuation marks. He also appropriately spaced his words and letters so the writing was easy to read. He had the initial sounds of the five words that he missed but he didn't get the medial or final sounds right. He had difficulties with /th/ for /t/, /o/ for /oa/, /ē/ for /y/, /ī/ for /ee/, the /br/ blend, and /gh/for /dge/ consonant digraph. (The Emergent Writing Stage Assessment can also be used to evaluate the student's writing; see Appendix.)

Instructional Implications B: Begin with making words with /oa/ and /ee/ vowel digraphs using word tiles. Then during separate lessons make words with the following: words ending in *y*, words containing /t/ and /th/, words with and a /br/ blend, past tense *-ed* with all three sounds (/ed/, /d/, /t/), and a brief lesson on /dge/ words.

Phonics Strategies: Letter and Sound Identification

The phonics strategies are divided into subtopics including: letter and sound identification strategies, phonic analysis strategies, analogy and structural cue strategies, context clue strategies, writing word strategies (spelling), and emergent print concept strategies.

General Purpose: To identify both the letter names and the sounds they represent. All of these strategies are suitable for grades K–1.

Basic Letter and Sound Identification

Procedure: Select a letter-sound correlation to teach based on student assessment or observation and the Phonics Skills for Grades K–3 chart (see Appendix), which will guide approximately what grade level to teaching the phonic elements. Generally begin with frequently occurring consonants followed by the others consonants, vowels, consonant digraphs, vowel digraphs, word endings, r-controlled vowels, and others. If the Letter and Sound Identification Assessment (see Appendix) has been administered, begin teaching the unknown sounds for which the student knew a word that began with that sound. When introducing each letter, point to it and say the letter name followed by the sound or sounds and then say a common word that begins with that sound, often illustrated by a picture. Have the students say it chorally with you, then echo you, and then by themselves.

Alphabet Books

Procedure: Read aloud alphabet books and then have students reread the books and consult them to think of keywords when making their own books about a letter.

Environmental Print

Procedure: Collect food labels, toy traffic signs, newspaper advertisements, and other environmental print for students to sort and use in identifying letters and words.

Keyword Alphabet Charts

Procedure: Use or make alphabet charts with a picture and word of a familiar object for each letter. Students must be familiar with the object or they won't remember the keywords. Recite the alphabet by pointing to each letter and saying "A- /ă/- apple" and so on.

Letter and Word Search

Procedure: While reading books, have students find a particular letter or words beginning with that letter. You could make circle-shaped letter frames from tag board, plastic bracelets, pipe cleaners, or wax-covered sticks for students to highlight particular letters on charts or in big books.

Letter Books and Posters

Procedure: Students can make letter books or posters with pictures of objects beginning with a particular letter on each page. They can add letter stamps or stickers.

Letter Containers

Procedure: Collect coffee cans or shoe boxes, one for each letter of the alphabet. Write upper- and lowercase letters on the outside and place several familiar objects that represent the letter in each container. Use these containers to introduce the letters. Students can use them at a center for sorting and matching activities.

Letter Stamps

Procedure: Students can use letter stamps and ink pads to stamp letters on paper or in booklets. They also can use letter-shaped sponges to paint letters and letter-shaped cookie cutters to make cookies or to cut out play dough letters.

Letter Tiles

Procedure: Given a variety of letters, students pick all examples of a letter or match upper- and lowercase letter forms. They also arrange the letters in alphabetical order and then use the letters to spell their names or other familiar words.

Making Letters

Procedure: Students practice making letters using pipe cleaners, play dough, shaving cream, colored hair gel in a bag, sidewalk chalk, with their fingers in the air, and with markers on white boards. Students should say the sound that each letter represents as they practice.

Show-and-Tell Bag

Procedure: At home, have students place items and pictures in a bag that represent a given letter or sound. They can share these items, or they can give clues as to what is in the bag for other students to guess.

Phonics Strategies: Phonic Analysis

General Purpose: To identify words by analyzing word parts. For emergent readers it is best to focus on high-frequency words and words the students will see regularly in their reading materials. The following general strategies are frequently taught in grades K–3, but older students also can use them to figure out unknown words they cannot determine from context.

Good Readers Bookmarks

Procedure: Give students the Good Reader Bookmark relevant to their grade level (see Appendix) and discuss each of the strategies lists on it. Prompt students to consider these strategies when they come to a word they don't know. For example, they could say the first three sounds and think about what makes sense, sounds right, and looks right; then, if it does not make sense or is not a real word, tell them to try breaking the word in parts or try a different sound.

Books With Specific Phonic Elements

Procedure: Read meaningful and predictable stories containing several examples of words that reflect the letter–sound pattern that is being taught. Ask students to find those letters in the words. Books such at *Cat on the Mat* (Wildsmith, 1982) encourage children to read through an interesting story with repetitive sentence structure that emphasizes the *-at* word family (*cat*, *sat*, *mat*). Beware, some books written for the purpose of teaching specific phonic elements are difficult to read because their story contains no real meaning; instead, they contain only a series of words with the same phonetic pattern such as "Nan can fan Dan." These types of books are not helpful when teaching.

Model Decoding Words

Procedure: Begin with small, familiar words. Model sounding out the letters left to right, blending the sounds together, searching for the word in memory, and saying the word.

Make-and-Break Words

Procedure: Students make words with magnetic letters or tiles. It is beneficial that the vowels and the consonants are different colors so that students know that every word has a vowel sound. Scramble the letters needed to make the word and have students reconstruct the word. Begin with two- and three-letter words that have one letter per sound and build to more complex words. Once they know some words, have students change the onset or rime to make new words. Have students find and read the word in the story.

Missing Vowel Cards

Procedure: Make index cards with each of the vowels then make cards with pictures of a variety of short-vowel CVC words (e.g., *cat, pen, pig, fox, cup*). Write the word under the picture, but make a blank line where the vowel should be. Have students sort the picture cards under the correct vowel.

Missing Vowel Mix and Match

Procedure: Make tiles or cards with the vowels on them. Put different vowels in each space to make multiple new words. Read and then write each real word.

Example: This could be made larger into a mat and the vowels could be cut apart to make words.

h __ t	b __ t	t __ p	c__t
s __ t	d __ g	f __ n	p__t
h __ m	m__ p	c __ b	g__t
a e i o u			

Sorting by Sounds

Procedure: Find a story that contains numerous examples of a single phonogram or phonograms with multiple sounds: *c* (/k/, /s/); *g* (/g/, /j/); *ch* (/ch/, /k/, /sh/);

ea (/ē/, /ĕ/, /ā/); *ed* (/ēd/, /d/, /t/). Make sound cards that represent the phonogram(s) in the story, and then ask students to sort word cards under the correct sound cards. Have students create new word cards as they find new words in print. Instead of teaching many phonic rules, teach students to try alternate sounds, starting with the most common sound.

Personal Word Chart

Procedure: Introduce a few high-frequency words as they are encountered in text. As words are introduced, students write them under the correct initial letter in a personal word chart or dictionary for ongoing reference. Students can draw picture clues if needed.

"Words I Know" and "Words I Am Learning" Envelopes or Boxes

Procedure: Make two envelopes or boxes labeled "Words I Know" and "Words I Am Learning." Put in word cards created from word wall words, sentence cut-ups, or other sight words the students are learning. As the students learn the words, they are moved from "Words I Am Learning" to "Words I Know." Keep the "Words I Am Learning" to no more than five to seven words. Help the students to break the new words into parts to read them.

Word Sort by Phonemes and Word Families

Source: Bear, Invernizzi, Templeton, & Johnston, 2000

Purpose: To identify the differences and similarities of words by sight or by sound (grades K–3).

Procedure: Select words that can be sorted by sight or by sound. Ask students to sort the words by how the vowel sounds. Students can also sort the words by similar spelling. You can include some exceptions to the spelling rules, once they learn the common spelling patterns.

Example: Sort words spelled with *-ea* into three sounds such as /ē/ (*eat*), /ĕ/ (*bread*), and /ā/ (*great*).

Published Dictionary or Glossary

Procedure: Provide instruction and practice in using the dictionary or glossary, including using guide words and understanding how to use the dictionary pronunciation key. Only after sufficient practice with dictionaries can they be used as an effective resource. (These resources are generally best for second-grade level readers or above.)

Phonics Strategies: Analogy and Structural Cues

General Purpose: To identify and compare phonic elements in known words to learn to read new words. These strategies are used to teach initial, medial, and final phonemes, as well as morphemes such as prefixes and suffixes. As readers begin to recognize sight words, they can use analogies to learn new words. For example, students who have seen the word *day* many times and who know the sound for the letter *m* will probably be able to recognize the word *may*. Building phonemic awareness for onsets and rimes helps students to identify simple words and syllables by analogy.

Activities that engage students in word family (*cat, sat, hat*) and initial consonant substitution ("What word would I have if I changed the *c* in *cat* to an *s*?") can assist emergent readers in being able to use analogies to read new words. Begin with small, familiar words, and teach the students to sound out the letters and blend them together, searching for the word in memory. Model sounding out the word, blending the sounds together, and then saying the word. The ability to sound out new words allows students to identify and learn new words on their own. Select one or two elements at a time on which to focus.

Teach more advanced readers to use structural cues to figure out how to decode and learn the meaning of new words. Help students to identify and learn meanings of prefixes and suffixes from the text. During reading, break words in parts (prefixes, roots, suffixes, compounds) by covering each affix. Add different suffixes to words (*play, plays, played, playing*) with magnetic letters or word cards. When learning contractions, substitute the apostrophe and subsequent letters with the word it replaces. The following are specific strategies that can be used to assist students in using analogy and structural cues to problem-solve unknown words.

Word Family, Phoneme, and Structural Analysis Books

Purpose: To identify an unknown word from the students' reading or writing and connect it to a similar known word or phoneme (grades K–5).

Procedure: Create minibooks using quartered index cards. Staple four to six minipages together on the left side. Write the known or keyword on the top page. The words should have the same rime, onset, or vowel sound. On each subsequent page, write the unknown word and other words with the same phonemes. You could underline the phonic element in each word, if necessary. You can make word family books (add consonants to rimes, such as adding *m* to *eat*), or affix books (adding prefixes such as *un-* to create *unfair, unhappy, unsure,* or suffixes such as *-ly* to create *quickly, slowly, quietly*) or compound words (add *fire* to *house, fly,* or *fighter*).

Comparing Visually Similar Words

Purpose: To correct a substitution of a visually similar word when reading (all grades).

Procedure: On paper or a dry-erase board, write what the students said directly above what was written in the text. Discuss the similarities and differences between the two words. Have students reread the correct word in the sentence.

Connecting Known to Unknown Words

Purpose: To help make connections between words that the student knows and the words written (all grades).

Procedure: When a student is reading and comes to an unknown word that has the same phonic element as a word he or she knows, write down, say, or point to the phonic element in the known word and say, "What is this word? The new word has the same sound. What it the new word?"

Flap Books

Purpose: To compare words with similar phonic elements (grades K–3).

Procedure: Using 1" × 3" strips of paper, make flap books that change one element of a word.

Example: Make silent -*e* flap books by adding a flap with *e* on it (change *mad* to *made* by adding *e*), contraction books (change *cannot* to *can't* by folding the *t* flap over the word *not*), or word family books (add different consonants to the word *at*).

H Brothers Poster

Purpose: To identify the sound of consonant digraphs (grades K–3).

Procedure: Using pictures of the four "H Brothers" (see Figure 3.1), point to each brother as you tell this story: "This brother plays with trains and says /ch/. This brother blows his whistle and says /wh/. This brother doesn't want to play and sticks his tongue out and says /th/. This last brother says mom is coming, /sh/." Students refer to the poster for reading or writing consonant digraphs. For example, the word *when* has the beginning sound of the brother who blows his whistle.

Figure 3.1. H Brothers Poster

Unpublished drawings by Andrea Newell.

Vowel Farm Bulletin Board

Purpose: To read and write words with the same vowel sounds using a keyword chart (grades K–3).

Procedure: Make a farm scene bulletin board containing all the visual images in the example below. Label each item with keywords for the vowel and underline the vowel.

Example: The word you want to write is like the /ā/ in hay, the /ā/ in pail, /ā/ in rake, /ē/ in sheep, /ē/ in wheat, /ē/ field, /ī/ in bike, /ī/ in light, /ī/ in silo, /ō/goat, /ō/ in post, /ō/ in scarecrow, /ō/ in backhoe, /ow/ in cow, /ow/ in mouse, /oo/ in goose and boots, /ar/ in barn, /or/ in horse, and /er/ in farmer.

Adaptation: It could also be used for consonant digraphs such as /ch/ in *chickens* or /sh/ in *sheep*.

Phonics Strategies: Context Clues

General Purpose: These strategies support students in using context clues such as their knowledge of background information, sentence structure, vocabulary, and meaning from the text and as well as graphic information to read and comprehend text. Although using phonics cues are important in learning to read, students benefit greatly from using context clues. While reading, you can prompt students to use context clues by asking them to read on or reread to collect clues to figure out unknown words. They can also ask themselves, "Does it make sense? Does it sound right?" These questions encourage students to be self-reflective. Pictures and graphics can also support students' reading, so when selecting books consider the support that the pictures and other graphics provide. Before reading, ask students to look at the pictures and graphics, discuss them, and predict what the text will be about. If applicable, direct students to look at the pictures or graphics and think about the story to figure out a word. Some emergent reader books have rebus pictures above the word or in place of the word to help the beginning reader. The strategies below are beneficial in assisting students in using context clues to figure out unknown words or concepts.

Predictable Language Approach

Purpose: To use context to read texts that contain predictable or patterned language (grades K–3).

Procedure: Have students read or chime in during the predictable or patterned part.

Example: *Brown Bear, Brown Bear, What Do You See?* (Martin, 1967)

"Brown Bear, Brown Bear, what do you see? I see a _____ looking at me."

Sequencing Sentences

Purpose: To sequence words to make a sentence (grades K–3).

Procedure: Using manipulatives such as word cards, have students put the word cards in order to make sentences. Nouns and verbs could be on different colored cards to be sure every sentence has one of each.

Cut-Up Sentences

Source: Clay, 1993b

Purpose: To sequence words, graphemes, and punctuation to make a sentence (grades K–3).

Procedure: Have students select a sentence that they like, or you select a sentence that students had difficulty reading from a song, poem, or book. Write the sentence on a thin strip of tag board. Cut between each word or word part, and cut off the punctuation. Write the sentence on an envelope. Have students read the sentence, turn over the envelope, and reconstruct the sentence. To make it more challenging, you can cut up individual words by onset/rime, by syllable, or by phonemes, depending on what students need to work on. This can then be sent home for homework.

Example: *Cat on the Mat* (Wildsmith, 1982)

The	dog	sat	on	the	mat	.

Cloze Procedure, or Guess the Covered Word

Source: Taylor, 1953; Cunningham, Hall, & Sigmon, 1999

Purpose: To use context clues to predict words (all grades).

Procedure: During reading, the student predicts the unknown word or part of the word that is deleted or covered with correction tape or sticky notes.

Example: *Where the Wild Things Are* (Sendak, 1963)

They gnashed their terrible _____ (teeth) and rolled their terrible _____ (eyes).

Phonics Strategies: Writing Words

General Purpose: These strategies can assist students in using conventional and inventive spelling to communicate ideas. Although spelling is important in order to accurately convey a written message, it is only one aspect of the writing process. Spelling ability is dependent on writers having a strong foundation of the sound-symbol correlations as well as being readers, so that they are familiar with how words look. Students should be taught to spell high-frequency words in the context of reading and writing sentences and use inventive spelling for unknown words. Students' writing will be stifled if they are limited by writing only words they can spell. Spelling skills are not necessarily sequential, so do not wait until students have mastered one spelling pattern before moving on.

For emergent readers and writers, introduce high-frequency, phonetically regular words first, followed by high-frequency, phonetically irregular words. Teach students to spell words by sounding them out into separate phonemes and writing the corresponding letters one by one. Model the sounding out and spelling process for students as they spell. Begin with short words students can sound out, because these words follow regular spelling conventions, for example, *at*, *can*, and *go* instead of *see*, *was*, or *have*. Next move to word family words and demonstrate how they are similar.

Sound Boxes

Source: Adapted from Elkonin, 1973

Purpose: To spell and recognize words based on the number of phonemes in a word (grades K–3).

Procedure: Draw one box for every phoneme. If more than one letter represents that phoneme then divide that box with dotted lines between each letter. For a silent -*e* at the end of a word, draw a line, because a box would indicate it has a sound. Have students predict the spelling and then write the letters in each box.

Example:

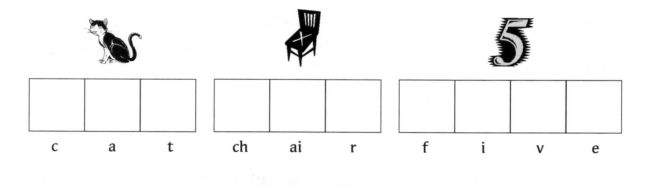

| c | a | t | ch | ai | r | f | i | v | e |

Magnetic Letters

Purpose: To read and spell new words based on the connection to known words or spelling patterns (grades K–3).

Procedure: Show students how to make new words by changing the onset (the initial consonants) or the rime (the vowel and the following consonants in a syllable).

Example: can (change the initial consonant to *f*, *m*, *pl*) fan, man, plan, plant (add a *t*)

Configuration Boxes

Source: Cunningham, Hall, & Sigmon, 1999

Purpose: To spell and recognize words based on their configuration (grades K–3).

Procedure: To assist memory of newly introduced words, draw the shape or outline around the words to indicate the pattern the letters make above the line (*b, d, f, h, k, l, t*), below the line (*g, j, p, q, y*), and between the lines for the rest of the letters. Then make blank configuration boxes that indicate the letters that are above, below, and between the lines to help students in spelling a word correctly. Tell the students the word and have them write it in the configuration box. This strategy is primarily used to aid in spelling the word. Although this strategy supports word identification, it cannot be used alone, as there can be numerous words with the same configuration.

Example: *play* and *happy*

Adaptation: Provide the configuration boxes and ask students to select the correct spelling word to match.

Read, Cover, Write, and Check Words

Source: McAndrews, 2004

Purpose: To read and write words from short-term memory rather than copying (all grades).

Procedure: Select two to five high-frequency words that students have difficulties with during reading or writing. These could be words that are visually similar. For advanced readers these could also be important content words. Fold a sheet of paper into four columns. In the first column write two to five new words to learn. The students read the first word, cover it up, write the same word in the second column, then open it up and check the spelling. Repeat this process in columns three and four. If a word is written incorrectly draw one line through it, reread the correct word, cover it, and write it again.

Example:

Read, Cover, Write, and Check three times each			
they	~~they~~ they	~~they~~ they	they
there	~~ther~~ there	there	there
their	their	their	their
they're	~~theyer~~ they're	they're	they're

Adaptation: Cut one side of a file folder into four equal flaps. Students put their paper inside the folder and lift each flap, write the word, cover, and open the first flap to check the word.

Chanting Words

Purpose: To spell words kinesthetically based on word configuration (grades K–2).

Procedure: Have the students chant the letters or sounds for each word. Add actions or arm movements as each word is spelled. For example, arms can be raised to the "attic" for tall letters that go above the line (*b, d, f, h, k, l, t*), arms can be out straight for "main floor" or letters that remain within the lines (*a, c, e, i, m*), and arms can go down to the "basement" for letters below the line (*g, j, p, q, y*).

Example: girl = *g* (arms down), *i* (arms out), *r* (arms out), *l* (arms up)

Word Study Notebook

Source: Bear et al., 2000

Purpose: The notebook serves as a record, assessment, and resource of the word study activities taught (grades K–5).

Procedure: Students write each learned spelling or sound pattern with examples on each page.

Example: *O* that says its name. (*boat, stone, so, grow*)

Word Wall

Source: Allington & Cunningham, 2002

Purpose: To use as a resource to spell and read explicitly taught common words (grades K–3).

Procedure: Introduce high-frequency words a few at a time. Model sounding out each word and provide a kinesthetic method for remembering how to spell and write it. Place words on the word wall underneath their initial letter. Have students refer to the word wall when they find words in books or want to write words that are on the wall. Word wall words are often written using an outline of the letter configurations as a clue.

Example: *Stop*

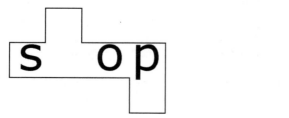

Framed Rhyming Innovations

Source: Walker, 2004

Purpose: To complete a sentence based on the author's pattern.

Procedure: You and the students rewrite a predictable book using the same pattern or frame but changing keywords.

Example: *The Very Hungry Caterpillar* (Carle, 1987)

On Monday I ate _____. On Tuesday I ate _____.

Keyword Spelling Chart

Purpose: To use a keyword chart to identify English spelling patterns associated with the long- and the short-vowel sounds.

Table 3.2   Keyword Spelling Chart

Vowel Sound	# of Spelling	Different Spellings
Long a /ā/	9	day, made, bait, straight, gauge, break, sleigh, obey, veil
Short a /ă/	4	pat, laugh, have, plaid
Long e /ē/	7	scheme, each, bleed, police, key, neither, niece
Short e /ĕ/	5	net, health, friend, heifer, said
Long i /ī/	11	die, mine, aye, aisle, geyser, stein, coyote, kind, light, height, my
Short i /ĭ/	6	pin, give, been, sieve, build, myth
Long o /ō/	9	cone, sew, mauve, soul, boast, dough, brooch, glow, toll
Short o /ŏ/	2	not, wasp
Long u /ū/	3	future, pewter, beauty
Short u /ŭ/	2	nut, some
Long oo /ö/	8	do, blue, broom, brute, bruise, move, through, group
Short oo /ŏŏ/	3	put, book, could
Diphthong /oi/	2	boy, join
Diphthong /ow/	3	how, mountain, sauerkraut
Schwa /ə/	7	basal, nickel, table, civil, Mongol, cherub, porpoise
Vocalic r /er/	6	her, first, nurse, works, early, grammar
r-controlled /ar/	1	arm
r-controlled /or/	1	for
l-, w-, and u-controlled	3	all, awful, auto
/aw/	8	claw, cause, broad, cough, gone, bought, boss, caught

Adapted from unpublished classroom materials, Bradley, 1996.

Procedure: Put the chart in Table 3.2 on the wall and make it available in the students' writing folders for a reference for spelling. Note that the long vowels have approximately twice the number of different spellings than the short vowels. This suggests that the short vowels may be easier to learn than the long vowels.

Message Writing

Purpose: To observe the writing process being modeled, so students will be able to write their own messages (grades K–2).

Procedure: While you write a message to the students or a dictated message from the students, segment words into their sounds by modeling the writing process on the board. Pronounce the word slowly and enunciate each word as you write it. Make connections to known words or parts of words.

Example: "I am going to begin by writing 'Dear Class.' What sound does the word *dear* start with? /d/. How do I write that sound? /d/. Because it is at the beginning of my greeting, I need a uppercase *D*. Next I hear /ē/, and that is written with two letters, *ea* like in *eat*. Finally I hear the /r/, written with the letter *r*. That word is done so I need a finger space. What is the next word? *Class*. It begins with the /k/ sound and it is written with the letter *c*, then /l/ă/s/ with two *ss*. Now I need a comma for the end of my greeting." Continue modeling the writing of the entire message and then chorally read the whole message.

Adaptation: Students could take turns dictating a message of the day while the teacher models writing it.

Phonics Strategies: Emergent Print Concepts

Directionality and One-to-One Matching

Purpose: To read from left to right, differentiate between the amount of space between letters and words, correlate one written word with every spoken word, and use the return sweep (grades K–1).

Procedure: When reading big books to the class, use a pointer to demonstrate reading from left to right and continuing on to the next line by pointing under each word. Have students take turns demonstrating these concepts using the big book and then demonstrate these same concepts on individual books with the same title. For one-to-one matching, make sure that students clearly point under each word as it is read. If the spoken and written words do not match up, such as if words have multiple syllables, remind students that they point only once for the entire word. Have students reread until they match one to one. One motivational technique would be to give students plastic fingertips with a long nail, found at a novelty store, to use when pointing.

These same concepts can be reinforced during writing instruction especially with finger spacing, the return sweep, capitalization, and punctuation.

Segmenting Sentences

Purpose: To segment sentences into separate words (grades K–2).

Procedure: Model and demonstrate how to break short sentences into individual words. Demonstrate with chips, cards, or other manipulatives how the sentence is made of separate words and how the order of the words matters.

Example: The sentence "Frogs eat bugs" has three words, so push up one chip for each word.

Understanding Punctuation

Purpose: To read with intonation and correct pausing marked by punctuation (all grades).

Procedure: Begin with declarative sentences that are marked with a period. Have the students point to each period on the page. Then read the sentences, taking a long breath after each period. Repeat this with choral reading. Remind students not to stop at the end of a line if it is midsentence. Then identify question marks and demonstrate this technique with interrogative sentences that are marked with a question mark. Point out that your voice goes up at the end of questions. Follow this same technique for exclamatory sentences that are marked with exclamation points. Point out that your voice rises with excitement and then falls. It is also important to introduce commas. Have students point to the commas. Then demonstrate pausing and taking a short breath after commas. Model the difference between the long breaths of ending punctuation and the short breaths of commas. For older students demonstrate this technique with colons and semicolons.

Quotation marks also need to be introduced, but do not emphasize them until students can read fluently at the primer level and quotation marks are found in their current reading. Have students point to the opening quotation mark and the closing quotation mark. Explain that the quotation marks show the words that the character says. Then read everything that is not in quotation marks and ask students to read what is in quotation marks.

CHAPTER 4

Oral Reading and Fluency

Understanding Oral Reading and Fluency

Oral reading is "the process of reading aloud to communicate to one another or to an audience" according to Harris and Hodges (1995, p. 173). During this social process, people read aloud or discuss the reading with others to share information, to further develop their understanding of the text, and for pure enjoyment of the text. Although not the primary purpose, oral reading can also be used for assessment and instruction when done properly. When students read materials in small groups or individually at their instructional level, oral reading provides a window into the reader's processing and provides opportunities to scaffold the instruction to enhance their problem-solving strategies.

Goodman's (1965) seminal work examines the sources of information students use while reading; these integrated sources are called the linguistic cueing system (Goodman, 1996), which is divided into three sources: (1) semantic (meaning), (2) syntactic (structure or grammar), and (3) graphophonic (symbol and sound). During the reading process, effective readers integrate semantic, syntactic, and graphophonic cues that interact with the reader's knowledge to support ongoing word identification and comprehension (Adams, 1990; Clay, 1991; Goodman, 1996; Rumelhart, 1994; see Figure 4.1). To monitor their reading, students can reflect on the following correlated questions: Does it make sense? (semantics), Does it sound right? (syntax), and Does it look right? (graphophonics). Familiarity with both syntax and semantics, through listening and reading a variety of texts, enables even very young readers to anticipate the format and predict the content of sentences in print (Singer & Ruddell, 1985). Oral reading strategies are the ways the reader makes sense of cues, such as the kind of cues that were used during reading, the cues that were used in making miscues, the cues that were used for self-corrections, and the cues that were used during cross-checking. A significant difference between efficient readers and developing readers is their ability to use a variety of strategies that integrate the cues in order to comprehend a passage (Clay, 1991; Goodman, 1996; Walker, 2004).

Although oral reading can be very beneficial during instruction, round-robin reading, a technique in which teachers call on students with different reading levels to read orally one after another, concerns some researchers and educators (Opitz & Rasinski, 1998). Students may get an inaccurate view of reading—that perfect word reading and following along in the text is the goal, rather than comprehending the text using effective reading. Students have fewer opportunities to problem-solve as others often correct them, and orally reading in front of more able readers may cause students to feel anxious or embarrassed about their reading. Because oral reading one by one is more time consuming than silent reading, less class time is spent reading, discussing, and comprehending the text (Opitz & Rasinski, 1998). Some students have difficulty

Figure 4.1   Cue System

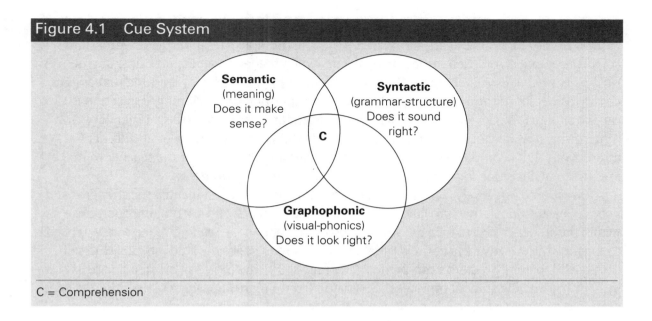

C = Comprehension

comprehending for a variety of reasons when other students read. Some students do not read loud enough, some do not read fluently enough or model ineffective strategies, and some read too fast for others to keep up. Not all students read at the same level or are able to use strategies to efficiently self-correct their miscues. It is very difficult to keep all students engaged during round-robin oral reading and therefore very few students benefit from this practice. In addition, it is inappropriate for the teacher and peers to critique a student's reading in front of the entire class as some students would feel embarrassed or self-conscious about their reading. Therefore, round-robin reading is not an effective oral reading practice.

Silent reading gives students an opportunity to read at their own pace, practice problem-solving and fluency strategies they have learned, focus on comprehension, have more time actually reading, and develop their interests in reading through self-selecting texts. During instructional time, give the students a purpose for reading silently and then discuss each section in order to monitor comprehension. Students then may reread sections orally in order to support answers or verify information found in the text.

Reading fluency is the ability to read in meaningful phrases with appropriate expression that reflects the meaning of the passage, to read smoothly and use efficient problem-solving strategies that often result in self-correction, and read at a conversational pace (Opitz & Rasinski, 1998).

There has been some confusion between reading fluently and reading quickly. The goal of reading is comprehension—not reading quickly. Because fluent readers do not have to concentrate on decoding the words, they can focus their attention on what the text means. Initially when students are learning to read, they often read slowly and have very few strategies for problem-solving unknown words. As students gain experience in reading and are able to efficiently integrate all three cueing systems, their pace of reading will improve. However, timing students' reading, in fact, may hinder their comprehension, as they will be less likely to engage in problem-solving strategies. Focusing on reading and understanding texts will develop efficient and effective readers (Opitz & Rasinski, 1998).

The two types of processing strategies are searching and monitoring. **Searching** includes gathering cues for an initial attempt to read, making multiple tries at difficult words, and self-correcting some errors. **Self-monitoring** occurs when readers evaluate attempts and decide if further searching is needed. Clay (1993) developed a theory of literacy learning that assigns a central role to monitoring strategies. An important question for beginning instruction is How can we support the development of a highly efficient and coordinated set of searching and monitoring strategies? Lyons, Pinnell, and DeFord (1993) attribute teacher and student interactions that promote effective literacy strategies and the ability of the teacher to make instructional decisions to the acceleration of students' reading progress.

In order to effectively facilitate students' reading, you must first identify the strengths and needs of each student, then provide wait time, scaffold prompts, and ask probing questions within the student's ZPD to help the students problem-solve while reading. Afterward you need to evaluate the effectiveness of the facilitation in order to enhance the students' ability to self-correct and therefore focus on comprehension of the story. An analysis of oral reading behaviors by both you and the student provides the basis for determining the student's strengths and needs as well as growth over time. Instruction is then adapted to support the student's use of reading strategies for self-monitoring in order to improve his or her comprehension. In addition, oral reading can be used authentically for sharing information and performing, which may enhance students' desire to read (Opitz & Rasinski, 1998).

This chapter focuses on small-group or individualized oral reading for assessment and instruction as well as developing oral reading and fluency when sharing information or performing for an audience. Oral reading should be paired with developing comprehension, which is described in Chapter 5.

Objectives for Oral Reading and Fluency

The following summary of oral reading objectives was adapted from Opitz and Rasinski (1998), Goodman (1996), and my own research. To improve oral reading and fluency, students will do the following:

- Listen to and read a wide variety of genres for enjoyment
- Listen to and read a wide variety of genres for vocabulary and comprehension development
- Read orally to share information with others
- Read orally to support answers or verify where information is found in the text
- Read orally to provide enjoyment to others
- Read orally for educators to identify the student's independent, instructional, and listening levels to select appropriate texts and instruction
- Read orally for educators, peers, and self to identify and improve problem-solving strategies
- Read orally to monitor their own reading
- Read fluently with appropriate phrasing, expression, smoothness, and pace

Oral Reading Assessments

Oral reading can be evaluated using an oral reading record to analyze specific miscues; an oral reading strategy checklist to identify oral reading strategies used; and a fluency assessment to evaluate phrasing, expression, smoothness, and pace. Once analyzed, all assessments can be used to teach oral reading and fluency strategies while reading a single text first and then applying the strategies to new texts. (Although comprehension should always be assessed with oral reading, comprehension is thoroughly covered in Chapter 5.)

Oral Reading Record and Analysis of Miscues

Source: S. McAndrews, 2004, 2006

Purpose: To accurately represent the student's oral reading behaviors while reading connected text in order to identify word accuracy and functioning levels and to analyze miscues and oral reading behaviors. This helps to scaffold instruction and select appropriate leveled texts in order to improve student's oral reading. The coding and analysis of oral reading was developed by integrating the procedures for running records (Clay, 1993a), miscue analysis (Goodman & Marek, 1996), and the Qualitative Reading Inventory, which has been updated in the fourth edition (Leslie & Caldwell, 2006). This assessment can be used as a pre- and posttest or an ongoing assessment to show growth over time. It helps the teacher determine a student's reading level, problem-solving abilities, and ability to orally read their current classroom texts or self-selected reading. The oral reading record and analysis is only the first part of the reading assessment; the second part is an analysis of comprehension, which is described in Chapter 5.

Procedure and Analysis: There are four parts to this assessment: the oral reading record, the analysis of miscues worksheet, the oral reading analysis of miscues summary, and the comprehension assessment and analysis (addressed in Chapter 5). To evaluate a student's oral reading behaviors during text reading, you can create an oral reading record on a typed, double-spaced copy of the text, on a photocopy of an actual text, or on blank paper. The Analysis of Miscues Worksheet (see Appendix) is the second form in which each miscue is written and analyzed by the type of miscue, the cues used in making the miscue, and whether it was self-corrected. The Oral Reading Analysis of Miscues Summary (see Appendix) is a third form that summarizes the scores and identifies the student's functioning levels.

The procedure itself is divided into four parts: text selection, coding oral reading behaviors, directions, and analysis of miscues and cueing sources.

1. Text selection: Select a current trade book, book from a published reading series, or electronic text to determine if the text is at the student's instructional or independent functioning level. To determine the student's reading grade level, select passages from an informal reading inventory or select benchmark texts that have been evaluated by the publisher or literacy specialist to be at a certain grade level or incremental level within a grade using a leveling system such as the Guided Reading Level Guidelines (Fountas & Pinnell, 1996).

When selecting texts for assessing reading, there are many factors to consider that influence a student's ability to read a given passage. Consider the student's interest, prior knowledge of the content and vocabulary, and ability to use strategies for self-monitoring. Examine the differences in text structure between narrative, expository, persuasive, and descriptive. Select a text believed to be at the student's instructional level based on the density of vocabulary or non–high-frequency words; the complexity of sentence structure; the complexity of concepts; the amount of picture, chart, or graphic support; and the typography, such as the size of text, headings, boldfaced print, and italics. (For more discussion about leveling and selecting books, see Chapter 7.) If the text has fewer than approximately 300 words, use the entire text; however, for longer texts, select a chapter or coherent passage within in the word count for the grade level according to the following general guidelines:

Preprimer–Primer: 40–60 words

First grade: 100–150 words

Second grade: 100–200 words

Third grade: 200–300 words

Fourth grade and above: 300–400 words

Which text you select depends on what information you want to gather. Sometimes reading a narrative text is easier than reading an expository text because of the reader's experience with that structure. However, selecting an expository text will provide more information about a student's problem-solving strategies while reading content area material. When selecting narrative and expository passages in an informal reading inventory, such as the Qualitative Reading Inventory-4 (Leslie & Caldwell, 2006), first find the student's instructional level on the word lists and then select a passage one grade level below. Reading familiar text reveals whether the difficulty level of the material the student is using is suitable and reveals in what ways the student is making use of the strategies that have been taught. Reading unfamiliar texts reveals the student's willingness to take risks and indicates the ability to use and integrate strategies independently (Walker, 2004). Selecting a text with one concept per page with strong picture support may enhance the student's oral reading, while choosing a longer text may overwhelm the reader. By selecting appropriate texts, you will be able to gather the information needed to make instructional decisions. Continue text reading until the student reaches frustration level.

2. Coding oral reading behaviors: The following coding system is a method for documenting the student's reading in such a way that the passage could be reread exactly how the student read it. To code the student's text reading, use the Coding and Scoring Oral Reading Behaviors Guide (see Appendix) to see how to mark each miscue. Record substitutions, omissions, insertions, hesitations, repetitions, and self-corrections above the word(s) in the text. Put commas between multiple attempts. For every two seconds of a hesitation, put a slash mark between words or letters. For repetitions, mark an *R* with a circle around it and draw an arrow back to where the repetition began. In this assessment, never tell students a word, as it may inflate the student's comprehension of the passage; this also sends a message to students that if they wait long enough, the teacher will tell them the word and they will not have to use problem-solving strategies. In a nonassessment setting, however, you may provide strategy prompts to help students problem-solve. In this event mark prompts by a *P* with a circle around it, and it is considered a miscue. The following is an example of coding miscues from the story *Annie and the Wild Animals* (Brett, 1985):

↓ s-c

The student read: Ann   fund ✓ cat cuddled ✓ ✓ /// s/t/r/ă/n/g/, strong plāks s-c

The actual text: Annie found her ^ curled up in   strange   places.

Notice that this example shows several types of miscues. If a student actually read like this, he or she would be at the frustration level.

3. Directions: Materials needed for the assessment include the text for the student to read, a sheet to document oral reading behaviors, a clipboard, a pencil, and a cassette recorder and tape (optional). You can use any of three formats to code the oral reading behaviors: a typed, double-spaced copy of the text, a photocopy of the text, or a blank sheet of paper. If you use a blank sheet of paper, one line of text should correspond to one line of coding marks. Use a checkmark (✓) for each correct word and write each miscue above the word in the text with a line between them. Sit next to and slightly behind the student so that you can see the student reading but can record the reading behaviors without the student seeing what is written. Then explain to the student what to do. Say, "Today I am going to listen to you read. I am going to mark down exactly what you say. I cannot help you while you are reading, so try your best if you come to a tricky part. When you are done, I will ask you about what you read. This story is called...." You may choose to provide a brief introduction to the story or ask questions to determine the student's prior knowledge. While the student is reading, code all reading behaviors. If the student reads too fast for you to keep up with the coding, ask the student to slow down. Until you become proficient at coding oral reading, audiotaping the reading is beneficial to verify that the coding was done accurately.

4. Analysis of miscues and cueing sources: A miscue is any deviation from the text including substitutions, insertions, deletions, repetitions, and self-corrections of words. Analyzing miscues provides information about how the reader constructs meaning with the text. This analysis is based on several theoretical assumptions suggested by Goodman and Marek (1996) and summarized by Walker (2004): Readers read to construct meaning, reading is not an exact process, some miscues or errors are more significant than others, miscues should be evaluated based on the degree to which they change meaning, and readers use a consistent pattern of correction strategies that indicate their text processing. In this analysis the type of miscue is analyzed as well as the cue source used.

All miscues, except repetitions and hesitations, should be recorded on the Analysis of Miscues Worksheet (see Appendix). For each miscue, mark the student's response, a slash, and then the word from the text. For insertions, write the word, a slash, and then a carat. For omissions, mark a hyphen, a slash, and the word. Although self-corrections are miscues and affect fluency, they are not incorrect responses, so they are not counted against word accuracy. Hesitations and omissions of punctuation are issues of fluency, not word accuracy, so they are also not included in the analysis of miscues. For each miscue put a checkmark (✓) indicating the type of miscue it is (self-correction, omission, insertion, decoded, or substitution). Mark *decoded* if a student sounds out a word or says a nonword, or mark *substitution* if a student substitutes a real word.

An analysis of the semantic (meaning), syntactic (structure or grammar), and graphophonic (visual and sound) cues used while making miscues provides an opportunity to examine the student's processing while reading. For each miscue, check the cue used during the initial attempt at the word (graphophonic, syntactic, or semantic). For graphophonic cues indicate whether the reader had the correct initial (I), medial (M), or final (F) sounds. Graphophonic cues are used when a reader predicts a word based on visual or sound similarities, such as the word *very* for *every* or when a reader attempts to sound out a word, such as /o/-/t/-/h/ for *other*. Syntactic cues are predictions of a word made on the basis of the sentence structure or what makes grammatical sense, such as the substitution of *run* for *swim* because they are both verbs. A student shows evidence of using semantic cues if the miscue has a similar meaning, such as the substitution of *little* for *small*. Generally, a student relies on the context and experience when making semantic miscues.

The last column is used to mark if the meaning of the text was retained even with or without a self-correction. Not all miscues have a significant impact on the meaning of the text. For example:

The student read: Toad put   the covers over his head.
The actual text: Toad pulled the covers over his head.

Put and *pulled* generally do not have the same meaning, but in this sentence the meaning of the text was retained, and therefore the miscue is considered acceptable. Mispronunciations are another example of how the text would maintain meaning; for example, saying /pŭskĕtē/ for *spaghetti*. Also, a student who says *gonna* for *going to* still maintains meaning. By comparing the accuracy and the acceptability score, you can see if the student's miscues still retain the meaning of the text. If a student has a higher acceptability score, then the student may be able to read more challenging text than the accuracy score would reflect.

Although word accuracy is important, the goal is comprehension. Even fluent readers make miscues. Because this assessment is also used to place students in appropriately leveled text, the acceptability of the miscues needs to be considered. Therefore, an acceptability, or meaning score, is also obtained. Once each of the miscues has been analyzed, each of the columns is totaled to determine the number of occurrences and to determine the student's strengths and needs in problem-solving unknown words.

Using the data from the Analysis of Miscues Worksheet (see Appendix), scores are obtained for word accuracy; acceptability; self-correction; and use of the graphophonic, syntactic, and semantic cues. The Oral Reading Analysis of Miscues Summary provides the formulas for calculating these scores (see Appendix). In calculating the accuracy score, self-corrections, repetitions, hesitations, and omissions of punctuation are not considered word accuracy errors. Self-corrections, self-correction attempts, repetitions, and hesitations are indications that the student is monitoring his or her reading in an attempt to understand it. The acceptability or meaning score includes the total correct words plus any uncorrected miscues that retained the meaning of the text.

Once the student's accuracy, acceptability, and comprehension scores are obtained, the functional reading levels can be determined. Betts (1946) was the first to set up three levels of reading made on the basis of the word accuracy score and the comprehension score: the independent level, the instructional level, and the frustration level (see Table 4.1). The purpose for identifying these levels is to determine the student's reading level and to select appropriate instructional materials that will challenge and support the reader. The independent level is the level at which the student reads fluently with good phrasing and excellent comprehension. It is also called the *recreational reading level* because a student should be able to read the material on his or her own and the student often has a high interest in the topic. Materials at this level should be for supplementary and independent reading.

The instructional level is the level at which the student can make progress in reading with instructional guidance. It is also called the teaching level or guided reading level because the reading material must be challenging but not too difficult. This level relates to Vygotsky's (1978) concept of the ZPD (see Chapter 1, page 14). Materials used for small-group instruction such as guided reading should be leveled within this zone.

The frustration level is the level at which a student is unable to pronounce many of the words or is unable to understand the material. This is the level to be avoided for instructional purposes. The material is too difficult and frustrates the student, thereby hindering reading development. However, it is appropriate for the teacher to read aloud material at this level if it is at the student's listening level (discussed further in Chapter 5). Students may enjoy looking through material at this level just because it is a topic of their interest, but it should not be used for instruction.

Although these levels have been proven historically useful to teachers looking for appropriate materials for instruction, remember that it is rarely possible to determine an exact reading level for a student, particularly for one reading beyond the primary levels. Familiarity or unfamiliarity with content, genre, and structure can cause great variability in a student's ability to read a selection with understanding. Students should have opportunities to read books at multiple levels for self-selected reading if they are interested in them.

If the student selects a book that is too challenging, give an option of the teacher continuing to read, the student perusing the book, or the teacher guiding the student in selecting a more appropriate text. The patterns in miscues can then be identified and instruction can be provided that supports the use of the other cues and additional strategies to increase comprehension and self-correction of miscues while reading. The following is an example of the Analysis of Miscues Worksheet and Summary.

Table 4.1   Functioning Levels

	Independent Level	**Instructional Level**	**Frustration Level**
Oral Accuracy	95%–100%	90%–94%	89% and below
Oral Acceptability	98%–100%	95%–97%	94% and below
Comprehension	90%–100%	70%–89%	69% and below

Adapted from Betts (1954).

Example and Analysis: Analysis of Miscues Worksheet, *The Mitten* (Brett, 1989)

Name:					Grade:				Date:	

Title: *The Mitten* by Jan Brett			Word Count: 310			Text Level: DRA Level 28			
	Type of Miscue					Type of Cues Used			Meaning Retained
Student Response/Text	Self-correction	Uncorrected miscue	Omission	Insertion	Decoded	Substitution	Graphophonic I = initial, M= medial, F = final	Syntactic	Semantic	
1. Nicholas/Nicki		✓				✓	I	✓	✓	yes
2. /k/nĭt/knit	✓			✓			M, F			yes
3. like/look		✓				✓	I	✓		
4. turning/tunneling		✓				✓				
5. decided/discovered		✓				✓	I, F	✓		
6. he/a	✓					✓				yes
7. something/things	✓						M, F	✓	✓	yes
8. with/the	✓					✓				yes
9. arg/argue		✓			✓		I			
10. picture, prediction, pickles/prickles		✓				✓	I			
11. there/through		✓				✓	I			
12. evered/eyed		✓			✓					
13. ^/and		✓		✓						yes
14. then/when		✓				✓	M, F			
15. dear/diggers		✓				✓	I			
16. The/A		✓				✓		✓	✓	yes
17. spid/spied		✓			✓		I			
18. pulled/plumped	✓					✓	I, F	✓		yes
19. tight/tightly		✓				✓	I, M		✓	yes
20. arg/argue		✓			✓		I			
21. a/an	✓					✓		✓	✓	yes
22. corn/acorn	✓					✓	M, F	✓	✓	yes
23. snap/shape		✓				✓	I, M			
24. dis/distance	✓				✓		I			yes
25. –/silhouetted		✓	✓							
Totals:	8	17	1	2	5	16	17	8	6	12, 4 not s-c

Example: Oral Reading Analysis of Miscues Summary

Name:	Grade: 3	Date: 10/13
Title: *The Mitten* by Jan Brett	Word Count: 198 of 310	Level: DRA 28
Text Type: Narrative or Expository	Reading Method: Oral, Silent, or Listening	

ORAL READING SUMMARY

Type of score	Calculation	Fraction	Percentage	Functioning level*
Word accuracy	Words correct = Word count – Uncorrected miscues ÷ Word count	$\frac{181}{198}$	91%	Instructional
Text meaning or acceptability	Words correct + Uncorrected meaning – Retained miscues ÷ Word count	$\frac{185}{198}$	93%	Instructional

Miscue Scores

Self-correction	$\frac{\text{Self-corrections}}{\text{Number of miscues}}$	$\frac{8}{25}$	32%	Sometimes used
Omissions	$\frac{\text{Omissions}}{\text{Number of miscues}}$	$\frac{1}{25}$	4%	Rarely used
Insertions	$\frac{\text{Insertions}}{\text{Number of miscues}}$	$\frac{2}{25}$	8%	Rarely used
Decoded sounds or nonwords	$\frac{\text{Decoded sounds}}{\text{Number of miscues}}$	$\frac{5}{25}$	20%	Sometimes used
Substitutions of real words	$\frac{\text{Substitutions}}{\text{Number of miscues}}$	$\frac{18}{25}$	64%	Often used

Cueing System Scores

Graphophonic	$\frac{\text{Number of graphophonic cues used}}{\text{Number of miscues}}$	$\frac{17}{25}$	68%	Often used
Syntactic	$\frac{\text{Number of syntactic cues used}}{\text{Number of miscues}}$	$\frac{8}{25}$	32%	Sometimes used
Semantic	$\frac{\text{Number of semantic cues used}}{\text{Number of miscues}}$	$\frac{6}{25}$	24%	Sometimes used

Functioning Levels for Text Reading

	Independent	Instructional	Frustration
Oral Reading Accuracy	95%–100%	90%–94%	89% and below
Oral Acceptability	98%–100%	95%–97%	94% and below
Comprehension	90%–100%	70%–89%	69% and below

Functioning Levels for Cueing System

75%–100%	Predominantly used cue
50%–74%	Often used cue
20%–49%	Sometimes used cue
19% and below	Rarely used cue

The student's oral reading was at an instructional level for the end of second grade. His comprehension as evaluated and analyzed in the comprehension chapter was also at the instructional level. When he came to an unknown word he often used the initial sounds. He sometimes used syntax and semantics during his predictions. He self-corrected 32% of his miscues, which is a significant improvement from when he rarely self-corrected. Most of his miscues were real words; however, some of them are still just decoded sounds.

Instructional Implications: The student should be praised for his number of self-corrections. He needs prompting to reread when he does not come up with a real word or the word does not make sense. Guessing the covered work might be an effective strategy to get him to predict real words that make sense.

Oral Reading Strategies Assessment

Purpose: The Oral Reading Strategies Assessment (see Appendix) is used to identify strategy use during reading. This is to be used for any oral reading that is at the instructional or frustration level for word accuracy.

Procedure and Analysis: While the student is orally reading, identify the strategies that are used in order to attempt to figure out words. Record a plus sign (+) if this strategy was used frequently, a checkmark (✓) if the strategy was used occasionally, or a minus sign (−) if the strategy was used rarely or not at all.

Example:

Oral Reading Strategies Assessment		
+ used frequently	✓ used occasionally	− used rarely
✓	Look at the pictures and think about the story	
✓	Say the beginning three sounds	
✓	Read on to collect clues and then go back	

–	Go back and read again
–	Break words into parts
–	Try different sounds
✓	Attempt to self-correct words that do not look right
–	Attempt to self-correct words that do not sound right
–	Attempt to self-corrects words that do not make sense
✓	Self-correct words

This student generally attempted to sound out the words when she came to words she didn't know. Usually only the first sound or two were correct. Sometimes she read on and figured out the word; however, she rarely reread, broke words into parts, or tried different sounds. She self-corrected 3 out of the 12 miscues. All of these self-corrections were for words that did not initially look like the word in the text.

Instructional Implications: Use the Oral Reading Strategy Checklists for Teachers, Peers, and Self to teach and reinforce word identification strategies (described later in this chapter; see also Appendix). Especially focus on rereading if the text doesn't make sense.

Published Informal Reading Inventories and Emergent Literacy Assessments

There are many informal reading inventories available. I selected the following four published literacy assessments as being the most influential in understanding the reading process of students: the Observational Survey (Clay, 1993a), the Illinois Snapshot of Early Literacy (ISEL; Barr et al., 2004), the Developmental Reading Assessment (DRA; Beaver, 2001), and the QRI-4, (Leslie & Caldwell, 2006).

Observational Survey: For assessing emergent literacy, Clay (1993a) developed the Observational Survey, which is used in her Reading Recovery program. This assessment includes letter identification, concepts about print, word tests, writing vocabulary, writing dictation, and text reading. Running records are taken from 30 leveled books between preprimer and third grade. For each book an introduction is provided and a running record of text is taken. A word accuracy score is obtained along with an analysis of errors.

Illinois Snapshot of Early Literacy (ISEL): Barr et al. (2004) developed the ISEL, which is based on Clay's work but which was designed as a screening instrument for classroom teachers to help evaluate all of the emergent literacy areas identified in the National Reading Panel report (NICHD, 2000). There are two separate tests. The kindergarten and first-grade test contains subtests in alphabet recognition, story listening, phonemic awareness, one-to-one matching and word naming, letter sounds, developmental spelling, vocabulary, passage accuracy and comprehension, and fluency. The second-grade test evaluates spelling, word recognition, fluency, extended written response, passage accuracy and comprehension, and vocabulary. Through extensive research, cut-off scores were obtained for the beginning and end of each grade level. I contributed to the piloting and adaptation of this assessment. (The ISEL is a free assessment and can be obtained online.)

Developmental Reading Assessment (DRA): If the student scores at or below the first-grade level on the word lists, the DRA (Beaver, 2001) can be selected for text reading because it subdivides each grade level into incremental levels. For example, grade one has differentiated reading levels from 1–16. These reading levels are similar to the Reading Recovery assessment stories (Clay, 1993b) but unlike Reading Recovery, an assessment of comprehension is included. This assessment is helpful when selecting appropriately leveled materials for guided and independent reading, especially at the emergent reading level. Many publishers are now identifying the levels of their books including DRA levels and Fountas and Pinnell Guided Reading levels. Although the initial DRA was designed for ease of use with students in grades K–3, it has limited nonfiction selections, and a more comprehensive miscue analysis, as described in this book, would be beneficial to understand the reading processes the student uses.

Qualitative Reading Inventory-4 (QRI-4): The QRI-4 (Leslie & Caldwell, 2006) is an informal reading inventory that identifies the oral, silent, and listening levels of the student using preprimer through 12th-grade word lists and expository and narrative passages. Although there are passages as low as preprimer in the QRI, the DRA has more incremental levels for emergent readers that can be correlated with book levels. There are five to six passages per grade level in the QRI-4. At the lower levels there are stories with pictures, and at the middle and high school levels there are longer passages based on the different content areas. To analyze the student's reading behaviors, oral reading records are taken during reading and then the miscues are analyzed. Comprehension of a passage is assessed through concept questions, retelling checklists, and explicit and implicit comprehension questions after reading the passage orally or silently. In addition, the listening comprehension level is useful in determining if a student can comprehend a passage even if it is at their frustration level for word accuracy. In a study, the QRI-3 was found to have the highest percentage of higher level questions when comparing it with seven other informal reading inventories (Applegate, Quinn, & Applegate, 2003).

Fluency Assessments

The following assessments reflect the complete concept of fluency, including phrasing, smoothness, and pace—not the limited fluency definition of words correct per minute that is used in some other assessments.

Fluency Assessment by Teachers and Peers

Purpose: The Fluency Assessment by Teachers and Peers (McAndrews, 2006) was developed on the basis of Zutell and Rasinski's (1991) three dimensions of fluency—phrasing, smoothness, and pace—as well as a compilation of other fluency elements. It can be used both by the teacher to plan instruction that reinforces and teaches appropriate fluency behaviors and by the peer to help students reflect on their fluency development (see Appendix).

Procedure and Analysis: While the student orally reads a passage, observe the student's fluency and compare it with the indicators for each of the fluency elements: reads in phrases (mostly in clauses or sentences), pays attention to end punctuation (period, question mark, exclamation point), pays attention to middle punctuation (comma, semicolon, colon), reads with expression, reads with emphasis for dramatization, reads smoothly (with only minor breaks), resolves word problems quickly (usually through self-correction), reads at an independent level (fewer than 5 meaning miscues per 100 words), reads at a conversational pace (not fast), and can comprehend or retell what was read. Mark each indicator with a plus sign (+) for generally fluent, a checkmark (✓) for sometimes fluent, or a minus sign (–) for rarely fluent. This assessment can be administered throughout the school year to plan appropriate fluency instruction and show growth over time.

Example and Analysis: Fluency Assessment by Teacher and Peers

Name: Maurice	Date:		
Title/Author: *Crickwing* by Janell Cannon (2005)	Level: Guided Reading O		Genre: Narrative
The student...	Generally Fluent (+)	Sometimes Fluent (✓)	Rarely Fluent (–)
Read in phrases score: ✓	Read sentences in meaningful phrases or clauses	Read in a mixture of appropriate phrasing and word by word	Read only one to two words at a time
Paid attention to punctuation score: ✓	Paused after end (period, question mark exclamation point) and middle punctuation (comma, semicolon, colon)	Usually paused at end punctuation, but not always middle punctuation	Rarely paused at punctuation
Read with expression score: –	Read with appropriate stress and intonation; changes voice for expression as needed; read with emphasis for dramatization or read with different voices	Read with some appropriate expression, and some changes in stress and intonation	Read with little expression or change in stress and intonation
Read smoothly score: ✓	Reading sounded smooth, with only a few short pauses for problem solving when needed	Reading was generally smooth, with some hesitations and repetitions	Reading sounded choppy, with several skipped words, hesitations, or repetitions

The student...	Generally Fluent (+)	Sometimes Fluent (✓)	Rarely Fluent (−)
Used problem-solving strategies efficiently score: −	After the first strategy was attempted, most meaning miscues were self-corrected	Two to three strategies were attempted and most meaning miscues were self-corrected	Multiple strategies were attempted and often did not result in self-correction
Read at a conversational pace score: ✓	The reading pace was like that of a conversation, not too fast or too slow for others to understand	The reading pace was either a little too fast or a little too slow	The reading was very slow and labored
Read at an independent word accuracy level score: ✓	Read at an independent word accuracy level (95% or higher word accuracy, less than 5 miscues per 100 words)	Read at an instructional word accuracy level (90-94% word accuracy, between 6-10 miscues per 100 words)	Read at a frustration level (89% or below word accuracy, 11 or more miscues per 100 words)
Comprehended or retold what was read score: −	Retold all of the elements of the story or the main idea and major details	Retold most of the elements of the story or the main idea and major details	Could not retell the important elements of the story or the main idea and major details

During this narrative passage, the student sometimes read in phrases, attended to punctuation, read smoothly, read at a conversational pace, and read at an instructional level. However, the student did not attend to expression even when Crickwing was yelling, "Oh, noooo!" or "Wait!" The student generally skipped unknown words and rarely used strategies to attempt to self-correct. He was unable to retell any of Crickwing's problems or how he saved the colony from army ants.

Instructional Implications: The student needs more opportunities to hear stories that are rich with expression being read aloud, and he needs discussion and practice on how and when to change one's voice to show expression when reading. The student would benefit from using the Good Readers Bookmarks (see Chapter 3 and Appendix) when he comes to words he does not know. Finally, think-aloud strategies or story maps could be used to identify each of the major events in the story and the resolution.

Ongoing Self-Evaluation of Fluency

Purpose: The Ongoing Self-Evaluation of Fluency (see Appendix) is a rubric, similar to the Fluency Assessment by Teachers and Peers, to help the students evaluate their own reading fluency and provide a guide for the indicators of fluent reading.

Procedure and Analysis: After students audiotape their reading, they replay the tape and evaluate their reading with a plus sign (+) for generally fluent, a checkmark (✓) for sometimes fluent, or a minus sign (−) for rarely fluent for each of the following indicators: I read in phrases, I paused at middle punctuation and end punctuation, My voice changed to show expression and match the meaning and emotions in the passage, I read smoothly, I used strategies to correct my reading if it didn't make sense, I read at a conversational pace, I can read most of the words, and I can retell what I read. Students can also practice rereading the same text and reevaluate their reading to identify any areas of improvement.

Oral Reading Fluency Strategies

General oral reading and fluency strategies include the teacher and students reading a variety of genres and having students reread familiar books. Encourage students to pause briefly at commas and longer after the end punctuation marks. Have them think after each sentence to see if it made sense. If it does not make sense, ask them try to figure out what would make sense. If students have difficulty keeping their place, suggest that they use a bookmark or keep their fingertips under each line. Have students tape record their reading and then listen to the tape to monitor their reading. Provide small-group reading opportunities that encourage problem solving during reading. Provide heterogeneous and homogeneous paired reading opportunities. Always include a self-reflection of reading.

The two most important strategies are the self-analysis of miscues and the oral reading strategy checklists (McAndrews, 1999, 2002, 2006), which are detailed in the following sections. There are three separate oral reading strategy checklists: one to be completed by teachers, one for peers, and the one for student self-evaluation (McAndrews, 1999, 2000, 2006; see Appendix). My recent data on the effectiveness of these checklists with first-through eighth-grade students has indicated that struggling readers whose teachers have implemented all three Oral Reading Strategy Checklists and provided the students with strategy bookmarks are able to self-correct during reading more often than struggling readers who have not been exposed to these assessments. The Oral Reading Strategy Checklists are more than just another tool; they are a way to improve student reading through reflection and analysis.

Because the difference between good readers and poor readers is the variety of strategies they can employ when they come to a word they cannot read, these strategy checklists can be used to scaffold students' problem solving while reading, thereby helping them to internalize reading strategies. Strategy instruction needs to occur during reading authentic literature. In order to internalize reading strategies, students need numerous opportunities to practice them in safe, risk-taking environments.

Self-Analysis of Miscues

Purpose: Based on concepts from retrospective miscue analysis (Goodman & Marek, 1996), these two self-assessments provide an opportunity for students to monitor and self-correct their own reading. The first method involves the interaction between the teacher and the student, and in the second method, the student does an analysis alone.

Procedure: You or the students select an interesting text that is near the students' instructional level. Before beginning, conduct a reading interview to determine the students' prior knowledge. Audiotape the students reading the text. After the initial session, you should code miscues on a printed version of the text and preselect miscues to discuss during retrospective miscue analysis. Sometimes, you may want the students to listen to the tape and stop when they hear a miscue. You and the students can listen to the tape and mark miscues on a printed version of text and then discuss miscues using the following seven questions taken from Goodman and Marek (1996, p. 45):

1. Does the miscue make sense?
2. Does the miscue sound like English language? Was the miscue corrected? Should it have been?

If the answers are "No" to the above questions, then ask the following:

3. Does the miscue look like what was on the page?
4. Does the miscue sound like what was on the page?

For all miscues, ask the following:

5. Why do you think you made the miscue?
6. Did that miscue affect your understanding of the text?
7. Why do you think that? How do you know?

Once the students have experienced several teacher–student sessions, they can use the following adapted method: The students read a story or passage into an audiotape recorder and then play back the tape while following along in the text. At each place of difficulty, students stop the tape and highlight the words. The students then answer the seven questions listed above.

Good Readers Poster

Purpose: To provide strategies that can be used when a reader cannot figure out a word or realizes that the reading does not make sense, sound right, or look right. The icons on the poster correspond to each strategy to help students identify the strategies on the checklist quickly (see Appendix).

Procedure: Display the Good Readers Poster in the classroom and provide each student with a personal Good Readers Bookmark (see Chapter 3 and Appendix). Explain to students that the heading "good readers" was selected because good readers, not poor readers, use strategies to figure out unknown words or to make sense of their reading. Read the strategies aloud according to the students' grade level, and provide examples for using each of the strategies while you read.

While students are reading, remind them to use their Good Readers Bookmark strategies when they come to words they do not know or if what they are reading does not make sense. These Good Readers Bookmarks can be used in conjunction with the Oral Reading Strategy Checklists.

Oral Reading Strategy Checklist for Teachers

Purpose: To help students efficiently identify words and correct their miscues by using oral strategies when students come to words they do not immediately recognize and to self-correct their reading when it does not make sense, look right, or sound right. This two-column checklist (see Appendix) can be used while students are reading to identify and analyze the strategies students use while problem-solving unknown words on the left column and to identify and analyze the prompts given to students to encourage the use of new strategies for word identification on the right column (grades 1 and above). By identifying and modeling the cues and strategies used by good readers, you can provide "critical moment teaching" (Goodman & Marek, 1996) and prompt for strategies that students can select when problem-solving on their own.

Procedure: Select a passage that is approximately at the student's instructional level. The first time the student is evaluated, do not preteach the strategies from the Good Readers Bookmark. Tell the student, "I am going to mark all the good things you do while reading." Then for subsequent evaluations, provide a copy of the Good Readers Bookmark for the student to use as a resource and say, "I am going to mark all the strategies you use during reading." Ask, "What do you think this story is about from the title, the pictures, or from what you have read so far?"

While the student is reading, make a tally mark corresponding to each of the strategies he uses on the left column of the checklist. Also tally the number of self-corrections. For each uncorrected miscue, note whether the miscue has a similar meaning, similar syntax, or is visually similar. After the student has read the passage or section, ask the student to retell the important events or ideas in the text.

After evaluating the student's strategy use, use the right column to tally each of the prompts you provided to support the student in correctly identifying the words. The words *wait time* at the top of the prompts column are to remind you to provide the student with at least three seconds of thinking time after making a miscue or wait until the student has finished reading the sentence or paragraph with a significant miscue prior to prompting him. This also gives you time to think about and plan what the most efficient prompt would be to help the student problem-solve. Mark each time you provide wait time. If the student needs support, ask, "What strategy from the bookmark could you try?" If the student is unsuccessful in self-correcting, suggest one of the strategies and mark it in the right column. Do not tell the student any words, as it prevents him from problem-solving, but continue to offer prompts until the student figures out the word.

Table 4.2 includes the prompts and when you should provide them. The strategy prompts are not presented in particular order but should be selected first by you and then by

Table 4.2 Oral Reading Strategy Prompts	
Strategy Prompt	**When Teacher Would Provide Prompt**
(Wait time)	Provide wait time before any prompting. Allow the student the opportunity to read to the end of the sentence before prompting.
Look at the pictures and think about the story.	Use if the picture, diagram, or the previous content can be used to figure out the unknown words.
Say the beginning three sounds. (Three was selected because it is more effective than predicting based only on the initial sound, and three is often more efficient than sounding out the entire word.)	Use if the student pauses for an extended time or makes a guess only on the basis of the initial sound.
Read on to collect clues.	Use if the context of the rest of the sentence would help. Then prompt the student to go back.
Go back and read again.	Use if the beginning of the sentence or the previous sentence will help.
Break words into parts.	Use if the student knows parts of the word or multisyllabic words.
Try different sounds.	Use when the student is mispronouncing phonemes. If necessary the correct sound can be provided.
Does that make sense?	Use when the student keeps reading and the miscue doesn't make sense.
Does that look right?	Use when the miscue doesn't look like the correct word.
Does that sound right?	Use when the miscue is the wrong part of speech.
Where is the tricky part?	Use when the student keeps reading well after the miscue.
Try that again.	Use to indicate there is one or more miscues and the student needs to figure it out.
Are you right? How do you know?	Highest Metacognitive Level: Use initially when the student is correct, to get the student to evaluate his or her own reading. Then use for both correct and incorrect reading.
What else can you do?	Use when the student was unsuccessful with the first strategy.
Summarize what you read.	Use to check comprehension of reading.

the student based on which strategies would result in the most efficient student correction of reading. Some prompts are very specific, while others allow for more metacognition on the part of the reader to analyze his own reading. Multiple prompts may be necessary to help a student problem-solve. Initially it may be necessary to provide specific prompts, such as "Look at the picture, what animal is that?" or "Try the long ā sound." As a student becomes more proficient at using the strategies, more general prompts can be given such as "try that again." Gradually you can provide more metacognitive prompts, such as "Does that make sense?" to allow the student to do more of the processing to become an independent reader. The prompts "Are you right?" and "How do you know?" are often initially used after the student has been able to self-correct and you want him to evaluate it for himself. Later these prompts can be used when the student is incorrect, but you do not want the student to rely on you to let him know if his reading is incorrect.

Using this right column helps you reflect on how you are prompting the student and begin to identify what prompts yield successful self-corrections and which do not. If the student predominantly uses graphophonic cues, for instance, then semantic or syntactic prompts may need to be provided. Students need to be reminded that rereading and self-correcting are strengths. Even unsuccessful attempts to use strategies need to be praised because before students can correct their reading they need to be aware that there is a problem.

As you analyze the checklist to determine instruction, first identify the strategies the student used and whether the strategies resulted in self-correction. Then identify the strategies the student might use efficiently to identify words. Also analyze the prompts you provided, and evaluate whether the prompts resulted in correction of the miscue. Point out to the student one or two strengths he demonstrated during oral reading, such as self-corrections or attempts at problem-solving strategies. If the student did not demonstrate these behaviors, then point out sentences with no miscues and ask if it those sentences made sense. Because it may not be practical or appropriate to review all of the miscues, first select those that affect meaning the most. Have the student reread the sentence to see if the miscue can be self-corrected. If the student does not self-correct, then read the sentence the way the student initially said it and ask where the tricky part is. Then proceed by prompting the student with strategies that eventually result in correcting the miscue. Afterward have the student reread the sentence to see if it makes sense, sounds right, and looks right. When the session is over, ask the student what strategies he tried that helped him figure out unknown words. Analyze the prompts that you provided for the student and evaluate whether the prompts resulted in correction of the miscue. Determine the strategies and prompts that were most effective for different types of miscues.

Oral Reading Strategy Checklist for Peers

Purpose: To identify strategy use in peers during small-group reading instruction, to reinforce peer use of strategies, and to help the recorder learn strategies they might use to facilitate their own strategy use when reading (grades 1 and above). It is easier to notice strategy use and miscues in others than in oneself; therefore, it is beneficial to provide opportunities for students to assess their peer's use of reading strategies before assessing themselves. This checklist provides peers with something positive to do rather than calling out words when the reader does not know them. The focus is on encouraging strategy use, not on the miscues made.

Procedure: Select a passage that is approximately at the student's instructional level. During small-group instruction, with students at the same or similar instructional level, select one student to focus on per day. Each time it is that student's turn to read, the other students listen for and identify the strategies the reader uses and mark them on the Oral Reading Strategy Checklist for Peers (see Appendix). When the students identify a strategy that the reader used, they place a stamp or use markers to mark the strategy on the checklist. This provides positive reinforcement of a student's strategy use while providing wait time for the reader to process. If the reader is unable to correct a word after adequate wait time, ask the group members if they could suggest a strategy that would help the reader determine the word. Sometimes a combination of strategies is helpful. The group members prompt the student to correct the miscue. After each reader's turn ends, the reader needs to summarize what has been read. The peers put a checkmark if the reader was able to do this.

At the bottom of the checklist is an evaluation where the students identify strategies that worked well and the strategies that might help the reader in the future. This activity leads to a discussion of how and when to use different strategies. When it is the next reader's turn to read, that student is more likely to try additional strategies and begin to internalize the use of strategies and problem-solve during reading.

Oral Reading Strategy Checklist for Self

Purpose: To help readers identify their own strategy use and evaluate when and which strategies to use, after listening to an audiotaped recording of their reading (grades 1 and above).

Procedure: This self-assessment, which is similar to the Oral Reading Strategy Checklist for Peers, is used only after the student is familiar with the strategies and has had practice using them during the teacher and peer assessments so that the student is better able to reflect on his own strategy use. The Oral Reading Strategy Checklist for Self (see Appendix) is similar to retrospective miscue analysis (Goodman & Marek, 1996), in that the student reads a passage into an audiotape recorder and then analyzes his reading after listening to the audiotape. When students use the oral reading strategies checklist, they not only identify specific strategies used or neglected but also may be able to correct some of their own miscues. Just like in the peer checklist, the student uses a stamp or marker to document each time a strategy is used, but this time he is listening to a recording of their own reading.

Once the checklist is completed, the student then selects a strategy that he feels was beneficial and one strategy that he thinks he should use more. If a student is unable to self-correct a word, he uses removable highlighting tape or a highlighter to mark it. Afterward you and the student discuss the strategies used and you provide additional prompts to figure out any unknown words.

Audiotapes can be kept for each student throughout the year, and the students can listen to them again and reflect on their progress. As students become more fluent readers, they are able to self-correct more often and select the most efficient strategies for problem solving. Students are often quite surprised at how much their reading had improved over the year.

General Fluency Strategies

The following strategies support students in fluently reading with appropriate phrasing, expression, smoothness, and pace.

Echo Reading

Source: Walker, 2004

Purpose: To provide a model of fluent reading that students can then repeat imitating the pronunciation of words, phrasing, intonation, and expression (grades K–2).

Procedure: Read one sentence with appropriate phrasing and intonation. The students read the same line immediately in order to remember how the text sounds, modeling your example. You and the students echo read the entire passage. Finally, the teacher increases the amount of text read for the students to model.

Choral Reading

Source: Opitz & Rasinski, 1998

Purpose: To improve fluency through guided practice reading aloud with others. Choral reading involves groups of students orally reading the same text in unison. This can be done for the whole text or a portion of the text (grades K–3).

Procedure: Select a text that is easy to read in unison, such as a poem, nursery rhyme, or a predictable book. Provide a copy of the text for everyone, or have it displayed in large writing such as on chart paper, overhead transparency, or computer projection. First, read the text aloud to the students to model choral reading. Next, read the text chorally several times the first day and then repeat it over several days.

Chunking

Source: Walker, 2004

Purpose: To encourage students to read in meaningful phrases by echoing your phrasing. Chunking facilitates comprehension and fluency by using thought units rather than word-by-word reading. This strategy is beneficial for students who are fairly proficient at word identification but need to improve their sentence comprehension (all grades).

Procedure: Tape record students reading a 100–200 word passage to review later. Model for the students how to read in meaningful phrases rather than word by word. Pause between phrases, such as between the subject, the predicate, and any prepositional phrase. The students then repeat or echo the same phrasing. You and the students continue echo reading the entire passage. When possible, you can increase the number of sentences chunked before the students repeat. As the students' ability to chunk meaningful phrases together increases, the students continue reading the passage without teacher modeling. Finally, tape record the reading of the passage again, and along with the students, compare the fluency, intonation, and phrasing of the two audiotaped readings.

Collaborative Reading

Source: Walker, 2004

Purpose: To read together incorporating shared reading, prediction, and discussion about the story. This is useful for students with a higher listening level and lower word identification skills (all grades).

Procedure: You and the students discuss what you think the book will be about. You read the story aloud, modeling appropriate intonation. While reading, stop periodically and ask questions such as What do you think will happen next? and Do you agree with what the character did? After the first reading, ask higher level, open-ended questions such as Which part of the story did you like best? Why? What would you change in the story? When reading the story a second time together, keep a fluent pace and invite the students to join in the reading. After the second reading, you and the students should review the troublesome phrases and ideas. On the third reading of the story, the students read alone and you prompt the students if they need help.

Language Experience Approach (LEA)

Source: R. Van Allen, adapted from Walker, 2004

Purpose: To enhance word identification in context and fluency through the repeated reading of students' dictated text. The story becomes the text for instruction and a collection of the stories becomes the students' first reader (grades K–3).

Procedure: Engage the students in a dialogue about a topic or an experience, asking for specific details. The students dictate the story while you write it. Then, ask questions such as What happened next? Is this what you wanted to say? How can you make a story using this information? You and the students read the story simultaneously to revise any statements that are unclear to them. Then you and the students read the story repeatedly, because repetition of the entire story will promote prediction during independent reading. The students read the story independently. Sentences or meaningful phrases can be written on sentence strips and cut up to be mixed and then resequenced by the students. This promotes a whole-part-whole philosophy of literacy learning. Stories can be collated into anthologies for the students to read. As the words are repeatedly read in context, you can check them off a word list, but do not assess word knowledge in isolation.

Paired Reading

Source: Opitz & Rasinski, 1998; Walker, 2004

Purpose: To increase intonation, fluency, and pace through simultaneous modeling (all grades).

Procedure: A slower paced reader and a proficient reader, either a peer or a teacher who serves as a model, read aloud simultaneously. Before reading, the two readers decide on a sign to be given when the slower paced reader wants to begin reading on his or her own and another one for when he or she needs help. This sign can be a nod or a tap. The pair begins reading in unison. The proficient reader sets a pace that is appropriate for the text, modeling intonation and phrasing. The proficient reader can move her finger along the print if necessary. As the slower paced student gains success, he signals the proficient reader to stop reading aloud, and then the slower reader continues to read on his own.

Repeated Readings

Source: Modified from Walker, 2004

Purpose: To orally reread a passage until students are able to read it fluently with 95% word accuracy, or independent level. This strategy is beneficial for students who read word by word and have some degree of word accuracy yet do not use syntactic or contextual cues while reading (all grades).

Procedure: Make a copy of the text so that miscues can be marked as the students read. The students read the passage orally while you record miscues and fluency behaviors. The reading could also be tape recorded for the students to mark miscues or to document oral reading improvement over time. Repeated practice helps students read more smoothly and automatically. Students practice silently rereading the passage while you listen to other students read or discuss their miscues and provide prompts for correction. The students then reread the passage orally while you record miscues with a colored pen. You and the students compare the initial reading with the final reading and discuss the students' progress. This progress can be charted on the Fluency Assessment by Teachers and Peers or the Ongoing Self-Evaluation of Fluency (see Appendix).

While some recommend timing the students' rate, I believe that timing detracts from the comprehension goal of reading. In order for students to comprehend a passage, it may be necessary for the students to use problem-solving strategies when reading, and these strategies take time to process. As students become more efficient at using strategies for figuring out unknown words, their reading pace will increase. Emphasis should be placed on improving word identification, phrasing, intonation, expression, and conversational pace—not on improving reading speed.

Reading With Expression

Purpose: To practice reading sentences with different expressions (all grades).

Procedure: Write words on index cards from four categories (Emotions, People, Actions, and Scenarios) that would indicate different ways to read with expression. Write a sentence on the board and have students read it aloud. Next have students take turns selecting an index card from a bag and reading a sentence using the expression indicated by that card. Example cards include: Emotions (excited, angry, confused, bored, panicked, joking); People (old lady, baby, a giant, Abraham Lincoln, Junie B. Jones, or another book character); Actions (whispering, sobbing, screaming, shuddering); and Scenarios (You just finished running a mile; You just received the best news in the world).

Talking Books

Source: Carbo, 1978; Walker, 2004

Purpose: To increase vocabulary, word recognition, and fluency by repeatedly reading along with a tape recording of a story until the students can read the text fluently with comprehension (all grades).

Procedure: Procure or make a tape recording of a story. Tape recordings should use natural phrases of language and should be segmented so the students can easily finish a tape in one sitting. Cueing the page numbers so the students can easily find the page is helpful, too. Students follow the line of print with a finger and listen to the tape recording to develop an overall understanding of the story. Next, students listen to and read along with the tape as many times as necessary until the text can be read fluently. The students rehearse the text alone and then read the text to the teacher. The teacher evaluates fluency and comprehension.

Computerized Books

Purpose: Similar to talking books, these interactive storybooks support word recognition and fluency (all grades).

Procedure: Students are able to hear the story read to them as the words in the text are highlighted. Students can click on any word and the computer will read it to them. Many programs come with additional phonics, word identification, and comprehension activities related to the story. (One popular series is Living Books, which you can often find by doing an Internet search.)

Sharing and Performing Oral Reading Strategies

One way of encouraging oral reading is for the teacher to read aloud daily, modeling appropriate fluency including phrasing, expression, intonation, smoothness, and conversational pace. The following are sharing and performing oral reading strategies.

Radio Reading Revised

Source: Greene, 1979; Searfoss, 1975, cited in Opitz & Rasinski, 1998

Purpose: To perform a reading fluently as if they are on the radio (grade 3 and above).

Procedure: Give students preselected portions of a text. After having an opportunity to rehearse the reading, the person reading takes on the role of a radio announcer and the others are the listeners. After reading each portion, the reader leads the group in a discussion about the text. This is preferable to round-robin reading because students have an opportunity to practice their part and the class discusses each section of the text.

Story Drama

Source: Walker, 2004

Purpose: To take on the roles of characters in a story in order to enhance fluency and comprehension (grade 2 and above).

Procedure: Students think about how a story might end or could end differently and role-play the scenes. By taking on the roles of various characters, the students take their knowledge of similar experiences as well as information from the story to act out their interpretation.

Display and Practice Poetry and Songs

Purpose: To learn poems and songs to enhance fluency and enjoyment of language (all grades).

Procedure: Display poems and songs large enough for everyone in the class to see. Read each one aloud a few times to the students. Have the whole class choral-read it together. Give students individual copies. Have them practice reading it in partners or independently. Finally, periodically come back and read the poem or song.

Poetry Chair

Purpose: To provide opportunities for each student to share poetry and have a purpose for reading fluently (all grades).

Procedure: Post a calendar and invite students to sign up to share a poetry selection for the day of their choice. Students should select a poem and photocopy it or write it on paper. Students practice reading their poem until it is their turn to share it from a chair in front of the class.

Readers Theatre

Source: Barchers, 1993; Braun & Braun, 1996; McAndrews, 2004; Walker, 2004

Purpose: To dramatically interpret a play, poem, fiction, or nonfiction story through a fluent oral interpretive reading to entertain and engage the audience; to motivate reluctant readers and provide fluent readers with the opportunity to explore different genres and characterization through intonation, inflection, and fluency of oral reading; to provide an opportunity for students to collaborate and communicate with one another; to provide ELLs with a language model (all grades).

Procedure: Select scripts that are at the students' interest and instructional level (90% or above word accuracy) so that the students can focus on intonation, inflection, and fluency, rather than on word identification. Most Readers Theatre scripts are literary adaptations, although others are original dramatic works. Initially, select works that are already written as scripts and divided into several different speaking parts. Scripts should be short enough to be completed and discussed within one class period.

There are several websites for Readers Theatre. Aaron Shepard explains Readers Theatre and provides free scripts and practice sheets at his website, www.aaronshep.com. Another excellent source for Readers Theatre scripts is the Scholastic website: teacher.scholastic.com/products/instructor/readerstheater.htm. The Playbooks website provides leveled books designed in a Readers Theatre format with each character's dialogue in a different color; you can get free samples of these books at playbooks.com.

When doing Readers Theatre, you should provide an introduction to the characters, setting, events, and problem for narratives or to the main idea and details of expository texts. Students select or are assigned appropriately leveled parts to read and are given separate scripts with each part highlighted. You should model and discuss appropriate elements such as those found in the Readers Theatre Rubric Analysis (see Appendix) including phrasing, punctuation, expression, volume, clarity, pacing, timing, facial and body language, interpretation, staging, and cooperation. Students read the script silently and then read their parts orally to themselves, practicing the elements on the rubric. Students perform the script with or without minimal sets, costumes, or props. Because the students read from the scripts, they do not need to memorize the text. Students convey the story line by their intonation and phrasing. Finally, listeners must use their imaginations to interpret the story line. Students' oral reading also can be evaluated for the elements on the Readers Theater Rubric Analysis.

Adaptation: You or the students can write original scripts based on stories, rewrites of stories, or nonfiction content being studied. This enhances the students' word recognition because they need to reread parts of the text several times, and it can improve their comprehension because they must decide what dialogue and narration are necessary to understand the story. Different reading levels can be included to allow readers of varying reading abilities to participate in the same activity.

CHAPTER

Reading and Listening Comprehension

Understanding Reading and Listening Comprehension

Comprehension is a complex thinking process in which the reader or listener interacts with the text to construct meaning; it is the most important of the literacy processes. The primary goal of comprehension is "constructing meaning by monitoring understanding, enhancing understanding, acquiring and actively using knowledge, and developing insight" (Harvey & Goudvis, 2007, p. 14). Proficient readers are better able to remember and apply what they have read, create new background knowledge for themselves, discriminate and carefully analyze the text and author, and engage in conversations or other analytical responses to what they read (Keene & Zimmermann, 1997).

Metacognition

Reading involves a high level of **metacognition**, which means being aware of our thinking as we perform specific tasks and then using this awareness to control what we are doing (Marzano et al., 1988). According to Baker and Brown (1984), there are four major aspects of metacognition in reading:

1. Knowing oneself as a learner—being aware of what you know and do not know, having reasons for your likes and dislikes, and being able to activate background knowledge

2. Regulating—knowing what to read, knowing how to read it, being aware of text structure, and knowing how to use this information

3. Checking comprehension—evaluating your own performance, being aware when comprehension is lacking or confused, knowing what information is important, and engaging in self-questioning to determine if your reading goals have been met

4. Repairing—taking steps to correct your comprehension, including problems caused by unknown words or concepts, misreading punctuation or phrasing, confusing relationships between ideas, misinterpreting main or important ideas, or having inadequate or conflicting prior knowledge

Metacognitive awareness involves self-questioning and has to be built into all literacy instruction. Gunning (2004) explains that instruction in metacognitive strategies must include the teacher modeling how he or she recalls prior knowledge, sets purposes for reading, decides on a reading strategy, carries out a strategy, monitors for meaning, takes corrective action, organizes information, and applies the knowledge gained from reading.

Schema Theory

According to Anderson (2004), **schema theory** involves an interaction between the reader's own knowledge and the text, which results in comprehension. There are two types of schemata: (1) content schemata, which is background knowledge of the world, and (2) formal schemata, which is background knowledge of rhetorical structure (Carrell, 1983). The reading process involves the identification of genre, formal structure, and topic, all of which activate schemata and allow readers to comprehend the text (Carrell, 1983). Readers can activate and build schemata through direct and indirect experiences. Direct experiences include experiments, field trips, videotapes, demonstrations, computer programs, Internet use, and guest speakers. An effective indirect experience is reading to and with the students from a wide variety of genres and having discussions to build content and formal schemata. Students need guidance in using their existing knowledge and experience, as well as visualization, to make sense of texts. Often this guidance involves providing motivational anticipatory sets; activating background knowledge; building text-specific knowledge; relating the reading to the students, other texts, and the world; providing a book introduction; previewing the text and text features; preteaching vocabulary and concepts; questioning and predicting; setting direction; and suggesting during- or postreading comprehension strategies. To enhance comprehension, readers need to make connections between the text and themselves, the text and other texts, and the text and the world (Farris, Fuller, & Walther, 2004). According to Carrell (1983), activating background knowledge is especially useful for ELLs to develop comprehension. Ask students to think about what they already know about a topic, author, vocabulary words, and text structure.

Activating prior knowledge and building connections before, during, and after reading enhances comprehension because it helps the reader or listener make connections between the text and their previous experiences and understandings, which is directly related to schema theory.

Classifications of Written Texts

There are two main divisions in written texts: fiction and nonfiction. **Fiction** is the telling of stories that are not entirely based upon facts. Genres of fiction include realistic fiction, historical fiction, science fiction, fantasy, mystery, folk tales (fairy tales, tall tales, fables), poetry, and drama. In contrast, **nonfiction** is an account or representation of a subject presented as fact. Genres of nonfiction include histories, biographies, autobiographies, journals, letters, essays, speeches, scientific papers, informational texts, textbooks, reference books, almanacs, dictionaries, manuals, narrative nonfiction, and some journalism. Although they are not traditional print texts, documentary films, photographs, and diagrams are also considered nonfiction.

There are four basic **modes of discourse** that describe the variety, conventions, and purposes of the major kinds of writing: (1) narrative, (2) descriptive, (3) expository, and (4) persuasive. **Narrative writing** describes a sequence of fictional or nonfictional events in the form of a story. **Descriptive writing** provides vivid details of a person, place, object, event, or feeling in a way that can be clearly seen in the reader's mind. This type of writing enables the reader to understand whatever is being described by using all the senses: sight, smell, touch, hearing, and taste. **Expository writing** is a mode of writing in which the purpose of the author is to inform, explain, describe, or define a subject to the reader. The content is presented as fact and the author often researches the topic to gain specific information. Examples include essays, journals, documentaries, histories, scientific papers, biographies, textbooks, technical manuals, legal and medical documents, articles, and other reference materials. **Persuasive writing** is designed to convince the reader to believe or do something; the writer argues a case from a particular point of view, often taking a position for or against an issue. Examples include speeches, advertisements, and some business letters. (Chapter 6 contains strategies for teaching students to write within these different modes of text.)

Narrative, descriptive, expository, and persuasive modes of writing can be written in different forms, such as essays, summaries, letters, reports, and brochures. Each of these modes differ in their purpose, organizational structure, language use, and printed format. The text could be to entertain, inform, or persuade. Knowing the text structure or organizational structure helps students understand the ideas in the text. Students may need to adjust the pace and style of their reading based on the purpose for reading and the text structure. The type of language used is dependent upon the purpose of the text. The format of the text, such as the information contained in the parts of a book or text, text features, graphic features, and typography, guide the reader in determining what the text is about and what is important. The parts of the book include the cover, title page, table of contents, glossary, index, and bibliography. The text features include the headings, subheadings, labels and captions, while the graphic features include illustrations, photographs, charts, graphs, and maps. The typography includes the type and size of font and the effects such as boldfaced or italicized words, as well as bullets and outlining structures.

Narrative texts have a sequence including the beginning, middle, and end, with descriptions of the characters, setting, plot or conflict, and resolution. These elements are often called the story grammar (Beck & McKeown, 1981). The plot can also be divided into the initiating event, internal response, attempt, consequence, and reaction. While generally sequential, plots could also include foreshadowing and flashback. More advanced narrative elements include characterization, stereotypes, theme, or point of the story (Buss & Karnowski, 2000). The author's style and use of language is generally more informal. These texts are written from a particular point of view and often include imagery, figurative language (similes, metaphors, hyperbole, irony), humor, allusion, mood, tone, motivation, suspense, inference, and exaggeration.

Expository texts contain one or more of the following organizational structures: generalizations or examples, question-answer, problem-solution, description, sequence, process, categorization, comparison-contrast, or cause-effect (Kletzien & Dreher, 2004). These organizational structures, while dominant in expository text, could also be embedded in narrative and persuasive texts. Each of these organizational structures, their definitions, and the words that often signal them can be found in Table 5.1, adapted from Kletzien and Dreher (2004). The language in expository text is more formal, containing specialized vocabulary, and the information is more densely packed. However, unlike most narrative texts, the format and text features in expository texts, such as headings, boldfaced important words, glossaries, and graphic information, support students' understanding if they know how to use them.

Table 5.1	Common Organizational Structures of Text	
Text Structure	**Definition**	**Signal Words**
Generalization-example	Gives a general statement and provides examples	for example
Question-answer	Presents a question and gives answers	who, what, why, when, where, how
Problem-solution	Presents a problem and suggests a solution	problem, because, cause, solution, so, so that, in order to, since
Description	Gives characteristics	color, size, other adjectives
Sequence	Explains something in time order	first, next, then, finally, last, number words
Comparison-contrast	Tells how two or more things are alike or different	different from, like, alike, compared to, similar to, same as, on the other hand
Cause-effect	Describes causes of certain events	because, cause, if, so, as a result of, since, in order to

Persuasive texts have four basic elements: (1) assertion, (2) supporting evidence, (3) opposing view, and (4) arguments against the opposing view. An assertion is a positive statement of fact or declaration of the writer's beliefs. The supporting evidence is found in the details in the text that provide reasons for the writer's point of view. The opposing view states what others may believe. The writer then provides reasons explaining why they disagree with the opposing view. Persuasive texts generally use the pro–con structure in which the writer discusses the positive and negative aspects of a topic. This structure is similar to cause-effect and compare-contrast structures. They may also include the problem-solution, in which the writer presents a problem and suggests a solution. The writer may try to emphasize a point by first discussing a topic and then restating it either through rephrasing it or explaining it using symbolism. Finally, the writer could integrate a narrative story within an expository or persuasive text in order to elaborate upon, personalize, or clarify a statement made. The language used depends on the audience for the persuasive paper and may include one or more propaganda techniques to convince the readers.

Comprehension Levels

My model of thinking and comprehension is based on the six levels of the revised Bloom's Taxonomy (1956)—remembering, understanding, applying, analyzing, evaluating, and creating—and Marzano et al.'s (1988) eight dimensions of thinking—focusing, information gathering, remembering, organizing, analyzing, generating, integrating, and evaluating. My literacy model organizes the comprehension process into the following categories: planning and monitoring, remembering, inferring, analyzing, evaluating, and creating. Each of these categories involves metacognition and self-questioning in order for students to actively engage in the comprehension process.

Planning and self-monitoring refers to what students do prior to and during reading. Students set purposes for their reading such as to learn about a topic, to solve a problem, to figure out how to do or make something, or for enjoyment. They decide which of the four reading styles matches their purpose for reading: (1) skimming, or reading quickly to obtain a general idea; (2) scanning, or reading quickly to find specific information; (3) intensive or study reading, which is careful reading for precise understanding of complex and detailed information; and (4) extensive or pleasure reading, which is reading fairly quickly for overall understanding and enjoyment.

The ultimate goal is for students to monitor their comprehension by generating and answering their own questions about their reading. **Question generation** is where readers ask themselves questions about various aspects of the text, the author, and themselves, and also set a purpose for reading. In **question answering**, readers answer questions posed by the teacher or themselves. Question generation and answering serves to guide students' thinking, develop comprehension, and assess comprehension. Too often, questions that teachers ask are designed to check comprehension rather than develop comprehension. Using questions to develop comprehension requires greater attention in the reading process. Questions can be used to help students monitor their comprehension.

During planning and monitoring comprehension, students gather information from the text by previewing the layout, graphics, and text features. Students ask metacognitive questions to activate their prior knowledge of the topic or genre, to predict or anticipate what the text will be about, to determine what they want to learn from the text, and to identify strategies for monitoring and comprehending the text.

Remembering is recalling and storing information that is directly stated, such as literal or explicit information. This involves identifying the story elements in narratives or the main idea and details in expository and persuasive text. It also includes sequencing events or processes, retelling, and summarizing the text.

Inferring is the ability to draw conclusions, make predictions, pose hypotheses, make generalizations, and visualize. Students use their prior knowledge of the content and text structure to infer information that is not directly stated in the text. Students are able to understand implicit story elements such as character's motivation, cause-and-effect relationships, and the meaning of figurative language. They can make connections between conclusions they draw and others' beliefs and knowledge.

Analyzing is the ability to classify, make comparisons, and identify cause-and-effect relationships and involves identifying and separating the ideas in the text into their component parts or organizational structures. Understanding organizational structures helps students determine the importance of the information being read and make decisions as to what parts of a text deserve the most attention. Not all information is of equal importance. Some details are secondary or just provide additional background information, while other details are essential for understanding.

Evaluating refers to making judgments. The reader can infer the writer's purpose and biases and then evaluate accuracy in comparison to other sources or experiences. Readers are able to discriminate between reality or fantasy and fact or opinion. Readers are able to examine the writer's style and use of language, including identifying various propaganda techniques. Finally, readers can make judgments about whether the text or ideas are valuable, appropriate, acceptable, interesting, and entertaining. These judgments often help readers decide what to believe or do. Students need instruction in viewing a text from different perspectives and need opportunities and instruction in locating, evaluating, and using reference sources. During evaluating, readers ask questions about who the writer is and whether he or she is an authority on the topic. Readers question the copyright date and the relevance to information now. In evaluating persuasive texts, the reader needs to determine whether the writer appealed to the reader's sense of fairness, goodness, or right and wrong.

Creating refers to applying the concepts or ideas to produce something new. Examples of this level of comprehension include written composition, oral presentation, demonstration, and dramatic or artistic interpretation.

Instructional Frameworks to Support Comprehension

Several flexible instructional frameworks have been developed to support comprehension: the Comprehension Strategy Framework (Dowhower, 1999); Scaffolded Reading Experience (Graves & Graves, 1994, in Tierney & Readence, 2005); and Guided Reading (Fountas & Pinnell, 1996). These frameworks are similar in that they include a planning or prereading phase to elicit and develop background knowledge and make connections including the topic, text, and strategy introduction; an implementation or active reading phase with scaffolded questions and prompts; and a postreading phase with experiences to revisit, respond to, and expand upon the text. In addition, guided reading, as defined by Fountas and Pinnell (1996), includes the important stage of analysis and evaluation of student learning to plan future instruction. Fountas and Pinnell developed an instructional framework for grades K–2 (1996) and grade 3–6 (2001), which includes guided reading (see also Chapter 1, p. 16). When constructing meaning, effective readers generate and answer questions before, during, and after reading in order to analyze, synthesize, infer, and evaluate information and then to apply this knowledge to create something new.

Objectives for Reading and Listening Comprehension

The following objectives are divided by the comprehension categories of planning and self-monitoring, remembering, inferring, analyzing, evaluating, and creating. Some objectives are specific to narrative, expository, or persuasive text and therefore are identified in parentheses.

Planning and Self-Monitoring Objectives

Prior to and during reading, students will do the following:

- Silently or orally state purpose for reading
- Preview text by looking at the cover, title page, table of contents, illustrations, captions, charts, graphs, headings, and boldfaced words
- Identify the text as being of a specific genre, such as narrative, expository, or persuasive

- Anticipate or predict what the text will be about based on text layout (title page, table of contents, glossary, index), graphics (illustrations, photographs, charts, graphs, maps), and text features (headings, captions, bullets, boldfaced and italicized words)
- Silently or orally state what they already know about this topic
- Silently or orally state what they want to learn about this topic
- Silently or orally state reading comprehension strategies they can use to understand this text
- Silently or orally state comprehension monitoring strategies at the sentence, paragraph, and passage level

Remembering Objectives

To enhance comprehension at the remembering level, students will do the following:

- Identify and describe characters, places, times (day, season, year) (narrative)
- Sequence the events in the story (narrative)
- Identify the stated problem and solution (narrative, expository, or persuasive)
- Identify and describe facts and details about living things, objects, places, events, concepts, and ideas (expository or persuasive)
- Sequence a process described in the text (expository)
- Define words or explain concepts (narrative, expository, or persuasive)
- Identify the directly stated main idea and supporting details in a paragraph or section (expository or persuasive)
- Retell the story or text (all)
- Explain events, process, or ideas (all)
- Summarize or paraphrase information directly stated in the text or section of the text (all)

Inferring Objectives

To enhance comprehension at the inferring level, students will use the text and their prior knowledge to do the following:

- Draw logical inferences, conclusions, and generalizations (all)
- Explain the implied problem or conflict (narrative)
- Explain the implied theme, plot, and resolution (narrative)
- Explain the implied main idea and supporting details (expository or persuasive)
- Explain the implied theme or purpose of the text (all)
- Explain the point of view of the author or characters (all)
- Explain inferred events, process, or ideas (all)

- Infer the definition of words or concepts (all)
- Infer connections and relationships (all)
- Make connections between conclusions they draw and others' beliefs and knowledge (persuasive)
- Interpret figurative language such as simile, metaphor, hyperbole, oxymoron, and personification (narrative and persuasive)
- Explain the author's use of irony, humor, allusion, flashback, mood, tone, point of view, motivation, suspense, inference, and exaggeration (narrative and persuasive)
- Generalize or form general concepts by inferring common properties of people, places, objects, and events (all)
- Predict or draw conclusions about what might happen to the characters, setting, or plot (narrative)
- Predict or draw conclusions about what the next part of the text will be about (all)
- Hypothesize, predict outcomes, or draw conclusions about ideas, problems, and solutions (all)
- Predict or draw conclusions about what may happen to the living things, objects, places, events, concepts, and ideas in the future (expository or persuasive)
- Visualize the setting, events, process, or ideas (all)
- Summarize or paraphrase inferred and explicit information from the text or a section of the text (all)

Analyzing Objectives

To enhance comprehension at the analysis level, students will do the following:

- Analyze or classify characters, setting, plot, and resolution (narrative)
- Analyze or classify main ideas and details about living things, objects, places, events, concepts, and ideas (expository and persuasive)
- Analyze or classify words or concepts (all)
- Compare and contrast characters, setting, plot, and resolution within and between texts (narrative)
- Compare and contrast main ideas and details about living things, objects, places, events, concepts, and ideas within and between texts (expository and persuasive)
- Compare and contrast words or concepts within or between texts (all)
- Compare and contrast characters, setting, plot, and resolution with your life or that of others (narrative)
- Compare and contrast main ideas and details about living things, objects, places, events, concepts, and ideas with your life or knowledge or that of others (expository and persuasive)

- Compare and contrast words or concepts with your knowledge or that of others (all)
- Identify cause-and-effect relationships between characters, living things, objects, places, events, concepts, and ideas (expository and persuasive)

Evaluating Objectives

To enhance comprehension at the evaluating level, students will do the following:

- Evaluate new information to determine if they need to change their existing knowledge to incorporate the new information (all)
- Discriminate between significant and irrelevant details in a paragraph or section (all)
- Determine importance of overall information (all)
- Evaluate the importance of words or concepts (all)
- Determine usefulness of information (all)
- Determine interest in the story or topic (all)
- Evaluate texts to select those that appeal to the emotions or affective domain (all)
- Rank information in terms of importance or interest (expository and persuasive)
- Evaluate your interest in the style of writing (all)
- Determine if events are based in reality or fantasy (narrative)
- Evaluate the accuracy and truthfulness of the material (expository and persuasive)
- Distinguish between facts and opinions (persuasive)
- Recognize valid arguments (persuasive)
- Compare material from several sources to verify or confirm information (expository and persuasive)
- Judge appropriateness, worth, desirability, and acceptability of the text for a specific purpose (all)
- Infer the author's biases or point of view (persuasive)
- Recognize the various propaganda techniques such as name-calling, glittering generalities, transfer, testimonials, card stacking, plain folks, bandwagon, and fear (persuasive) (Institute for Propaganda Analysis, 1938)

Creating Objectives

To enhance comprehension at the creating level, students will do the following:

- Combine prior knowledge with the knowledge, attitudes, or insights gained from reading to create something new (all)
- Apply reading to one's own life for problem solving or gaining understanding (all)
- Express a personal response to the text or subject (all)

- Apply knowledge about the characters, setting, plot, and resolution to create something new, such as drama, illustration, a model, or other artistic representation (narrative)

- Apply knowledge about the characters, setting, plot, and resolution to rewrite the story in another genre or to compose a new story (narrative)

- Apply knowledge about the topic to represent information in a new form such as a chart, graph, outline, illustration, or model (expository)

- Apply knowledge of the text to add information or go beyond the text (all)

- Apply knowledge from the text to solve a problem, conduct research, demonstrate a concept, or give a persuasive speech (expository and persuasive)

- Use the text or combination of texts as a guide to compose your own narrative, expository, or persuasive writing; oral communication; or artistic interpretation (all)

Reading and Listening Comprehension Assessments

Comprehension is strategic, interactive, engaging, and constructive. Assessment must also reflect the idea that reading comprehension is a complex process, which involves a more in-depth analysis of an individual student's reading growth. Comprehension is dependent upon several factors including adequate background knowledge; understanding of important concepts, vocabulary, and organizational structures and features; effective use of monitoring strategies; basic decoding skills and fluency; motivation and the ability to concentrate; and well-developed thinking and language skills (Gunning, 2007). Comprehension should be evaluated through diagnostic assessment followed by formative and summative assessment.

Diagnostic assessments not only help identify a student's reading or listening comprehension ability, but more importantly they identify the levels of comprehension, the story grammar elements, the main ideas and details, the expository organizational structures, and the concepts and vocabulary the student is able to comprehend and those she will need instructional support to understand. Diagnostic assessments should be from different genres and include prior knowledge and prediction questions, a retelling checklist, and explicit and implicit comprehension questions. Critical and creative questions may also be included. An informal reading inventory such as the QRI-4 (Leslie & Caldwell, 2006) can be used for this purpose, as it contains these essential elements. To evaluate a student's reading or listening comprehension on a given text, you can develop your own evaluation using the guidelines in the Comprehension Retelling and Questioning Assessment described in this section. For formative or summative assessment, you can use your observations and notes or student writing on discussions and responses to texts, checklists for retelling or comprehension elements, graphic organizers, teacher-made or publisher-made tests, or evaluations based on the use of additional comprehension strategies. Standardized tests provide overall measures of comprehension, but they contain generally low-level, multiple-choice type of questions, and do not provide the students the opportunities to construct their own responses (Gunning,

2007). Effective comprehension assessments should provide opportunities for multiple levels of comprehension.

Comprehension Retelling and Questioning Assessment and Comprehension Analysis Summary

Purpose: To analyze a student's prior knowledge before oral or silent reading and his comprehension after reading by retelling and responses to comprehension questions with and without looking back in the text. Listening comprehension can be assessed after the student has heard a fluent reading of the text in person or through any form of audio media such as a tape, CD, or computerized reading. The Comprehension Retelling and Questioning Assessment is used to determine the student's ability to comprehend when the task of reading is removed. It is always given to students who read at or below the preprimer level. It can also be given to any student to determine their listening comprehension level. This assessment should be administered regularly to select appropriate texts and instructional strategies on the basis of the students' comprehension strengths and needs. Because this assessment is created by the teacher for a specific text or is part of a published informal reading inventory there is not a specific assessment form contained in this resource. There is, however, a narrative and an expository example that I created along with the accompanying Comprehension Analysis Summary (see Appendix).

Procedure and Analysis: Choose a narrative, expository, or persuasive text from a trade book, reading series, reference material, or Internet site, depending on which type of comprehension you want to evaluate. To determine the student's comprehension grade level, use an informal reading inventory such as the QRI-4 (Leslie & Caldwell, 2006). The QRI-4 is particularly valuable because it contains multiple narrative and expository passages at each level. It also contains background knowledge questions, retelling checklists, and explicit and implicit questions. The text selected should be a complete passage or a complete meaningful section of a passage. If the text has fewer than 300 words, use the entire text. The following is a general word count guide for text length by grade level:

- Preprimer–Primer: 40–60 words
- First grade: 100–150 words
- Second grade: 100–200 words
- Third grade and above: approximately 200–300 words

Decide whether the story should be read orally or silently by the student or if you should read it to the student. If the student reads the passage out loud, you can analyze his miscues. (See the Analysis of Miscues Worksheet in Chapter 4, p. 101.)

Develop background knowledge questions and ask for a prediction about the story. Develop a retelling checklist with the important narrative or expository elements. Develop approximately 6–10 explicit, implicit, and critical questions that address important concepts in the text. Include a final question that would address a connection between the text and the student, the world, or another text. Mark each question with E for *explicit*, I for *implicit*, and C for *critical*. You can also include questions to define important vocabulary words or concepts. To help develop questions, use the Active Reading Questions (described in the strategies portion of this chapter), as well as the Narrative Comprehension Guide and the Expository Comprehension Guide presented in the strategies portion of this chapter and questions at a variety of levels of Bloom's Revised Taxonomy described in Chapter 1.

It is beneficial to audiotape the student's responses to review for accuracy, but always write the student's responses during the procedure. Ask the student background knowledge questions about what he already knows about the topic. Hand the student the text and read the title. Ask the student to scan through the text and predict what it will be about. Write down the student's background knowledge and prediction responses and score each response with a plus sign (+), checkmark (✓), or minus sign (−), depending on the accuracy and detail of the response.

Next, tell the student, "After you read, I will ask you to tell me everything you remember about the story and then I will ask you questions about what you read." If the student is to read the story orally, follow the directions for recording and analyzing their miscues as described in the Oral Reading Analysis of Miscues Summary in Chapter 4. If oral reading is not to be analyzed, the student can read silently. To find the student's listening level when comprehension of the passage is to be isolated without concern for student's reading ability, the passage is read to the student in person by a fluent reader or through a fluent recording.

After reading, say to the student, "Tell me everything you remember about the story," and then write the response. Use a retelling checklist to evaluate the student's recollection of essential elements of the text. Ask questions about the text, write the student's responses, and score with a plus sign (+) or a minus sign (−) based on their accuracy. Do not give partial credit. If the student gives an incomplete response, write *T.P.* for *teacher prompt*, and write a clarifying question such as "Anything else?" Then have the student look back into the text to find the evidence for his responses. Document his ability to verify his accurate responses and correct any answers based on looking back at the text. Write *L.B.* for *looking back*. Put a checkmark (✓) next to any response that was corrected after looking back.

To determine instructional needs, first analyze the accuracy and depth of the student's background knowledge and prediction by marking the response with a plus sign (+) for accurate and complete responses, checkmark (✓) for some knowledge, and minus sign (−) for no knowledge or incorrect responses. Then analyze the student's ability to retell and answer different types of comprehension questions (explicit, implicit, and critical). Analyze comprehension to determine independent, instructional, and frustration levels as well as specific reading strengths and needs. Although the retelling and comprehension questions are separate, they can be used to determine student's comprehension functioning level. If the student is able to correctly retell or answer 90%–100% of the questions correctly, he is at an independent level for comprehension. The student is at the instructional level if his comprehension score is 70%–89%. A comprehension score of 69% and below indicates the frustration level.

A passage that the student reads orally or silently at the frustration comprehension level may be read to the student to see if it is within his listening capacity level. The listening capacity level, although not identified by Betts, is the level at which a student can understand the material that is read to them with a comprehension score of 75%–100%. This level is also called the potential level, because if the student was able to read fluently, he would be able to comprehend. In order to determine the student's functioning level when the word accuracy and comprehension score are different, Leslie and Caldwell (2006) offer the guidelines presented in Table 5.2.

A student's comprehension can be affected by a variety of factors. To plan future instruction, you need to reflect on the following questions: Did the student have background knowledge of the topic? Was the student able to use concepts of texts such as title, headings, typography and graphics to predict what the text would be about? If the text was read orally, was the student able to read it at least at the instructional level for word accuracy? Was the student able to retell essential elements? If not, what elements were neglected? Was the student able to answer explicit questions, implicit questions, and critical questions? Was the student able to look back into the text to verify or correct responses? Does the student comprehend narrative or expository passages better? How do the factors above affect each other? During instruction select texts that are at the student's instructional level and select strategies that would enhance the student's comprehension in the areas of need above.

Using informal reading inventories, such as the QRI-4 (Leslie & Caldwell, 2006) and the DRA (Beavers, 2001), is another method to assess comprehension based on oral reading, silent reading, or listening to reading. The QRI-4 is particularly valuable because it contains both narrative and expository passages at each level. It also contains background knowledge questions, retelling checklists, and explicit and implicit questions. Informal reading inventories are especially useful for determining the student's reading level, not just his ability to comprehend a specific text.

The following narrative text comprehension example is a continuation of the Oral Reading Analysis of Miscues Summary example in Chapter 4.

Table 5.2   Overall Functioning Levels for Text Reading

Word Accuracy		Comprehension		Total Passage Level
Independent	+	Instructional	=	Instructional
Independent	+	Frustration	=	Frustration
Instructional	+	Independent	=	Instructional
Instructional	+	Frustration	=	Frustration
Frustration	+	Independent	=	Instructional
Frustration	+	Instructional	=	Frustration

From Leslie, L., & Caldwell, J. (2006). *Qualitative reading inventory-4* (4th ed.). Boston: Pearson. Adapted with permission.

Example and Analysis: Comprehension Retelling and Questioning Assessment—Narrative Text

Title/Author: *The Mitten* (Brett, 1989)	Level: DRA 28 (End of Grade 2)

Genre: Narrative, folktale

Prior knowledge questions:
   Have you read this book before? *No.*
✓ What is a mitten? *Things for your hands.*
₌ What is knitting? *I don't know.*
± What happens if you lose something? *My mom gets mad.*

Prediction: What do you think this story is going to be about?
Animals in the snow

Student retelling: *There is a little boy. Grandmother made mittens. He was climbing a tree and dropped a mitten. A mole came through. The rabbit and porcupine. Then the owl, badger, fox, bear, and the mouse.* (T.P.)Anything else? (T.P.)Then what happened? *He went home.*

Retelling checklist:

Characters:
✓ boy,   ___Nicki
✓ grandmother, ___Baba
___ animals

Setting:
___ in the house
___ in the snow in the woods
___ back to house

Plot:
✓ Grandmother knits a pair of white mittens.
___ Grandmother warns Nicki to be careful not to lose the mittens because they are hard to find in the snow.
___ Nicki plays in the snow.
✓ Nicki climbs a tree.
✓ Nicki drops a mitten in the snow.
✓ A mole finds the mitten in the snow and crawls inside.
✓ A snowshoe rabbit finds the mitten.
___ The mole complains there is not enough room, but the rabbit climbs in.
___ The grandmother's knitting holds as the mitten stretches.
___ A hedgehog finds the mitten.
___ Each time the others complain there is not enough room.
___ Each time they crawl.
___ The grandmother's knitting holds as the mitten stretches.
✓ An owl, ___ a badger, ✓ a fox, ✓ a bear finds the mitten.
✓ Finally a mouse finds the mitten.
___ There is no more room in the mitten.
___ Nicki searches for the mitten.
___ Uses verbs to describe how the animals moved, such as *swoop, lumber, trot, snuffle, bump, jostle.*

Resolution:

____ The mouse causes the bear to sneeze.

____ The mitten and all its animals go flying.

____ Nicki sees the mitten it the air and gets it.

____ Nicki goes back to grandmother with the mittens.

____ The grandmother notices how stretched out the mitten is.

Comprehension Questions: *The Mitten* (Brett, 1989)

Score +/−	Question	Answer
+	What is the grandmother doing at the beginning of the story? (E)	*She's making mittens.*
−	What did the grandmother warn Nicki about? (I)	*I don't know. She made him mittens.*
+	How did Nicki lose his mitten? (E)	*He was climbing a tree. He dropped it.*
+	Which animals found the mitten? (At least 5) (E)	*mole, rabbit, owl, fox, bear, mouse*
+	What did the animals do when they found the mitten? (E)	*They went inside.*
+	Why do you think the animals went into the mitten? (I)	*They were cold.*
−	According to the story, what does it mean to lumber over to the mitten? (I)	*Wood*
−	Why do you think that the mitten didn't break? (I)	*It was a big mitten.*
−	How did Nicki find his mitten? (E)	*It was on the ground.*
+	How do you think the grandmother would have felt if Nicki lost the mitten? Why? (I)	*She would have been mad because she made the mitten.* (Stronger response—because she warned him not to lose it.)

Critical Questions (Note: These are not used for assessing the comprehension of text but to evaluate the text and make connections.)

+	What do you think Nicki could do to keep from losing his mittens again? (C)	*Put those clip things to hold them on the coat.*

−	In real life when do you think that the mitten would break? (C)	*When the mouse climbed in.*
−	Why do you think that the author made illustrations on the outside of the picture in the middle? (C)	*To make it look pretty.* (Note: It tells two different stories, one of grandmother knitting and the other of the animals climbing in the mitten.)
+	What is your favorite part of the story? Why? (C)	*I like the part when all of the animals were in the mitten because it got really big.*

Example: Comprehension Analysis Summary—Narrative Text

Name: Laura	Grade: 3	Date: 10/13
Title: *The Mitten* (Brett, 1989)	Word Count: 198 of 310	Level: DRA 28
Text Type: Narrative	Reading Method: Oral	

COMPREHENSION SUMMARY

Prior Knowledge (+, ✓, —)	✓
Prediction (+, ✓, —)	✓
Retelling (+, ✓, —) Narrative Expository Characters/Main Idea Setting/Details Plot/Main Idea Resolution/Details	 C= ✓ S= — P= ✓ (animals in the mitten, but not much else) R= —

Comprehension Score	Without Look Backs	With Look Backs*
Explicit ?: right there	4/4 = 100%	____/____ = ____%
Implicit ?: inference	2/6 = 33%	____/____ = ____%
Total correct	6/10 = 60%	____/____ = ____%
Critical?: evaluative*	2/4 = 50%	____/____ = ____%

Comprehension Functioning Level	Frustration		

* Not used for determining level

Functioning Levels for Comprehension

	Independent	Instructional	Frustration
Oral Reading Accuracy	95%–100%	90%–94%	89% and below
Oral Acceptability	98%–100%	95%–97%	94% and below
Comprehension	90%–100%	70%–89%	69% and below

Although this text is at the student's instructional level for oral accuracy, it is at the frustration level for comprehension, so reading instruction should be at a lower text level.

Instructional Implications: Point out to the student that he was successful in identifying information that was right in the text. Then model using the think-aloud method on how to use information from different parts of the text and prior knowledge to answer the implicit questions in this text. On an easier text, teach the student to answer implicit questions and have the student describe what information he used from the story and his background knowledge to answer the questions.

Example and Analysis: Comprehension Retelling and Questioning Assessment—Expository Text

Title/Author: *What on Earth Is a Chuckwalla?* (Ricciuti, 1994)
Genre: Expository

Grade Level: Grade 5
Guided Reading Level: T

Prior knowledge questions:
Have you read this book before? *No.*
–What is a chuckwalla? *I don't know.*
✓ Describe the desert. *It is hot.*
✓ How do animals adapt to their environment? *They change.*

Prediction: What do you think this story is going to be about?
A lizard (looked at the front cover)

Retelling checklist:
___✓ Main idea: What does it look like?

Details:
___ large head
___✓ big, flat belly
___ long, thick tail
___ folds of skin hang from throat, neck, and shoulder
___ skin is rough and scaly

___✓ in rocky places in the desert
___✓ Main idea: Food

Details:
___✓ It eats only plants—leaves, fruits, and flowers
___ likes yellow flowers on the prickly pear cactus and the creosote bush
___ food for hawks and big birds

✓ dark skin with spots of yellow or gray

___ is about 18 inches long

___ Main idea: How is it classified?

Details:

✓ Chuckwalla is a lizard

___ related to iguanas in the family Iguanids

___ scientific name *Sauromalus obesus*

___ *sauros* means *lizard* and *omalus* means *flat*

✓ Main idea: Habitat

Details:

___ lives in the Southwest United States (California, Nevada, Utah, Arizona, and Baja California)

___ Main idea: Reproduction

Details:

___ mate between 4 and 7 years

___ male attracts mate by bobbing its head and selecting a place with plenty of food and rocks

___ lays 6–30 eggs in a burrow and fills it up

___ in three months the young dig out

✓ Main idea: Survival

___ burrows to get out of the heat

___ eats in the morning and evening when it is not hot

✓ wedges itself between cracks in rocks

✓ puffs up its lungs so it can't be pulled out

Comprehension Questions: *What on Earth Is a Chuckwalla?* (Ricciuti, 1994)

Score +/−	Question	Answer
+	1. What does a chuckwalla look like? Describe at least three physical characteristics. (E) Large lizard with a large head, a fat body, and a thick tail; about 18 inches long (46 cm.) and weighs more than 3 pounds (1 kilogram). Folds of skin droop from its throat, neck, and shoulders. It is usually has dark, scaly skin with yellow or gray dots sprinkled on its back.	*A big lizard with a big belly and loose skin.* (T.P.) Anything else? *It has spots all over.*
+	2. Describe its habitat. (E) It lives in the desert, especially in rocky places.	*It lives in the rocks in the desert.*
+	3. On the map, where does it live? (E) It is found in southern California, southern Nevada, and Utah, western Arizona, northern Mexico, and an island in Mexico's Gulf of California.	*In the United States* (T.P.) Specifically where? *Like California, Arizona, and Mexico*
+	4. How does it adapt to living in the desert? (I) When it is hot it crawls into holes. It eats in the morning and evening because it is not too hot or too cold.	*It goes into holes when it is too hot.*
+	5. What kind of defense does it have against its enemies? (E) It goes into a crevice, inflates its lungs with air. The body swells so it cannot be pulled out.	*It goes between rocks and gets fat and nothing can pull it out.*

+	6. What does it eat? (E) It eats only plants—leaves, fruits, and flowers. They are attracted to yellow flowers.	*They eat yellow flowers. (T.P.) Anything else? Just plants.*
− LB+	7. How do male chuckwallas attract mates? (E) They bob their heads and stake out a territory with plants and boulders.	*They call them.*
− LB−	8. How do changes in the environment affect mating? (I)	*I don't know.*
+	9. What dangers do chuckwallas face? (I) They are hunted by hawks and large birds, their habitats are being destroyed, and people are taking them as pets.	*Birds can eat them. (T.P.) Anything else? People take them.*
− LB−	10. Why do you think chuckwallas lay so many eggs? (I) Because the desert is hot and dangerous and many won't live. They have to dig out themselves out after they are hatched. They have to be at least four years old to mate.	*Because there are a lot of them.*
+	11. Would a chuckwalla be comfortable living where you live? Why or why not? (C)	*No, because it is too cold here and they couldn't eat.*
+	12. How might you protect chuckwallas? (C)	*Don't let people tear up the land and take them home.*

Example: Comprehension Analysis Summary—Expository Text

Name: Katherine	Grade: 6	Date: April 4
Title: *What on Earth Is a Chuckwalla?* (Ricciuti, 1994)	Word Count:	Level: G.R. T Grade 5.2
Text Type: Expository	Reading Method: Silent	

COMPREHENSION SUMMARY

Prior Knowledge (+, ✓, −)	✓			
Prediction (+, ✓, −)	✓			
Retelling (+, ✓, −) Expository Main idea (MI) and details (D)	MI= Looks ✓ MI= Classified − MI= Habitat ✓	D = ✓ D = − D = ✓	MI: Food ✓ MI: Reproduction − MI: Survival ✓	D = − D = − D = ✓

Comprehension Score	Without Look Backs	With Look Backs*
Explicit?: right there Implicit?: inference	5/6 = 83% 2/4 = 50%	6/6 = 100% 2/4 = 50%

Total Correct	7/10 = 70%	8/10 = 80%
Critical ?: evaluative*	2/2 = 100%	8/10 = 80%

Comprehension Functioning Level	Instructional	

* Not used for determining level

Functioning Levels for Comprehension

	Independent	Instructional	Frustration
Comprehension	90%–100%	70%–89%	69% and below

This text was one grade level below the student's current grade. She did not have any background knowledge on chuckwallas and her response was limited to how animals adapt to their environment. She read the story silently. During her retelling, she mentioned how it looks, the habitat, food, and survival. She did not mention how it was classified or anything about reproduction. She did not provide many of the important ideas or details in the text. However, for the comprehension questions, she was able to answer all but one explicit question and two out of the four implicit questions. After the assessment when she looked back into the text she was able to answer the two explicit questions but not the implicit ones.

Instructional Implications: Have the student orally read sections that would contain clues to the implicit questions. Explain that the answers were not directly in the text but had to be inferred from the information in the text and her own knowledge. Continue teaching using this level of materials and focus on implicit questions.

Nonfiction Layout and Text Features Assessment

Purpose: To determine if a student can identify and use nonfiction text concepts such as title, author, illustrator, table of contents, illustrations, tables, charts, glossary, index, and typographical information (grades 2–8).

Procedure and Analysis: The Nonfiction Layout and Text Features Assessment (see Appendix) can be administered individually or in a group if each student has a copy of the selected text. Select a nonfiction text that contains the text concepts listed in the assessment. This assessment may be read to the students, especially if they read or write at or below third-grade level. However, the students can also independently read and answer the questions in writing. Either you or the students can write the responses. Evaluate by writing a plus sign (+) next to correct responses. (Note: If any of the features are absent from the text, write *N/A* and change the denominator of the fraction for the total number of questions.)

Example and Analysis: Nonfiction Layout and Text Features Assessment

Book Title: *Habitats: Tropical Rain Forests*   Author: Libby Romero (2005)

	Questions	Response	Score
1.	What is the title of the book?	*Tropical Rain Forests*	+
2.	Who is the author of the book?	*Libby Romero*	+
3.	Who is the illustrator of the book?	*It doesn't say.*	N/A
4.	Is there any information about the author or illustrator? If yes, write one fact.	*No* (Teacher: There is author information on the back cover.)	−
5.	What is the copyright date?	*2005*	+
6.	Why is it important?	*It's a new book.*	+
7.	Who is the publisher?	*I don't know.* (Teacher: Try to find it.)	−
8.	Where is the table of contents?	*Right here* (Student: pointed)	+
9.	What information do you find there?	*What's in the book and page number.*	+
10.	What page can you find "What Lives in Tropical Rain Forests?" on?	*Page 1*	+
11.	Where is the glossary?	*I don't know.*	−
12.	What information do you find there?	*Words* (Teacher: Anything else?) *No*	−
13.	What is the definition of *habitat*?	*Where stuff lives* (Not from book)	−
14.	Where is the index?	*Right here* (Student: pointed)	+
15.	What information do you find there?	*Words* (Teacher: Anything else?) *No*	−
16.	What page is *deciduous* on?	*Page 9*	+
17.	Where is a heading?	*Page 4*	+
18.	What information does it tell you?	*What are tropical rain forests?*	+
19.	Where are boldfaced or italicized words?	*Tropics*	+
20.	Why are they boldfaced or italicized in the text?	*They're important.*	+
21.	Where is a caption?	*I don't know.*	−
22.	What information does it tell you?	*I don't know.*	−
23.	Where is a photograph or illustration?	(Student: pointed)	+
24.	What information does it tell you?	*It's a Howler monkey.*	+
25.	Where is a diagram or map?	(Student: pointed to page 4.)	+
26.	What information does it tell you?	*It's the world.* (Teacher: Anything else?) *It's where the rainforests are.*	+
27.	Where is a table or chart?	(Student: pointed to page 9.)	+

28.	What information does it tell you?	*Stuff about rain forests?*	–
29.	Where can you go to get additional information on this topic?	*On the Internet*	+
30.	Looking through the book, what do you think it is going to be about?	*It's about rain forests.* (Teacher: Anything else?) *Where they are and what's in them*	+
Total Correct			20/29

Answer the following questions to analyze and evaluate the student's understanding of the layout and text features: Can the student locate and know the purpose for information on the title page such as the title, author, illustrator, copyright date, and publisher (questions 1–7)? Can the student locate and demonstrate the purpose for each of the following parts of a book: table of contents, glossary, and index (questions 8–16)? Can the student locate and know the purpose of typographical text such as headings, captions, boldfaced and italicized words (questions 17–22)? Can the student locate and describe the graphic information that can be found in illustrations, tables, and charts (questions 23–28)? Can the student identify other resources where information can be found (question 29)? Does the student understand that reading is a comprehension process and information can be obtained from these text concepts (question 30)? Identify the concepts the student has not yet mastered and reinforce them during instruction.

Instructional Implications: Point to all of the text features that the student was unable to locate and then ask the student to describe the information found there. For example, point out the information about the author, publisher, glossary, and captions. Then discuss what each one is for. For reinforcement, ask these questions with other nonfiction texts containing these features.

Guided Reading Checklist

Purpose: The Guided Reading Checklist (see Appendix) can be used to evaluate students during guided reading. It is divided into three categories: reading silently, reading orally, and comprehension. This checklist was developed from multiple sources, including my assessments, Fountas and Pinnell (2001), and Robb (2001).

Procedure and Analysis: Evaluate all students in the reading group during guided reading. Mark each element with a plus sign (+) if students usually exhibit the behavior, a checkmark (✓) if the students occasionally exhibit the behavior, or a minus sign (–) if the students rarely or never exhibit the behavior. Add comments to clarify behaviors.

Example and Analysis: Guided Reading Checklist

	Score: + / ✓ / –
Reading Silently	
Stays on task	✓
Chooses to read	+
Uses parts of the book such as the table of contents, glossary, and index to clarify information	–
Refers back to parts already read to clarify or extend new information	–
Reads for detail rather than always skimming	
Participates actively in discussion of the text	+
Contributes to discussion and questioning that indicates an appropriate level of comprehension	✓
Connects text to self, other texts, or to the world	✓
Reading Orally	
Accuracy	
Uses a variety of strategies to problem-solve unknown words	–
Rereads if the reading doesn't make sense, look right, or sound right	✓
Self-corrects miscues that affect the meaning of the text	–
Makes fewer than 5 miscues in 50 words	–
Uses resources to gain meaning of unknown words	–
Fluency	
Reads in phrases	✓
Pauses at punctuation	✓
Changes expression and intonation according to the author's style	–
Generally reads smoothly and resolves any problems quickly	–
Adjusts pace according to material and purpose	✓
Reads at a conversational pace	✓
Comprehension	
Predicts content based on cover page, table of contents, graphic information, headings, or reading the first paragraph	✓
Identifies the genre and can explain how	+
Makes inferences and evaluates them during reading	–
Rereads to clarify meaning	–
Uses resources or asks questions to clarify meaning	–
Can identify and explain the narrative story elements in own words	✓
Can identify and explain the main ideas and details of expository texts	–
Can identify and explain the expository text structures in own words	–
Can summarize the text in own words	✓
Makes connections within the text, to other texts, to self, and to the world	✓
Evaluates the text for author bias, content, and interest	✓

This student generally participates in the group discussion of the text. Through group discussion, she is beginning to better understand the texts. She needs to remember to use resources such as the glossary when she doesn't know the meaning of a word. She needs support in using a variety of strategies to figure out unknown words, especially strategies that result in self-correcting miscues that affect the meaning of the text. With support, she is learning to use parts of the book and visual information to make predictions about the text. She can identify the genre but has difficulty identifying text structures. She is getting better at summarizing, making connections to the text, and evaluating the content and her interest in the text.

Instructional Implications: The first lesson should include learning how to use parts of a book such as table of contents, glossary, index, and headings. Next, show her how to use this information to predict what the text is about. Teach the student that the main purpose for reading is to understand what the author is communicating and how it is similar or different from what we already know. Use the Good Readers Bookmark (see Appendix) to teach the student multiple strategies to use when she comes to unknown words or concepts. Later lessons would include identifying organizational structures and strategies for comprehending texts with those structures.

Oral or Written Story Retelling Analysis

Purpose: To analyze oral or written retellings of narratives.

Procedure and Analysis: Give students a copy of the Oral or Written Story Retelling Analysis sheet (see Appendix). Say, "Tell me (or write) everything you remember about the story, in order." Mark each element with a plus sign (+) if students provide a complete correct response, a checkmark (✓) if it is a partial or partially correct response, or a minus sign (−) if the response is incorrect or not given. Add comments to clarify behaviors.

Reading and Listening Comprehension Strategies

Instruction that actively engages students in asking questions, summarizing and synthesizing text, and identifying important ideas improves comprehension (Keene & Zimmerman, 2007). This book includes strategies for enhancing comprehension before reading, during reading, and after reading. The comprehension strategies are organized by the following headings: Predicting Strategies, Monitoring Strategies, Connecting and Visualizing Strategies, Questioning Strategies, Inferring Strategies, Summarizing Strategies, Critical Comprehension Strategies, Narrative and Expository Structure Comprehension Strategies, Information Organizing Strategies, Group Comprehension Strategies, Bloom's Taxonomy Strategies, Creative Comprehension Strategies, Emergent Listening Comprehension Strategies, and General Strategies for All Readers. (Additional strategies that support comprehension in the area of vocabulary and concept development can be found in Chapter 2, and strategies for oral reading and fluency can be found in Chapter 4. Chapter 6 also includes writing strategies that can be used to extend comprehension beyond the text. Some of these strategies are helpful when used alone, but many are more effective when used as part of a multiple-strategy method and through collaborative experiences in which students comprehend text with the support of their peers.)

The goal of these comprehension strategies is for students to be able to use them on their own to enhance their comprehension. The following are general procedures for teaching all of these strategies:

1. Select a text that is the same genre as what the students will be reading.
2. Read the text on your own.
3. Select a strategy that would be helpful in understanding that text.
4. Practice using the strategy on your own. Write out your thinking, speaking, reading, and writing responses.
5. Explain in class the purpose for reading the text and the purpose for the strategy you selected.
6. Read the text or a coherent section of the text aloud.
7. Model the strategy, explaining your thinking along the way.
8. Try not to break up the text too much, otherwise comprehension could be impeded.
9. Select a text that is judged to be at students' independent or instructional comprehension level.
10. Provide guided practice with this strategy, asking specific questions to guide comprehension.
11. Provide paired or independent practice using this strategy.
12. Explain when, why, and how the students could use this strategy on their own.
13. Have students keep a list or a notebook of strategies they have learned as a reference.

Predicting Strategies

Prediction Maps or Logs

Source: Walker, 2004

Purpose: To predict and then revise predictions during reading to enhance comprehension.

Procedure: Ask students to predict what the text is about before and during reading based on cover, introduction, or the beginning sentences. Make a visual map of predictions and revisions or verification, or write a log of the predictions and changes.

Example: *Holes* (Sachar, 1998)

Predictions	Revisions or Verification
The boys dig holes to plant trees.	They have to dig holes to please the rancher in search of buried treasure.
He runs away and gets help.	He runs away and gets caught.

THIEVES

Source: Manz, 2002

Purpose: To provide background knowledge and organizational structure for expository texts by surveying parts of a textbook or other nonfiction text.

Procedure: Before reading an expository text, the students preview each element in the acronym and then write or think about each of the questions shown in Figure 5.1.

Figure 5.1 THIEVES Questions

T	**Title:** What is the title? What do I already know about this topic? What does it have to do with the preceding chapter? Does the title express a point of view? What do I think I will be reading about?
H	**Headings:** What does this heading tell me I will be reading about? What is the topic of the paragraph beneath it? How can I turn this heading into a question that is likely to be answered in the text?
I	**Introduction:** Is there an opening paragraph? Does the first paragraph introduce the chapter? What does the introduction tell me I will be reading about? Do I know anything about this topic already?
E	**Every first sentence in a paragraph:** What do I think this chapter is going to be about based on the first sentence in each paragraph?
V	**Visuals and vocabulary:** Does the chapter include photographs, drawings, maps, charts, or graphs? What can I learn from the visuals? How do the captions help me better understand the meaning? Is there a list of key vocabulary terms and definitions? Are there important words in boldfaced type? Do I know what the boldfaced words mean? Can I tell the meaning of the boldfaced words from the sentences around them?
E	**End-of-chapter questions:** What do the questions ask? What information do they identify as important? What information do I learn from the questions? (Keep in mind the questions while reading and note where the important information is located.)
S	**Summary:** What do I understand and recall about the topics covered in the summary?

From Manz, S.L. (2002). A strategy for previewing textbooks: Teaching readers to become THIEVES. *The Reading Teacher, 55*(5), 434–435. Reprinted with permission.

Story Impressions

Source: McGinley & Denner, 1987

Purpose: To give students an opportunity to predict what is going to happen in the story before the students see the text (all grades).

Procedure: Create a list of words or 2–3 word phrases from the story that shows key aspects of the story, including setting, character names or descriptions, plot, and resolution for fiction or nonfiction narratives. Students write a short story using these words and phrases in the order in which they were given. The stories are shared with the class. The students then read the original text. Then they compare and contrast their stories to the one they read.

Text Introduction

Purpose: To elicit and provide background knowledge and a purpose for reading.

Procedure: Sit comfortably where you and the students can see the pictures and read the title, author, and illustrator. Give students a purpose for reading the book. Do a picture walk, looking at the graphics and the text features, and ask the students to predict what the text might be about. Discuss important vocabulary words. For complex or phonetically irregular words, have students predict what the initial letters would be and locate them in the text. Add information or relate information in books to something that is familiar to students. Engage them in a discussion of the topics and help them make connections between what they already know and the story; ask them to think about the author, topic, events, structure, or visually similar words.

Nonfiction Layout and Text Features

Purpose: To identify whether students know how to use the parts of nonfiction books and text features to enhance comprehension of texts (grade 3 and above).

Procedure: Select a text containing parts of the book (title page, table of contents, glossary, index), graphic information (pictures, charts, graphs), and typographic information (headings, captions, boldfaced and italicized words). Model and provide students with practice in identifying and describing the purpose for each of the parts or features.

- Title page—First page of a book that tells the title, author, illustrator, and publisher

- Preface—Introduction to the book
- Table of contents—List of chapters with their page numbers
- Appendix—Extra information put near the end of a book
- Glossary—Alphabetical list of definitions and pronunciations of special or unusual words
- Index—Alphabetical list of topics and their page numbers placed at the very end of a book
- Bibliography—Alphabetical list of references used in the text
- Headings—Words that appear boldfaced and big to show what the text below is about. There can be different levels of headings, main headings, and subheadings.
- Captions—Words describing a picture, illustration, chart, or graph
- Boldfaced and italicized words—Words with a change in font to show importance

These concepts should be taught when introducing a new science or social studies textbook or when using a text with many these features. Take turns with students asking and answering questions to demonstrate their understanding of each of these parts or features. Example pages can be shown using a transparency projector or a computer projector. For independent practice, students each should have a copy of the text and demonstrate their understanding of the text concepts by finding and explaining the purpose for each of the text concepts while you walk around. Discuss why these parts and features are important and how they can help them while reading and writing their own texts.

Anticipation Guide

Source: Vacca et al., 2006

Purpose: To evaluate statements prior to reading to assess students' current knowledge or beliefs. An anticipation guide is a series of oral or written statements, including key concepts and vocabulary words that individual students respond to before reading the text.

Procedure: Prepare a document for students to read or listen to that includes statements about key concepts and vocabulary words. The types of responses can include agree–disagree, true–false, fact–opinion, or a Likert scale of 1–5 of how strongly the students believe a statement. Discuss students' predictions and anticipations before reading. After reading discuss and reevaluate the statements to see if their ideas remained the same or changed.

Example: *The River Road* (Goldish, 2000)

True or False

- The Mississippi river is the longest river in the United States. (T)

- In this book, cars drive on the river road. (F; The river road is for the barges)
- Barges carry many people down the river. (F; The barges carry materials and goods)
- People live along the river in farms, towns, and cities. (T)
- The river is useful to carry people and goods. (T)

Monitoring Strategies

As they are reading, students need to be aware of what they do not understand, to identify what they do not understand, and to use strategies to resolve problems in comprehension. At the sentence level students can use the oral reading strategies on the Good Readers Bookmarks (see Appendix) to problem-solve words, such as rereading sentences and pausing at the periods to see if the text makes sense. At the paragraph level, students also need to stop and think if what they are reading makes sense. The student may need to look back or skim through the previous sections of text to remember important information. Also looking at the pictures, graphs, maps, diagrams, charts, or illustrations may help to clarify the text. Using the context, glossary, or dictionary can provide the meaning for unknown words. Students can also use an encyclopedia, reference book, or the Internet to clarify confusing concepts. If the text is difficult the student may need to slow down their rate of reading.

Self-Questioning

Purpose: To make explicit students' thinking process about monitoring reading comprehension (all grades).

Procedure: Tell students to ask themselves the following questions: Did I understand what I was reading? How do I know that I understand what I am reading? Did I have any problems reading any word or understanding ideas? What did I do to solve those problems? Was it successful? What else might I try?

Everyone Reads To... (ERT)

Source: Cunningham, Hall, & Sigmon, 1999

Purpose: To read sections of a text for a purpose.

Procedure: Pose a question to students based on a selected text. Students read silently (or orally to themselves) an identified page, paragraph, or section or until they find the answer. Then discuss what was read.

Example: Jackie Joyner-Kersee in *And Not Afraid to Dare: The Stories of Ten African-American Women* (Bolden, 1998)

Question:	We found out:
Read to the end of page 189 to find out why Pop Miles decided to mentor Jackie Joyner to be an Olympian.	Pop ran the community center where Jackie participated in sports activities. He noticed that she had high athletic aptitude. She had the talent and character to be a champion.

Think-Pair-Share

Source: Lyman, 1981

Purpose: To increase student engagement in comprehension by sharing ideas with peers.

Procedure: Pose a topic to discuss or ask a question. Students think about it, find a partner, and discuss their thoughts. You should monitor the conversations and ask a few students to share with the class.

Connecting and Visualizing Strategies

Text Connections

Source: Harvey & Goudvis, 2000

Purpose: To make connections while reading texts (analyzing) (all grades).

Procedure: Explain to students that there are three main types of connections that we make while reading texts:

1. Text-to-Text Connection—This reminds me of something else that I read....

2. Text-to-Self Connection—This reminds me of when I....

3. Text-to-World Connection—This makes me think about....

While reading a text to the students, stop at least three times—one time for each type of connection—and tell students your connection and which type it is. After students have had sufficient practice making text-to-self (T-S), text-to-text (T-T), and text-to-world (T-W) connections, assess their learning by having students read a text and write down their three types of connections and label them using the abreviations.

Structured Overviews

Source: Baron, 1969, cited in Gunning, 2004

Purpose: To use vocabulary words to relate new ideas in the text to familiar knowledge in the text (all grades).

Procedure: Select two to four important concepts and related vocabulary. Then arrange the words into a diagram to show their interrelationships with lines connecting the words. Add known words to show how they relate to new words and evaluate whether the major relationships are clearly shown. Then introduce the diagram to the students, and explain why the words were arranged that way.

Adaptation: Students could make their own structured overview after one has been modeled.

Photographs of the Mind

Source: Keene & Zimmermann, 1997

Purpose: To visualize while reading the text and to make connections to the ideas (all grades).

Procedure: The students preview the text to be read. They read the text. Then at pre-determined or self-selected points in the text, stop and sketch a visualization related to the reading. After reading, share the sketches in small groups.

Graphic Prediction

Purpose: To predict the content of the text and activate background knowledge (all grades).

Procedure: Students page through the text and look at each of the pictures, graphs, charts, maps or other visual information. Students then predict the main idea of the text and share what they learned with a partner before reading.

Prereading Plan (PREP)

Source: Langer, 1981

Purpose: To provide background knowledge about the topic to improve the comprehension of the text (all grades).

Procedure: First, engage students in group discussion on a key concept such as a word, phrase, or picture. Students then brainstorm to make associations between the concept and prior knowledge. Write students' responses on the board. Students then orally reflect on these associations in order to refine and expand their knowledge of concepts.

Visual or Guided Imagery

Source: Walker, 2004

Purpose: To increase active comprehension and activate background knowledge about situations and characters in fiction or key concepts in nonfiction text (all grades).

Procedure: Use sensory images related to the story line to introduce the text. For example, to introduce the book *On the Far Side of the Mountain* (George, 1990), you might begin by saying to students, "Close your eyes and picture yourself in the mountains. What can you hear, what can you see? You are all alone. How are you going to eat? Where are you going to sleep?"

K-W-L and K-W-L Plus

Source: Carr & Ogle, 1987; Ogle, 1986

Purpose: To monitor reading of expository texts by identifying prior knowledge, questioning what the students want to learn, and documenting what they have learned (all grades).

Procedure: Make three columns on a chart labeled "What I *Know*," "What I *Want* to Know," and "What I *Learned*" and then elicit student responses to complete each column. K-W-L Plus involves creating a map or web to organize concepts of what topic was learned and then summarizing the text.

Example A: K-W-L chart: *Time for Kids: Mammals* (Housel, 2005)

What I *Know*	What I *Want* to Know	What I *Learned*
Mammals are animals. Dogs and cats are mammals. Bears are mammals.	What is a mammal? What are other kinds of mammals?	D: Mammals are warm blooded because their body temperature stays the same.

Mammals have fur. *
Lions and tigers are animals.
They live on the ground. *

Where do mammals live?
How many mammals are
there?

D: They are vertebrates because
they have backbones.
G: There are 4,550 kinds of
mammals.
E: Rabbits and seals are
mammals.
L: Some mammals, like whales,
live in the sea.
D: All mammals breathe with
their lungs.
D: Most mammals grow inside
their mothers and are born alive.
D: They are born helpless, so
they need their parent's care.
D: They drink their mother's
milk.
G: Primates are a group of
mammals.
E: Humans, apes, and monkeys
are types of mammals.
E: Wolves, lions, and otters are
carnivores.
G: Rodents are a group of
mammals.
E: Chipmunks are a type of
mammal.
G: Hoofed mammals are
herbivores.
E; Deer, giraffes, and cows are
types of mammals.
E: Bats are the only mammals
that can fly.
G: Marsupials have pouches, like
kangaroos, and they live in
Australia.
G: Monotremes-Platypuses lay
eggs but drink milk.

D = description; G = groups of mammals; E = examples of mammals; L = live where?
* = partially correct student statement

Example B: K-W-L Plus Map: *Time for Kids: Mammals* (Housel, 2005).

```
                    Mammals
```

Description	Group and Example	Where They Live
• Vertebrate • Warm blooded • Breathe air • Born alive and helpless • Drink milk • Fur (most)	• Primates: Humans, apes, and monkeys • Carnivores: Cats, dogs, lions, and tigers • Herbivores: Deer, giraffes, and cows • Marsupials: Kangaroo • Rodents: Chipmunks There are 4,550 kinds of mammals.	• Most mammals live on land. • Some mammals, such as whales, live in the sea. • Monkeys live in rain forests. • Marsupials live in Australia.

Say Something

Source: Walker, 2004

Purpose: To provide a personal response to the text.

Procedure: Students take turns saying something at intervals during the reading of the story. They can make comments about what they have learned, what is surprising, what it reminds them of, how it is different from or similar to something else, or questions they have about it.

Adaptation: Use sticky notes for students to mark their comments.

Response Journal

Purpose: To express in writing personal reactions and to wonder about events, themes, and ideas in a book (all grades).

Procedure: Read a book or section of a book and write reflections. These may be shared with peers or the teacher.

Guided Writing Procedure

Source: Smith & Bean, 1980

Purpose: To activate and synthesize students' prior knowledge. This can also provide a variety of purposes to guide the reading of a selection (grade 4 and above).

Procedure: Identify the key concept in the selection to be read (e.g., pollution). Ask students to brainstorm any associations they have with the word and record their responses on the board (e.g., smoke, ponds, cars, noise, garbage, factories, oceans, death, diseases). Through a class discussion, group the responses into categories and label the categories. Then use the categories to create an outline of information. Next, have students write a passage, perhaps one or two paragraphs in length, using the information in the outline. Ask a few students to read their passages aloud to demonstrate that even though every class member used the same outline, each person's writing is unique. Finally, have students read the selection to compare the outline and text, identify points of agreement and disagreement, and identify additional information in the text that could be used to enhance or clarify their passages. After reading, discuss the text selection in terms of these purposes.

Example: Pollution

POLLUTION
  I. Sources
    A. Cars
    B. Factories
  II. Products
    A. Smoke
    B. Noise
    C. Garbage
III. Water Pollution
    A. Ponds
    B. Oceans
IV. Results
    A. Diseases
    B. Death

Questioning Strategies

The following are some guidelines for questions that help develop comprehension created by C. McAndrews (2004). There are six types of questions that are asked before, during, and after reading by active readers: predicting, questioning, clarifying, making connections, summarizing, and evaluating.

To help your students to comprehend as they read and generate their own questions, try the following general ideas:

- Ask good metacognitive questions that require students to think about how they are thinking.
- Ask questions about what is going to be read. This enhances higher-level thinking.
- Ask important questions.
- Ask questions that follow naturally from an initial question.
- Avoid using too many diversionary questions such as "What would you do in this situation?"
- Ask questions that access prior knowledge and encourage students to use what they've already read.
- Ask predictive questions that explore more than one possibility.
- Ask questions during the story that clarify meaning or make the reader want to read more.
- Ask questions that center on story problems.
- Save some of the good thought-provoking questions until after the reading is completed.
- After reading, reflect on and analyze the story.

The remainder of this section details specific strategies to help build question generating and question answering.

Active Reader Questions

Purpose: To guide comprehension of narrative and expository reading (grades 3–12).

Procedure: There are six types of questions that are asked before, during and after reading by active readers: predicting, questioning, clarifying, making connections, summarizing, and evaluating. Students use the following questions to monitor their reading comprehension.

Predicting

All texts—What is my purpose for reading? What is the author's purpose? What is the text going to be about based on graphics and text? What do I already know about this topic? As I read, are my predictions changing? What new questions do I have as I read?

Narrative—What will happen next? Why do I think so? What effect will that have on the story or the text?

Expository—What will the next section be about? What do I already know about this topic?

Questioning

All texts—What information is important after I read each paragraph or section? What questions do I have about what I am reading?

Narrative—Who is involved? Who is telling the story and why? Where and when does the story take place? What are the characters doing? Why? What do they want? Why? What is the situation or problem? How might it be solved? How was it solved?

Expository—What do I want to learn? Why? What is the main idea or topic? What did I learn after each section? What else do I want to learn? How can I use what I am learning? If the author provided questions, can I answer them?

Clarifying

All texts—Did I understand what I read? Can I recognize when I do not understand something and help myself to understand as I read? What part do I not understand? Does this word, sentence, or idea make sense? What strategies can I use? If my strategies don't work, where else can I get help? Can I restate what I learned?

Making Connections

All texts—How does the information in the text relate to my experiences and understanding? How does information from one part of the book or text relate to other parts of the text? How does the information in the book or text relate to others texts? How does information in the texts relate to the world?

Summarizing

All texts—Can I restate what I read in my own words?

Narrative—What happened in the beginning, middle, and end? Why did it happen? What was the theme? What was the main problem? How was it solved?

Expository—What was the text mostly about? What details supported this? What new information did I learn?

Evaluating

Narrative—What did I like about the story, characters, or the way the author wrote? Do I agree or disagree with the characters actions? Would I recommend this book? Why?

Expository—What new information did I learn? Was the information accurate? How do I know? Why is this information important?

Self-Directed Questioning

Source: Walker, 2004

Purpose: To improve comprehension through self-questioning.

Procedure: Students write questions before and during reading and then answer them after reading. This can be done on sticky notes for the class members to organize and answer.

Question-Answer Relationships (QAR)

Source: Raphael, 1982

Purpose: To identify the type of response necessary to answer comprehension questions (grade 4 and above).

Procedure: Students read each question and identify the type of question and response needed from the following list:

- Right There—explicit comprehension—the answer is in the text and easy to find
- Think and Search—explicit comprehension—the answer is in the text, but students need to put together different parts of the text to find it
- Author and You—implicit and critical comprehension—the answer is not in the text, and students need to combine what they already know with what the author states
- On My Own—creative comprehension—the answer is not in the text and can be answered by using students' own experiences

Students then answer the questions.

Adaptation: Students can use highlighting tape to identify the answers to "right there" (explicit) questions within the text.

Example:

Title: *F Is For Freedom*	Author: Roni Schotter (2000)
Right There (Explicit) Who got out of one of the sacks of grain?	Author and Me (Implicit) Why do you think Amanda says that there are probably Christmas presents behind the locked door?
Think and Search (Explicit) Where does Father put the mysterious family when they get inside the house?	On My Own (Implicit) Can you name a place in your house or a friend's house where you could hide?

Question Generation Strategy

Source: Walker, 2004

Purpose: To question and identify important ideas in a text.

Procedure: Before, during, and after reading, the students write and answer questions about important information in their reading. These questions and answers are then compared with those the teacher wrote.

Reciprocal Questioning or Request Procedure

Source: Manzo, 1969

Purpose: To model effective questioning to enhance comprehension.

Procedure: Students and teacher read the text and take turns asking and answering one another's questions before, during, and after reading the text.

Guided Questioning Activity

Purpose: To guide reading comprehension during text reading.

Procedure: Divide the text into sections based on important stopping points. Develop questions to ask after each stopping point.

Example: *Ronald Morgan Goes to Bat* by Patricia Reilly Giff (1990)

Book	What sport are they playing? *Baseball*
Introduction	How do you think the boy in the picture feels? *Nervous. If he strikes out he may have to wait a long time. He may be scared because the ball may hit him.*
Page 7	How did Ronald feel now? Why? *He was excited because he got to play baseball.*
Page 10	Do you think that boy knows how to play baseball? Why? *No, because he was holding the bat wrong.*
Page 13	What might Ronald do after he heard someone say he is the worst? *He might punch him or do something to him.*
Page 16	What will keep happening if Ronald keeps his eyes shut when he swings? *He's going to keep striking out.*
	Why does he close his eyes? *He's afraid of the ball. It might hit his glasses and then he won't be able to see.*
Page 23	What was Ronald doing when he should have been watching the ball? *He was playing with a stick and drawing things with it.*
Page 25	Why did the kids want Ronald on their team? *Because he helps them feel good.*

Page 29   What did Ronald's father help him do? *Open his eyes.*

Ending   How do you think Ronald feels at the end of the story? Why? *Happy, because he is going to be a good player and his dad practiced with him and taught him to open his eyes.*

Radio Reading Procedures

Source: Steward & Borgia, 2004

Purpose: To comprehend a text using literal, inference, and evaluative questions.

Procedure: First, teach about types of questions: literal, inference, and evaluative. Cut text being read into parts for each reader. Instruct all students to read their parts silently, looking for unfamiliar vocabulary. They should use resources or discuss the word meanings and then read silently again. Students then write a question for the other students to answer later. Review speaking and listening rules. One student then uses a microphone to read the part to rest of the class and ask the question. The class answers the question and the speaker verifies the correctness.

Inferring Strategies

Think-Alouds

Source: Wilhelm, Baker, & Dube, 2001

Purpose: To share metacognitive thought processes by teachers or students, such as making predictions, visualizing, making connections, monitoring comprehension, and using self-correction strategies.

Procedure: Read aloud to students; verbalize your thinking to make inferences that help you comprehend the text. Locate evidence from the text from which you draw your inferences. As you read, think aloud, showing students how to put together prior knowledge and facts from the text. Model this inferencing procedure until students can begin to take over. Examples include, "Hm, what does that mean? Let me reread. Well I know...so maybe it could be.... Let me keep reading to see if that makes sense. I wonder what that means." Students then work with partners while they take turns reading and orally demonstrating their thinking processes. Students practice these strategies while reading silently. Students can write their thinking process and self-questions on sticky notes. Finally, the students apply think-alouds to their everyday reading. After reading, you can ask students to discuss their compression processes.

Directed Reading Thinking Activity (DRTA)

Source: Adapted from Stauffer, 1969

Purpose: To infer information and justify responses (all grades).

Procedure: Students draw on prior knowledge and text information to hypothesize what the text is about and monitor their thinking by providing a rationale for their predictions. Before reading, students predict and develop purposes for reading. They question what the text might be about, what might happen next, and why they think that. During reading, the students read a predetermined amount of text and think about what they are reading. They confirm or deny their predictions and ask what new information verifies this. After reading, the students reexamine their purposes for reading, ask if their prediction is still possible, determine whether they want to change their prediction, and predict what will happen next.

Generative-Reciprocal Inference Procedure

Source: Walker, 2004

Purpose: To read and write paragraphs that require making an inference (grade 2 and above).

Procedure: Select paragraphs with an inference as the key idea and project it for the students to read. (Short mysteries are good for this purpose.) Explain that inferences are not directly stated in the text. Highlight keywords that may help the students identify the key idea. Pose questions to help students identify the inferred idea. On subsequent examples, the students identify the keywords and the inference. In pairs, the students write their own inference paragraphs and then share with others to predict what happened.

Inference and Questioning Strategy

Purpose: To make inferences (all grades).

Procedure: Have students draw three columns on a paper. In the first column, they write down questions as they read. In the second column, they answer the question What can you infer from what you have read already? In the third column, they write the evidence that supports their inferences.

Summarizing Strategies

Story Frames

Purpose: The goal of a story frame is to help students construct models of appropriate sets of responses and to guide students to places in the stories where information can be found. The same story frame can be applied to a wide range of reading abilities. As students attempt the problem of completing a frame in order for it to make sense, you can determine when and if to guide a group toward a more explicit response. Over time, students' ability to use the same frame may demonstrate growth in specific comprehension skills. As independent assignments, frames can be used to help students deal with a variety of ideas, concepts, and information. In addition, story frames are an excellent tool to use for quick, informal evaluation (all grades).

Procedure: A story frame is a sequence of spaces hooked together by key language elements. In most cases, these language elements are transition words, and they often reflect a specific line of thought or argument. Once a frame is constructed, it can be used with new passages as long as the passage can support the line of thought or argument implied with the frame. Story frames are especially effective in the primary grades and in remedial classes. They can be used to help students organize information in order to identify important ideas, analyze characters and their problems, make comparisons, and summarize passage content. Frequent use of story frames is particularly helpful for students who have trouble keeping to the point of a question or writing conversationally rather than in the style of written language. Select or adapt one of the story frames for students to complete.

Example:

Important Idea or Plot	Setting
In this story, the problem starts when _____ _____. After that, _____.	This story takes place in _____. It takes place during _____.
Next, _____.	I know this because the author used the
Then, _____.	words " _____."
The problem is finally solved when _____ _____.	Other clues that show when the story takes
The story ends _____.	place are _____.

Somebody Wanted but So (Cunningham & Allington, 2003)

(Somebody)_____ wanted _____.

But _____. So _____.

Character Analysis	Character Comparison
_____ is an important character in our story. _____ (character's name) is important because _____. Once, he/she _____. Another time, _____. I think that _____ (character's name) is _____, because _____ _____ (character trait).	_____ and _____ are two characters in our story. _____ (character's name) is _____ (character trait), while _____ (other character's name) is _____ (trait). For instance, _____ tries to _____ and _____ tries to _____ _____. When _____ learns a lesson of _____.
Story Summary With One Character Included	**Topic Comparison**
Our story is about _____ _____. _____ is an important character in our story. _____ (character) tried to _____. The story ends when _____ _____.	_____ and _____ are main ideas in our text. _____ (one main idea) is _____ (meaning) _____ (another idea) is _____ (meaning) These two ideas are similar because _____ _____. These two ideas are different because_____ _____.
Subject Analysis	**Text Summary With One Main Idea**
_____ is an important idea/subject in out text. _____ is important because _____. One example is _____. One way it is used is _____. I think that _____ is _____ because _____.	The article is about_____. _____ is an important fact in our article. _____ (event or fact) resulted in or influenced _____ _____. In summary, then _____ _____ _____ (what happened and why).

Story Summary

_____ Story takes place in _____ (place) during _____ (when).

_____ is an important character who _____.

A problem occurs when _____.

After that, _____.

The problem is solved by _____.

The story ends when _____.

Predict, Organize, Rehearse, Practice, and Evaluate (PORPE)

Source: Simpson, 1992, in Tierney and Readence, 2005

Purpose: To actively plan, monitor, and evaluate content learning; to prepare for essay exams; and to use process writing to learn content (grade 5 and above).

Procedure: Students will predict potential essay questions and clarify their purpose for reading. They then organize key information to answer predicted questions; summarize and synthesize the material and outline or make concept maps of the answers; and rehearse the key ideas, examples, and organization to put it into long-term memory. Students should practice writing out in detail what they rehearsed in the rehearsal step. They should then evaluate the quality of their own answers based on how they think the teacher would. You should model each of these steps.

R.A.P.Q.

Source: Adapted from Schumaker, Denton, & Deshler, 1984

Purpose: To identify main ideas, question reading, and summarize paragraphs (grade 3 and above).

Procedure: The acronym stands for Read, Ask, Put, and Question. Teach students the following steps: *R*ead the paragraph; *A*sk and answer questions about the main ideas and important details; *P*ut the paragraph in your own words; create a *Q*uestion about what you read, write it on a notecard, and put the answer on the back. Students can then use these cards as a study guide.

Example:

Read a paragraph or a section of the material you are working on.	"The Hopi are thought to be descendants of the Anasazi, who lived in the area hundreds of years earlier. Like the Anasazi they built large pueblos. These buildings had many levels and were made from sun-dried bricks of mud and straw called adobe. Towns were usually placed atop high mesas—flat-topped hills or mountains with cliff-like sides." McNally (1994), p. 52.
Ask yourself what the main ideas are.	Hopi are probably descendants of the Anasazi.
Put the main ideas in your own words.	Hopi, who are probably descendants of the Anasazi, live in adobe pueblos with many levels on top of mesas.
Question about the reading	[front of notecard] What do the Hopi towns called pueblos look like? [back of notecard] The buildings have many levels and are made of straw and brick. They are built on top of flat mountains with steep sides.

Reciprocal Teaching

Source: Palincsar & Brown, 1986

Purpose: To predict, summarize, clarify and ask questions while reading (all grades).

Procedure: With a partner, students predict what the text or the next part of the text will be about. They read a section of text and then summarize in one to two sentences what the passage was mainly about or the main idea. Students clarify what they did not understand, such as a word, phrase, or statement, and then they ask each other questions about what they just read.

SQ3R

Source: Walker, 2004

Purpose: To study content area texts and monitor comprehension and learning (all grades).

Procedure: The acronym SQ3R includes five steps:

1. Survey—Skim the passage to construct framework

2. Question—Students develop questions that will be answered in the text

3. Read—Read to answer the questions

4. Recite—Construct answer and possibly write important information

5. Review—Review questions and answers and then relate the information to the framework of the text

Summaries

Purpose: To write short summaries containing the important information (all grades).

Procedure: Read a section of text and write a summary of your own. Then share with students why only the important information is included and why some information is not included. Students then work in groups, pairs, and individually to write their own summaries.

Study Guides

Source: Herber, 1978

Purpose: To help students develop multiple levels of understanding when reading a text (all grades).

Procedure: Students will analyze content and identify major concepts and important details. You or they can create a study guide by developing questions at all three levels of understanding:

Explicit level—information is given right on the page

Implicit level—think and search for information

Experience-based level—find the information on your own

Assign the study guide and engage students in small-group discussions.

Triple Read Outline

Source: Walker, 2004

Purpose: To identify the main idea and supporting details and then write a summary of an expository text (all grades).

Procedure: You tell students that the purpose for the first reading is to identify the main idea of each paragraph, and then you model it by writing it in the margin of a photocopy of the text. During the second reading, the purpose is to identify the supporting details. The third reading is to organize the information into an outline. You then write a summary of the passage using the main idea as the topic sentence and include details to support it. Point out the irrelevant information that you have left out. The students then follow the same procedure on their own using a new passage and compare their outline with what you wrote.

GIST Procedure

Source: Cunningham, 1982

Purpose: To improve students' abilities to comprehend the GIST of the paragraphs: *G*enerating *I*nteractions between *S*chemata and *T*ext.

Procedure: First, select a paragraph. Ask students to read the first sentence and generate a summary. Next, read the first two sentences and ask students to generate a summary for sentences one and two. Continue with this procedure for the remainder of the paragraph and finally move from sentence approach to the paragraph approach.

Critical Comprehension Strategies

Critical comprehension is reasoning by the reader to go beyond the ideas in the passage and make inferences or conclusions about them. Examples include recognizing the author's purpose; identifying the author's overall organizational pattern; and recognizing explicit and implicit relationships between the words, phrases, and sentences. It involves making connections between personal conclusions and other's beliefs and knowledge and making critical or analytical judgments about what they read, as well as perceptions of biases and assessment of truth and values. Finally, it involves aesthetic value such as enjoyment, usefulness, or enlightenment.

Questioning the Author (QTA)

Source: Beck, McKeown, Hamilton, & Kucan, 1997, cited in Tierney & Readence, 2000

Purpose: To provide a model for questioning the author's writing.

Procedure: Identify major understandings that the students are to construct and potential problems students might face while reading. Then divide the text into meaningful segments and write a series of initiating, follow-up, and narrative queries such as What is the author trying to say here? Does the author explain it clearly? How does this connect to what the author has already told us? Does the author tell us why? Given what the author already told us about the character, what do you think will happen? How does the author let you know something has changed? Strategically guide students' contributions and discussions to help them construct an understanding of the ideas in the text.

Dialogical Thinking-Reading Lesson

Source: Commeyras, 1993, cited in Tierney & Readence, 2005

Purpose: To engage elementary students in reflection and critical thinking about issues in narrative text reading (all grades).

Procedure: Select a text that can be viewed from multiple viewpoints and that the students would find interesting. After the students read, discuss a central question, such as What should a particular character do? Discuss two hypothesized conclusions. Next, students dictate the reasons for the hypothesized conclusions and you write their reasons on the board. Next evaluate the reasons with (T) for true, (F) for false, and (D) for it depends. Mark (Y) if the reason is relevant and (N) if it is not. Finally, each student draws his or her own conclusion about the central question. This can be shared orally or in writing.

Inquiry Chart

Source: Tierney & Readence, 2005

Purpose: To study a topic in depth from multiple texts with possibly different points of view and enhance critical thinking (grade 4 and above).

Procedure: You or the students determine the topic, develop two to four questions, create the inquiry chart (I-Chart), and collect texts from multiple sources. Example questions include What are the characteristics of marine mammals? How are they similar to other mammals? How are they different? How are mammals grouped? Then ask students about their prior knowledge and record it under the correct guiding question. Additional information is recorded under interesting facts and students' new questions. Students then read from a variety of sources and you record what they learned. The students generate summary questions for each of the guiding questions. The students then compare the information from each of the sources with their prior knowledge. The students continue to pose new questions and research the answers. The inquiry chart can become an individual or group research project. Finally, the students report their findings to the whole class.

Example:

	Guiding Questions					
Sources: Topic	1.	2.	3.	4.	Interesting Facts and Figures	New Questions
What we know						
1.						
2.						
3.						
Summary						

Group Investigation Approach

Source: Walker, 2004

Purpose: To study and present a topic in cooperative groups (grade 4 and above).

Procedure: You or the students select a topic to investigate and gather resources. Then students develop a list of questions to investigate, and the list is organized by key categories and subtopics. Organize research groups around subtopics. Students select appropriate resources to read. They summarize their learning and share it during reporting sessions. Each group prepares a product (webpage, PowerPoint, poster, etc.) to share the information the members learned about their subtopic. Finally, you and the students develop summary questions to ask the class. Students write a reflection about what they learned from each group.

Critical Reflections

Purpose: To examine the text for challenges to your beliefs and values (all grades).

Procedure: As you read a text for the first time, mark an *X* in the margin at each point where you feel a personal challenge to your attitudes, beliefs, or status. Make a brief note in the margin about what you feel or about what in the text created the challenge. Now look again at the places you marked in the text where you felt personally challenged. What patterns do you see?

Fact, Opinion, or Inference

Purpose: To help distinguish between a statement of fact, an opinion, or an inference (all grades).

Procedure: Define facts, opinions, and inferences for your students as follows:

Fact—reports information that can be directly observed or can be verified or checked for accuracy

Opinion—expresses an evaluation based on a personal judgment or belief which may or may not be verifiable

Inference—offers a logical conclusion or a legitimate implication based on factual information.

Write a list of statements that contain examples of each. Have the students mark each statement with *F*, *O*, or *I*. Afterward, select texts that contain facts, opinions, and inferences such as newspaper articles and historical narratives. Have students find examples of each.

Persuasive Analysis Strategy Argument Chart

Source: Moss, 2004

Purpose: To identify elements of a persuasive argument (grade 4 and above).

Procedure: Create a simple four-column chart. Write what the author is asserting, what the supporting evidence for this assertion is, what the opposing views are, and finally what the arguments against the opposing view are.

Example:

Analysis of _____ (Title)

Assertion	Supporting Evidence	Opposing View	Arguments Against the Opposing View

Narrative and Expository Structure Comprehension Strategies

Narrative Comprehension Guide

Purpose: To help students comprehend a narrative text.

Procedure: During and after reading, students ask themselves the following questions to help them understand the story better:

Characters

- Who are the main characters of the story?
- How are they related to one another?
- How do the characters act?
- Do the characters do things that are generally good or bad? What kind of things?
- Do any of the characters change in the story? How?
- Do I like the characters? Why or why not?

Setting

- Where does the story take place? Does it change?
- What is the place like?
- When did the story take place? How do I know?
- What time of year does the story take place? How do I know?
- Is the setting similar to a place I am familiar with? How?

Plot

- What are the main events that happened in the story?
- As you read, ask, What do I think will happen next? Why?
- What the problem in the story?
- What were the attempts to solve the problem?
- What would I have done differently if I were the character?

Mood

- How did this story make me feel in the beginning, middle, and end?
- What was the most exciting thing that happened?
- What is the funniest or saddest or strangest thing that happened?
- What will I remember most about this story?

Style

- What interesting words or phrases does the author use?
- What do I like about the way the author wrote the story?
- What do I dislike about how the author wrote the story?

Theme

- Why do I think the author wrote the story?
- Is there a message in the story? What was the message?

Point of View

- Who is telling the story?

Author

- What is the author trying to say about this book?
- What did the author have to know to write this book?
- Do I want to read other books by this author? Why?

Illustrator

- Who is the illustrator?
- How did the illustrations help me to understand the story?
- Do I like the illustrations? Why or why not?

Retelling of Advanced Narrative Story

Purpose: To identify story elements (grade 6 and above).

Procedure: Select appropriate grade-level books and identify the story elements each exemplifies. Introduce the definitions to the students and provide examples in short stories. Have students read and discuss the text. Individually or in groups, the students can explain orally or in writing how the book uses each story element. The following are definitions for elements of the plot and literary techniques:

Allusion—a reference to another work of fiction, a film, a piece of art, or even a real event.

Climax—the point of highest interest in terms of the conflict; a major turning point in the action

Conflict—the problem that controls or triggers the action in the story

Exposition—the introduction of setting, situation, and main characters

Falling action—the sequence of events that follow the climax and end in the resolution

Flashback—a point in the story that goes back to an earlier time to fill in missing information

Foreshadowing—when the author gives clues about what will happen

Irony—what is said and what is meant do not match

Mood—the feeling the reader gets from the story

Moral—the lesson to be learned from the story

Point of view—the angle from which the story is told; depends on who is telling the story

Resolution—the point of the story when the conflict is resolved

Rising action—the series of events that lead to the climax of the story, including the conflicts or problems of the main character

Surprise ending—twist in the plot at the end of the story

Suspense—tension or excitement that makes you want to read more

Tone—the author's attitude or feeling about a story

Expository Comprehension Guide

Purpose: To help students better understand expository texts through questioning (grades 3–12).

Procedure: During and after reading, students ask themselves some of the following questions.

Text Structure

- What kind of structure is used to present the information?
- Does it give information in a sequence?
- Does it just list information?
- Does it compare something or tell how things are different?
- Does it tell what causes something to happen and the effect of that cause?
- Does it tell about a problem and about a solution to a problem?
- Does it tell a main idea or topic and then give details to support the idea or topic?

Content

- Explain the organizational structures that I answered yes from above.
- What is the topic of the book or chapter?
- What do the headings tell me about the topic?
- What facts do I find most interesting?
- Would I like to read more books on this topic? Why?
- What else would I like to learn about this topic?

Illustrations and Pictures

- What information did I get from the illustrations, pictures, charts, and graphs?
- Did the illustrations help me understand the information? How?
- Which illustrations or pictures are the most interesting? Why?

- What could the author or illustrator do to make the information easier to understand?

Accuracy

- What information do I know about the author?
- What qualifies the author to write on this topic?
- What would I want to ask the author?
- What research did the author have to do to write this information?
- What is the copyright date? Does this book provide recent information?
- Where else can I find current information on this topic?
- Give examples of how the author lets the reader know he is stating facts or opinions.

Style

- Do I understand what the author is saying?
- What did the author do to make it easier or harder to understand?
- Do I want to read more books by this author? Why?
- How is this book similar or different from other books I have read?

Identifying Expository Organizational Structure

Source: Tierney & Readence, 2005

Purpose: To recognize and use expository organizational structures to better understand and recall information (grade 6 and above).

Procedure: Select a text with a clear expository structure (refer again to Table 5.1 on page 129). Define each structure for the student. Demonstrate the text structure through a think-aloud and point out signal words for each given type. Students learn to recognize the structure as you walk them through the text by asking questions based on text structure and writing. The students then produce the text structure on their own using a graphic organizer or outline of the passage.

There are also language features that are distinctive to expository texts. In addition to specialized language, the overall organization of the content is different. The language structures and the signals that identify them are also unique. The language in expository text is more formal and the information is more densely packed. The author's purpose and subject matter affect language choice and text organization in the text.

Information Organizing Strategies

The graphic organizers in the following pages are intended to help students to arrange ideas in all phases of learning from brainstorming ideas to presenting findings; to think about information in new ways; to select keywords and focus on the connections; to use in reviewing concepts and demonstrating understanding; to show a large amount of information in a single picture or graphic; to reduce the amount of time to edit, revise, and quickly add to a visual map; to use as an informal assessment of level of comprehension; to translate their understanding; and to use these tools to structure their own ideas.

There are six main structures that support the organization of information: (1) simple description, (2) problem-solution, (3) compare-contrast, (4) sequence, (5) classification, and (6) cause-effect. The descriptions, questions they might answer, and examples are listed on the following pages.

Simple Description

General Purpose: To list characteristics, features, and examples of a specific topic. A simple description can be extended so that the characteristics, features, and examples of that specific topic are described. It can also be used to clarify vocabulary words, answering questions such as What are you describing? What are its qualities? Examples: Radial Diagram, Story Pyramid, Five Senses Chart, and a variety of story maps (all grades).

Radial Diagram

Purpose: To show relationships to core idea.

Procedure: Write the topic in the center and then add descriptors and examples on each of the outer circles.

Example:

Story Pyramid

Procedure: Follow the directions for each line: Write one word for the name of a character; write two words that describe the setting, write three words that describe the character, write four words in a phrase that describe one event, and write five words in a phrase that describe another event.

Example: *Sarah, Plain and Tall* (MacLachlan, 1985)

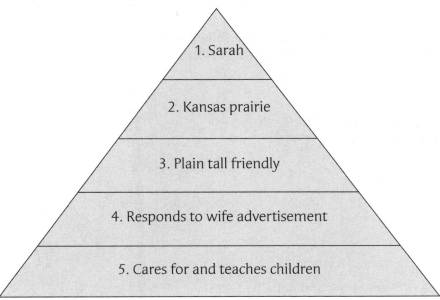

1. Sarah

2. Kansas prairie

3. Plain tall friendly

4. Responds to wife advertisement

5. Cares for and teaches children

Five Senses Chart

Procedure: List details from the story that are related to each of the five senses.

Example: *Harry Potter and the Sorcerer's Stone* (Rowling, 1998)

Hear	See	Feel	Smell	Taste
The snitch whizzed through the air as Harry tried to capture it on his Nimbus 2000 broom.	The owls delivered millions of letters to Harry through every crack in the house, inviting Harry to go to Hogwarts.	The electricity ran through Hermione's body as she used her wand.	They entered the musty chamber past the sleeping three-headed dog to get the Sorcerer's Stone.	They sat down to a delicious feast of meats and fruit in the great hall when Harry's team was awarded the cup.

Retelling Word Sort

Procedure: You or the students can write important words from each chapter. Students then do a word sort that organizes the words by their relationship to one another and retells the important information.

Story Map

Source: Walker, 2004

Procedure: As a whole class or individually, students write each element on a story map, which contains vertical boxes for each element with sequential plot episodes.

Example:

Name of Book: *Ronald Morgan Goes to Bat*
Author: Patricia Reilly Giff

Setting: At baseball practice
Where: Park
When: Spring

Main Character(s): Ronald Morgan, Coach
Other Characters: Mom, Dad, and Ronald's friends

Important Events in the Story:

Event 1:

He was bad at baseball.

Event 2:

He did not open his eyes when he was at bat.

Event 3:

His dad helped him and he was able to hit the ball.

But the most important thing in this story is...
To try your best in whatever you do.

Herringbone Map

Procedure: Write responses to who, where, when, what, how, and why on each of the fish bones. On the backbone, write the main idea.

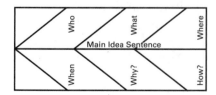

Beach Ball

Procedure: Toss a beach ball with story element questions written on it. Students answer the question that a specified part of their hand touches.

Comprehension Origami-Folded Fortune Tellers

Source: www.reallygoodstuff.com

Procedure: Using a square piece of paper, students make an origami fortune teller. Number each square on one side with 3, 4, 5, and 6 and number each triangle on the other side with 1-8. Write story element questions on each of the flaps: 1. Title, 2. Author and Illustrator, 3. Setting, 4. Description of Main Character, 5. Description of Additional Characters, 6. Main Problem, 7. Events, and 8. Solution. Students take turns asking and answering questions based on the story elements.

Adaptation: Choose different topics to put on the flaps, such as words and their definitions.

Manipulative Retell

Procedure: Use or make puppets, pictures, or felt cut-outs. Put them in order and then retell or explain the sequence of events.

Problem-Solution

General Purpose: To present information as a problem and list one or more solutions for that problem. This type of graphic organizer can be used to look at how a main character acts and reacts.

Problem-Solution Story Map

Procedure: This type of map can be used to identify the problem, examine how a main character acts and reacts, and the solution.

Example: *The Three Little Javelinas*   Author: Susan Lowell

Setting:	Sonoran Desert in Arizona
Characters:	First Little Javelina, Second Little Javelina, Third Little Javelina, and Coyote
Problem:	Coyote wants to eat the Javelinas.
Event 1:	The first little Javelina built a house of tumble weeds.
Event 2:	The coyote blew it down and the first little Javelina ran to brother's house.
Event 3:	The second little Javelina built a house of saguaro cactus ribs.

Event 4:	The coyote blew the house down and the first and second Javelina ran to their sister's house.
Event 5:	The third little Javelina built her house with adobe brick.
Solution:	The coyote huffed and puffed and couldn't blow down the adobe house. He squeezed into the stove pipe where the third little Javelina lit a fire. The coyote howled and ran away. If you ever hear a coyote's voice way out in the desert at night...well, you know what he's remembering!

Question-Answer Problem-Solution Map

Procedure: Create a simple two-column chart in which a question is posed in the left column and an answer or answers are given in the right. Questions could include What is the problem in the story? What attempts are made to solve the problem? How does the main character solve the problem? Why does the resolution come about?

Story Web

Procedure: Draw a large circle in the center, and write the title and author. Then draw circles that border the center circle, each containing the following headings: Main Characters, Setting, Problem, and Solution. Students can then fill in the information in the appropriate circles and draw lines back to the center showing the relationship of the information.

Example: Arthur's Pet Business (Brown, 1990)

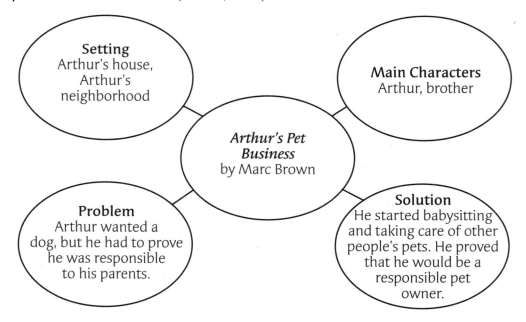

Circular Story Map

Procedure: Divide a circle into six sections and write the following information in each: (1) characters, setting, place; (2) first event and problem; (3, 4, 5) attempts and result; (6) resolution.

Compare-Contrast

General Purpose: To explore two or more elements within the story, or to compare the story with another story in order to develop a listing of similarities and differences. Comparing two characters is just one use for this type of graphic organizer. Questions to answer include What are the similar and different qualities of these things? What qualities of each thing correspond to one another? And in what way?

Venn Diagram

Purpose: To compare two or three items.

Procedure: Make a circle for each item. Characteristics that are unique go in the large part of the circle and those that are shared go in the intersections of the circles. If a concept is shared by all three, put it in the center.

H-Chart

Purpose: To compare two topics, characters, or texts.

Procedure: Draw a large, two-dimensional letter H. On the left, write characteristics of only topic 1; on the right, write characteristics of only topic 2. In the center bar, write similarities.

Compare-Contrast Diagram

Procedure: Compare two characters or topics using categories of information, answering questions such as How are they alike? How are they different? Students could create charts in numerous ways; two examples are shown here.

Example A: Comparing characters in *The Diary of Anne Frank* (Goodrich & Hackett, 1996) and *Hitler's Daughter* (French, 2003)

How are they alike? Both were born in Germany; both are in hiding.

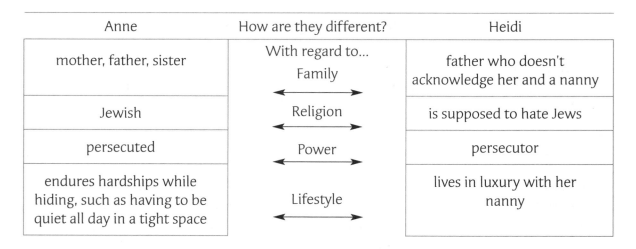

Example B: Comparing topics in *Amphibian: Eyewitness Books* (Clark, 2000)

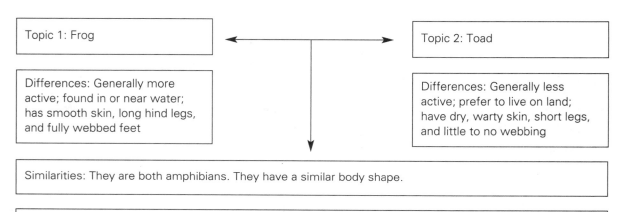

Sequence

General Purpose: To place events from the text in sequential order and to examine the significance of this ordering. This type of graphic organizer can be used for ordering events in a story or creating an outline for a student's original story. Questions to ask include What happened? What is the sequence of events? What are the substages?

Flow Chart

Procedure: Write the events in a story or a process in order.

Timeline

Procedure: Put the events in chronological order. Label them by date or event.

Cycle Diagram

Procedure: Draw a circular progression of arrows to show a process with a continuous cycle, such as in the process of plants making food in photosynthesis. Add words or pictures between arrows.

Example: *The River: A First Discovery Book* (Jeunesse, 1992)

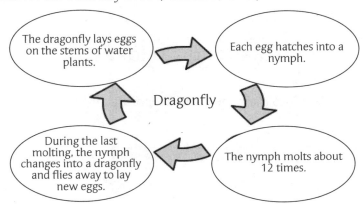

Story Board

Procedure: Divide a sheet of paper in a 2 × 3 grid. Think about six major events in the text and draw or write the main events in order in each section. Be sure to provide details.

Classification

General Purpose: To explore information from the text and organize it into classes or groups. The general connection between multiple items can be examined using these tools. Questions to ask include What sort of thing is this? What are the subcategories? What other things can go into these subcategories? (all grades)

Hierarchy Diagram

Purpose: To show hierarchical relationships between topic and subordinate and coordinate ideas; organize the concepts by their relationships.

Procedure: Draw boxes and lines to show how these concepts are related.

Example:

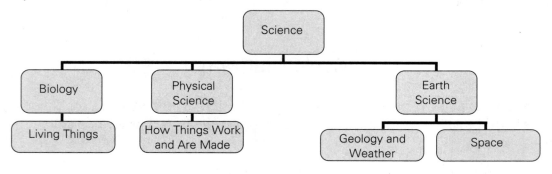

Stacking Up Ideas

Purpose: To organize ideas into main idea, subcategories, and details.

Example:

The Three Branches of the United States Government								
Legislative Branch			Executive Branch			Judicial Branch		
Makes laws	Senate	House of Representatives	President/ Vice President	Cabinet members	15 major departmental secretaries	Supreme Court	Oversees the court systems of the United States	1 Chief Justice, 8 Associate Justices

Cluster Web

Purpose: To identify a main concept in the story or text and add details about that concept in the circles connected to it.

Procedure: List supporting details in the additional circles. Insert additional circles if needed.

Cause-Effect

General Purpose: To identify the cause or causes and the resulting effect or effects. Events from within the story or text are looked at for their connections. Ask What are the causes and effects of this event? What might happen next? This story map can be also be used to show how events are affected by the characters actions.

Cause-Effect Map

Procedure: Write the cause(s) on left and effect(s) on the right.

Example: Title: *Rabble Rousers*, "Ida Bell Wells-Barnett" (Harness, 2003)

Cause:		Effect:
People were being sold as slaves.	→	13th Amendment made slavery illegal in 1865.
Fever struck.	→	Ida's parents and brother died.
Ida was asked to leave the train car because she was black.	→	Ida sued the railroad for discrimination and was awarded $500.
This decision was overturned in the state Supreme Court.	→	She wrote about courtrooms where blacks were unfairly tried and harshly punished.
Ida described the school where she taught as being shabby and poorly equipped.	→	Ida lost her teaching job at the school for black children.
Three black businessmen were jailed and hanged for false charges.	→	She began gathering and publishing evidence that more than 1,000 black men, women, and children had been hanged.
She feared for her safety.	→	She formed antilynching societies in the United States and Great Britain.

Group Comprehension Strategies

Literature Circles

Source: Short, Harste, & Burke, 1996

Purpose: To engage in student-led discussion groups around self-selected reading (grade 2 and above).

Procedure: Each member of the group is given a role sheet with required roles: discussion director, literary luminary/passage master, connector, and illustrator. (Optional roles might include researcher, summarizer, character captain, vocabulary enricher/word master, and travel tracer/scene setter.) Each role sheet includes guiding questions and responses. The discussion director guides the group's discussions and develops a list of questions to ask the group. The literary luminary (or "passage master") selects key sections of the text that the group would find interesting. The connector thinks of ways the story connects to themselves, other group members, their community, and experiences. The illustrator draws a picture, chart, web, or cartoon, and explains it to the group. The summarizer prepares a summary and the key points of the reading for the day. At the end of the literature circle, each group determines what to share with the rest of the class. These roles should be rotated so students get an opportunity for each role.

Book Club

Source: Raphael, Pardo, & Highfield, 2002

Purpose: To engage students in conversations about books and a framework to develop reading and writing for all ages.

Procedure: There are four parts to the framework: community share, book club discussions, reading, and writing. In community share, you introduce and model strategies including those for communication, and you also introduce conventions and vocabulary. Students hear and use language of literacy and discussion and share their discussions from their book club group. The book club discussions are authentic conversations between students in the group (who are not necessarily grouped by ability). Students learn to focus more on appreciating others' ideas rather than competing with others.

During reading, the students read for at least 15 minutes per day by themselves, with peers, or with the teacher. Emphasis is given to reading strategy development. Writing is important for personal responses and involves extending thinking with analysis and synthesis of the text. This can include reading logs and think sheets. The writing includes planning, revision, and publishing.

Bloom's Taxonomy Strategies

Bloom's Revised Taxonomy Questions and Strategies

Source: Anderson & Krathwohl, 2001, based on Bloom, 1956

Purpose: To comprehend both narrative and expository texts using multiple levels of Bloom's Taxonomy (all grades).

Procedure: Use the verbs of the cognitive domain to develop objectives for instruction before, during, and after reading: Creating, Evaluating, Analyzing, Applying, Understanding, and Remembering. There are several strategies that use the six levels of thinking. Questioning Strategies Based on Bloom's Revised Taxonomy (see Table 5.3) includes guidelines for asking questions, starting at the highest level of questioning, which is creating, and moving to the lowest level, which is remembering. Comprehension of Narratives Based on Bloom's Revised Taxonomy (see Table 5.4) contains literacy questions and activities that can be used to assess the student's understanding of a narrative story at each of the Revised Bloom's Taxonomy Levels.

Creative Comprehension Strategies

There are a variety of strategies that can extend beyond the text through oral, written, and visual communication. For the sake of brevity, the following is a list of several strategies:

- Share orally or in writing a favorite, interesting, or thought-provoking part.
- Share orally or in writing a scenario in which you meet a character or become a character and what that would be like.
- Make oral or written connections to your own experiences.
- Use a response journal to write about your feelings, what you know, what you don't understand, and to draw what is happening in the chapter and orally explain it.
- Share books through oral, written, or visual reports; stories; and newspaper articles.
- Create book reviews, newspaper articles, travel brochures, letters to the author, letters to the characters, or oral reading advertisements such as those found at the end of *Reading Rainbow* segments on television.
- Design and illustrate a book jacket and a biography of the author for the book.
- Think about a place in the book and write five words that describe it and draw a picture.
- Draw two additional pictures for the book and write a caption describing each of them.
- Make a comic strip about one part in the story.
- Write a story with a different ending, a sequel, a spin-off with different characters, setting, or problem, based on another story.
- Make puppets and act out the story.
- Write poetry or a song based on or adapted from the reading.
- Write an acrostic poem using the letters of a character or a topic and provide descriptions that start with each letter.

Table 5.3   Questioning Strategies Based on Bloom's Revised Taxonomy

Bloom's Taxonomy Level	Keywords	Questions
Creating: Combines elements or parts in meaningful construction; compiles information together in a different way	Build Create Design Integrate Compose Predict Formulate Imagine Elaborate Plan Propose Modify Choose Suppose Solve Construct Invent Hypothesize Organize Produce Rewrite Perform	What changes would you make to solve...? What would happen if...? Suppose you could ___, what would you do? Can you elaborate on the reason...?
Evaluating: Presents and defends opinion by making judgments about information	Determine Choose Defend Judge Prove Justify Compare Estimate Appraise Support Decide Interpret Rate Prioritize Disprove Criticize Predict Assess	How would you prove...? How could you determine...? What information would you use to support the view...? Why was it better than...? Why do you think he should?
Analyzing: Examines information and separates elements or parts using meaningful categories	Analyze Compare Contrast Categorize Classify Examine Simplify Survey Differentiate Dissect Test for Conclude Inspect Classify Divide Deduce Discover Motive Separate Research Distinguish Relate Outline Separate Diagram Discriminate	What motive is there..? What conclusions can you draw...? What evidence can you find...? Can you make the distinction between...?
Applying: Uses abstract concepts/ideas to solve problems to new situations by applying acquired knowledge	Apply Develop Interview Construct Organize Solve Plan Model Identify Utilize Select Make use of Build Choose Experiment Transfer Compute Produce Demonstrate Draw Paint Show Change Prepare Dramatize	How would you use...? How would you solve _____ using what you've learned? What approach would you use to...? What facts would you select to show? What would you do if...?
Understanding: Demonstrates understanding of facts and ideas by working with main ideas; uses examples or paraphrasing	Compare Translate Show Extend Infer Explain Summarize Relate Contrast Interpret Classify Illustrate Outline Demonstrate Tell Discuss Restate Illustrate Paraphrase Review Report	How would you compare...? Contrast? What facts or ideas show...? How would you summarize...? Which statements support...? Explain in your own words....
Remembering: Exhibits memory of previously learned material by recalling, remembering or locating facts, terms, basic concepts, and answers	Who What Where When Name Label Choose Find Match Recall Recite Write List Spell Count Show Define Select Describe Identify Sequence Quote	Who are the characters? What happened at the end of the story? When and where did the story take place? What definition is given for ___?

Table 5.4 Comprehension of Narratives Based on Bloom's Revised Taxonomy

Creating: This level provides the student with an opportunity to put parts from the story together in a new way to form a new idea or product. Success at this level will be evidenced by the student's ability to	• Create a story from just the title before the story is read (prereading exercise). • Write three new titles for the story that would give a good idea what it was about. • Create a poster to advertise the story so people will want to read it. • Create a new product related to the story. • Restructure the roles of the main characters to create new outcomes in the story. • Compose and perform a dialogue or monologue that will communicate the thoughts of the main character(s) at a given point in the story. • Imagine that he or she is one of the main characters and write a diary account of daily thoughts and activities. • Create an original character and tell how the character would fit into the story. • Write the lyrics and music to a song that one of the main characters would sing if he/she/it became a rock star, and perform it.
Evaluating: This level provides the student with an opportunity to form and present an opinion backed up by sound reasoning. Success at this level will be evidenced by the student's ability to	• Decide which character in the selection he or she would most like to spend a day with and why. • Judge whether or not a character should have acted in a particular way and why. • Decide if the story really could have happened and justify reasons for the decision. • Consider how this story can help the student in his or her own life. • Appraise the value of the story. • Compare the story with another one the student has read. • Write a recommendation as to why the books should be read or not.
Analyzing: This level provides the student with an opportunity to take parts of the story and examine these parts carefully in order to better understand the whole story. Success at this level will be evidenced by the student's ability to	• Identify general characteristics (stated and/or implied) of the main characters. • Distinguish what could happen from what couldn't happen in the story in real life. • Select parts of the story that were the funniest, saddest, happiest, and most unbelievable. • Differentiate fact from opinion. • Compare and/or contrast two of the main characters. • Select an action of a main character that was exactly the same as something the student would have done.

(continued)

Table 5.4 Comprehension of Narratives Based on Bloom's Revised Taxonomy (Continued)

Applying: This level provides the student with an opportunity to use information from the story in a new way. Success at this level will be evidenced by the student's ability to	• Classify the characters as human, animal, or thing and list them on a chart. • Transfer a main character to a new setting and tell how the story would be different. • Make finger puppets and act out a part of the story. • Select a meal that one of the main characters would enjoy eating. Plan a menu and a method of serving it. • Think of a situation that occurred to a character in the story and write about how he or she would have handled the situation differently. • Give examples of people the student knows who have the same problems as the characters in the story.
Understanding: This level provides the student with an opportunity to demonstrate a basic understanding of the story. Success at this level will be evidenced by the student's ability to:	• Interpret pictures of scenes from the story, and describe it in your own words. • Explain selected ideas or parts from the story in his or her own words. • Draw a picture showing what happened before and after a passage or illustration found in the book. • Write a sentence explaining what happened before and after a passage or illustration found in the book. • Predict what could happen next in the story before the reading of the entire book is completed. • Construct a pictorial timeline that summarizes what happens in the story. • Explain how the main character felt at the beginning, middle, and end of the story.
Remembering: This level provides the student with an opportunity to recall fundamental facts and information about the story. Success at this level will be evidenced by the student's ability to:	• Match character names with pictures of the characters. • Match statements with the characters who said them. • List the main characteristics of one of the main characters in a "Wanted" poster. • Arrange scrambled story pictures in sequential order. • Arrange scrambled story sentences in sequential order. • Recall details about the setting by creating a picture of where a part of the story took place. • Write one sentence from the story that tells what the main character did first.

Adapted from Teacher Created Materials. (n.d.). *Celebrate Literature and Critical Thinking Notebook*

- Research the same topic or books by the same author.

- Integrate reading with social studies, science, and math concepts.

- Create mnemonic devices for remembering sequences of events or concepts in the text such as *My Mama Eats Vegetables Just Standing Up Near Papa* (Mercury, Mars, Earth, Venus, Jupiter, Saturn, Uranus, Neptune, Pluto).

- Develop art, construction, cooking, or music activities related to the reading.

Emergent Listening Comprehension Strategies

Many students, especially those at lower reading levels, can comprehend a text better when it is read orally to them because they can concentrate on the meaning rather than on decoding the text. It is important for students to be able to hear, discuss, and comprehend text at and above their reading or word accuracy level to develop reading comprehension and a love of literature. According to Harris and Hodges (1995, p. 140), a student's listening comprehension level is "the highest grade level of material that can be comprehended well when it is read aloud to the student."

- Reread their favorite books and introduce new ones.

- Begin instruction not with phonics, but with opportunities to develop language skills through discussion of ideas and sharing books.

- Use prediction based on the sentence structure and the meaning. Beginners with well-developed language can use prediction to help them read. They can make educated guesses about what will come next.

- Read the story with expression and use different voices for different characters to get your students more involved in the story.

- Point to details in the picture that show what you read, such as "Look, there are two cats," or "That's where the mouse is hiding."

- Encourage students to wonder while reading narrative and expository texts. For example, "I wonder what Pooh will do now?" "How do you think the father feels?" or "I wonder what frogs do in the winter? Do you think that's a problem? Why?" and "What do you think is going to happen next?"

- Use a modified oral cloze procedure when the reader omits words for the listener to provide. Encourage the student to chime in on repeated phrases or patterns, by stopping to see if your student can supply the repeating phrase or the last word of the rhyme. For example, from *Green Eggs and Ham* by Dr. Seuss (1960): Would you could you in a boat? Would you could you with a _____? (goat). Or, try a phrase from The Three Little Pigs: He huffed and he puffed and _____ (he blew the house down).

- Talk about the pictures and words your student may not understand, such as "Look, there's a baby sheep; it's called a lamb."

- Point out unfamiliar words and explore their meaning. Revisit these words frequently and encourage students to use them in their own conversations.
- Make brief comments during the story and answer students' questions.

After reading, have a conversation about the story. Ask questions such as What was your favorite part? Or, talk about how the story is similar or different from students' lives. Ask questions such as Where does *your* cat sleep? or How is this character like you?

Encourage your students to read or to pretend to read by retelling from the pictures. Say, "Now why don't you read to me? Remember to look at the pictures." You could also suggest that students draw a picture related to the story or their lives. Have students tell you about the picture and write down what they say above or below the picture. Help students to write their names or their ideas on the paper. Connect their writing and art activities to the reading in unique ways, such as making puppets based on the books to help the students expand their vocabulary.

General Strategies for All Readers

- Read aloud to all students daily from a variety of genres and generally above their reading level, as it helps their language to grow.
- Model fluent reading of text by reading with appropriate expression, intonation, and pace. Use different voices or dialects for stories with dialogue.
- Help students extend their experience with the words, language, and ideas in books by interactively reading harder texts with them and to them every day.
- While reading books, point out the pictures, diagrams, and charts and talk about them.
- Point out vocabulary or concepts students may not be familiar with.
- Talk about similarities between the reading and previous experiences students have had or heard about.
- Take every opportunity to point out the ways in which reading is essential to the communications of everyday life (e.g., on labels, instructions, signs).
- Show your students that you read books, magazines, newspapers, and computer resources.

CHAPTER 6

Emergent Writing and Writing Composition

Understanding Emergent Writing

Emergent writing includes the preconventional forms of writing, such as scribbling, drawing, nonphonetic letterings, and phonetic or inventive spelling, that occur prior to conventional writing (Sulzby & Teale, 1991). Early writing development begins with children making marks on a paper just for fun. This progresses into communicating visual messages on paper to creating texts (Morrow, 2005).

Sulzby and Teale (1991) describe the development of children's writing. Once they learn letter forms, children create strings of letters for their written messages without regard for the sounds represented by the letters. Children then learn that the formation of letters equates to sounds, which can be strung together to write words and ideas. They begin to use invented or phonetic spelling that typically includes the most dominant sounds in a word, such as the beginning and ending sounds. However, it takes some time before they use phonetic clues to read what they write, and often they try to recall what was written or they use the pictures to remind them. Finally, children are able to write the majority of the sounds in the words needed to communicate a message and they are able to read it back.

Children need early experiences with writing materials and observing others writing to communicate information. It is important to model that what students say can be written down and what is written down can be read by others to share information. The focus of emergent writing is on communicating a message. Through emergent writing, children refine their understanding of the written language system (Jensen, 1984), which not only helps them communicate their ideas but also enhances students' phonics and spelling development (see Chapter 3). Handwriting is an additional skill needed for emergent writers to communicate their ideas.

Understanding Writing Composition

Writing composition is the "process or result of arranging ideas to form a clear and unified impression in order to create an effective message" (Harris & Hodges, 1995, p. 38). Writing is essential to life. As Routman (2005) states, "I want students to write with passion and ease. I want them to be motivated, confident writers who see writing as an everyday, useful, even enjoyable tool" (p. 1). Writing instruction is sometimes neglected in the teaching curriculum and is often a neglected topic in national and state legislation and research reports. The National Reading Panel report (NICHD, 2000) identified five important areas of reading instruction (phonemic awareness, phonics, fluency, vocabulary, and reading comprehension) but unfortunately, writing was not listed as an important area—even though reading and writing are related processes. Both the IRA and the National Reading Council have embraced the need for effective writing instruction, and in *Standards for Reading Professionals—Revised 2003* (IRA, 2003), both reading and writing instruction are addressed.

Composing and comprehending are interrelated processes; readers *and* writers compose meaning (Tierney & Pearson, as cited in Jensen, 1984). The more students use reading and writing together the more they learn from both. Learning to comprehend in a given genre supports the written composition in that same genre, just as learning to compose supports comprehension of the same genre. When introducing each genre, read aloud examples of effective writing and discuss the writing elements. Students should know the criteria on which they are graded, and a rubric or checklist should be provided and explained to them. Panman and Panman (2006) identify writing genre elements that you can use to determine what elements need to be specifically taught for each genre (see Table 6.1).

The most important method of supporting students' writing composition is to provide instruction and clear expectations prior to beginning writing. Lessons should be taught on each of the writing criteria for content and conventions that are to be evaluated: ideas and details, organization, voice, sentence fluency, word choice, grammar, punctuation, capitalization, and spelling.

Handwriting should be addressed if necessary. At the primary level, students should be instructed on the correct formation of letters, writing within the lines and the margins. In the upper grades, students tend to develop their own style of handwriting. Handwriting should be addressed in the upper grades only if it affects the reader's ability to read the writing easily and without having to predict what is written.

Genres and Forms of Writing

The same genres exist in reading instruction as in writing instruction; however, some are emphasized more than others during the writing process. It is important to make explicit the elements of each genre as they are taught during the reading process; this allows students to become successful in including these elements during writing. Panman and Panman (2006) outline several kinds of writing that are often taught in schools, including essays, reports, and letters. Writing using technology has also been added.

One of the most common forms of writing is the essay. The essay tells a story, such as in a **narrative** with a beginning, middle, and an end. It creates vivid images for readers, such as in a **descriptive** piece that describes a person, place, thing, or idea. It presents facts, explains ideas, gives directions, or defines terms so that they can be easily understood, such as an **expository** essay. A **persuasive** essay tries to convince the reader to support a certain point of view.

Another type of writing is report writing. Students can write a short report, such as a newspaper or magazine article. They can write reviews of books, movies, music, or other media. They can write about a specific topic or a person. Reports contain an introduction, development of the topic, and a conclusion. Older students can write a research paper, which is similar to a report in that it contains the same headings, except there are more development paragraphs and students use multiple references to support their writing. In addition to

Table 6.1	Writing Genre Elements
Narrative	**Introductory paragraph:** Captures the reader's attention and introduces the characters and the setting **Development paragraph:** Gives details about the characters and what's happening to them, builds the plot, and leads to the point of the story **Concluding paragraph:** Summarizes the story, expresses a reaction to the events, offers an opinion, or reaches a conclusion
Descriptive	**Introductory paragraph:** Gets the reader's attention, uses vivid details to introduce the setting, creates the mood, and provides an overview **Development paragraph:** Focuses on the details of one event using appealing to the author's senses **Concluding paragraph:** Builds to a conclusion
Expository	Gives directions about how to do something, how to get somewhere, explains how something works, or how something happens **Introductory paragraph:** Defines the topic and provides an overview **Development paragraph:** Explains the process and gives supporting facts; uses transition words such as *first*, *second*, *third*, or *before*, *after*, *sometimes* **Concluding paragraph:** Restates or supports the topic and draws a conclusion
Persuasive	**Introductory paragraph:** States the purpose, identifies the audience, introduces the subject, includes the status of the writer, provides two reasons in support of the idea, and provides the opinion of the author **Development paragraph:** Gives the topic sentence for the first reason of support, includes several sentences explaining the reason and then restating the reason, includes subsequent paragraphs for reasons two and three **Concluding paragraph:** Includes a sentence that restates the topic, a sentence or two that supports this reason, and a summary of the author's opinion and a conclusion
Short report, book report, research paper	Gather resources, take notes, group notes by topic, make an outline with headings, and sequence notes to put in outline **Introductory paragraph:** Introduces the topic, the audience, and the author's reason for writing about it; defines the topic and answers who, what, where, when, and why; includes a conclusion sentence that provides a transition from the introduction to the development paragraphs **Development paragraph:** Provides details and cites the specific sources of your information **Concluding paragraph:** Restates the topic, explain the up-to-date status of the topic or what was learned so far and what you hope to learn in the future, provides your personal view and conclusion
Friendly letter, business letter	Return address, date line, inside address, greeting **Introductory paragraph** (explain why you are writing) **Development paragraph** (develop your ideas) **Concluding paragraph** (summarize what you want the reader to know or do) Closing and signature block
Résumé	Identification heading, career goal, work experience, education, special skills, interests and hobbies, awards and achievements, references

writing traditional papers, students can also create PowerPoint or other media presentations to share the information they have learned.

Letter writing is another important form of writing. There are many purposes for writing a letter. It can be a friendly letter or thank-you note. It can be a business letter asking for information, requesting something, or making a complaint. It can also be for employment, as a cover letter for a resume. Less formal forms of letter writing are e-mail, instant messaging, and text messaging. There are unique aspects to these electronic forms of writing.

Finally, there is descriptive writing, such as journaling, poetry, song lyrics, plays, and advertising jingles and slogans. Each of these forms of writing needs to be taught and practiced. The most effective method is through reading, sharing, and discussing how others have written using these forms of writing. It is not the content but *how* others write that needs to be stressed. It is important to share with your students your own writing, including the multiple drafts. Finally, give students numerous opportunities to write in a variety of genres for a variety of purposes.

The Writing Process

Solley (2000) gives a historical perspective on the writing process. In the past, writing was taught in school as a product, not a process. Teaching the writing process began in the early 1970s when Emig (1971) began studying the writing process of high school students. Harste, Woodward, and Burke (1984) began studying the thinking process of emergent writers at the preschool age. Think-aloud protocols were developed by Flower and Hayes (1981) and extended by Graves (1983) and Calkins (1983) to understand the thought processes of children and adults as they write. This was the beginning of a writing process model that included rehearsal, drafting, revising, and editing. This developed into the Writers' Workshop Model, developed by Graves (1983) and Calkins (1983), which added conferring and publishing to the process. Atwell (1987) expanded this model for use with middle-level students. Routman (2005) added specific elements for teaching the writing process. The complete writing process approach includes publishing one's writing; however, not all writing must go through all stages of the "writing process." Students should select those pieces that are most meaningful to take all the way through the publishing stage.

The writing process includes prewriting activities, first draft, revising, editing, conferring, revising subsequent drafts, and publishing. During prewriting activities, the students identify purpose and audience for writing, identify writing genre (narrative, expository, persuasive, or creative), brainstorm ideas for writing, make a graphic organizer of major ideas, and sequence ideas in an outline. During the first draft stage, students write their ideas on every other line to allow room for revising and editing, they read the draft aloud, and then research more ideas and details on the topic. Revising is the next stage. During revising, students reread multiple times while focusing on revision of ideas, organization, voice, word choice, and sentence fluency; they then reread. During the editing stage, students edit for grammar and usage, paragraphing, punctuation, capitalization, and spelling. They then reread again.

In the conferring stage, students share their writing with a partner and get feedback. The partner needs to be instructed to look for the revision concepts first and then the editing concepts. The writer reflects on and revises subsequent drafts based on self and peer evaluation. The writer rereads in order to refine writing and uses an editing checklist to complete final edit of content and mechanics. The writer shares the writing with a partner again and then with the teacher to get feedback. Final revisions are made in preparation for publishing.

During the final publishing stage, students type or rewrite their compositions in their finest handwriting and then illustrate or add graphics. If a composition is multiple pages in length, students can create a cover and title page and bind their work. Finally, students share writing orally or display it for an audience. This is the basic model of the writing process. However, depending on the style of writing, specific criteria may need to be added to the process.

Objectives for Emergent Writing

Students will do the following:

- Draw pictures to communicate information
- Dictate stories for others to write
- Write letters to represent sounds or words
- Write strings of letters to represent ideas
- Write uppercase and lowercase letters with the correct formation
- Write letters and words from left to right
- Return to the left for the next line using the return sweep
- Use proper spacing between letters and words
- Use inventive spelling of words
- Use resources to spell words
- Write phrases to communicate ideas
- Write using sentence frames or patterned sentences
- Write using transitional spelling, with letters representing every sound
- Write high-frequency words correctly
- Write sentences with initial capitalization and end punctuation
- Write for a variety of purposes
- Write more complete sentences
- Write stories of three sentences on one topic
- Begin to recognize mistakes in content, punctuation, capitalization, spelling, and grammar

Objectives for Writing Composition

Students will do the following:

- Read with a writer's perspective and apply that knowledge to their own writing
- Write for a specific audience and with a meaningful purpose
- Compose writing of different genres: narrative, descriptive, expository, persuasive, and poetic

- Demonstrate daily functional writing such as making lists, making notes, completing forms, and writing thank-you cards
- Compose personal and dialogue journals, stories, poems, and songs
- Compose writing to demonstrate comprehension of a text or concept such as content journals, notetaking, book reports, and response to essay questions
- Compose writing to share or request information: letters, e-mails, invitations, directions, reports, presentations, newsletters, speeches, persuasive essays, and webpages

- Use prewriting strategies such as drawing, brainstorming, diagramming or outlining, and sharing
- Use drafting strategies such as elaborating on initial ideas in complete sentence
- Use revising strategies
  - Write ideas and details clearly, in an organized manner, using appropriate transitions
  - Elaborate on ideas by providing details, support, and descriptions of people, places, objects, processes, and events
  - Use voice in writing such as tone (friendly, formal, distant), word choice (everyday words, complex words, specific content words), sentence patterns, and personal style
  - Use different language structures such as figurative language, dialogue, sensory descriptions, humor, cause and effect, sequencing, compare and contrast, and point of view
  - Write using varied, specific, and interesting nouns, verbs, adjectives, and adverbs.
- Write using a variety of sentence structures such as compound and complex sentences
- Use editing strategies to check for appropriate grammar, punctuation, capitalization, spelling, and legible handwriting
- Share writing orally or make it available for others to read such as publishing for the classroom, library, family, community, newspaper, or Internet

Emergent Writing Assessments

Emergent Writing Development Stage Assessment

Purpose: To document a student's emergent writing behaviors, from exploring with writing materials to writing complete sentences; to identify the student's emergent writing stage. l developed the Emergent Writing Development State Assessment (see Appendix) with descriptors adapted from Beaty (1994) and Morrow (1993). (grades K–1)

Procedure and Analysis: Observe and collect several writing samples from the student. Read each of the descriptors in the checklist and evaluate it using a plus sign (+) to indicate that the student exhibited this behavior frequently, a checkmark (✓) to indicate that the behavior was sometimes exhibited, or a minus sign (–) to indicate that the student rarely or never exhibited this behavior.

There are five stages of emergent writing development. Kindergarten includes stages 1–4 and the expectation for first grade is stage 5. The stage with the most checkmarks or plus signs is the student's emergent writing stage. Review the student's specific areas of strength and need in writing and plan instruction to reinforce the strengths and develop the areas of need. Add comments to record clarifying information.

Example and Analysis: This assessment is based on first-grade writing samples from Tanisha's journal dated August 20, September 18, and October 20. On August 20 she drew a picture of herself. I asked her to tell me about the picture. She said, "I play soccer." I asked her, "Do you know how to write *I*?" She wrote *A*. I asked her, "Can you write *play*?" She wrote *B*. So I wrote her sentence on the paper. I asked her to read the sentence and she said "soccer" and could not point one-to-one. I asked her if she could write her name and she wrote *T*. On September 18 she wrote *I P M S*. I asked her to read it and she said, "I play with my sister." She wrote *TAN* again for her name.

On October 20 she wrote, *I GO 2 the PK W MI DG*. I asked her to read it and she said, "I go to the park with my dog." She was able to draw a detailed picture and write her name in all uppercase letters.

Score +/✓/–	Descriptor	Date Observed, Comments
Stage 2		
	CONTENT	
+	Dictates sentences to be written	8/20 Journal
✓, +	"Reads" story with consistent oral text	8/20, 9/18 Journal
✓, +	Differentiates between picture and story	8/20, 9/18 Journal
	HANDWRITING	
N/A	Symbols or scribbles represent letters, words, or strings of words	
✓	Writes mock letters or letters but they have no phonetic representation	8/20 wrote *AB* for *I play*
✓	Begins to write alphabet letters	8/20 *A* and *B*
Stage 3		
	CONTENT	
✓	Dictates more complete stories to be written	9/18, during Language Experience

N/A	Completes sentence frames or patterned sentences	
✓	Draws recognizable pictures	8/20 she drew a picture of her
–	Attempts to label pictures and writes letters for words	8/20 didn't write anything until prompted
	SPELLING	
✓	Writes letters to represent a word or idea	9/18 wrote correct initial letter for 3 of 4 words
✓	Attempts inventive spelling of words with some correct sound-symbol association	9/18 initial letters, 10/20 initial and final letters
✓, +	Hears and writes letters for beginning consonant sounds	9/18 wrote correct initial sounds, except for *w*, 10/20 wrote correct initial sounds
✓, +	Hears and writes letters for ending consonant sounds	10/20 wrote most of the correct ending sounds
	HANDWRITING	
✓	Awareness of letter and word spacing begins	10/20 beginning to space between words
	Awareness of left-to-right sequence of letters and words	9/18, 10/20 wrote letters left to right
✓	Begins to copy words	10/20 copied *the* from word wall
✓	Most letters are recognizable, may mix between uppercase and lowercase letters	10/20 letters are recognizable except wrote *2* for *to*, still mostly uppercase

Stage 4

	CONTENT	
✓	Writes on a self-selected topic	10/20 Journal
N/A	Writes on a teacher-selected topic	
+	Illustrations match text	9/18, 10/20
	SENTENCE STRUCTURE	
✓	Writes one sentence with at least four words	10/20 3 of 8 words spelled correctly
	CAPITALIZATION/PUNCTUATION	
–	Some use of correct capitalization	10/20 mostly uppercase
–	Some use of correct end punctuation	10/20 no punctuation
	SPELLING	
✓	Writes short sentences using inventive spelling	10/20

✓	Writes name and some sight words correctly	10/20 wrote name, *I*, *GO*, and *the* correctly
✓	Writes words with beginning and ending consonant sounds	10/20 6 of 8 words had the correct beginning and ending sounds
–	Writes words with some vowel sounds	*I*, *GO*, and *the* are the only words with vowels
✓	Begins to use written resources for spelling	10/20 wrote *the* using word wall
	HANDWRITING	
✓	All letters are recognizable	10/20 all letters except *2* for *two*
–	Lowercase letters are generally used	10/20 capitals
–	Beginning to write within lines	10/20 not on lines
✓	Writes from left to right	9/18 and 10/20 wrote from left to right
–	Begins to use appropriate spacing between words	10/20 words and letters still bunched together

This student is in first grade. Based on the descriptors, her writing is at stage 3. Her picture and text match and tell a story. She was able to write her ideas with letters representing many of the initial and final consonant sounds. She was able to use the word wall to spell the word *the*. She does not yet represent all of the sounds in the words, use upper- and lowercase letters appropriately, or use any punctuation.

Instructional Implications: This student needs daily opportunities to practice communicating her ideas using inventive spelling. During journal writing, she should be encouraged to sound out each word and write the letters for the sounds she hears. Provide sound boxes for each of the common unknown words to help her include vowel sounds. Initially select phonetically regular words, such as *dog*, from her journal, and have her say a letter that could represent each sound. To write the words with lowercase letters, provide an alphabet strip with lower- and uppercase letters. Have her find each lowercase letter on the strip and copy it to write the words in her sentence. Use a familiar book to show her that the first letter of every sentence has an uppercase letter and that there is a period at the end of every statement. Have her select her favorite journal page to rewrite.

Handwriting Rubric Assessment

Purpose: To determine a student's strengths and needs based on handwriting standards (grades K–4).

Procedure and Analysis: The Handwriting Rubric Assessment (see Appendix) can be used with any writing assessment or writing sample to assess the student's specific development in handwriting. Using the criteria listed in the rubric under the columns labeled Exceeds, Meets, and Does Not Meet, mark a plus sign (+), checkmark (✓), or minus sign (–) for each of the standards. Using the school-adopted style of manuscript or cursive, compare the student's handwriting with the expected standard and identify areas of strength and need such as letter formation, spacing, directionality, reversals, and capitalization. However, because the goal of writing is communication, focus on legibility over exact handwriting style.

Writing Composition Assessment

Purpose: To analyze a student's writing based on his ideas, organization, voice, sentence fluency, word choice, and conventions. Writing composition assessment is an important part of any complete literacy evaluation. It initially provides you and the student with baseline data about how the student is able to communicate his ideas in writing. This assessment can be repeated, such as at the end of every grading period, to identify areas of growth and need in the student's writing.

Procedure and Analysis: There are three tools you can use to assess writing composition: the Writing Composition Assessment Summary, the Writing Composition Rubric for Writer and Teacher, and the Writing Process Rubric for Writer and Teacher.

The Writing Composition Assessment Summary (see Appendix), provides a summary of the student's strengths and needs in writing composition based on specific prompts. Select a genre for the student to write and then provide a prompt such as one of the following:

- For a narrative sample: "Write about an important event in your life."
- For a descriptive sample: "Write a poem or song about something you like."
- For an expository sample: "Write about a specific topic or how to make something."
- For a persuasive sample: "Write about what you would like to change in your school."

For grades K–1, have the student draw a picture first and then write about it. Because emergent writing may be difficult to read, have the student read what he or she has written while you write what the student says. You could provide the Writing Composition Assessment Summary form as a reference so the student would know what he is going to be evaluated on. Explain to the student that he will be evaluated on content and conventions. You or the student then select a purpose for writing and genre in which he will write.

Give the student a prompt such as the ones above and say, "I want you to think about an event or topic you know well. Tell me about it. Now explain it in writing with as much detail as possible. Please write on every other line. When you are done, please reread it and make any changes to help the reader understand what you wrote." Although this is not a timed assessment, the student should be encouraged to continue to write or revise for the allotted time based on his grade (Grade K–1: 15 minutes, Grade 2–3: 30 minutes, Grade 4–5: 45 minutes, and Grade 6–12: 1 hour) or developmental ability.

For each writing element, examine the indicators and mark in the left column a plus sign (+) if it is excellent, a checkmark (✔) if satisfactory, or minus sign (–) if it needs work or incomplete, and then in the right column write descriptive statements for each element. In the analysis section, indicate areas of strength or need. Also give comments about the length of the writing and any evidence of prewriting or revisions. Additional notes can be made if the handwriting is a concern; the Handwriting Rubric Assessment (see Appendix) also may be used. An evaluation of this information is used to plan lessons to further develop the student's writing. This writing composition could be used as a rough draft, and then after instruction it could be edited and revised as a published piece of writing.

Using the Writing Composition Rubric for Writer and Teacher (see Appendix), you can evaluate the content elements (ideas and details, organization, voice, sentence fluency, and word choice) and the convention elements (grammar, punctuation, capitalization, and spelling). Use the rubric as a guide throughout the writing process or afterward as an initial evaluation of student writing. Circle either student or teacher in the score column. After reading the entire composition, read each of the descriptors in the rubric and mark each element with a plus sign (+) for excellent, a checkmark (✔) for satisfactory, or a minus sign (–) for needs improvement. Underline any descriptive words that seem appropriate. Then analyze with specific examples from the composition.

The Writing Process Rubric for Writer and Teacher (see Appendix) is used to evaluate the student's use of each of the steps of the writing process when he decides to publish his writing.

Writing composition assessment is an important part of any complete literacy evaluation. It initially provides the literacy specialist with baseline data about how the student is able to communicate ideas in writing. This assessment can be repeated, such as at the end of every grading period, to identify areas of growth and need in the student's writing.

Example and Analysis: One day I wos on a hill. As I was go (^ing) dawn (down) the hill. I had bowt feet on the front tier to mack it sawnd. (^ like a moter sicol) I staer did doing a front flip with a owt a hamit.

(Spelling translation: One day I was on a hill. As I was going down the hill, I had both feet on the front tire to make it sound like a motorcycle. I started doing a front flip without a helmet.)

Writing Composition Assessment Summary

Prompt: Circle one.

(Narrative)	"Write about an important event in your life."
Descriptive	"Write a poem or song about something you like."
Expository	"Write about a specific topic or how to make something."
Persuasive	"Write about what you would like to change in your school."

Title or Topic: Going down the hill on a bike

Content

✓	Ideas and details: He had four events that he described with some detail, but did not complete the story.
–	Organization: He had the beginning of the story and a lead up to an event, but it didn't occur and there was no ending.
✓	Voice: You could tell that this was a personal event that happened to him.
–	Sentence fluency: His sentences flowed from one to another. He had one fragment: "As I wos go dawn the hill." He had one sentence that didn't make sense: "I staer did doing a front flip with a owt a hamit."
✓	Word choice: He used several adjectives (both, front, motor). He added a description of what he sounded like.

Conventions

✓	Grammar: Correct except for "I staer did doing a front flip…"
✓	Punctuation: All correct except for the sentence fragment starting with "As…"
✓	Capitalization: All correct except for the sentence fragment starting with "As…"
–	Spelling: Most spelling mistakes were decodable but common words: *wos/was*; *bowt/both*, *tier/tire*, *mack/make*, *sawnd/sound*, *moter/motor*, *sicol /cycle*; *with owt/without*; *hamit/helmet* One misspelling affected the meaning of the sentence: *staer/started*

Length:　　Number of sentences **4**　　Number of paragraphs **1** (incomplete)
Average number of words per sentence **10**　Appropriate length for topic: (yes or ⓝⓞ)
Evidence of prewriting: He talked about it.
Evidence of revision and editing: He correctly changed *go* to *going* and *dawn* to *down*. He added new descriptive information *like a motor sicol* and changed *with a* to *with out*.

This student was able to communicate some initial ideas about an event, but the story ended abruptly. The student did some revision and editing.

Instructional Implications: Instruction should begin with rereading the story orally to see if everything makes sense and then developing a story structure with a beginning, middle, and end. Have the student revise this initial piece because it is a good beginning. Begin phonics and spelling instruction with words that have vowels, vowel diphthongs, and r-controlled vowels.

Emergent Writing Strategies

Emergent writing begins with scribbles. However, students quickly learn that writing communicates a message when they are provided daily opportunities to see writing modeled;

have their ideas written down by others; and begin seeing that their sentences are made up of words, the words are made up of sounds, and the sounds can be written with letters. By guiding students to represent their ideas by writing letters for the sounds they hear, most kindergarten students can meet the expectation of composing a complete sentence by the end of the year. The following strategies support students in communicating a message by matching the sounds they hear to writing letters. Be sure that the students have a personal alphabet chart with pictures so they can use it as a model for writing letters. It is beneficial to begin with teaching students to write their name, because this is a very important word and it is needed to document the author or the illustrator of their work. These strategies are all useful with primary-grade children.

Students' Names

Purpose: To learn to write their name in order to sign their work (grades K–3).

Procedure: On a lined sentence strip write the students' preferred first and last name using the school-selected handwriting style. Keep it available for them to see. Model for students how to write their names with the initial letters uppercase and the rest of the letters lowercase. Have them write their names with a variety of media such as markers, crayons, paints, and pencils. Be sure to remind students to put their names on their drawing and writing.

Drawing and Dictating

Purpose: To model for students that what they say can be written and what is written can be read (grades K–2).

Procedure: After students draw a picture, ask them to tell you about it. Write what they say on the paper using the school-selected handwriting style. Then reread each student's writing, pointing to each word and asking them to "read" it to you.

Drawing and Labeling

Purpose: To correlate sounds in words with writing letters (grades K–3).

Procedure: Provide blank paper and ask students to draw a picture and then label their drawing. In developmental stages, suggest that students write the letter for the initial sound of each word. They can use a personal alphabet chart with picture cues to help them with selecting the appropriate letter. When students are successful, ask them to write letters for other sounds they hear in the word; often these are the consonants, and eventually they begin to include letters for the medial sounds.

Sentence Frames

Purpose: To provide a structure or model for students writing in sentence form (grades K–3).

Procedure: Select a sentence that students could complete based on a pattern in a book or based on a topic. Write the sentence frame on each student's paper or on the chalkboard, leaving an underline for words that need to be inserted. For example, after reading *Brown Bear, Brown Bear, What Do You See?* (Martin, 1967), students could write the same sentence pattern substituting a color and an animal for the underlines, such as <u>Red ant, red ant</u>, what do you see? Students then could illustrate their writing.

Message Writing

Purpose: To observe the writing process being modeled, so that the students will be able to write their own messages (grades K–3).

Procedure: While you write a message to the students or a dictated message from the students, segment words into their sounds by modeling the writing process on the chalkboard. Pronounce each word slowly and enunciate each word as you write it. Make connections to known words or parts of words. For example, say "I am going to begin by writing *Dear Class*. What sound does the word *dear* start with? /d/. How do I write that sound? Because it is at the beginning of my greeting, I need a capital *D*. Next I hear /ē/, and that is written with two letters *ea* like in *eat*. Finally I hear the /r/, written with the letter *r*. That word is done, so I need a finger space. What is the next word? *Class*. It begins with the /k/ sound and it is written with the letter *c*, then I/ă/s/ with two *Ss*. Now I need a comma for the end of my greeting." Continue modeling the writing of the entire message and then chorally read the whole message.

Adaptation: Students could take turns dictating a message of the day while the teacher models writing it.

Emergent Journal Writing

Purpose: To provide opportunities for students to write in a journal every day (grades K–3).

Procedure: This should be a free-writing experience. Sometimes it is helpful if students draw a picture first, talk about it, and then write about it. For writing unknown words, teach students to say each word slowly and to write letters for all of the sounds that they hear. They can also use resources such as the word wall, personal dictionary, and posters. You could have charts listing color, number, and topic words. If you keep a personal journal, share parts of it with your students and encourage them to "write" about their day.

Emergent Functional Writing

Purpose: To provide opportunities for writing for authentic purposes (grades K–2).

Procedure: Students make a grocery list, things-to-do list, or wish list. Students decide what to write on letters, thank-you cards, and invitations. Make pretend checks, prescriptions, airline tickets, menus, or grocery lists for your students to write on while they are playing.

Handwriting Strategies

Although handwriting is a minor part of writing, it needs to be addressed. The purpose for writing is to communicate ideas, and if the readers cannot easily read what is written, the writers need to improve their handwriting. Here are a few suggested strategies.

Writing Utensils: For emergent writers or those with fine motor coordination difficulties, select a writing implement such as a large-diameter pencil, pen, marker, or crayon. To motivate students, change the media. If students hold the implement improperly or too tightly, provide a pencil grip—some varieties even have an indentation for each finger to encourage proper grip.

Paper: For emergent writers, begin with unlined paper until their letters become small enough for lines. Begin with the widest ruled paper available in landscape format, and for older students use regular ruled notebook paper. Some primary-grade paper has textured and colored lines, such as green at the bottom, yellow in the middle, and blue at the top. This is beneficial when instructing students on letter formation.

Letter Formation: Begin by forming large letters in the air, then on the sidewalk with chalk or with a paintbrush drenched in water, and finally on paper. As students form each letter, have them say the letter name and the sound(s) that are represented by it. Although the D'Nealian handwriting style is popular in schools, I have found that the Zaner-Bloser, or ball-and-stick, style is easier for many students to write because it doesn't have the added stroke of a tail on the letters. Sometimes teaching letters together that use the same motions are helpful. For example, teach the "2 o'clock letters" together: *c, o, a, d,* and *g.* These all start at the 2 position on a clock and go left to 12 and around counterclockwise. Have students evaluate their own handwriting by putting a smiley face above the letter or word they wrote the best. Remind the students to have good posture when writing, placing their feet on the floor and pushing their chairs in. One technique for tracing letters is to write letters, words, or sentences with a color-changing marker. Have the students use another marker on top that changes the original color. It works only if the students trace directly over the original writing. You can add texture to the letters for the students to follow with their fingertips by writing on a textured fluorescent light cover with a crayon. Have students trace letters of their names and high-frequency words using textured letters or color-changing markers. The sooner students are able to create their own writing compositions the better. Sharing your ideas with others is a motivating factor in writing legibly.

Word Spacing: Students use a finger between words or they can place a "space person," or a decorated craft stick, between words to make sure the words are spaced appropriately.

Margins: Students fold left and right margins in their paper and should be instructed not to write outside these margins. Do not encourage hyphenating words, but suggest the entire word be written on the next line.

Writing Composition Strategies

Routman (2005) identifies five important things she does to ensure students become excellent writers:

- Demonstrate that I am a writer who always writes with a reader in mind and make the writing process visible.
- Connect writing to reading through literature; and notice what authors do.
- Guide students to choose topic they care about (by offering them choice within structure) and give students time to talk and write about them.
- Teach students the strategies they need to draft, revise, edit, polish, and publish.
- Rely primarily on regular conferences with students to assess and evaluate: note strengths, give feedback, teach, and set mutual goals. (p. 8)

Guided Writing Blocks

Source: Fountas & Pinnell, 2001

Purpose: To organize instruction so that students have experience with shared writing, interactive writing, guided writing, and independent writing (all grades).

Procedure: For shared writing, work with students to compose messages and stories; then support the process as scribe. For interactive writing, as in shared writing, you compose messages and stories with the students that are written using a "shared pen" technique that involves the students in the writing. In guided writing or writers' workshop, students engage in writing a variety of texts. You guide the process and provide instruction through minilessons and conferences. In independent writing, students write their own pieces, including stories, informational pieces, retellings, labeling, speech balloons, lists, and so forth.

The Writing Process

Purpose: To improve writing by using each of the steps in the writing process (all grades).

Procedure: There are a variety of steps in the writing process, depending on the resource. I selected the following steps to use when instructing the writing process: prewriting, drafting, conferring, revising, editing, publishing, and sharing. Between each of these steps is rereading. Although there are many strategies for writing depending on the genre or purpose, it is important that students reread what they write to be sure that it accurately and clearly conveys the message they want to communicate. To improve in their writing development, students need to write on a daily basis and for different purposes. They should also be given models to read of the type of writing that is expected. The Writing Process Rubric for Writer and Teacher (see Appendix) can be used to evaluate students at every stage in the writing process. Although not all writing is published, those pieces that are published need to go through the writing process. The following are strategies to improve writing composition at each stage of the writing process.

Prewriting Strategies: During prewriting students identify the purpose, audience, and genre for writing (narrative, descriptive, expository, persuasive, or poetic) and then they organize their ideas for their topic. Students should write for authentic purposes. Writing can help people to discover ideas, relationships, connections, and patterns in their lives and in their world. Writing is also used to communicate by sharing ideas and information with an audience. The audience could be themselves, peers, educators, family, community, business people, or people with whom they may never come in contact. To guide their writing, students should read and examine the writer's craft in examples of the genre in which they want to write. Next, students brainstorm ideas for the topic of their writing, talk to others about what they want to write, draw pictures, make a graphic organizer of major ideas, and sequence their ideas in an outline. When planning the writing, students may need to do research, read about the topic, interview others about the topic, narrow the focus, and decide what is most important to include. Rog (2003) describes a variety of strategies for prewriting, such as making a class chart of shared experiences, dividing a paper in four quadrants and having the students draw a quick picture in each (such as a favorite person, a special place, food they love, and something they like to do), and making a writing ideas Bingo card with story starters.

Drafting Strategies: During the first draft stage, students write their initial ideas in complete sentences. Explain to students that the first draft can be simply free-writing where students just write continuously for a period of time, or it could be organized writing based on a prewriting graphic organizer or outline. Sometimes it helps to write on every other line to allow room for revising and editing later. Students should focus on the content and not be concerned with spelling at this time. If they are unsure how to spell a word, they should use inventive spelling by sounding it out and writing letters for each sound they hear and then circle the word so they can return to it later. The ideas are the most important at this stage. One drafting strategy from Rog (2003) is the Five-Finger Planner: Students draw an outline of their hand. In the palm they write their topic, on each finger they write a detail about that topic and on their thumb they write how they feel about that topic. After drafting, the students should reread what they wrote to be sure it says what they want it to say.

Conferring Strategies: In the conferring stage, which can occur at multiple times during the writing process, the students share their writing with a partner and then with you to get feedback. The feedback needs to include identifying specific strengths in writing followed by questions on the ideas and organization of the writing. Leave the editing for the final conference before publishing. Teachers and peers can use the think-aloud strategy in which they respond to or question the student's writing as they are reading it. This process could be first modeled using the process of thinking about their own writing and then students can use this same process as they revise.

Revising Strategies: Revising is the next stage, where students reread their drafts and revise the content. Students will reread multiple times, focusing on revision of the first five traits identified in the 6-Trait Writing model (Spandel, 2004). Students begin by clarifying the ideas and details and verifying that they are accurate and complete. They may need to research the topic more to expand on or clarify the information. They need to organize and sequence the information. Depending on the genre and style of writing, students may need to include specific elements and types of language and structures. The writing should include descriptive and topic-specific vocabulary. They should add their personal voice to the text, selecting powerful and interesting words. To improve sentence fluency, students can use a variety of sentence structures and transitions to make the sentences flow from one idea to the next. Specific sentence combining and expanding strategies can be used (see page 218, later in this chapter).

Editing Strategies for Word Choice: Reread to check if the words are accurate, specific, and interesting. One strategy is to make a chart of the words used in each sentence. The headings for the chart could be first word, noun, verb, adjective, adverb, and number of words per sentence. For each sentence fill in the words in the chart horizontally. When the chart is finished, it will be very clear if the student used different beginning words, strong verbs, and interesting adjectives and adverbs and if the student varied the sentence length.

Editing Strategies for Grammar, Punctuation, and Spelling: Students can use an editing checklist such as the Primary Narrative Revising and Editing Checklist or the Advanced Revising and Editing Checklist (see Appendix) to help them focus on one type of editing at a time. When introducing the checklists for the first time, select a piece of writing that matches the genre and grade level. Review each element of the checklist and evaluate that piece of writing together. Then have the students work in pairs to evaluate a piece of writing, and finally they work individually to evaluate their own writing. Students should reread their story multiple times for different purposes. The first rereading should be to examine sentence structure.

Another strategy is to read backward, sentence by sentence. This helps to identify incomplete sentences or sentences that do not make sense. Each sentence should be carefully checked for punctuation. Finally, examine the spelling. First, sound out all of the words to make sure all of the sounds are included. An excellent spelling strategy is to use resources. Students should see if the word they want to spell is in a book, on the word wall, or around the room. They can then use a dictionary or type it in the computer and use spell-check.

Students could also use Editing and Revising Bookmarks (see Appendix).The first bookmark is for emergent writers to revise and edit their writing. The second bookmark is a checklist to revise and edit narrative/story writing, and the last bookmark is to revise and edit expository/descriptive writing. Prior to writing, go over each step with the students. During writing, the students refer to the checklist and then do a self-assessment after they complete their writing. Point out that the first step is to reread what they have written. This is an essential step in improving the students' writing composition.

Sharing and Publishing Strategies: It is important that students have an audience for their writing. Students should share their writing orally or make it available for others to read, such as in the classroom, library, in a newspaper, or online publishing. The Young Author's Conference, which is held in most states, is another forum for students to share their writing.

The Author's Chair Strategy is when the students sit in a chair in front of the class and share their writing with an audience. The audience asks questions of the author and vice versa. Students can read their writing to their peers, to younger students, and to their families. Students can even put on a school or community performance such as poetry or creative writing or reading.

Students often take pride in their writing when they illustrate and bind their books. The binding could be stapled, taped, or sewn. The covers could be paper, cardboard, cloth, or contact paper. Books can be made in a variety of shapes and sizes. Books can even be sent away to be bound. They can also display their books in the classroom or school library for others to see and read.

Writing Portfolios

Purpose: There are two types of writing portfolios: process and showcase. The **process portfolio** is used to guide and evaluate student writing and provide data to inform specific writing instruction. The **showcase portfolio** is used to celebrate the student's published works (all grades).

Procedure: Students create their own writing portfolios by designing a cover and writing their name on it. Students' process portfolio can contain many documents, including self-made lists of topics to write about; open-ended writing prompts; drawings and graphic organizers for planning writing; lists of authors and books whose style of writing the students prefer; lists of powerful and intriguing words that one could use (verbs, adverbs, adjectives); lists of high-frequency words as a reference for spelling; revising and editing checklists and bookmarks; the students' writing record; the students' journal writing and students' writing in different stages of the writing process; conference forms; and assessments on writing such as the Writing Composition Assessment Summary (see Appendix), the Writing Composition Rubric for Writer and Teacher (see Appendix), and the Writing Process Rubric for Writer and Teacher (see Appendix). The writing process portfolio should be used for daily writing.

The showcase portfolio contains a table of contents and the student's published pieces of writing with copyright dates so you and the student can see progress over time.

Writing Record

Source: Adapted from Solley, 2000

Purpose: To keep a record of students' writing (all grades).

Procedure: Students write daily on a chart information such as the date, topic and stage of writing, the plans for tomorrow, things done well, and things to work on.

Example:

Date	Topic and stage of writing	What I want to work on tomorrow
9/10	First draft of story about our camping trip	Reread and revise story

I can do these things well	I'm working on these things	I plan to learn these things
I wrote the whole time and I stayed on the topic.	Add details to setting up camp and the raccoon getting in the tent	New words that mean fun and name and location of the campground and park

Anecdotal Records

Purpose: To document your observations of the students' writing process, such as their thinking and interaction with others (grade 3 and above).

Procedure: Write anecdotal comments on the form for students' thinking or writing processes. See Appendix for a reproducible Anecdotal Record Form.

Peer Conference Summary

Purpose: To help students improve their peer editing. Records such as these could be part of the students' writing portfolio (grade 2 and above).

Procedure: In pairs, students ask and answer the questions on the Peer Conference Summary Form (see Appendix). The Writing Composition Assessment Summary could be readministered at the end of each grading period and then analyzed to demonstrate growth or need in the students' writing development over time.

Writing Genre Strategies

Purpose: To use the appropriate structures and elements when writing in a given genre (all grades).

Procedure: When introducing each genre, read aloud examples of effective writing in that genre and discuss each genre's writing elements. Students should know the criteria in which they will be graded and a rubric or checklist should be provided and explained to them. (Refer to the writing genre elements in Table 6.1 on page 199 to identify what elements need to be specifically taught for each genre.)

Guided Writing Procedure

Source: Smith & Bean, 1980, as cited in Tierney & Readence, 2000

Purpose: To diagnose and teach content and written expression in a content area through guided instruction that facilitates the synthesis and retention of text material (all grades).

Procedure: First, record everything students say about the topic to be learned. Then the students organize the main ideas and details in an outline or graphic organizer and write one or two paragraphs. The teacher analyzes the paragraphs for content and conventions using the Writing Composition Rubric for Writer and Teacher (see Appendix), the Revising and Editing Checklists (see Appendix), or your own checklist based on the genre and your specific purposes for the writing.

To develop rubrics or checklists you must first envision the students' best performance and then, along with the students, generate criteria, indicators, or scales. It is beneficial to get a class set of writing assignments and use the rubric or checklist. For writing beginning, rising and ending actions in personal narratives, I developed a Personal Narrative Action Rubric (see Appendix). For report writing, I created the Report Writing Checklist (see Appendix), using the Project Based Learning website by Advanced Learning Technologies (2006), pblchecklist.4teachers.org. This website allows you to select criteria and add your own criteria to develop a checklist or rubric for multiple writing or project assignments.

To teach content and written expression, students read about the topic from a text. Display a draft or compilation of drafts on a transparency along with the writing rubric or checklist used to evaluate the content, organization, word choice, spelling, grammar, and other conventions of writing. You and the students then contribute ideas to revise and edit the paragraph. Finally, the students edit their own paragraph.

Sentence Structure Writing Strategies

Writing Half Sentences

Source: Fitzpatrick, 1999

Purpose: To determine the subject and predicate of a simple sentence (grades 1–5).

Procedure: Make a "Build a Sentence" poster that shows somebody doing something. Put the poster on the chalkboard. Alongside the poster write incomplete sentences, leaving enough space for the missing words. Review the parts of a sentence. Explain that the sentences on the chalkboard are only partially complete—that either the subject (somebody or something) or the predicate (doing or being) is missing. Invite students to play a "whodunit" game by having them use their imaginations to decide which subject and which predicate is missing from each sentence. Share their answers aloud as you write the corresponding words on the chalkboard. Complete the activity by drawing separate boxes around the subject and the predicate of each sentence.

Example:

The funny clown _____.

_____ was driving the new car.

The big black bear was _____.

_____ is swimming in the water.

Sentence Expanding

Purpose: To increase the complexity and detail in sentences (all grades).

Procedure: Model this process by writing a noun and a verb. Ask students to add words to make an interesting sentence. Add parts of speech such as articles, adjectives, adverbs, conjunctions, prepositions, and pronouns. Students then edit their own writing by expanding their sentences.

Sentence Combining

Source: Walker, 2004

Purpose: To assist students in combining sentences to make compound and complex sentences that show the relationship between the ideas (grade 1 and above).

Procedure: Using students' examples of short related sentences, show how to delete repeated words or phrases and combine sentences with a variety of conjunctions and prepositions. Students can then edit their own writing by combining sentences.

My Writing Seek and Find

Purpose: To identify sentence types and parts of speech in the students' own writing (grade 3 and above).

Procedure: Instruct students to look in their writing portfolios to find an example of one of each of the following types of sentences and copy it: declarative sentence, interrogative sentence, imperative sentence, a sentence with a compound subject, a sentence with a compound predicate, a compound sentence, a sentence with a concrete noun, a sentence with a proper noun, a sentence using a plural noun that does not end in *s*, a sentence using a collective noun, a sentence with an appositive, a sentence with a simile, and a sentence with figurative language. Then ask students to write 10 words they have learned how to spell. Adaptations include selecting only a few of the choices above or finding examples in published texts.

Paragraph Writing Strategies

Four-Square Writing

Source: Gould & Gould, 1999

Purpose: To develop prewriting and organizational skills in writing details that support a topic. This strategy can be applied to narrative, expository, persuasive, and descriptive forms of writing (all grades).

Procedure: Fold paper into four equal squares and write a topic in the middle of the paper. In the first three squares, write details to support the topic. In the last square, write feelings or concluding statements about the topic. Then draw a picture in each box that describes the sentences. Finally use the information on the four-square writing organizer to write a complete text. This strategy can be adapted to be used with words, phrases, or whole sentences in each box.

Example: Topic—It takes great responsibility to take care of a dog. Box 1—First, you need to make sure they have food and water every day. Box 2—Next, you need to make sure their place to live is clean and has enough room. Box 3—Finally, they need lots of exercise to stay healthy. Box 4—Proper care is rewarded with love and attention from the dog.

Six-Sentence Accordion Paragraph

Source: Auman, 2005

Purpose: To develop a six-sentence paragraph with a topic sentence, two details, explanation or examples, and restatement of the topic (grade 2 and above).

Procedure: Select a writing prompt. Give students color-coded strips of paper that correlate to the traffic light in this order: green, yellow, red, yellow, red, green. Green means *Go*, and students write a topic sentence. Yellow means *Slow Down*, give a reason, detail, or fact and use a transition. Red means *Stop*, explain, and give an example. On the second yellow strip, students write another reason, detail, or fact. On the second red strip they explain or give an example of the detail on the previous yellow strip. The final green strip means *Go Back* and write a sentence that reminds the reader of your topic. Students then write a first draft of their paper using the sentence strips.

Narrative, Descriptive, and Creative Writing Strategies

Narrative Writing Guide

Purpose: To provide an organizational structure for writing narratives (grade 2 and above).

Procedure: Students answer the questions presented in Table 6.2 before, during, and after writing. After writing the initial draft, students reread it and revise it for meaning, edit for grammar and conventions, and share it with others.

Table 6.2	Narrative Writing Guide
Parts	**Questions to Answer With Your Writing**
Setting	Where and when does your story take place? Identify and provide details of the setting (place, time period, time of year, time of day)
Initiating event	What happened to the character to cause him or her to do something?
Problem	What is the problem?
Character's feelings	What are the character's feelings about what happened? (emotions, goals, desires, intentions, thoughts)
Events	What does the character(s) do? Sequence the story and add details that include the five senses.
Attempt	How does the character attempt to solve the problem?
Additional attempts	What else does the character do?
Consequence	What happened as a result of the attempts? Are there any complications?
Resolution	How does the character feel about the consequence?

Alternate Endings

Purpose: To use the author's style of writing as a model to change the ending of a story (grade 2 and above).

Procedure: After reading a complete story or reading up to the point of the resolution, write an original ending to the story.

Adaptations of Stories

Purpose: To rewrite a story changing one or more of the story elements (grade 2 and above).

Procedure: First, model this by sharing different versions of stories such as Cinderella and the Three Little Pigs. Then, discuss the common elements and what was different. For example, the characters and the setting could be different and the problem could be modified to fit the new setting.

Writing as a Character

Purpose: To identify elements of characterization by writing in the role of a character (grade 2 and above).

Procedure: Students will write a letter to the author or another character in the role of one of the characters. Students examine the actions, motivations, feelings, regrets, limitations, aspirations, experiences, and appearances of the character. They also examine the other characters' comments and actions toward the character. The student then takes on that personality and writes to the author or another character about how she is feeling and what she would like to do.

Dear Diary

Purpose: To connect reading and writing instruction by writing a diary entry for a selected character (grade 2 and above).

Procedure: Tell students a diary is a place to write down the events of the day and personal feelings. Students create a diary for a character in the book they are reading. The following are possible questions to consider in the journal writing and can be adjusted based on the book or topic: What kind of day have you had? What is one feeling you've had today? Has anything special happened to you today? (describe events), Where were you? (setting), Why do you think this happened? Is there anything else you'd like to tell us? By writing in the diary, students become actively involved in the story and "become" the character.

Personal Narrative Action Rubric

Purpose: To write using beginning, rising, and ending actions in personal narratives (grade 2 and above).

Procedure: Write an example of a problem that you have had. Show the students the Personal Narrative Action Rubric (see Appendix) and help them to identify the problem, rising action, and ending action in your writing. Then have the students write a personal narrative about a problem that they had, the events leading up to the solution, and how the problem was solved.

Example:

Problem—We moved to a new house and my dog ran away.

Rising Actions—We went looking for her. We called the police and put up signs with her picture. We got a phone call from a man saying he found our dog.

Ending Action—We went to his house and brought her home. We got her new dog tags and made sure she didn't get out again.

Personal Journals

Purpose: To provide opportunities for self-selected writing for students' own purposes (all grades).

Procedure: Provide a journal for all students and give them time to write in it every day. Even kindergarteners can use the resources in their environment and their knowledge of phoneme–grapheme correlations to draw pictures and write in their journals. For unknown spelling of words, ask students to slowly say the word, write the sounds heard, and then circle the word to show monitoring.

Dialogue Journals

Purpose: To provide regular opportunities for the students to communicate with you (grade 1 and above).

Procedure: You and the students write back and forth on a topic of their choosing or you could provide prompts. This could be done weekly, and you could assign students to turn it in on different days so that you would have time to respond to each student.

Letter Writing

Purpose: To write for authentic purposes and to demonstrate the correct format for letter writing (grade 1 and above).

Procedure: Provide examples of friendly letters and business letters. Identify all of the parts of a letter. Students write to pen pals, authors, friends, and family members. Students' letters can be mailed or e-mailed.

Use Your Senses

Purpose: To develop description using sensory images (grade 1 and above).

Procedure: Tell students to select an event in their lives and then write a word or phrase in the column under each sense that describes the event. Then write a personal narrative.

Example: Bicycle accident

See	Hear	Smell	Taste	Touch	Emotion
a deer leaping, not seeing each other	car crashing into bike, squealing tires	burning rubber, asphalt	metallic taste of blood in my mouth	slamming on brakes, face colliding against hard metal, cuts on face and body, pain	embarrassed

Name That Emotion

Source: Newingham, 2008

Purpose: To develop voice such as mood or personality in student writing (grade 2 and above).

Procedure: Write each of the following emotion words on a card: *happiness, excitement, fear, confusion, anger, boredom, jealousy, envy, greed, joy, guilt, pride, compassion, arrogance, hunger, relief, satisfaction, love, regret, sadness, gratitude, panic, embarrassment, empathy, sympathy, hope, anxiety, concern, loneliness, surprise, shame, curiosity, disappointment, shock, exhaustion, confidence, disapproval,* and *remorse.* Give each student a card. Students write a paragraph describing the emotion on their card. The students then read their paragraph to the class and the other students try to guess the name of the emotion. Students must include at least one of their emotion words in their next piece of narrative or descriptive writing.

Similes and Metaphors

Purpose: To interpret and write similes and metaphors (grade 5 and above).

Procedure: Provide poems with examples of similes and metaphors. Ask students questions such as What are some ways authors write to make their details more vivid? What are some good describing words to describe a (give an example)? How can we write things to show comparisons?

Next, provide definitions for similes and metaphors. Use a list of sample similes and metaphors and have the students identify each. Also have the students identify what is being compared in the examples. Ask students to change the similes to metaphors and the metaphors to similes. As a class, choose a person from television or an era in history and write several similes and metaphors to describe the person. Afterward, students write their own similes and metaphors and share them. Assess students' similes and metaphors: Did they use *like* or *as* in similes? Did they use comparisons? Is the information accurate about the person they chose?

Hyperbole

Purpose: To identify hyperboles and determine when to use them in writing (grade 5 and above).

Procedure: Define a hyperbole as an exaggeration or overstatement used to make a point but that is not taken literally. Hyperbole is appropriate to use in narratives but not in essays or reports. Provide examples such as "I've told you a million times not to exaggerate" or "This box weighs a ton." Provide examples within poems or short stories. Have students dictate as many hyperboles as possible and discuss their meanings. Students then work in pairs to write a poem or short story with characters that use hyperboles repeatedly.

Poems and Songs

Purpose: To write creative poems and songs (grade 2 and above).

Procedure: Read several poems or song lyrics and then write class poems or songs. Students write or rewrite their own poems and songs. Examples include the following ideas:

Acrostic—Select a topic and write words or phrases about that topic using each of the letters in the topic name.

> *R*elaxing in a chair
>
> *E*scaping reality
>
> *A*nticipating the climax
>
> *D*elighting in my favorite book

Haiku—A Japanese poem with 3 lines of 5, 7, and 5 syllables, respectively.

> A pond under trees
>
> the sound of a frog jumping
>
> in cool, green water

Limerick—A humorous Irish poem containing a five-line, A-A-B-B-A rhyme pattern.

> There once was a man from Nantucket
>
> Who kept all his cash in a bucket.
>
> But his daughter, named Nan,
>
> Ran away with a man
>
> And as for the bucket, Nan took it.

Cinquain—A five-line poem with adjectives based on a single topic and following this pattern:

> Line 1—a one-word title (two syllables)
>
> Line 2—a two-word phrase that describes your title or you can just use two words (four syllables)
>
> Line 3—a three-word phrase that describes an action relating to your title or just action words (six syllables)
>
> Line 4—a four-word phrase that describes a feeling relating to your topic or just feeling words (eight syllables)
>
> Line 5—one word that refers back to your title (one syllable).

Name Poem—A poem about yourself following this pattern:

> Line 1—Your first name
>
> Line 2—"It means" and then three adjectives that describe you
>
> Line 3—"It is the number" and then any number you choose
>
> Line 4—"It is like" and describe a color but don't name it
>
> Line 5—"It is" and name something you remember experiencing that makes you smile
>
> Line 6—"It is the memory of" and name a person who is or has been significant to you
>
> Line 7—"Who taught me" and two abstract concepts (such as "honesty")

Line 8—"When he/she" and then refer to something that person did that displayed the qualities in line 7

Line 9—"My name is" and your first name

Line 10—"It means" and in one to two brief sentences state something important you believe about life

Collaborative Writing Strategies

Alternate Writing

Source: Walker, 2004

Purpose: To compose a story among a group of students and yourself (all grades).

Procedure: Writing for a specified time—five minutes, for example—each person alternately continues the development of a cohesive story line. They must first read what has been written so far and then continue the story. When it is completed, read the story to the class.

Dot-to-Dot Narrative Writing

Purpose: To collaboratively write stories about people, places, and problems that students share with the class (grade 2 and above).

Procedure: Review the story elements of characters, setting, and problem, and select three colors of sticker dots (e.g., yellow, red, blue) to represent them. Put one dot on index cards and distribute one card to each student. Students who receive yellow dots write the name of a person, students with red dots write the name of a place, and students with blue dots write a problem. Form groups of three with one student representing each color. Students share with their group what they wrote on their cards. Instruct each group to write a story using all three elements, thus connecting the dots.

After students write their stories, they share their stories with the class. Students will be surprised at how different their stories are even though they had the same elements.

Adaptation: Form groups with more than one problem, place, or person in each group. After the group writes the first story, instruct one student from each group to rotate to a new group and write a new story with the elements.

Partner Writing

Purpose: To collaboratively write using correct grammar and elements of short stories such as plot, setting, character, theme, climax, and so forth. (grade 2 and above).

Procedure: Divide students into pairs and give topics or beginning prompts on the chalkboard. The first student writes a topic or prompt and then begins to write a story. After a certain amount of time, instruct students to switch. Students must stop writing and pass their paper to their partner, even if one student is in midsentence. The second student reads what is written and continues with the story. This continues until writing time is almost up. It is best to tell students when it is about "half time" and when there are five minutes left, to let partners know they need to start wrapping up their stories.

Adaptation: This is a great activity to target certain areas of story writing. At times, quotations and use of speech could be stressed, while at other times action or sensory words could be emphasized.

Expository Writing Strategies

Expository Writing Guide

Purpose: To provide an organizational structure for writing expository texts (grade 1 and above).

Procedure: The teacher selects short texts with the five expository text structures: description, sequence, comparison, cause and effect, and problem and solution. Students identify which type of text it is, based on the description and the clue words. Students then select one of the text structures to use for their writing depending on their purpose. They answer the questions in the Expository Writing Guide for that text structure before, during, and after writing (see Table 6.3). Be sure to use clue words when writing. After writing the initial draft, reread it and revise it for meaning, edit for grammar and conventions, and share it with others.

Traveling Paragraphs

Purpose: To review and write main ideas and supporting details in students' paragraphs. Students practice writing details for support in paragraphs and practice writing complete sentences and using correct punctuation. Students are given main ideas and they write supporting details in groups (grade 1 and above).

Table 6.3	Expository Writing Guide	
Pattern	**Description**	**Cue Words and Phrases**
Description	The author describes a topic by listing characteristics, features, and examples	*for example* *characteristics are*
Sequence	The author describes a process or events in numerical or chronological order.	*first* *second* *third* *next* *then* *finally*
Comparison	The author explains how two or more ideas, objects, events, or people are similar and/or how they are different.	*different* *in contrast* *alike* *same as* *on the other hand*
Cause and Effect	The author lists one or more causes and the resulting effect or effects.	*reasons why* *if...then* *as a result* *therefore* *because*
Problem and Solution	The author states a problem and lists one or more solutions for the problem. A variation of this pattern is the question-and-answer format in which the author poses a question and then answers it.	*problem is* *dilemma is* *puzzle is solved* *question...answer*

Procedure: In preparation, write five main idea sentences on strips of paper or sticky notes. For example, "The weather looked threatening" or "The children had a great time at the party." Organize students into groups of five. Distribute one main idea sentence to each student. Give each student one minute to write a supporting detail for his or her main idea. When time is up, instruct students to trade paper strips with another group member. Give students another minute to read this new main idea and its detail and to add a different supporting detail. Then have students trade papers again. Continue in this manner until each student has written a supporting detail for all five ideas and traded to get his or her original paper strip back.

Adaptation: Have students share paragraphs with the class, allowing students to listen very carefully for details. Instruct them to give it a thumbs up, thumbs sideways, or thumbs down, and discuss reasons.

Content Journals

Purpose: To keep a daily journal for content learning (all grades).

Procedure: Students write about each subject area and reflect on their thinking and learning.

Newspapers and Newsletters

Purpose: To write a story answering who, what, where, when, why, and how questions about an event (grade 1 and above).

Procedure: Students create their own class newspaper and publish their own expository writing about what they are learning and upcoming events. This could also be a place to publish creative writing as features.

Adaptation: When reading narratives, students write a newspaper article about the events in a story.

Reports

Purpose: To enhance content knowledge of a specific subject (grade 1 and above).

Procedure: Students research and write reports about a variety of topics using the Report Writing Checklist (see Appendix). Remind them to include text features such as headings, illustrations, graphs, tables of contents, and glossaries.

Recipes and How-To Books

Purpose: To write specific directions (grade 1 and above).

Procedure: Students read examples and then write their own recipes or books on how to make something.

PowerPoint and Media Presentations

Purpose: To use technology to present information in a visually engaging manner (grade 4 and above).

Procedure: Students create PowerPoint presentations to share information from group or individual projects.

Webpages or Blogs

Purpose: To create a personal or class webpage or blog to share student writing (grade 2 and above).

Procedure: Teachers and students create individual class webpages or blog . A class webpage or blog should be maintained by the teacher and can include regular entries of class or school events, commentary, assignments, teacher and student writing, messages to families, photos, and video.

A **blog** is a website, but the entries are commonly displayed in reverse chronological order. Readers can leave comments in an interactive format in a blog. Some blogs could discuss a certain topic or function as an online diary.

Persuasive Writing Strategies

Persuasive Writing Guide

Purpose: To provide an organizational structure for writing persuasive texts (grade 2 and above).

Procedure: The teacher selects short persuasive texts. Students identify the persuasive elements in the text. Students then select a topic that is important to them, such as why they should be allowed to participate in an after-school activity. They answer the questions in the Persuasive Writing Guide before, during, and after writing (see Table 6.4). After writing the initial draft, reread it and revise it for meaning, edit for grammar and conventions, and share it with others.

Power of Persuasive Writing

Source: Norris & Brock, 2001

Purpose: To engage students in reading and writing persuasively using the Internet, to analyze and conduct research for persuasive techniques, to use critical reading skills to

Table 6.4 Persuasive Writing Guide	
Parts	**Questions to Answer With Your Writing**
Assertion and Introduction	What do I believe? Why is it important to me?
Supporting Evidence	What are the reasons I believe it?
Opposing View	What do others say they believe?
Arguments Against the Opposing View	Why do I disagree with them?
Summary	What do I want you to do?

deconstruct advertisements and articles, to discriminate between the stated and inferred, to differentiate between fact and opinion, to articulate how persuasion in media can affect and manipulate people's thinking, to relate what has been learned by creating a final multimedia or webpage project reflecting an effective advertisement, and to develop an awareness of advertisements and persuasive writing that is a part of our daily lives (grade 4 and above).

Procedure: This lesson is a three-week unit that begins with the students and teacher searching magazines and the Internet for advertisements and articles. After modeling of persuasive techniques, the students compare and contrast ideas in the advertisements. Teams of students select a role to focus on—photographer, lawyer, poet, politician, comedian, or newspaper reporter—and then research Internet and primary sources. Each team works together to design a multimedia or webpage project reflecting an effective advertisement, while you provide questions to guide their research and project. Students are evaluated on the basis of their response to the following questions: What is persuasive writing? How do new opportunities of the 21st century challenge the advertising? What makes your project an effective persuasive example? Discuss how persuasion techniques in media are a part of daily life.

Letters to the Editor or Election Speeches

Purpose: To write a persuasive letter or speech to convince a reader or listener to support an opinion (grade 3 and above).

Procedure: Students write letters or speeches persuading someone to do something. This writing can be mailed or presented as a speech.

CHAPTER 7

Attitudes and Motivation

Understanding Attitudes and Motivation

Students' attitude and motivation toward reading and writing are key factors affecting reading and writing performance. Positive attitudes and motivation can compensate for relatively weak skills, and negative attitudes can prevent students from applying existing knowledge or from acquiring new information (Paris, Olson, & Stevenson, 1983, as cited in Lipson & Wixson, 2003). According to attribution theory, an individual's expectation of an event's outcome, feelings about an experience, and motivation toward future experiences have great impact on their learning (Winograd & Niquette, 1988). Learned helplessness contributes to reading and other problems.

Winograd and Niquette (1988) also conclude that learned helplessness contributes to reading and other problems. **Self-efficacy**, according to Bandura (1994), is people's beliefs about their capabilities to produce at a certain level of performance and has an influence over events that affect their lives. Self-efficacy beliefs determine how people feel, think, motivate themselves, and behave. People with high assurance in their capabilities approach difficult tasks as challenges to be mastered rather than as threats to be avoided. In contrast, those who doubt their capabilities shy away from difficult tasks that they view as personal threats.

According to Zimmerman (2000), social cognitive theorists contend that the interdependent relationship among cognitive, behavioral, and environmental factors helps to improve self-regulation toward learning. Cognitive factors affect whether students have a positive attitude about their own ability. Are they able to set learning goals that are challenging rather than simple performance goals, which are not as challenging but simply involve task completion? Do students have a positive self-efficacy in which they believe they can learn what is being asked? Are they able to use metacognition to think about the process of their thinking? Do they have knowledge of strategies to problem-solve? Do students perceive the task or learning to be valuable? Do they have a positive view of the task or learning? You can have a great impact on students' self-efficacy by helping them make decisions in terms of tasks and materials.

Behavioral factors affect whether students choose to self-monitor their learning, how they make self-judgments about what and how they are learning, and how they decide to react to the learning or task. To promote self-regulation, you can provide experiences that require a higher level of engagement in the tasks and give students strategies to set goals and self-evaluate their own learning throughout the process, not just the product. Students' belief about their ability to use self-regulatory learning strategies influences their confidence with which they approach academic tasks, and this correlates with reading and writing success (Zimmerman, Bandura, & Martinez-Pons, 1992).

Finally, environmental factors affect whether students have a positive attitude about the learning climate. The climate is influenced by the students' feeling of acceptance by teachers and peers, their physical comfort, and their feeling of a sense of order. Your decisions about the classroom environment and how you interact with students can also shape students' attitudes and motivation toward learning.

Objectives for Attitudes and Motivation

Students will do the following:

- Make statements to indicate they believe they can learn what is being asked
- Set challenging yet attainable learning goals
- Monitor their own learning
- Demonstrate problem-solving behaviors
- Assess their own learning
- Make decisions that promote learning
- Engage in meaningful self-selected reading, writing, speaking, and listening activities
- Engage in meaningful teacher-selected reading, writing, speaking and listening experiences
- Use reading, writing, speaking, and listening to accomplish authentic daily functions
- Read, write, speak, and listen for pleasure
- Read, write, speak, and listen to share and learn information

Attitudes and Motivation Assessments

This chapter offers four inventories you can use to identify students' attitudes, beliefs, and motivation toward reading and writing in order to plan instruction: Interest and Activities Inventory, School Attitude Inventory, Reading Interest Inventory: Elementary, and Reading Interest Inventory: Middle Level and Secondary (see Appendix). In addition, there are numerous interviews and surveys included in the following pages. The procedures for administering all of the interviews or surveys are generally the same but can be approached in any of three ways:

1. It is best to administer these assessments as individual interviews, in which you read the questions and write the student's responses. This approach provides the most accurate information and does not require the student to write his or her own responses.

2. These assessments can be given to the student as a homework assignment to complete with the help of their parents. This is beneficial for the parents to engage

their child in conversations about their interests. Parents may be able to provide additional prompting on the basis of their family experiences.

3. The assessments can be given to a student who reads at or above second-grade level to complete independently. However, the student may not read or respond to them thoughtfully and thoroughly when being asked to complete them independently.

First, analyze the assessments based on content. Ask yourself what the student's responses were and how you can use this information to inform your instruction, including selection of materials and topics of discussion. Second, if the assessments were administered orally, you can evaluate the student's speech and language to see if further assessments are needed. For example, did the student comprehend the questions or statements? Was the student able to answer the questions easily, without significant delays or nonresponses? Did the student use a variety of vocabulary words and sentence structures? Was the speech clear and at an appropriate volume? By learning about students' interests and abilities, you can personalize instruction for each student by selecting or suggesting interesting books or writing topics.

Interest and Activities Inventory

Purpose: To gain background information about students, such as the names of their family members and pets as well as the students' interests and activities (all grades).

Procedure and Analysis: See the general procedures above for administration. It is suggested that the Interest and Activities Inventory (see Appendix) be administered prior to any other assessment, especially if you are not familiar with the student. Students tend to be more relaxed about assessment if it begins with questions about themselves with no right or wrong answers. Typically this assessment would only be given once and filed for reference for those who work with the student.

All responses are useful to determine the types of literacy materials the student might like as well as conversation starters. The names of family members and pets can be used as a resource for the student to correctly spell during writing activities. The final two questions address the amount of time the student spends reading and writing outside of school.

School Attitude Inventory

Purpose: To identify identifies students' attitudes toward school. The eight questions and prompts on the School Attitude Inventory are generally open ended to allow for a range of responses (see Appendix).

Procedure and Analysis: Ask the questions and write down the student's responses. See the general procedures for administration. Use this information to determine if the student has a generally positive or negative attitude toward school. Students with a positive attitude may be able to be pushed to higher achievement levels more quickly, while students with a negative attitude may need to have more successful experiences before continuing on.

Reading Interest Inventories

Purpose: To identify the genres of literature that students like to listen to or read. There are two separate reading interest inventories: Reading Interest Inventory: Elementary is intended for students in grades K–5 (see Appendix) and Reading Interest Inventory: Middle Level and Secondary is intended for students in grades 6–12 (see Appendix).

Procedure and Analysis: Tell the student, "This is a list of types of reading or genres. As I read each of these types, tell me whether you would like to read or listen to them. (You or I) will put a checkmark under the happy face for yes and the sad face for no." If it would not be too time consuming, you can give the student an option of who will make the checkmarks. The elementary level interest inventory contains additional prompts at the bottom. For this section, say, "I am going to read you some statements. If these statements are true, (you or I) will make a checkmark under the happy face for yes, but if it is not true mark the sad face for no." See the general procedures for administration, and analyze results to select literature that is likely to be of interest to the student and to encourage recreational reading.

Literacy Process Interview

Purpose: To determine students' perceived reading and writing strategies, strengths, and needs. This 10-question Literacy Process Interview is based on Carol Burke's Reading Interview (Goodman, Watson, & Burke, 1987) and is appropriate to give to students who read and write at or above first-grade level (see Appendix).

Procedure and Analysis: Ask the questions and write down the student's responses. See general procedures for administration. Use the results of this assessment to determine whether the student is oriented toward phonics, grammar, meaning, or a combination of these cue sources. Ask the following questions: Does the student focus on graphophonics or sounding out words? Does the student focus on semantics and syntax by trying to figure out the meaning of words or choose words that would sound right in that sentence? Does the student mention a combination of strategies? If so, the student has a more integrated view of the reading process. In the writing section, ask these questions: Does the student focus on being able to spell words? Does the student focus on communicating ideas in writing? Does the student emphasize handwriting or being able to correctly form the letters? What are the student's perceived strengths and needs that you can build upon during instruction? What strategies did the student say they employ during writing? Compare what the student states with the strategies observed during the other assessments. During teaching, reinforce strategies used and prompt for neglected strategies.

Example and Analysis: Literacy Process Interview, second-grade student

Reading Questions

When you are reading and you come to a word you do not know, what do you do? Do you do anything else?   *Look at the picture.*

When you are reading and you do not understand something, what do you do? Do you do anything else?   *Sound it out. Cover up the last part of the word.*

How would you help someone who is having trouble reading?   *Tell them the word they are stuck on, if I knew it.*

What do you think you do well at during reading? Why?   *I can read bigger words because I can sound them out.*

What would you like to change about your reading? Why?   *I would want to read faster. I want to be like Molly.*

Writing Questions

When you are writing and you come to a difficult part, what do you do? Do you do anything else?   *I try to find the word on a poster or in my dictionary.*

If you are given a writing assignment, what would you do first? Next? Then what? Last?   *I put my name on it. Then I think of what to write and I write it.*

How would you help someone who is having trouble writing?   *I'd give them a dictionary like mine.*

What do you think you do well at during writing? Why?   *I write my letters good. People tell me I write good.*

What do you like to change about your writing? Why?   *That I could always spell stuff right, cause I am not good at spelling.*

Adapted from Goodman, Watson, & Burke (2005).

Analysis of Reading Questions: This student states that he uses three different strategies for figuring out unknown words: Look at the picture, sound it out, and cover up the ending. He thinks that a good reader is one who knows the words and can read fast. He has a predominant focus on phonics.

Instructional Implications for Reading: Reinforce known strategies and suggest new ones such as read on, go back, and think about what makes sense. Absent from these comments is the idea that the purpose for reading is to learn something or for enjoyment, not reading quickly. This needs to be made explicit in teaching.

Analysis of Writing Questions: The student uses resources to figure out how to spell words he wants to write. He thinks that he is a good writer because he has good handwriting. He also thinks that spelling is important.

Instructional Implications for Writing: The student needs to be commended for using resources for spelling and having neat handwriting. Although it is beneficial to have neat handwriting, it is more important that he understands that the real purpose is to communicate ideas. He needs opportunities to write to communicate his ideas and needs to be shown how to use inventive spelling and to circle words for which he is unsure of the correct spelling.

Garfield Reading and Writing Attitude Surveys

Purpose: To assess K–6 grade students' reading and writing attitudes. In addition to the assessments in this resource, you can administer the Elementary Reading Attitude Survey (McKenna & Kear, 1990), and the Elementary Writing Attitude Survey (Kear, Coffman, McKenna, & Ambrosia, 2000).

Procedure and Analysis: Ask the student to respond to these 20-question assessments by circling the Garfield the Cat cartoon picture that best represents their feelings from very happy to very upset. Analyze the scores on the basis of student's attitudes toward academic and recreational reading and writing.

Developing Positive Attitudes and Motivation

Students who have a positive attitude have successful experiences and have some choice in their reading, writing, speaking, and listening experiences. They are more likely to be risk takers and can be challenged to the leading edge of their ZPD so they can learn at an accelerated rate. In contrast, students who have a poor attitude and less successful experiences may need more scaffolding and practice at the instructional level with smaller, incremental changes and more choice in what they do. Furthermore, students with a positive attitude often learn at an accelerated rate, as compared with those students who have a less positive attitude. Through decisions about learning climate, learning tasks, and materials, you can enhance students' attitudes and motivation to learn.

Learning Climate

The learning climate refers to the students' need to feel that their teacher and their peers accept them and their need to be physically comfortable in the classroom. Marzano (1992) explains that you can support students' feelings of teacher acceptance by greeting them when they walk in the door and initiate conversations with them by asking about their well-being or bringing up known topics of interest. During instruction, make eye contact, call on students by their preferred name, and move close to them during learning experiences.

You can provide a supportive, risk-free environment by responding positively to students' questions, comments, or responses and providing wait time before calling on students. Dignify students' responses, restate or paraphrase questions, and provide guidance such as hints or clues to help students answer questions or problem-solve. Students should not be expected to read and write perfectly or quickly. Mistakes or miscues can be used to understand students' learning process and help select appropriate problem-solving strategies. Students should have numerous opportunities to practice reading, writing, speaking, and listening for authentic purposes.

Support students' beliefs that they are accepted by their peers by encouraging them to respect one another, work together, and support one another in the learning process. Encourage especially younger students to treat one another with respect by referring to everyone in the class as friends. You can make statements such as "Can you help your friend by showing her which paragraph you might find the answer?" or "Our friend Katherine is home sick today; can you help me write a get well card to her?" For all grades, it is important that you take time to point out when students or colleagues help or treat others kindly. You also must stop and address any and all statements and behaviors that can be hurtful. Students' feelings of self worth are often related to what people say and how they react to them. As they leave your class, wish students a good day and let them know you are looking forward to seeing them tomorrow.

To address students' physical comfort, carefully arrange furniture for ease of movement with space for group and individual work. Be sure the students' chairs, desks, or tables are at the appropriate height so students can sit comfortably. Provide an organized space for the classroom library, computers, and materials for writing and publishing. Proudly display new student work throughout the classroom. Carefully select what is put on the walls so that it is meaningful and interesting to the students but not too overwhelming. Organize classroom materials so students have easy access to them. Provide opportunities for students to take breaks, go to the restroom, or get a drink of water as needed. Finally, to fulfill students' sense of order, provide clear expectations of routines, tasks, and behavior. These should be taught initially and then reinforced throughout the year.

Learning Tasks

You can significantly influence students' attitudes and motivation by carefully selecting appropriate tasks that are meaningful, engaging, and authentic. To select appropriate tasks, you first need to have an understanding of students' interests, background knowledge of the task and the content, their functioning level, and their ability to use strategies to problem-solve. This can be accomplished by using data from diagnostic or formative assessments, observations, and interactions, and then selecting tasks that are meaningful, interesting, and within the students' ZPD, whereby students can successfully complete the task with the scaffolded support of an adult or more capable peer.

While teaching, use the gradual release of responsibility model. Expectations should be realistic, clearly stated, and with the appropriate level of support. At first, provide a significant amount of support by helping the students connect to their background knowledge, providing additional information and by modeling the task that the students are expected to do by thinking aloud or by stating what you are thinking about as you are reading and writing. Next, give students guided practice and suggest strategies that they might try in order to monitor their learning and successfully complete the task. Give them opportunities to practice with the support of their peers while you provide reflective questioning and feedback. Although students appreciate specific praise, they gain the most confidence when they feel their own sense of accomplishment. If students understand your expectations, including monitoring their thinking, they are more likely to be engaged in the learning process and be motivated to continue learning. Finally, students complete the task independently, you and the students evaluate their learning, and you both identify specific strengths and needs. If students are successful, they feel a great sense of accomplishment when they achieve the high-but-reasonable expectations. You can then select new objectives and tasks that build on their prior learning. If students are not completely successful, identify the area of difficulty and reteach objectives in another way.

Although it is not always appropriate, providing opportunities for students to select the type of task not only gives the students choices but also takes into account different learning styles. For example, if students are studying a science or social studies unit, they could demonstrate their understanding through a variety of projects including presentations, reports, demonstrations, dioramas, or plays. Guided choice could include giving the students options or asking them which task they would prefer to complete first.

Teacher- and Student-Selected Materials

Students' attitude and motivation toward a task is often related to the reading and writing materials selected or available for self-selection. What follows are suggestions for the types of texts in classroom and school libraries, why students should read a variety of texts, the criteria for evaluating texts, and methods of measuring readability and leveling texts.

Types of Texts in Classroom and School Libraries

Through wide reading, students acquire knowledge about the world, specific content, vocabulary, and the language and form of written text (Illinois Board of Education, 2000). It is crucial that students have access to a variety of genres, formats of text, and levels of text in both their classroom and school libraries. A listing of important genres can be found in Table 7.1. Texts should be of high interest to the students and include authentic multicultural literature, especially literature that represents the diverse cultures and interests of the students in the classroom and school. It is beneficial to have books by the same author or on the same topic because it may encourage students to read additional books and students can

Table 7.1 Literature Genres

Fiction or Narrative	Nonfiction or Informational
Traditional literature: Myths Religious stories Ballads and folk songs Traditional rhymes and riddles Poetry and verse Plays Folk tales: Animal tales, fairy tales, fables, pourquoi tales, noodlehead stories, tall tales, cumulative tales, ghost stories, epics, heroic legends Fantasy: Animal fantasy, toy fantasy, enchanted journeys and imaginary lands, heroic or quest fantasy, supernatural and time fantasy, science fiction and space fantasy Modern folk tales Westerns Romance Horror Thrillers Mysteries Contemporary realistic fiction Historical fiction	**Informational books:** Science and nature: Biology and the human body, environmental science, earth science and the universe, physical science and technology Social science Community and culture Fine and applied arts Sports History Geography Government and citizenship Human development and behavior Language and communication Mathematics: Sorting and patterning; number concepts and place value; operations (add, subtract, multiply, divide); fractions, decimals, and percents; measurement (length, area, volume, weight) Algebra Geometry Estimation and probability Graphs and charts Problem solving
Early childhood books: Concept books: animals, shapes, colors, opposites, prepositions, human body Label books Alphabet books Counting books Songs Rhymes Finger plays Pattern picture books Wordless picture books Picture story books	**Biography and autobiography:** Political leaders, sports and athletes, entertainment, military leaders, religious leaders, adventurers, documentaries, writers, scientists, fine artists, infamous people, other historical figures **Resources:** Dictionaries (English, other languages, picture, medical, rhyming); thesauruses; encyclopedias; almanacs; atlases; maps; globes; newspapers; magazines; journals; brochures; procedural texts (recipes, how-to books); Internet and Intranet; computer programs for reading and writing; teacher- and student-made books and materials

extend learning by conducting author or topic studies. Having multiple texts related to the topics taught in class provides opportunities for students to compare and contrast or verify information from multiple sources.

Recent studies show the scarcity of expository books as compared with narratives in classroom libraries (Duke, 2000). In addition to narratives and poetry, classroom libraries should include a variety of expository books, magazines, newspapers, and technology resources on science, social science, and math topics to enhance student reading and learning. Class-made and student-made books should also be available. The books in the classroom library can be organized by topic to facilitate book selection. In addition, resources materials should be available, such as picture dictionaries and dictionaries in other languages, thesauruses, atlases, maps, globes, encyclopedias, almanacs, magazines, and technology including the Internet and computer programs.

It is essential that students are exposed to quality literature. The following resources contain lists of high-quality expository or narrative books for students: Kletzien and Dreher (2004), Gunning (2000), Headley and Dunston (2000), and Griffiths and Clyne (1991). The American Library Association and their Association for Library Service to Children Division give awards to authors and illustrators. A list and criteria for these awards can be found online at www.ala.org/ala/alsc/awardsscholarships/literaryawds/literaryrelated.cfm. The awards include, but are not limited to, the following:

- The John Newbery Medal is awarded to the author of the most distinguished contribution to American Literature for Children.

- The Randolph Caldecott Medal is awarded to the artist of the most distinguished American picture book for children.

- The Coretta Scott King Book Awards is given to African American authors and illustrators for outstanding inspirational and educational contributions.

- The Pura Belpré Award is presented to a Latino/Latina writer and illustrator whose work best portrays, affirms, and celebrates the Latino cultural experience in an outstanding work of literature for children and youth.

- The Robert F. Sibert Informational Book Award is awarded annually to the author(s) and illustrator(s) of the most distinguished informational book published in English.

- The Theodor Seuss Geisel Award is given annually to the author(s) and illustrator(s) of the most distinguished American book for beginning readers published in English.

- Children's Notable Award identifies the best of the best in children's books, recordings, videos, and computer software.

In addition, there are other organizations that give book awards:

- International Reading Association and Children's Book Council Teachers' Choices, Children's Choices, and Young Adult Choices booklists (www.reading.org/resources/tools/choices_childrens.html)

- Children's Book Council booklists and awards (www.cbcbooks.org)

- National Science Teachers Association Outstanding Science Trade Books for Students K–12 (www.nsta.org/publications/ostb/)

Organizing the Library. In order to help students with their book selections, you can arrange your library by book level and teach students some simple guidelines. Books can be placed in specified baskets or have colored labels indicating their level. Although providing appropriate leveled books is important, providing opportunities for self-selection of interesting books is equally, if not more, important in motivating students to read.

Encouraging Wide Reading. Promote interest in a variety of topics, genres, or authors. Enthusiastically read portions or entire texts to students from different genres. Share newspaper or magazine articles with students. Model book talks and have students give book talks on self-selected texts. Have students conduct author studies or topic studies and then share with the class. Identify students' interests and recommend books to them. Connect texts to topics in the curriculum or of student interest. Have students share information they learned from the Internet that is related to classroom experiences and topics. Have students select poems, jokes, and riddles to read to the class. Give students regular opportunities to discuss texts and connect them to their lives, other texts, and the world. Provide opportunities for individual, paired and small-group reading experiences. Prominently display new additions to your classroom library.

Why Include Fiction Texts in Your Classroom Library?

For many students, fiction or narrative texts are quite entertaining and provide opportunities to expand their imaginations. Fairy tales and Mother Goose rhymes are often passed down from generation to generation. Many of these stories have a predictable story structure and often include repetitive lines, which make these texts easier to read. Bookshelves for young students continue to be filled with Dr. Seuss books, Bridwell's Clifford the Big Red Dog series, and fairy tale books redone by Disney with the "happily ever after" ending. Older students enjoy classics such as Swift's *Gulliver's Travels*, Twain's *The Adventures of Tom Sawyer*, London's *Call of the Wild*, and Verne's *Twenty Thousand Leagues Under the Sea*, as well as more contemporary titles such as Paulsen's *Hatchet* and Rowling's Harry Potter series. Most children's books in school and at home are fictional narratives.

Why Include Nonfiction Texts in Your Classroom Library?

Most of the material children read outside of school is nonfiction or expository, and most of the reading we do as adults is nonfiction (Harvey, 1998). Yet elementary school reading programs have traditionally been dominated by narrative texts. As a result, when children reach the upper grades and encounter content area texts and research materials, many students struggle to comprehend nonfiction texts (Caswell & Duke, 1998; Rog, 2003). Children's difficulty with nonfiction texts in the upper grades may be caused by lack of experience in primary grades (Caswell & Duke, 1998; Donovan & Smolkin, 2001). If children are to survive in this age of advancement of information and technology, they will need greater familiarity with nonfiction texts (Moss, Leone, & Dipillo, 1997).

Young children are not only capable of interacting with nonfiction texts, but when they are provided with multiple opportunities to engage in them, their ability to comprehend nonfiction texts dramatically increases (Duke & Kays, 1998; Kamil & Lane, 1997 as cited in Yopp & Yopp, 2000). Not only are nonfiction texts beneficial to gain content knowledge, children are motivated by them. Doiron (1994) suggests that the use of nonfiction books be increased at all levels for affective reasons. He argues that nonfiction books need to be included in read-alouds, guided reading, and independent reading because children are curious about and interested in learning about the world around them. Yopp and Yopp (2000) explain that nonfiction texts can capitalize on children's interests and lead them to be more purposeful and active readers.

With the emphasis in the United States on state standards and national legislation, it is important that teachers provide elementary students with experiences and texts that motivate them to read in order to not only enhance their reading development but also to provide them with valuable content knowledge. Because nonfiction texts make up a larger portion of state and district tests, it is beneficial to devote more instructional time to them. In addition, pairing fiction and nonfiction books on the same topic, along with interactive strategies, can boost students' understanding and enjoyment (Camp, 2000; Taberski, 2001).

Criteria for Evaluating Texts

Select quality texts for your classroom library on the basis of inviting design, engaging linguistic style, accurate content, and clear organization. Consider the following points to evaluate each text.

Inviting Design. Does the text include quality eye-catching illustrations, photographs, maps, drawings, charts, or figures? Do the illustrations support and enhance the text? Are they clearly labeled and appropriately integrated within the text? Is the font easy to read? Is the placement of the text easy for the reader to follow? For excellent examples of design, look at any book in the Eyewitness series, such as *Hurricane and Tornado* (Challoner, 2004). This text contains photographs, models, illustrations, and experiments related to hurricanes and tornadoes, including details about Hurricane Katrina.

Engaging Linguistic Style. The linguistic style should be engaging and appropriate for the students' interest or reading level. Does the author create excitement for the subject? Is the author's style and language appropriate for the age and development of the students? Do the texts vary in difficulty from easy-to-read picture books to challenging texts for independent and instructional reading as well as for read-alouds and browsing? Higher-level books can be explored by looking at the pictures or by having an adult or a more capable peer read selections or the whole book to the students.

Accurate Content of a Nonfiction Text. Answer the following questions about the accuracy of the text: Is the content accurate? Is the factual information clearly distinguished from fiction? What are the credentials of the author and the references? Is the information current? Is the content appropriate for students? Is the factual information clearly distinguished from fiction? Do the materials accurately represent diversity in people? Are stereotypes avoided? Do the materials appeal to a wide range of students' interests and social, cultural, ethnic, and linguistic backgrounds? Do the materials relate to curricular topics or provide other learning opportunities for the students?

Clear Organization of a Nonfiction Text. Although the organization of nonfiction texts varies, the structure should be clear. Does the text include a table of contents, index, glossary, and references? Does it contain headings, subheadings, or bulleted information? Does the text include boldfaced or italicized fonts to identify important concepts? All of these organizational structures help guide the reader for improved comprehension. Freeman (1990) and Harvey (1998) describe the importance of using nonfiction text in the classroom. Kobrin (1995) describes more than 800 nonfiction books in her resource book. McAndrews (2004) offers a list of quality nonfiction books for primary-grade students. Students enjoy magazines such as *National Geographic Kids*, *National Geographic World*, *Ranger Rick*, *Your Big Backyard*, *Sports Illustrated for Kids*, *Time for Kids*, and *Zoobooks*.

Elements of a Fiction Text. Read the text and evaluate it based on these questions: Is the plot believable? Does it contain specific details? Did the main character overcome the problem but not too easily? Did the characters seem real? Did the characters have strengths and weaknesses? Is the setting accurate to the time or place? Was the theme worthwhile? Did the rest of the language sound natural? When reading, could you picture yourself in the story? (These questions were adapted from Norton, 1995.)

Measuring Readability and Leveling Texts

The readability of a text is dependant upon a variety of factors. The primary factor is the reader's interest or choice in reading the text. Background knowledge that is required of reader is another significant factor. The passage length and the density of information such as the amount of elaboration or use of examples also affect readability. The type of content and the way in which new vocabulary is used are also factors. The genre (e.g., fiction, nonfiction) or the passage format (e.g., expository, narrative, persuasive) are important factors. The organizational structure (e.g., headings, diagrams, pictures) can enhance the readability. The style of the writing, along with the grammatical complexity such as predictable sentence patterns and word choices, or complex structures that clearly reveal causality, can facilitate comprehension. The readability of a text depends upon not only the text but the reader as well.

Although the readability of a text cannot be determined exactly for a given student, books can be assigned an approximate reading level. There are several ways in which books have been leveled. Historically, starting with the McGuffy Readers in 1879, books were divided by grade level based on factors such as what teachers thought children should know and read at a given age, but there was not much consistency in book leveling. In 1977, Edward Fry developed a readability formula and graph to help judge the difficulty of a text based on the number of syllables in each sentence and the number of sentences in three 100-word samples of a text. (Fry's readability graph can be found in Fry, Kress, & Fountoukidis [1993] or Walker [2004].) Since then there have been several readability formulas, some of which looked at factors such as the number of words used that were not on high-frequency word lists. These and other formulas were used to identify book levels. Publishers have begun to put book levels on the back of books. Book levels are often denoted by *R.L.* for *reading level* and a single number standing for the grade level, or by the addition of a decimal indicating the number of months beyond the beginning of that grade. A comparison chart of the different types of book levels for elementary school can be found in Table 7.2, which compares the grade level, Reading Recovery levels (Clay, 1993), Guided Reading levels (Fountas & Pinnell, 1996), DRA levels (Beaver, 2001), Basal Equivalent levels, and Lexile levels (MetaMetrics, no date).

Table 7.2 Reading Level Correlation Chart

Grade Level	Reading Recovery	Fountas-Pinnell Guided Reading	DRA	Basal Equivalent	Lexile
Kindergarten	A,B	A	A	Readiness	
	1		1		
	2	B	2	Preprimer 1	
	3	C	3		
Grade 1	4		4	Preprimer 2	
	5	D	6		
	6				
	7	E	8	Preprimer 3	
	8				
	9	F	10	Primer	
	10				
	11	G	12		
	12				
	13	H	14	Grade 1	
	14				
	15	I	16		200–299
	16				
Grade 2	18	J, K	20	Grade 2	300–399
	20	L, M	28		400–499
Grade 3	22	N	30	Grade 3	500–599
			34		
	24	O, P	38		600–699
Grade 4	26	Q, R, S	40	Grade 4	700–799
Grade 5	28	T, U, V	44	Grade 5	800–899
Grade 6	30	W, X, Y		Grade 6	900–999
Grade 7	32	Z		Grade 7	1000–1100
Grade 8	34	Z		Grade 8	

If a text is not already leveled, one way of identifying its level is by examining readability factors such as interest, background knowledge, and complexity. These are the general criteria used in leveling books for kindergarten through grade 12 (Clay, 1993). Clay, who developed the Reading Recovery program, examined hundreds of texts and created her own numbering system that divided grade K–2 books into several distinct levels per grade. Table 7.3 provides a description of these Reading Recovery levels, which formed the basis for later leveling systems. A similar numbering system was used by Beaver (2001) to level books in her DRA. Fountas and Pinnell, who are both Reading Recovery Teacher Trainers, developed another system of leveling using letters called Guided Reading Levels. The Fountas and Pinnell (1996) text provides guidelines for leveling books using letters, with Level A for preprimer and Level Z for grade 6.

The most well-known readability formula is Fry's Readability Scale; however, there are now many computerized readability formulas to help determine the readability of a text. It is important to note that no formula can take into account a student's background knowledge and interest and therefore a formula should be used with caution.

Fry's Readability Scale (Fry, 1977). This is based on the number of sentences and syllables in a 100-word passage. You can find the Fry Readability Scale at school.discovery.com/schrockguide/fry/fry.html.

Readability Using Microsoft Word. Open the Word program, key in text passages at random with approximately 100 words per passage. Be sure to use all of the punctuation and paragraphs of the original text. Pull down the Tools menu and go to Options. Click on Spelling and Grammar and check the box that says "Show readability statistics." Click OK. Highlight the

Table 7.3   Reading Recovery and DRA Book Levels

Level	Description
1–4	Consistent placement of print, repetition of one to two sentence patterns (one to two word changes), oral language structures, familiar objects and actions, and illustrations provide high support.
5–8	Repetition of two to three sentence patterns (phrases may change), opening, closing sentences vary, varied simple sentence patterns, predominantly oral language structures, many familiar objects and actions, and illustrations provide moderate to high support.
9–12	Repetition of three or more sentence patterns, or varied sentence patterns (repeated phrases or refrains), blend of oral and written language structures, or, fantastic happenings in framework of familiar experiences, and illustrations provide moderate support.
13–15	Varied sentence patterns (may have repeated phrases or refrains), or repeated patterns in cumulative form, written language structures, oral structures appearing in dialogue, conventional story and literary language, specialized vocabulary for some topics, and illustrations provide low to moderate support.
16–20	Elaborated episodes and events; extended descriptions; links to familiar stories; literary language; unusual, challenging vocabulary; and illustrations provide low support.

From Peterson, B. (1988). *Characteristics of texts that support beginning readers.* Unpublished doctoral dissertation, The Ohio State University, Columbus, OH. Adapted with permission.

text. Pull down the Tools menu and go to Spelling and Grammar (Note: If you have not made a spelling or grammar error, click YES to continue testing). A box will appear that gives you the Flesch–Kincaid Grade Level equivalency. For better accuracy, check at least three samples from different parts of the book.

ATOS (Advantage-TASA Open Standard). This computer formula uses number of words per sentence, characters per word, and average grade level of words. You can find it at www.renlearn.com.

Lexile Scale. This computer formula includes measurement of sentence length and word frequency. You can find it at www.lexile.com.

Degrees of Reading Power. Measures sentence length, number of words not on the Dale List of words known by fourth graders, and average number of letters per word. For levels of content area text books, go to www.tasaliteracy.com.

Readability Plus Formulas. Using this software program from Micro Power and Light Co., you can scan or type the text, and then select the readability formula (Dale–Chall, Flesch, Fry Graph, FOG, SMOG, Powers–Sumner–Kearl, FORCAST, and the Spache) to obtain an approximate grade level. This program also allows you to compare the passage with a graded vocabulary list and identify all the words not on the list.

Leveled Booklists. The following websites contain lists of leveled books. For an excellent leveled book database, go to registration.beavton.k12.or.us/lbdb/. Reading Recovery and grade level lists can be found at www.pps.k12.or.us/curriculum/literacy/leveled_books. Scholastic Reading Counts has an e-catalog that identifies books by author, title, or keyword and the interest level, reading level, Guided Reading level, and Lexile level. Go to src.scholastic.com/ecatalog for more information. It is important to note, however, that all book levels are approximate and a students' success in reading a specific book can significantly differ on the basis of prior experience with the content and vocabulary as well as their familiarity with the text structure.

Guided Reading Levels. Use the book *Matching Books to Readers: Using Leveled Books in Guided Reading, K–3* (Fountas & Pinnell, 1999) to learn how to level books. This resource also contains booklists organized by title, author, and level. Their website, www.FountasandPinnellLeveledBooks.com, also provides a link to a booklist with more than 18,000 leveled books that are searchable by level, title, author, or publisher.

Publishers' Posted Levels on the Internet. Look up titles on the Internet to see if publishers have already leveled the text. Many publishers such as the Wright Group, Scholastic, Sundance Publishing, Troll, and New Bridge have a list of all of their books with levels on their websites.

Leveling by Comparison. Compare characteristics such as sentence structure and vocabulary of known leveled books with unleveled books. For any leveling method, always use your professional judgment to adjust book levels on the basis of experience with students or the text.

Functioning Level

To get the most out of text in all grade levels, it is best to match the text with the students' interest and functioning levels. As noted previously, Betts (1946) developed three functioning levels: Independent, Instructional, and Frustration. Students are reading at the independent level if they have 95%–100% word accuracy, at the instructional level if they have 90%–94% word accuracy, and at the frustration level if their word accuracy is below 89%. For sustained silent reading or independent reading, students should select books within their independent level, and for classroom instruction books, students should select books at their instructional level. Books read during teacher read-alouds should be at the students' frustration level. The book is discussed, and students should be able to comprehend the book afterward. It is important to read aloud more complex text in order to expand students' interests, language, and knowledge as well as to model appropriate fluency and phrasing.

To verify the appropriate reading level of the text, you need to use both the Oral Reading Analysis of Miscues Summary and Comprehension Analysis Summary (see Appendix) to determine a student's functioning level in a text passage. If the student reads the passage at the independent level with full comprehension, they can probably read the text on their own. If the passage is read at the instructional level with some comprehension, the student can read it with support. If the student reads the passage at the frustration level with little comprehension, they should select another text, have the text read to them, or use the text to browse the pictures and read parts that are interesting.

Attitude and Motivation Strategies

Identifying your students' strengths, needs, and interests, and providing for self-selection of topics and materials are important strategies for motivating reading, writing, and speaking through self-selection. Students may need some guidance in their self-selection. Parents may also need support in understanding what is appropriate for their child. The following are some strategies to enhance the students' attitude and motivation toward literacy activities.

Identifying Your Students' Strengths, Needs, and Interests

The method for understanding your students is through observation, interaction, and analysis of assessments and interest surveys, such as those described in this book. Because success breeds success, it is important to select objectives, strategies, and materials that are within the students' ZPD or instructional level. This can be done by analyzing informal and ongoing assessments and adapting instruction as needed to scaffold students' learning. By observing and having conversations with students, you become aware of their interests. Make it a point to incorporate these topics in discussions and lessons. Seek out materials and writing opportunities related to these topics. For example, if you know a student likes horses, say "Here are some Walter Farley books about the Black Stallion that I enjoyed reading. I like this one especially because you wonder what happens to the Black Stallion as he travels across the ocean." If you are writing examples on the chalkboard, you might include the student's name and something you learned about them. Providing appropriate instruction enhances students' engagement and interest in learning.

Self-Selection of Reading Materials

Here are five guiding questions you can teach students to help them select appropriate reading materials:

1. Does the book look interesting?

2. Does the book look as hard as other books I have read? To figure out if the book is too hard, use the "Five Finger Rule": Read approximately 50 words and put up one finger for every word you cannot read or understand. Five or more mistakes indicate the text is probably too hard.

3. Can I understand what the book is saying?

4. Am I able to explain what I just read?

5. Am I choosing reading materials from different genres and authors?

Students should have opportunities to select materials even if they are not always on their instructional level. Easier or independent-level books provide recreational reading and fluency practice, while more difficult books may pique their interest and encourage experience with more complex text and more diverse vocabulary.

Leveling Bookmarks for Books Sent Home

Children come home from school with a variety of books. Parents may not know what level reading is appropriate for their child. It is important that you communicate with parents about how the books should be read at home. I developed three leveled Text Selection Bookmarks (see Appendix) to help parents: "Read to me!" (for books that are too hard for the student to read, and that are approximately at their frustration level but that are interesting to them), "Read with me!" (for books that are approximately at the student's instructional level) and "I can read this on my own!" (for books that the student already has read or could probably read).

For example, if a student selects a book from the library because she is really interested in the Hubble Space Telescope but it is above her reading level, put the "Read to me!" bookmark in the book when it goes home with her. Students should have opportunities to select books based on their interests, even if the books are too hard to read. If the student can read most of the book but it has several unknown words, put the "Read with me!" bookmark in it. If the student has had several opportunities to practice the book or it is at her independent level, put the "I can read this on my own!" bookmark in the book. It is hoped that using these bookmarks will alleviate some of the problems parents encounter, such as making a child sound out every word in a book that is at their frustration level. In addition, it is helpful if literacy specialists and teachers send home the Good Reader Bookmarks in the Appendix.

At-Home Reading Log

In order to monitor the student's reading at home, you can send home a simple At-Home Reading Log (see Appendix). You record the date, the title, and the level of the book. In the far-right column, a family member signs after listening to the child read and then indicates how well their child read the book by writing a plus sign, checkmark, or minus sign.

By getting this feedback, the literacy specialist or teacher can adjust the level of books sent home. For example, the student presented in Figure 7.1 was able to successfully read Reading Recovery Level 16 and 17 books, which equate to Guided Reading Level I. When the teacher moved her up to RR 18 or GR J, the book was too hard. It is a nonfiction title, so the teacher should try again at the same level; if the next one is too hard, the student can read a book from one level lower.

Writing Experiences

In order to help students have a positive attitude and be motivated to write, they need to have many opportunities to write for authentic purposes, write for audiences other than just the teacher, and be able to select what they write about. (Specific writing strategies are described in Chapter 5.) Students should write on a daily basis, including some free-writing such as journaling or diary writing. Although formula writing provides a guide, it often leads to contrived and less imaginative writing, so allow freedom of expression. The literature genres listed in Table 7.1 on page 240 are the same genres students should have an opportunity to write. Reading and discussing examples from a given genre before students are expected to write it helps them understand the essential elements of each genre. It is often beneficial for students to have an opportunity to talk about and brainstorm ideas before writing, as it enhances their engagement and motivation to write.

Here are four guiding questions for helping students select appropriate writing or speaking topics and genres:

Figure 7.1   At-Home Reading Log

Name: Katherine

Directions: Listen to the child read, talk about the story, sign this form, and mark a plus sign (+) if it was read very well with almost no help, a checkmark (✓) if it was read pretty well with some help, and a minus sign (–) if it was read with difficulty and with a lot of help. Then return the log and book to school the next day.

Date	Title and Level Reading Recovery Level = RR Guided Reading Level = GR Grade Level = GL	Signature and Evaluation +/✓/–
Aug. 25	A Kiss for Little Bear (Minarik, E.) RR 16 , GR I, GL 1.8	SLM ✓
Aug. 26	My Visit to the Dinosaurs (Aliki) RR 16, GR I, GL 1.8	SLM +
Aug. 27	There's a Nightmare in My Closet (Mayer, M.) RR 16, GR I, GL 1.8	SLM +
Aug. 28	Hungry, Hungry Sharks (Cole, J.) RR 17, GR I, GL 2.0	SLM ✓
Aug. 29	How Kittens Grow (Selsam, M.) RR 18, GR J, GL 2.1	SLM –

1. Did I choose a topic that I am interested in?

2. Do I have knowledge about this topic or have resources to learn more about it?

3. Have I read examples of this type of genre?

4. Have I experimented with using different types of writing or speaking (narrative, expository, descriptive, persuasive)?

Ask emergent writers to draw a picture and then tell what they drew. They can use inventive spelling to write their ideas. If the ideas cannot be read clearly, take dictation on the same page so that others may read the ideas the writer intended. Older writers can make a story map or graphic organizer to help them before writing.

Although not all writing needs to be published, an audience is often motivating, so students should have opportunities to share their writing with classmates, friends, teachers, school, family, and community members.

Speaking and Listening Experiences

Students need many experiences in speaking and listening every day and should have choices about what they share. Every student should orally communicate during every lesson. This can be done by the Think-Pair-Share strategy in which the teacher poses a question or a statement, and then each student thinks about it and turns to a partner to talk about it. You can regularly use this strategy for students to tell one another what they learned from the lesson or how it connects to their lives. Students should also work in small, collaborative groups where more interaction occurs rather than just listening to the teacher. Encourage students to participate in class and group discussions; they should share what they are thinking. Teach them to be good listeners by restating what was said and by asking thoughtful questions of the person speaking or presenting. Have students select topics for show and tell or presentations that are interesting to them. Engage class members, families, and community members in presenting and listening to one another during several planned events.

In conclusion, students become more engaged and motivated to read, write, speak, and listen when they feel that they are capable of doing it; when they feel it is meaningful and interesting; when they feel accepted and supported by their teacher and peers; and when they have some choice of what they do based on their diverse interests, experiences, and understandings. You can support your students by creating a positive learning environment; getting to know your students' interests and abilities; providing appropriate tasks, strategies, and materials; and engaging them in meaningful reading, writing, speaking, and listening experiences. The assessments and strategies provided in this resource have been found to not only improve students' attitudes and motivation toward literacy but also support them in developing into lifelong readers and writers.

APPENDIX

Assessments and Resources

ASSESSMENTS AND THE RELATED LITERACY PROCESSES

Literacy Processes

Assessments	Language Development	Vocabulary	Phonological Awareness	Phonics and Spelling	Word Identification	Oral Reading and Fluency	Reading and Listening Comprehension	Emergent Writing	Writing Composition
Inventories: Interest and Activities; School Attitude; Reading Interest	•	•							
Literacy Process Interview	•	•		•	•	•	•	•	
Language Observation Scale	•	•					•		
Oral Presentation Assessment	•	•							
Synonym and Antonym Vocabulary	•	•			•				
Emergent Text Concepts		•	•	•	•				
Auditory Discrimination (Consonants-1, Vowels-2)			•						
Phoneme Blending and Phoneme Segmentation			•		•				
Letter and Sound Identification				•					
Reading Words (Fry's and Graded Reading)				•	•				
Writing Words (Fry's and Graded Reading)			•	•	•			•	
Sentence Dictation (K–Primer, 1–2, 3, and above)			•	•				•	
Oral Reading Analysis of Miscues Summary (Reading Record and Analysis of Miscues Worksheet)		•			•	•	•		
Oral Reading Strategies Assessment		•			•	•	•		
Fluency Assessment by Teacher, Peer, and Self	•	•							
Nonfiction Layout and Text Features Assessment	•	•							
Developmental Reading Assessment						•	•	•	

(continued)

ASSESSMENTS AND THE RELATED LITERACY PROCESSES
(continued)

Literacy Processes

Assessments	Language Development	Vocabulary	Phonological Awareness	Phonics and Spelling	Word Identification	Oral Reading and Fluency	Reading and Listening Comprehension	Emergent Writing	Writing Composition
Qualitative Reading Inventory-4					•	•	•		
Illinois Early Literacy Assessments: ISEL	•	•	•	•	•	•	•		
Emergent Writing Stage Assessment								•	
Handwriting Rubric Assessment								•	
Writing Composition Assessment Summary	•	•	•	•			•		•
Writing Composition Rubric for Writer and Teacher	•	•	•	•			•		•
Writing Process Rubric for Writer and Teacher	•	•	•	•			•		•
Inventories: Interest and Activities; School Attitude; Reading Interest (Elementary and Middle-Secondary)	•	•							
Literacy Process Interview	•	•		•	•	•	•	•	•

PURPOSES FOR ASSESSMENTS

Assessments	Which Students? When?	Purpose: To Identify...
	Pre- and Postdiagnostic Assessments	
Language Observation Scale	Grades K–12, if speech or language difficulties are noted	Speech or language problems that may require further assessment by speech-language pathologist
Oral Presentation Assessment	Grades 3–12, give or adapt for all oral presentations	Important elements in oral presentations
Inventories: Interest, Activities, School Attitude	Grades K–12, give if you do not know the students' interests	Interests and activities for reading and writing
Reading Interest Inventory	Grades K–12, give if you do not know the genre students like to read	Genres students are interested in for book selection and writing prompts
Literacy Process Interview	At least first-grade reading level; if reading or writing difficulties	Strategies students use for reading and writing
Synonym Vocabulary Reading/Listening	Grades K–12, if possible low language; start listening level at frustration vocabulary reading level	Synonym vocabulary knowledge and to inform text reading starting level
Antonym Vocabulary Reading/Listening	Grades K–12, if possible low language. Start listening level at frustration reading level.	Antonym vocabulary knowledge and to inform text reading starting level
Emergent Text Concepts Assessment	Grades K–2, if not reading at or above first-grade level	Concepts of directionality, letter/words, and punctuation
Nonfiction Layout and Text Features Assessment	Grades 2–12, if students do not show use or knowledge of nonfiction text concepts	Concepts such as the use of title page, parts of books, graphic information, and typographical features
Phoneme Blending	At or below first grade on reading word lists	Orally blending sounds as needed for reading
Phoneme Segmentation	At or below first grade on writing word lists	Orally segmenting sounds as needed for writing
Letter and Sound Identification Assessment	At or below first grade on reading or writing lists	Known and unknown letters, sounds, and example words
Auditory Discrimination: Consonants, Vowels (long/short and diagraphs)	Those with difficulties in blending or segmenting phonemes, at or below first grade on reading or writing, or substituting similar sounds	Hearing differences in phonemes in words
Graded Reading Words Assessment	Grades K–12, start at least two grade levels below actual grade	Known sight words and ability to identify new words
Oral Reading Record and Oral Reading Analysis of Miscues	Grades K–12, students who may have difficulties decoding and identifying words; often paired with comprehension assessment	Word identification and strategy use to select materials and instructional strategies

(continued)

PURPOSES FOR ASSESSMENTS (continued)

Assessments	Which Students? When?	Purpose: To Identify...
Pre- and Postdiagnostic Assessments		
Comprehension Retelling and Question Assessment	Grades K–12, use after all oral reading records and to monitor comprehension only	Comprehension of narrative and expository texts
Oral Reading Strategies Assessment	Grades K–12, students who may have difficulties decoding and word identification	Oral reading strategy use and selection of additional strategies
Fluency Assessment by Teacher, Peer, and Self	First-grade reading level and above	Phrasing, intonation, expression, smoothness, and pace
Developmental Reading Assessment (DRA) Oral and Listening Levels	Best for preprimer to second-grade reading levels 2–4 times per year (available for grades K–3 and 4–6)	Words in context, oral and listening comprehension of narrative texts; identify sublevels within each grade
Qualitative Reading Inventory-4 (QRI-4)	All grades 3–5 as initial screening; grades 3–12 students with reading difficulties 2–4 times per year (available for grades K–12)	Words in context; oral, silent, and listening comprehension of narrative and expository texts
Graded Writing Words Assessment	All grades K–3 as initial screening; grades K–12 students with spelling difficulties	Spelling of high-frequency words (K–5) and commonly misspelled words (6–12)
Sentence Dictation Assessment	All grades 1–3 as initial screening; grades 1–12 with spelling difficulties.	Phoneme–graphemes correlation and developmental spelling level
Emergent Writing Stage Assessment	Grades K–1 or anyone who does not yet write sentences	Letters, phonetic spelling, words, and a sentence
Handwriting Rubric Assessment	Grades K–2 or anyone with difficulties with handwriting	Formation and spacing within lines, words, and page
Writing Composition Assessment Summary	Narrative (K–12), Expository (2–12), Persuasive (3–12); annual pre- and posttest	Writing elements such as content, organization, and conventions
Writing Composition Rubric for Student and Teacher	Grades K–12, for all writing throughout the year	Content, organization, and conventions
Writing Process Rubric for Student and Teacher	Grades K–12, for all published writing throughout the year	Prewriting, drafting, conferring, revising, editing, publishing

EXAMPLE LITERACY LESSON PLAN FORMAT

Heading:	Your name, name of student or group, grade, instructional level, and date of the lesson
Objectives With Learning Standards:	Based on student strengths and needs, what will the students do in observable and measurable terms? What is the purpose of the task? How will you assess learning? Identify the state or IRA/NCTE language arts standard that is met by each objective. Share the objectives with students. • Oral reading/fluency objective • Language/vocabulary objective • Comprehension objective • Writing composition objective • Phonics/spelling objective
Materials:	Include titles and authors of books and all curricular or prepared materials.
Procedure:	(Put the following headings in order of instruction)
Text/Concept Introduction:	Write a summary of what you are going to say to students to get their interest in the text or concepts. Include an introduction to the genre, concepts, characters, vocabulary words, pictures, and connection to students' prior learning or experiences. Read the title, author, illustrator, preview the text, and discuss the pictures or other graphic information to make predictions.
Reading Method:	Describe how the text is going to be read (guided, paired, shared reading, by the paragraph or page, echo, oral, or silent)
Oral Reading/Fluency Strategies:	For instructional level reading, identify and discuss specific graphophonic, syntactic, and semantic oral reading strategies students can use to problem-solve unknown words. For independent level reading, identify and discuss fluency strategies such as reading in meaningful phrases, pausing for punctuation, problem-solving efficiently, reading with expression, reading smoothly and at a conversational pace.
Assessment/Evaluation:	How will you assess student learning? How did students do? For example, write down oral reading strategies used, self-corrections, miscues, strategies prompted, and fluency behaviors. Analyze miscues for graphophonics, syntax, and semantics. Analyze students' ability to use strategies for unknown words. Are there specific phonetic elements the students need to work on?
Language/Vocabulary Strategies:	List unknown vocabulary words or phrases and the strategies for teaching them. The definitions or explanations of these words may be discussed before, during, or after reading.
Assessment/Evaluation:	How will you assess student learning? Evaluate by recording a +, ✓, or – after each word, depending on how well the students demonstrated the meaning of the word. Analyze their ability to use vocabulary strategies and comprehend vocabulary.
Reading or Listening Comprehension Strategies:	Describe the strategies or questions used to assess comprehension before, during, and after reading the text at a variety of the Revised Bloom's Taxonomy levels. For narratives, students may describe the characters, settings, plot, events, and resolution; for expository texts, students may describe the main idea and details.

(continued)

EXAMPLE LITERACY LESSON PLAN FORMAT (continued)

Assessment/Evaluation: How will you assess student learning? It is often beneficial to tell students in advance what you want them to know and do after reading. Write down and evaluate with a +, –, or ✓ the students' retelling, answers to questions, or responses to activities. Make a statement regarding comprehension improvement or need.

Writing Composition Strategies: Emergent writers should write at least one complete sentence, and those at or above the second-grade writing level should write multiple sentences.

1. Introduce the writing content and genre: Provide a writing prompt based on the text or students' experiences. Suggest prewriting strategies and resources they can use to enhance content.

2. Introduce writing criteria: Make a scoring guide in advance and preteach students your criteria for evaluating the content, genre, and conventions. Suggest resources for students to use to help with vocabulary and spelling.

3. Revising and editing writing: How are you going to help students revise the content and edit the conventions in their writing? Will the students publish their writing?

Assessment/Evaluation: State the assessment tool or criteria for assessing the students' writing. Evaluate student writing on the basis of the predetermined elements above, using a rubric or scoring guide. How did the students do? Provide examples of specific responses and specific changes made. Write down areas of improvement or need.

Phonics and Spelling Strategies: Identify specific phonemes or graphemes to work on within the context of common words. Include strategies such as make-and-break words, "read, cover, and write," sound boxes, or personal dictionary. For spelling, focus on approximately three to five high-frequency words the students had trouble reading or spelling.

Assessment/Evaluation: Write how will you assess their learning. How well did students learn the strategy and words? Record a +, ✓, or – after each word depending on the level of independence with which students were able to read or write.

Modifications/Adaptations: How did you preplan or change the lesson to meet the students' specific needs?

Extensions/Technology: How are you going to extend learning? How did you include technology?

Closure With Students' Reflection: Ask the students what they learned in the lesson. If they did not mention all of the objectives, discuss them and ask students if they felt they learned them. Ask what the teacher or peers did to help them learn better.

Evidence of Student Work: Write down the names of the materials completed during the lesson. Keep examples of the actual student and teacher work for the portfolio.

Family Communication: This is for notes or discussions with the family. Share a summary of the students' strengths and needs during the lesson, and give suggestions for support at home. Ask for family feedback and document any information that is shared with you.

Your Reflection: This is a reflection of your teaching, student learning, and students' affect. Provide specific evaluation of your teaching and the students' learning of each of the objectives. What went well and why? What didn't go well and why? What did you learn? What will you do differently in the future? Based on your observations and documentation of student learning, what do they need instruction on next? Discuss additional ideas with colleagues. If applicable, write any concerns.

Diagnostic Literacy Assessments and Instructional Strategies: A Literacy Specialist's Resource by Stephanie L. McAndrews. © 2008 by the International Reading Association. May be copied for classroom use.

LANGUAGE OBSERVATION SCALE

Name: _____ Grade: _____ Date: _____

Directions: After observing the student over time, circle the number on each of the scales below that best describes the student's communicative behavior.

Scoring: Mark each behavior on a scale from 1–4.
1 = Almost no evidence of this behavior; communication is significantly interrupted
2 = Rarely exhibits the correct behavior; frequently interfering with communication
3 = Sometimes exhibits the correct behavior; some interference with communication
4 = Predominantly exhibits the correct behavior; almost no interference with communication

Articulation, Pronunciation, and Fluency	Score			
1. Articulation: Correctly produces speech sounds	1	2	3	4
2. Pronunciation: Correctly pronounces words and does not add or delete sounds	1	2	3	4
3. Linguistic fluency: Speech is fluent and not disrupted by repetitions, revisions, unusual pauses, and fillers such as *um* or *like*	1	2	3	4

Comments:

Syntax and Grammar	Score			
4. Uses a variety of long, complex, and compound sentences	1	2	3	4
5. Uses conjunctions (coordinating: *and*, *but*, *or*; subordinating: *because*, *when*, *unless*)	1	2	3	4
6. Uses action verbs	1	2	3	4
7. Uses adverbs	1	2	3	4
8. Uses adjectives	1	2	3	4
9. Uses prepositions	1	2	3	4
10. Uses correct subject–verb agreement	1	2	3	4
11. Uses the copula (*to be*) correctly	1	2	3	4
12. Uses correct past tense irregular verbs	1	2	3	4
13. Uses correct past tense *-ed* appropriately: /ed/, /d/, /t/	1	2	3	4
14. Uses present progressive *-ing* with auxiliary verb	1	2	3	4
15. Uses regular and irregular plurals correctly	1	2	3	4
16. Uses possessives correctly	1	2	3	4

Comments:

(continued)

LANGUAGE OBSERVATION SCALE (continued)

Word Choice	Score			
17. Uses words in the correct context including question words	1	2	3	4
18. Uses a variety of words	1	2	3	4
19. Uses content-specific vocabulary	1	2	3	4
20. Uses pronouns correctly so that the reference is clear	1	2	3	4
21. Uses specific terms instead of "stuff" or "things" when the listener has no way of knowing the reference	1	2	3	4

Comments:

Language Use	Score			
22. Communication of ideas: Statements and questions are clearly understood	1	2	3	4
23. Prompt responding: Pauses less than 2 seconds before responding to a question or other verbal stimulus	1	2	3	4
24. Appropriate responses: Speaker's utterances seem to follow naturally what has been said or asked previously by someone else	1	2	3	4
25. Introduces topic appropriately: Gets listener's attention and provides listener with sufficient background information	1	2	3	4
26. Topic maintenance: Maintains a topic appropriately while adding new and relevant information and keeps topic going	1	2	3	4
27. Changes topic appropriately: Speaker provides information to the listener when changing topic to help the listener follow the conversation	1	2	3	4
28. Asks questions for clarification: Asks for clarification when uncertain of information	1	2	3	4
29. Repetition not needed: Student requires or does not request repetition for apparently clear statements or questions	1	2	3	4
30. Responds to speaker's request for clarification: Responds to requests such as "Tell me more" or "I don't understand"	1	2	3	4
31. Follows three-step instructions: Repetitions and visual cues are not required in order to understand	1	2	3	4
32. Changes language style for listener: Uses appropriate register for adults, family, and peers	1	2	3	4

Comments:

Analysis:

ORAL PRESENTATION ASSESSMENT

Presenter: _____ Grade: _____ Date: _____

Topic: _____

Directions: Provide a copy to the student before planning his or her presentation. During the presentation, the teacher writes down specific observations under each heading and scores it. After the presentation, the student completes a self-evaluation and then the teacher provides the student with specific feedback on the effective elements of the presentation and suggestions for improvement.

Scoring: During the presentation evaluate each element with a plus sign (+) if all of the descriptors were clearly observed, a checkmark (✓) if most of them were, or a minus sign (–) if they were rarely or never observed.

Score	Did the presenter...
_____ _____ _____ _____ _____ _____	**Language:** Use appropriate language for the audience? Convey the information clearly to the audience? Use appropriate and specific vocabulary? Pronounce words correctly? Use grammatically correct sentences? Use complex and compound sentences with adjectives, adverbs, prepositions, and conjunctions? Observations:
_____ _____ _____ _____	**Organization:** Have an interesting introduction? State main ideas and details clearly and in an appropriate order? Have smooth transitions? Summarize main ideas at the end? Observations:
_____ _____ _____ _____	**Content:** Include accurate information? Clearly describe and support information with illustrations, evidence, and examples? Follow the directions of the assignment? Teach the audience new information? Observations:

(continued)

ORAL PRESENTATION ASSESSMENT (continued)

Score	Did the presenter...
_____ _____	**Visual media:** Use visual materials directly related to the topic? Use visual materials that improved audience understanding of the content? Observations:
_____ _____ _____ _____	**Manner:** Maintain good eye contact? Speak clearly, at the appropriate volume, and at an understandable pace? Convey enthusiastic interest in the topic? Maintain the attention of the audience? Observations:
_____ _____ _____	**Audience participation:** Ask questions or ask the audience to do anything during or after the presentation? Provide adequate time for questions after the presentation? Answer questions to the best of his or her knowledge? Observations:

Analysis:

SYNONYM VOCABULARY ASSESSMENT

Name: _____ Grade: _____ Date: _____

Reading or Listening (circle one); if both, mark each level (R) for reading and (L) for listening.

Reading Directions: Tell the student, "Read each line of words. Circle the word that means the same or almost the same as the first word in each line." Continue until the student reaches the frustration level or becomes frustrated and then repeat that grade level by having the student listen as you read the words. Continue again until the student reaches the frustration level.

Listening Directions: Tell the student, "Follow along as I read the words in each line and circle the word that means the same or almost the same as the first word in each line."

Scoring: In front of each line number, put a plus sign (+) if correct and a minus sign (–) if incorrect. Write total correct to determine functioning level.

Functioning Level: Independent (90%–100%), Instructional (70%–80%), Frustration (60% and below)

Practice Item	**A**	**B**	**C**	**D**
1. fast	run	more	look	quick

LEVEL 1   Functioning Level: _____   Score: ___ /10 = ___ %

+/–		**A**	**B**	**C**	**D**
	1. see	run	more	look	us
	2. little	come	long	away	small
	3. say	talk	goes	like	just
	4. mom	dog	mother	many	with
	5. start	begin	last	round	slow
	6. big	door	right	fun	large
	7. hop	hard	ball	dark	jump
	8. alike	grew	pot	same	most
	9. glad	happy	sail	rope	hold
	10. street	time	thin	very	road

LEVEL 2   Functioning Level: _____   Score: ___ /10 = ___ %

+/–		**A**	**B**	**C**	**D**
	1. go	anything	leave	rest	summer
	2. pair	read	should	two	middle
	3. cut	last	round	slow	slice
	4. thin	shout	skinny	live	under
	5. hear	kind	magic	help	listen
	6. car	secret	chew	automobile	juice
	7. fear	afraid	lunch	yellow	welcome
	8. stir	hospital	stood	mix	know
	9. below	live	place	under	took
	10. all	this	every	find	lunch

(continued)

SYNONYM VOCABULARY ASSESSMENT (continued)

LEVEL 3	Functioning Level:			Score: /10 = %	
+/–		A	B	C	D
	1. like	cure	enjoy	tall	high
	2. beautiful	tired	asleep	seven	pretty
	3. close	shut	grow	leg	fat
	4. choose	busy	select	exactly	figure
	5. fix	busy	city	stop	repair
	6. gift	present	play	test	earth
	7. find	control	discover	listen	learn
	8. forest	job	desert	woods	book
	9. wrong	keep	kind	loose	incorrect
	10. cried	rabbit	wept	years	enough

LEVEL 4	Functioning Level:			Score: /10 = %	
+/–		A	B	C	D
	1. drink	beverage	taco	salt	clover
	2. harm	meadow	misty	injure	enjoy
	3. perhaps	maybe	necklace	squeeze	strange
	4. vacant	machine	empty	hopefully	wrapper
	5. divide	frighten	separate	finally	statue
	6. quarrel	wander	grab	argue	puppet
	7. prison	meter	handle	churn	jail
	8. collect	through	young	belong	gather
	9. heal	cure	join	prepare	bring
	10. gloomy	scratch	dreary	creature	ocean

LEVEL 5	Functioning Level:			Score: /10 = %	
+/–		A	B	C	D
	1. slender	language	piece	thin	valley
	2. able	capable	sudden	goal	entire
	3. toil	suddenly	tongue	model	work
	4. achieve	grant	start	accomplish	youth
	5. careful	shout	cautious	agree	state
	6. motion	dangerous	cellar	movement	shriek
	7. drapes	daze	curtains	treasure	giggle
	8. thief	pebble	blanket	gallop	criminal
	9. ascend	climb	harpoon	stitch	swung
	10. continue	persevere	separate	finish	level

(continued)

SYNONYM VOCABULARY ASSESSMENT (continued)

LEVEL 6   Functioning Level: Score: /10 =   %

+/−		A	B	C	D
	1. grateful	detest	appreciative	response	attain
	2. protect	shelter	officer	bounce	porch
	3. prohibit	engaged	possess	restrict	detest
	4. conceal	lawyer	female	hide	braids
	5. deposit	fountain	gophers	knotted	leave
	6. think	contemplate	assist	develop	discover
	7. delete	tardy	silent	repair	omit
	8. renew	restore	attend	wound	recent
	9. conclude	end	ransom	salt	fortress
	10. liquid	prejudice	fluid	radish	distemper

LEVEL 7–9   Functioning Level: Score: /10 =   %

+/−		A	B	C	D
	1. surplus	design	hearth	extra	mansion
	2. revise	alter	computer	militia	museum
	3. reduce	oxygen	condense	chariot	pliers
	4. erupt	allowance	huff	incredible	explode
	5. deport	ooze	banish	turret	walrus
	6. exhibit	trophy	accountant	privacy	display
	7. solitary	gravel	starvation	tassel	alone
	8. pout	bolt	wizard	sulk	fertilizer
	9. recede	lemonade	market	bruising	ebb
	10. precious	valuable	embarrass	smolder	injection

LEVEL 10–12   Functioning Level: Score: /10 =   %

+/−		A	B	C	D
	1. hazardous	aluminum	lavender	dangerous	famine
	2. elongate	portrait	stretch	retrieve	pigeon
	3. fierce	indelible	lariat	diplomat	savage
	4. caribou	scaffold	slalom	reindeer	awesome
	5. competition	rivalry	quench	ogre	sculpture
	6. demeanor	vanish	parallel	behavior	vertical
	7. inexhaustible	chancellor	derrick	infamy	tireless
	8. dissuade	dislocate	arouse	discourage	jovial
	9. aggregate	egret	total	obsidian	veer
	10. advisor	transistor	riveter	pageant	consultant

Diagnostic Literacy Assessments and Instructional Strategies: A Literacy Specialist's Resource by Stephanie L. McAndrews. © 2008 by the International Reading Association. May be copied for classroom use.

ANTONYM VOCABULARY ASSESSMENT

Name: _____ Grade: _____ Date: _____

Reading or Listening (circle one); if both, mark each level (R) for reading and (L) for listening.

Reading Directions: Tell the student, "Read each line of words. Draw a circle around the word that means the opposite of the first word in each line." Continue until the student reaches the frustration level or becomes frustrated, then repeat that grade level by having the student listen as you read the words. Continue again until the student reaches the frustration level.

Listening Directions: Tell the student, "Follow along as I read the words and draw a circle around the word that means the opposite of the first word in each line."

Scoring: In front of each line number, put a plus sign (+) if correct and a minus sign (–) if incorrect. Write total correct to determine functioning level.

Functioning Level: Independent (90%–100%), Instructional (70%–80%), Frustration (60% and below)

Practice Item	A	B	C	D
1. stop	boy	go	her	luck

LEVEL 1	Functioning Level:			Score: /10 = %
+/−	A	B	C	D
1. hot	red	help	cold	up
2. in	to	out	down	way
3. big	fast	little	give	her
4. wet	soon	help	dry	like
5. easy	hard	liked	old	look
6. tall	come	well	short	see
7. sick	well	dark	sing	call
8. up	made	down	love	come
9. happy	car	pit	sad	silly
10. kind	big	before	play	mean

LEVEL 2	Functioning Level:			Score: /10 = %
+/−	A	B	C	D
1. sit	play	stand	help	be
2. true	need	able	false	part
3. push	pull	name	fall	love
4. front	back	lower	side	simple
5. sweet	small	taste	sour	eat
6. smile	near	mean	frown	pretty
7. wrong	part	first	quiet	right
8. over	sign	under	listen	care
9. early	on	late	bump	moon
10. forget	lost	hurry	school	remember

(continued)

ANTONYM VOCABULARY ASSESSMENT (continued)

Functioning Level: Score: /10 =   %

+/−		A	B	C	D
	1. quick	tired	rough	draw	slow
	2. moist	dry	exit	taste	scent
	3. alone	perfect	together	camp	light
	4. weak	strong	sweet	guard	ring
	5. empty	long	different	moment	full
	6. poor	polite	hour	wealthy	missing
	7. neat	messy	drive	regular	cook
	8. dull	same	waste	bright	game
	9. add	follow	subtract	pay	fancy
	10. deep	shallow	never	warm	sell

LEVEL 4   Functioning Level: Score: /10 =   %

+/−		A	B	C	D
	1. certain	county	honest	cause	doubtful
	2. enjoy	trust	dislike	punish	attack
	3. southern	eastern	western	northern	map
	4. despair	hope	shy	clumsy	change
	5. nervous	pleased	relaxed	calm	asleep
	6. ashamed	middle	proud	curious	friendly
	7. forgive	blame	send	drive	promise
	8. expert	fitness	building	amateur	object
	9. confident	trust	insecure	forget	hungry
	10. vanish	hide	allow	jealous	appear

LEVEL 5   Functioning Level: Score: /10 =   %

+/−		A	B	C	D
	1. poverty	support	replay	wealth	inform
	2. rejected	related	special	interested	accepted
	3. alive	deceased	ancient	predator	attention
	4. abundance	scarce	liar	increase	profit
	5. solate	improve	disagree	reassure	include
	6. genuine	intelligent	natural	artificial	serious
	7. shrink	desire	expand	rotate	dissolve
	8. illegal	clumsy	compromise	lawful	observe
	9. reluctant	enthusiastic	increase	remain	begin
	10. avoid	honor	confront	replace	surrender

(continued)

ANTONYM VOCABULARY ASSESSMENT (continued)

LEVEL 6   Functioning Level: Score: /10 =   %

+/–		A	B	C	D
	1. vacant	mammal	occupied	rested	irresponsible
	2. authentic	impossible	elderly	imitation	physical
	3. cease	begin	minor	respect	measure
	4. apathetic	exhausted	concerned	motivated	professional
	5. disregard	active	understand	consider	believe
	6. excess	shortage	deny	gather	expensive
	7. destruction	association	foundation	reconsider	creation
	8. oblivious	typical	aware	frustrated	cheap
	9. arrogant	humble	official	convinced	brutal
	10. fatigue	heavy	energy	careless	imply

LEVEL 7–9   Functioning Level: Score: /10 =   %

+/–		A	B	C	D
	1. novice	experienced	praise	reprimand	cascade
	2. assault	resolve	expand	attempt	absorbent
	3. exhibit	concave	conductive	conceal	condescending
	4. conform	relocate	porous	revolt	distract
	5. withdrawn	outgoing	levitate	abrasion	implicit
	6. mediator	juvenile	legislator	adversary	monarch
	7. abolish	establish	apprehensive	diminish	aggressive
	8. sporadic	strict	optional	constant	restless
	9. extravagant	revived	restrained	intricate	retained
	10. harmless	tranquil	appeased	calamity	detrimental

LEVEL 10–12   Functioning Level: Score: /10 =   %

+/–		A	B	C	D
	1. harmony	reliable	discord	tentative	incline
	2. flustered	composed	hostility	slender	modest
	3. redundant	obliged	mediocre	concise	undeserving
	4. collaborate	flatter	resist	condescend	incapable
	5. discriminate	stabilized	generalize	hesitate	justifiable
	6. degrade	successful	retrospect	assessment	compliment
	7. naïve	sophisticated	pilgrim	fictitious	superficial
	8. precarious	tentative	emulate	stable	agitated
	9. substantiate	challenge	avoid	admire	incoherent
	10. expedite	irritable	impede	extensive	strict

CONSONANT AUDITORY DISCRIMINATION ASSESSMENT

Name: _____ Grade: _____ Date: _____

Directions: Sit shoulder to shoulder with the student, but facing away from one another so the student cannot see the words pronounced. Toward the student's ear say, "I am going to say two words, and I want you to tell me if they are the same or different."

Scoring: Record the student's response as *S* for same and *D* for different. Score with a plus sign (+) for correct and minus sign (–) for incorrect. Write the total score to determine functional level.

Functioning Level: Independent (36–40 correct or 90%–100%), Instructional (28–35 correct or 70%–88%), Frustration (27 correct and below or 68% and below)

Functioning Level: _____   Score: _____ / 40 = _____ %

	Response/Score			Response/Score
1. let-wet			21. pet-bet	
2. pass-pass			22. van-fan	
3. nine-line			23. wake-rake	
4. much-much			24. not-not	
5. think-sink			25. what-hut	
6. jet-jet			26. time-dime	
7. hiss-his			27. head-head	
8. map-nap			28. zoo-shoe	
9. hit-wit			29. pot-tot	
10. quick-quick			30. came-game	
11. big-dig			31. been-been	
12. kite-tight			32. quit-kit	
13. fat-that			33. gate-date	
14. gave-gave			34. where-where	
15. sell-shell			35. sun-sung	
16. right-right			36. jump-chump	
17. yell-well			37. some-some	
18. jeep-sheep			38. men-when	
19. share-chair			39. this-this	
20. come-come			40. dim-gym	

Analysis:

SHORT AND LONG VOWEL AUDITORY DISCRIMINATION ASSESSMENT

Name: _____ Grade: _____ Date: _____

Directions: Sitting shoulder to shoulder with the student but facing away from one another so the student cannot see the words pronounced, say, "I am going to say two words, and I want you to tell me if they are the same or different."

Scoring: Record the student's response as *S* for same and *D* for different. Score with a plus sign (+) for correct and minus sign (–) for incorrect. Write the total score to determine functional level.

Functioning Level: Independent (36–40 correct or 90%–100%), Instructional (28–35 correct or 70%–88%), Frustration (27 correct and below or 68% and below)

Functioning Level: _____   Score: ____ / 40 = ____ %

	Response/Score		Response/Score
1. get-get		21. cake-cake	
2. hat-hot		22. jean-June	
3. pet-pat		23. high-hay	
4. had-had		24. bite-beat	
5. nut-not		25. home-home	
6. him-him		26. tube-tube	
7. lad-lid		27. line-loan	
8. ham-hum		28. mule-mail	
9. pin-pen		29. week-week	
10. hip-hop		30. heap-hope	
11. tub-tub		31. rude-ride	
12. rod-red		32. name-name	
13. hut-hit		33. not-note	
14. job-job		34. teen-ten	
15. bet-but		35. mop-mop	
16. heat-heat		36. cute-cut	
17. tone-tune		37. big-big	
18. we-way		38. Tim-time	
19. hike-hike		39. mad-made	
20. cope-cape		40. feet-feet	

Analysis:

DIPHTHONG AND CONTROLLED VOWEL AUDITORY DISCRIMINATION ASSESSMENT

Name: _____ Grade: _____ Date: _____

Directions: Sit shoulder to shoulder with the student, but facing away from one another so the student cannot see the words pronounced. Toward the student's ear say, "I am going to say two words, and I want you to tell me if they are the same or different."

Scoring: Record the student's response as *S* for same and *D* for different. Score with a plus sign (+) for correct and minus sign (–) for incorrect.

Functioning Level: Independent (18–20 correct or 90%–100%), Instructional (14–17 correct or 70%–85%), Frustration (13 and below or 65% and below)

Functioning Level: _____   Score: _____ /20 = _____ %

	Response/Score		Response/Score
1. hall-hail		11. grow-grew	
2. pool-pole		12. shook-shook	
3. few-few		13. town-tune	
4. her-here		14. talk-took	
5. bowl-boil		15. shoot-shut	
6. foot-foot		16. cloud-clawed	
7. fair-far		17. our-or	
8. mood-mud		18. fund-found	
9. care-care		19. pull-Paul	
10. stir-steer		20. fur-for	

Analysis:

PHONEME BLENDING ASSESSMENT

Name: _____ Grade: _____ Date: _____

Directions: Say to the student, "Today we're going to play a word game. I'm going to say separate sounds, and I want you to say the word. For example, if I say '/o/-/l/-/d/', you should say 'old.'"(Note the words are not written phonetically but the way they are spelled.)

Practice Items: /r/i/de/, /g/o/, /m/a/n/

Scoring: Write a plus sign (+) for correct blending and minus sign (–) for incorrect blending and write the incorrect response.

Functioning Level: Independent (20–22), Instructional (15–19), Frustration (14 and below)

Functioning Level: _____ Score: /22 = %

	+ or – and response		+ or – and response
1. c/a/t		12. d/ay	
2. s/ee/d		13. p/l/a/ce	
3. m/i/ne		14. t/o	
4. g/o		15. th/r/ee	
5. h/e		16. j/o/b	
6. s/a/ve		17. th/i/s	
7. b/l/ue		18. r/i/ce	
8. wh/e/n		19. u/s	
9. b/e/d		20. s/t/o/p	
10. sh/e		21. m/y	
11. d/o/g		22. f/i/sh	

Analysis:

Adapted from Yopp, H.K. (1995). A test for assessing phonemic awareness in young students. *The Reading Teacher, 49*(1), 20–29.

PHONEME SEGMENTATION ASSESSMENT
(YOPP–SINGER TEST OF PHONEME SEGMENTATION)

Name: _____ Grade: _____ Date: _____

Directions: Say to the student, "Today we're going to play a word game. I'm going to say a word, and I want you to break the word apart. You are going to say each sound in the word in order. For example, if I say 'old,' you should say '/o/-/l/-/d/.'"

Practice Items: *ride*, *go*, *man*

Scoring: Write a plus sign (+) for correct segmenting and minus sign (–) for incorrect segmenting and write the incorrect response.

Functioning Level: Independent (20–22), Instructional (15–19), Frustration (14 and below)

Functioning Level: _____ Score: _____ /22 = _____ %

	+ or – and response		+ or – and response
1. dog	d/ŏ/g/	12. lay	l/ā
2. keep	k/ē/p	13. race	r/ă/s
3. fine	f/ī/n	14. zoo	z/ö
4. no	n/ō	15. three	th/r/ē
5. she	sh/ē	16. job	j/ŏ/b
6. wave	w/ā/v	17. in	ĭ/n
7. grew	g/r/ö	18. ice	ī/s
8. that	th/ă/t	19. at	ă/t
9. red	r/ĕ/d	20. top	t/ō/p
10. me	m/ē	21. by	b/ī
11. sat	s/ă/t	22. do	d/ö

Analysis:

From Yopp, H.K. (1995). A test for assessing phonemic awareness in young students. *The Reading Teacher*, *49*(1), 20–29. Reprinted with permission.

LETTER AND SOUND IDENTIFICATION ASSESSMENT

Name: _____ Grade: _____ Date: _____

Directions: Give the student a copy of the letter chart and place an index card under the first rows of letters. Say, "I want you to tell me the names of each letter and the sound or sounds it makes." Point to the first letter and say, "What letter is this?" Write the student's response on this record sheet. Ask, "Do you know what sound it makes?" If the letter is marked with an asterisk (*) there are multiple sounds so ask, "Do you know what other sound it makes?" If the student does not know a sound ask, "Do you know a word that starts with that letter?"

Scoring: Write a plus sign (+) for each correct letter and sound and minus sign (–) for incorrect and write out all incorrect responses. If a student says, "I don't know," write *IDK*. See the Sound column for correct responses.

Total Uppercase Letter Names: /26   Total Lowercase Letter Names: /28
Total Letter Sounds: /26

	Letter	Sound	Word		Letter	Sound	Word
B		/b/		b		/b/	
O*		/ŏ/ /ō/ /ö/		o*		/ŏ/ /ō/ /ö/	
S		/s/ /z/		s		/s/ /z/	
A*		/ă/ /ā/ /ŏ/		a*		/ă/ /ā/ /ŏ/	
W		/w/		w		/w/	
Z		/z/		z		/z/	
F		/f/		f		/f/	
H		/h/		h		/h/	
K		/k/		k		/k/	
J		/j/		j		/j/	
U*		/ŭ/ /ū/		u*		/ŭ/ /ū/	
				ɑ*			
C*		/k/ /s/		c*		/k/ /s/	
Y*		/y/ /ē/ /ī/ /ĭ/		y*		/y/ /ē/ /ī/ /ĭ/	
L		/l/		l		/l/	
Q		/kw/		q		/kw/	
M		/m/		m		/m/	
D		/d/		d		/d/	
N		/n/		n		/n/	
X		/ks/		x		/ks/	
I*		/ĭ/ /ī/		i*		/ĭ/ /ī/	
P		/p/		p		/p/	
E*		/ĕ/ /ē/		e*		/ĕ/ /ē/	
G*		/g/ /j/		g*		/g/ /j/	
R		/r/		r		/r/	
V		/v/		v		/v/	
T		/t/		t		/t/	
				g*			
Total	/26	/26		Total	/28	/26	

Analysis:

(continued)

Adapted from Clay, M.M. (1993b). *Reading recovery: A guidebook for teachers in training.* Portsmouth, NH: Heinemann.

B	O	S	A	W	Z
F	H	K	J	U	
C	Y	L	Q	M	
D	N	X	I	P	
E	G	R	V	T	

b	o	s	a	w	z
f	h	k	j	u	a
c	y	l	q	m	
d	n	x	i	p	
e	g	r	v	t	g

INDIVIDUAL PHONICS SUMMARY

Name: _____ Grade: _____ Date: _____

Directions: Use after literacy assessments have been completed and then after instruction. Highlight in yellow the elements missed while reading. Highlight in blue the elements missed while writing. Highlight in green the elements missed in both reading and writing. After instruction, circle each element once the student is able to read and write it correctly.

Consonants	Vowels
Initial Consonants b c d f g h j k l m n p qu r s t v w y z x /z/	Short Vowels a, e, i, o, u, y (/ĭ/) also a in "father", o in "to", o in "gone"
Final Consonants b d f g k l m n p t x z s /z/, /s/ v (followed by e)	Long Vowels a, e, i, o, u, y (/e/, /ī/, /ĭ/) Spelling: change y to i when adding suffix.
Initial Blends bl br cl cr dr fl fr gl gr pl pr sc scr sk sl sm sn sp spl st str squ tr thr tw	Long and Short Vowels With Silent -e a_e, e_e, i_e, o_e, u_e
Final Blends -ct -ld -mp -np -nk -nt -rb -rk -rl -rm -sk -sp	Vowel Digraphs ay, ai, ea, ee, ei, eigh, ey, ie, igh, oa, oe, oo in good, ö in moo, ou /ŭ/, ow /ō/, uy in buy
Consonant Digraphs With New Sound th (voiced, voiceless), wh, ch (/ch,/k/,/sh/), ph, ng, ck, dge, sh, ti, ci (/sh/) si (/sh/ or /zh/)	Diphthongs oi, oy, ou in ouch, ow in cow,
Consonant Digraphs With Silent Consonants gh kn wr pn rh	-ough Digraphs and Diphthongs /ō/, /oo/, /ŭf/, /ŏf/, /aw/ /ŏw/
Hard and Soft C /k/ /s/	-r, -l, -w, and -u controlled vowels /ar/ /or/; /al/ in all, /aw/ in saw, /au/ in autumn, /ew/ in new
Hard and Soft G /g/ /j/	Vocalic -r /er/: er, ir, ur, wor in work, ear in early, ar in grammar
Verb Tenses: -s, ing, -ed (/ed/ /d/ /t/) Suffixes: -er, -est, -ly	Plurals: -s, -es, irregular Plurals changing y to i
Doubling Consonants: following short vowels or when adding suffixes	

PHONICS SKILLS FOR GRADES K–3

Name: _____ Grade: _____ Date: _____

Directions: Use this as a grade level instructional guide or assessment.
Scoring: + or –

Skills Introduced and Mastered in Kindergarten

_____ Identifies all lowercase letters

_____ Identifies all uppercase letters

_____ Identifies the sounds of the following consonant letters: ___b, ___d, ___f, ___h, ___j, ___k, ___l, ___m, ___n, ___p, ___qu, ___r, ___s, ___t, ___v, ___w, ___x, ___y, ___z

_____ Identifies the hard sound of ___c: cat; ___g: get

Skills Introduced in Kindergarten

_____ Identifies the sounds of the short vowels: ___a, ___e, ___i, ___o, ___u

_____ Identifies the sounds of the long vowels: ___a, ___e, ___i, ___o, ___u

_____ Identifies the soft sounds ___/c/: city; ___/g/: giant, followed by e, i, or y

_____ Writes all letters correctly

_____ Uses inventive spelling, writes words with several correct consonants

Skills Mastered in First Grade

_____ Identifies both sounds of the following consonant letters: ___c, ___g, ___s

_____ Identifies the sound of /ck/ when it follows a short vowel

_____ Identifies the sounds of the vowels: ___a: at, ate, want; ___e: end, me; ___i: is, I; ___o: on, open, do; ___u: up, use, put; ___y: my, baby, gym

_____ Identifies the long-vowel sound with a silent e at the end of a word

_____ Identifies the sounds of the consonant digraphs: ___th: the, think; ___sh: she; ___ch: chair, school, ___wh: when

_____ Identifies the endings ___-ing; ___-ed: wanted, smiled, jumped; -s: cats

_____ Writes phonetically regular words correctly

_____ Uses inventive spelling, write words with most of the correct sounds

_____ Reads at least 100 words and writes at least 50 words on Fry's Instant Sight Word List

Skills Introduced in First Grade

_____ Identifies the sounds of the vowel digraphs: ___ie: pie, piece, friend; ___ei: either; ___ea: eat, great, bread; ___ee: see; ___oa: boat; ___ai: sail; ___ay: say; ___ui: fruit

_____ Identifies the sound of igh: night

_____ Identifies the sounds of digraphs/diphthongs: ___ou: out, four, you, should; ___ow: cow, grow; ___oi: oil; ___oy: boy; ___ew: new

_____ Identifies the sounds of ey: they, key

_____ Identifies the sounds of oo: moon, book, floor

_____ Identifies the sounds of the vocalic r: ___er: her; ___ir: first; ___ur: nurse; ___or: works; ___ear: early; ___ar: grammar

_____ Identifies r-, l-, w-, and u-controlled vowels: ___ar, ___or, ___al, ___aw, ___au

_____ Identifies the ending ___-es, ___-ly

_____ Identifies the sound of /ng/: sing, song

_____ Identifies the sound of the consonant digraph ___ph

(continued)

PHONICS SKILLS FOR GRADES K–3 (continued)

Skills Mastered in Second Grade

_____ Identifies the sounds of the vowel digraphs: ___ie: pie, piece, friend; ___ei: either; ___ea: eat, great, bread; ___ee: meet; ___oa: boat; ___ai: rain; ___ay: say; ___ui: fruit

_____ Identifies the sound of igh: night

_____ Identifies the sounds of the digraphs/diphthongs: ___ou: out, four, you, should; ___ow: cow, grow; ___oi: oil; ___oy: boy; ___ew: new

_____ Identifies the sounds of ey: they, key

_____ Identifies the sounds of oo: moon, book, floor

_____ Identifies the sounds of the vocalic r: ___ er: her; ___ir: first; ___ur: nurse; ___or: works; ___ear: early; ___ar: grammar

_____ Identifies r-, l-, w-, and u-controlled vowels: ___ar, ___or, ___al, ___aw, ___au

_____ Identifies the sound of /ng/: sing, song

_____ Identifies the sound of the consonant digraph ___ph

_____ Reads at least 200 words and writes at least 100 words on Fry's Instant Sight Word List

Skills Introduced in Second Grade

_____ Identifies the sound of /kn/: knock

_____ Identifies silent l and b: walk, climb

_____ Identifies the sound of /dge/ used after a short vowel

_____ Identifies the sound of /gh/: ghost, used at the beginning of a word

_____ Identifies the sound of /wr/: wrap

_____ Identifies words that end in a /v/ sound are followed by an e: have, love

Skills Mastered in Third Grade

_____ Identifies the sound of /kn/: knock

_____ Identifies silent l and b: walk, climb

_____ Identifies the sound of /dge/: dodge

_____ Identifies the sound of /gh/: ghost

_____ Identifies the sound of /gn/: gnat, reign

_____ Identifies the sound of /ei/: veil, forfeit

_____ Identifies words that end in a /v/ sound are followed by an e: have, love

Skills Introduced and Mastered in Third Grade

_____ Identifies the sounds of /ough/: though, through, rough, cough, thought, bough

_____ Identifies the sounds of /eigh/: eight, height

_____ Identifies the sounds of ___ /ti/: nation; ___ /si/: session, vision; ___ /ci/: special; ___ /ch/: machine

_____ Identifies all the previous phonics skills

_____ Reads at least 300 words and writes at least 200 words on Fry's Instant Sight Word List

EMERGENT TEXT CONCEPTS ASSESSMENT

Name: _____ Grade: _____ Date: _____

Title/Author: _____ Level: _____

Directions: Select a picture book with a picture and two to three lines of print on each page. For questions 1–7, first ask the questions then read the page. For questions 8–25, read each page and then ask the questions. Fill in the blanks on questions 15–17.

Scoring: Write the student's responses and a plus sign (+) if correct and a minus sign (–) if incorrect. If any of the concepts are absent write "N/A" and change the denominator of the fraction for the total number of questions.

What You Do	What You Say	Response
Hold book with spine to the student.	1. Where is the front of the book?	
Show the cover and read the title and author of the book. Ask the question. Read the statement.	2. What do you think this book is going to be about? I'll read this story and you can help me.	
Find the first page with a picture and print. (Read any text on preceding pages without pictures and then stop.)	3. Where do I begin reading? Read the page.	
On the next page that has at least two lines of text, ask questions and then read the page.	4. Show me where to start. 5. Which way do I go? 6. Where do I go next? 7. Point to each word as I read.	
On the next page, read the following prompts:	8. Point to the first word on the page. 9. Point to the last word on the page. 10. Show me the bottom of the picture.	
Read along until you come to a period, question mark, comma, and quotation marks, then stop, point, and ask questions.	11. What's this for (.)? 12. What's this for (?)? 13. What's this for (,)? 14. What are these for ("")?	
Find two letters that have both an uppercase and lowercase on that page. Point to the uppercase letter and ask...	15. Can you find a lowercase letter like this? (point to uppercase ____) 16. Can you find a capital or uppercase letter like this? (point to lowercase ____)	
Read until you find a page with two words that start with the same lowercase letter. Select the second.	17. Can you find the word _____?	
Find a page with preferably one line of text or cover one line of text. Read the page. Hand the student two index cards and demonstrate how to close them like a curtain.	18. I want you to close the cards like this until all you can see is one letter. 19. Now show me two letters. 20. Show me just one word. 21. Now show me two words. 22. Show me the first letter of a word. 23. Show me the last letter of a word. 24. Show me an uppercase letter.	
Read to the end of book.	25. What was this story about?	
Analysis:		Score: /25

Adapted from Clay (1993a). *An observation survey of early literacy achievement.* Portsmouth, NH: Heinemann.

GRADED READING WORDS ASSESSMENT

Name: _____ Grade: _____ Date: _____

Directions: Give the student a copy of the appropriate reading word list and an index card. For emergent readers, write the words on index cards and present them one at a time. Say, "Read each word and then move the card down as you read each line. I cannot help you, so if you do not know a word, try to figure it out."

Scoring: Above each word, write a plus sign (+) for correct and a minus sign (–) for incorrect and phonetically write all incorrect responses, with vowels marked. Put a slash for every two seconds the student pauses and between decoded parts of words. Try to finish all the words within one grade level. Continue until the frustration level is reached.

Functioning Level: Independent (18–20), Instructional (14–17), and Frustration (13 and below)

Preprimer Reading Words   Functioning Level: _____

Automatic Score: _____ / 20 words = _____%   Total Score: _____ / 20 words = _____%

a	to	in	is	he
I	at	have	go	see
cat	can	like	the	mom
on	dog	dad	and	we

Primer Reading Words   Functioning Level: _____

Automatic Score: _____ / 20 words = _____%   Total Score: _____ / 20 words = _____%

by	what	are	for	his
then	with	my	this	all
you	from	she	do	made
was	her	how	saw	that

Grade 1 Reading Words   Functioning Level: _____

Automatic Score: _____/ 20 words = _____%   Total Score: _____ / 20 words = _____%

of	about	many	each	when
why	which	there	play	down
little	they	new	out	one
some	good	said	going	other

Analysis:

(continued)

Name: _____ Grade: _____ Date: _____

Grade 2 Reading Words   Functioning Level:_____

Automatic Score:_____ / 20 words = _____%   Total Score: _____ / 20 words = _____%

very	before	right	goes	always
around	works	great	their	don't
where	use	would	who	your
wanted	first	please	talked	long

Grade 3 Reading Words   Functioning Level:_____

Automatic Score:_____ / 20 words =_____%   Total Score: _____ / 20 words = _____%

favorite	really	family	because	people
friend	again	another	everyone	sometimes
thought	walked	called	writing	carried
doesn't	early	once	we're	believe

Grade 4 Reading Words   Functioning Level:_____

Automatic Score:_____ / 20 words =_____%   Total Score: _____ / 20 words = _____%

been	different	they're	beautiful	piece
pretty	knew	sign	brought	finally
trouble	learned	usually	excited	whether
half	weight	whole	through	tomorrow

Analysis:

(continued)

GRADED READING WORDS ASSESSMENT (continued)

Name: _____ Grade: _____ Date: _____

Grade 5 Reading Words   Functioning Level:_____

Automatic Score:_____ / 20 words = _____%   Total Score: _____ / 20 words = _____%

heard	couldn't	conclusion	library	environment
watched	sure	laughed	terrible	excellent
knowledge	experience	certain	athletic	difference
separate	height	probably	opinion	picture

Grade 6–8 Reading Words   Functioning Level:_____

Automatic Score:_____ / 20 words =_____%   Total Score: _____ / 20 words = _____%

absence	challenge	government	humorous	curious
business	attendance	emergency	unnecessary	exercise
secretary	similar	straight	thorough	sincerely
receipt	success	restaurant	special	familiar

Grade 9–12 Reading Words   Functioning Level:_____

Automatic Score:_____ / 20 words = _____%   Total Score: _____ / 20 words = _____%

achievement	beneficial	accidentally	extraordinary	analyze
permanent	exception	especially	independence	naturally
acceptable	efficiency	conscientious	committee	technique
tournament	vision	ridiculous	guarantee	acquaintance

Analysis:

(continued)

GRADED READING WORDS ASSESSMENT (continued)

Name: _____ Grade: _____ Date: _____

a	by	of	very
to	what	about	before
in	are	many	right
is	for	each	goes
he	his	when	always
I	then	why	around
at	with	which	works
have	my	there	great
go	this	play	their
see	all	down	don't
cat	you	little	where
can	from	they	use
like	she	new	would
the	do	out	who
mom	made	one	your
on	was	some	wanted
dog	her	good	first
dad	how	said	please
and	saw	going	talked
we	that	other	long

(continued)

Diagnostic Literacy Assessments and Instructional Strategies: A Literacy Specialist's Resource by Stephanie L. McAndrews. © 2008 by the International Reading Association. May be copied for classroom use.

GRADED READING WORDS ASSESSMENT (continued)

Name: _____ Grade: _____ Date: _____

favorite	been	heard	absence	achievement
really	different	couldn't	challenge	beneficial
family	they're	conclusion	government	accidentally
because	beautiful	library	humorous	extraordinary
people	piece	environment	curious	analyze
friend	pretty	watched	business	permanent
again	knew	sure	attendance	exception
another	sign	laughed	emergency	especially
everyone	brought	terrible	unnecessary	independence
sometimes	finally	excellent	exercise	naturally
thought	trouble	knowledge	secretary	acceptable
walked	learned	experience	similar	efficiency
called	usually	certain	straight	conscientious
writing	excited	athletic	thorough	committee
carried	whether	difference	sincerely	technique
doesn't	half	separate	receipt	tournament
early	weight	height	success	vision
once	whole	probably	restaurant	ridiculous
we're	through	opinion	special	guarantee
believe	tomorrow	picture	familiar	acquaintance

(continued)

FRY'S INSTANT SIGHT WORDS: FIRST HUNDRED

Name: _____ Grade: _____ Date: _____

Reading or Writing Assessment (circle one)   Score: /100 =   %

Reading Directions: Give the student a copy of this word list and an index card. For emergent readers, write the words on index cards and present them one at a time. Say, "Read each word and move the card down as you read each line. If you do not know a word, try to figure it out."

Writing Directions: Give the student lined paper and fold it in columns. Read each word clearly to the student. If the word is a homophone, provide a sentence. Say, "Write each word I say and then go to the next line. If you do not know a word, try to write as many letters as you can."

Scoring: Write a plus sign (+) for the correct word and minus sign (–) for an incorrect word, and write all incorrect responses phonetically.

a	can	her	many	see	us
about	come	here	me	she	very
after	day	him	much	so	was
again	did	his	my	some	we
all	do	how	new	take	were
an	down	I	no	that	what
and	eat	if	not	the	when
any	for	in	of	their	which
are	from	is	old	them	who
as	get	it	on	then	will
at	give	just	one	there	with
be	go	know	or	they	work
been	good	like	other	this	would
before	had	little	our	three	you
boy	has	long	out	to	your
but	have	make	put	two	
by	he	man	said	up	

From Fry, E.B., Kress, J.E., & Fountoukidis, D.L. (1993). *The reading teacher's book of lists* (3rd ed.). Upper Saddle River, NJ: Prentice Hall.

FRY'S INSTANT SIGHT WORDS: SECOND HUNDRED

Name: _____ Grade: _____ Date: _____

Reading or Writing Assessment (circle one)   Score: /100 =   %

also	color	home	must	red	think
am	could	house	name	right	too
another	dear	into	near	run	tree
away	each	kind	never	saw	under
back	ear	last	next	say	until
ball	end	leave	night	school	upon
because	far	left	only	seem	use
best	find	let	open	shall	want
better	first	live	over	should	way
big	five	look	own	soon	where
black	found	made	people	stand	while
book	four	may	play	such	white
both	friend	men	please	sure	wish
box	girl	more	present	tell	why
bring	got	morning	pretty	than	year
call	hand	most	ran	these	
came	high	mother	read	thing	

From Fry, E.B., Kress, J.E., & Fountoukidis, D.L. (1993). *The reading teacher's book of lists* (3rd ed.). Upper Saddle River, NJ: Prentice Hall.

FRY'S INSTANT SIGHT WORDS: THIRD HUNDRED

Name: _____ Grade: _____ Date: _____

Reading or Writing Assessment (circle one)　　　　　　　　Score:　　/100 =　　%

along	didn't	food	keep	sat	through
always	does	full	letter	second	today
anything	dog	funny	longer	set	took
around	don't	gave	love	seven	town
ask	door	goes	might	show	try
ate	dress	green	money	sing	turn
bed	early	grow	myself	sister	walk
brown	eight	hat	now	sit	warm
buy	every	happy	o'clock	six	wash
car	eyes	hard	off	sleep	water
carry	face	head	once	small	woman
clean	fall	hear	order	start	write
close	fast	help	pair	stop	yellow
clothes	fat	hold	part	ten	yes
coat	fine	hope	ride	thank	yesterday
cold	fire	hot	round	third	
cut	fly	jump	same	those	

From Fry, E.B., Kress, J.E., & Fountoukidis, D.L. (1993). *The reading teacher's book of lists* (3rd ed.). Upper Saddle River, NJ: Prentice Hall.

GRADED WRITING WORDS ASSESSMENT

Name: _____ Grade: _____ Date: _____

Directions: Give the student lined paper and fold it into two columns. Read each word clearly to the student. If the word is a common homophone, as indicated by an asterisk (*), provide a sentence for the student to understand the context of the word. Say, "Write each word I say, then go to the next line. If you do not know a word, try to write as many letters for the sounds as you can." For the preprimer list, ask the student to write their name, the words on the list, and then if at the frustration level ask if they can write any other words.

Scoring: Above each word, write a plus sign (+) for the correct word and a minus sign (–) for the incorrect word and write all incorrect responses. Be sure to record reversals and uppercase letters. Continue until frustration level is reached.

Functioning Level: Independent (18–20), Instructional (14–17), and Frustration (13 and below)

Developmental Spelling Stage:

Conventional	Transitional	Phonetic	Semiphonetic	Prephonetic
The word is spelled correctly.	Overgeneralizes when applying simple spelling rules. All sounds are represented graphically.	Use of a vowel; at least half of the sounds are graphically represented.	Some sound-symbol relationships, 1–2 letters could represent a word.	Letters or shapes are written but do not represent the sounds.

Preprimer Writing Words   Functioning Level: _____   Score: _____ / _____ words asked = _____ %
Developmental Stage:

Ask, "Can you write your first name and last name?" _____

a	to*	in	is	he
I	at	have	go	see*
cat	can	like	the	mom
on	dog	dad	and	we

Do you know how to write any other words?" _____

_____

_____

Analysis:

(continued)

GRADED WRITING WORDS ASSESSMENT (continued)

Name: _____ Grade: _____ Date: _____

Primer Writing Words   Functioning Level: _____   Score: _____ / 20 words = _____%
                             Developmental Stage:

by*	what	are	for	his
then	with	my	this	all
you	from	she	do*	made
was	her	how	saw	that

Grade 1 Writing Words   Functioning Level: _____   Score: _____ / 20 words = _____%
                              Developmental Stage:

of	about	many	each	when
why	which*	there*	play	down
little	they	new*	out	one*
some*	good	said	going	other

Grade 2 Writing Words   Functioning Level: _____   Score: _____ / 20 words = _____%
                              Developmental Stage:

very*	before	right*	goes	always
around	works	great*	their*	don't
where*	use	would*	who	your*
wanted	first	please	talked	long

Grade 3 Writing Words   Functioning Level: _____   Score: _____ / 20 words = _____%
                              Developmental Stage:

favorite	really	family	because	people
friend	again	another	everyone	sometimes
thought	walked	called	writing	carried
doesn't	early	once	we're	believe

Analysis:

(continued)

GRADED WRITING WORDS ASSESSMENT (continued)

Name: _____ Grade: _____ Date: _____

Grade 4 Writing Words   Functioning Level: _____   Score: _____ / 20 words = _____%
Developmental Stage:

been	different	they're*	beautiful	piece*
pretty	knew*	sign	brought	finally
trouble	learned	usually	excited	whether*
half	weight*	whole*	through*	tomorrow

Grade 5 Writing Words   Functioning Level: _____   Score: _____ / 20 words = _____%
Developmental Stage:

heard*	couldn't	conclusion	library	environment
watched	sure	laughed	terrible	excellent
knowledge	experience	certain	athletic	difference
separate	height	probably	opinion	picture

Grade 6–8 Writing Words   Functioning Level: _____   Score: _____ / 20 words = _____%
Developmental Stage:

absence	challenge	government	humorous	curious
business	attendance	emergency	unnecessary	exercise
secretary	similar	straight	thorough	sincerely
receipt	success	restaurant	special	familiar

Grade 9–12 Writing Words   Functioning Level: _____   Score: _____ / 20 words = _____%
Developmental Stage:

achievement	beneficial	accidentally	extraordinary	analyze
permanent	exception	especially	independence	naturally
acceptable	efficiency	permanent	committee	technique
tournament	vision	ridiculous	guarantee	acquaintance

Analysis:

SENTENCE DICTATION ASSESSMENT

Name: _____ Grade: _____ Date: _____

Directions: Give the student lined paper. Say, "I am going to read you a story, and then I will go back and read one word at a time. Write down each word I say. If you do not know how to write a word, say the word to yourself, and write down the letters for the sounds you hear."

Scoring: Write a plus sign (+) above all the correct words and a minus sign (–) for deleted words. For misspelled words write the student's response above the word. Count each correct underlined phoneme-grapheme correlation and total them. Continue to the next grade level until the frustration level is reached.

Functioning Level: Independent (90%–100%), Instructional (70%–89%), Frustration (69% and below)

Kindergarten and Primer   Functioning Level: _____   Score: _____ /41 graphemes

I have a big dog at home. Today I am going to take him to school.

Clay, M. (1993)

First and Second Grade   Functioning Level: _____   Score: _____ /51 graphemes

The farmer saw the black and white toy boat out on the water.

It floated under the shiny steel bridge to a small beach.

McAndrews, S.L. (2005)

Third Grade and Above   Functioning Level: _____   Score: _____ /157 graphemes

Today I saw a little girl walking in the cool water along the breezy beach in Florida. She asked, "Chris, do you know where my two blue toy sailboats are?" I said, "I think they floated under that new bridge and the huge waves might have brought them up on the jagged shore over there." "Why don't you put on your shoes because you could get hurt climbing?" We found only a small piece of one boat in the soil. I exclaimed, "Let's head back, it's getting quite dark! Now don't worry, we'll start looking again early tomorrow."

Analysis: Use the headings on the Individual Phonics Summary and list graphemes not represented correctly or write a plus sign (+) if all of them are correct.

GOOD READERS BOOKMARKS

Primary Bookmark

Intermediate Through High School Bookmarks

Good Readers:

- Look at the pictures and think about the story

- Say the beginning three sounds

- Read on to collect clues

- Go back and read again

- Break words into parts

- Try different sounds

- Think:

    - Does it make sense?

    - Does it sound right?

    - Does it look right?

- Self-correct

- Summarize

Good Readers:

- Look at the graphics and headings and think about the text

- Say the beginning three sounds and predict word

- Read on to collect clues

- Go back and read again

- Break words into parts (think about meaning of prefix, suffix, and root)

- Try different sounds

- Use glossary or dictionary

- Think:

    - Does it make sense?

    - Does it sound right?

    - Does it look right?

- Self-correct

- Summarize

Good Readers:

- Look at the graphics and headings and think about the text

- Say the beginning three sounds and predict word

- Read on to collect clues

- Go back and read again

- Break words into parts (think about meaning of prefix, suffix, and root)

- Try different sounds

- Use glossary or dictionary

- Think:

    - Does it make sense?

    - Does it sound right?

    - Does it look right?

- Self-correct

- Summarize

ANALYSIS OF MISCUES WORKSHEET

Name: _____ Grade: _____ Date: _____

Title: _____ Word Count: _____ Text Level: _____

Student Response/Text	Type of Miscue						Type of Cues Used			Meaning Retained
	Self-Correction	Uncorrected Miscue	Omission	Insertion	Decoded	Substitution	Graphophonic I = Initial, M = medial, F = final	Syntactic	Semantic	
1.										
2.										
3.										
4.										
5.										
6.										
7.										
8.										
9.										
10.										
11.										
12.										
13.										
14.										
15.										
16.										
17.										
18.										
19.										
20.										
21.										
22.										
23.										
24.										
25.										
26.										
27.										
28.										
Totals:										

ORAL READING ANALYSIS OF MISCUES SUMMARY

Name: _____ Grade: _____ Date: _____

Title: _____ Word Count: _____ Level: _____

Text Type: Narrative, Descriptive, Expository, or Persuasive

ORAL READING SUMMARY

Type of score	Calculation	Fraction	Percentage	Functioning level*
Word accuracy	Word count – Uncorrected miscues / Word count			
Text meaning or acceptability	Words correct + Uncorrected meaning – Retained miscues / Word Count			
Miscue Scores				
Self-correction	Self-corrections / Number of miscues			
Omissions	Omissions / Number of miscues			
Insertions	Insertions / Number of miscues			
Decoded sounds or nonwords	Decoded sounds / Number of miscues			
Substitutions of real words	Substitutions / Number of miscues			
Cueing System Scores				
Graphophonic	Number of graphophonic cues used / Number of miscues			
Syntactic	Number of syntactic cues used / Number of miscues			
Semantic	Number of semantic cues used / Number of miscues			

Functioning Level*	Independent	Instructional	Frustration
Oral Accuracy	95%–100%	90%–94%	89% and below
Oral Acceptability	98%–100%	95%–97%	94% and below
Comprehension	90%–100%	70%–89%	69% and below

Functioning Levels for Cueing System
75–100%   Predominantly Used Cue
50–74%   Often Used Cue
20–49%   Sometimes Used Cue
19% and below Rarely Used Cue

* To obtain a true functioning level, comprehension must also be assessed.

Analysis:

CODING AND SCORING ORAL READING BEHAVIORS GUIDE

Behavior	Example Student Response	Example Word From List or Text	Description (Record above the correct word)
Correct pronunciation of word	+ or ✓	come	Plus sign for word lists or checkmark for text reading
Substitution: With another word	house	horse	Word said
Substitution: Nonword with different vowel sounds	rēb	red	Write phonetic pronunciation, mark all incorrect vowels with breve (ĕ short) or macron (ē long)
Substitution: With alternate consonant sounds	dēkīd	decide	Use dominant letter such as *k* for hard /c/, and *s* for soft /c/, *g* for hard /g/ and *j* for soft /g/
Substitution: Decoded with pauses between sounds	m/ă/d	mad	Put slashes for pauses, mark all incorrect vowels with short or long marks
Substitution: Chunked sounds	/to/get/her/	together	Put slashes between each group of sounds
Substitution: Spelled letter	r-e-a-d	read	Hyphens for each letter said
Substitution: Mispronunciation is due to articulation	pŭskĕtē	spaghetti	Record phonetic pronunciation with vowels markes. If in doubt ask for a sentence. Not an error.
Substitution: Mispronunciation is due to reader's dialect	goin'	going	Record phonetic pronunciation. If in doubt ask for a sentence. Not an error.
Omission of word	–	friends	Hyphen for omitted word
Insertion of word	little	^	Caret for inserted word during text reading
Multiple attempts	thr, three	there	Write each attempt with a comma between them.
Self correction*	saw, /w/ s-c	was	Word(s) said incorrect initially and then self-corrected
Hesitation*	// ✓	He // laughed	1 slash per 2 seconds. Not an error.
Repetition of word or phrase*	✓ ®	because ✓ ®	Check and put a circled *R* each time repeated and score as correct. During text reading put an arrow back to where the repetition began.
Correct then incorrect	✓ three	there, three	Put a check and then write incorrect response, scored as incorrect

* Not counted against word accuracy in text reading

ORAL READING STRATEGIES ASSESSMENT

Name: _____ Date: _____

Directions: While the student is orally reading, identify the strategies that are used in order to figure out words. This can be used for a single text reading or a summary of readings.

Scoring: Record a plus sign (+) if this strategy was used frequently, a checkmark (✓) if the strategy was used occasionally, and minus sign (–) if the strategy was used rarely or not at all.

	Look at the pictures and think about the story
	Say the beginning three sounds
	Read on to collect clues, then go back
	Go back and read again
	Break words into parts
	Try different sounds
	Attempts to self-correct words that do not look right
	Attempts to self-correct words that do not sound right
	Attempts to self-corrects words that do not make sense
	Self-corrects words

FLUENCY ASSESSMENT BY TEACHERS AND PEERS

Name: _____ Date: _____

Title/Author: _____ Level: _____ Genre: _____

The student...	Generally Fluent (+)	Sometimes Fluent (✓)	Rarely Fluent (−)
read in phrases score:	Read sentences in meaningful phrases or clauses	Read in a mixture of appropriate phrasing and word by word	Read only one to two words at a time
paid attention to punctuation score:	Paused after end (period, question mark, exclamation point) and middle punctuation (comma, semicolon, colon)	Usually paused at end punctuation but not always middle punctuation	Rarely paused at punctuation
read with expression score:	Read with appropriate stress and intonation; changes voice for expression as needed; read with emphasis for dramatization or read with different voices	Read with some appropriate expression and some changes in stress and intonation	Read with little expression or change in stress and intonation
read smoothly score:	Reading sounded smooth, with only a few short pauses for problem solving when needed	Reading was generally smooth, with some hesitations and repetitions	Reading sounded choppy, with several skipped words, hesitations, or repetitions
used problem-solving strategies efficiently score:	After the first strategy attempted, most meaning miscues were self-corrected	Two to three strategies were attempted and most meaning miscues were self-corrected	Multiple strategies were attempted and often did not result in self-correction
read at a conversational pace score:	The reading pace was like that of a conversation, not too fast or too slow for others to understand	At times, the reading pace was either a little too fast or a little too slow	The reading pace was very slow and labored
read at an independent word accuracy level score:	Read at an independent word accuracy level (95% or higher word accuracy, less than 5 miscues per 100 words)	Read at an instructional word accuracy level (90%–94% word accuracy, between 6–10 miscues per 100 words)	Read at a frustration level (89% or below word accuracy, 11 or more miscues per 100 words)
Comprehended or retold what was read score:	Retold all of the elements of the story or the main idea and major details	Retold most of the elements of the story or the main idea and major details	Could not retell the important elements of the story or the main idea and major details

Analysis:

ONGOING SELF-EVALUATION OF FLUENCY

Name: _____ Date: _____

Title/Author: _____ Level: _____ Genre: _____

	Generally Fluent (+)	Sometimes Fluent (✓)	Rarely Fluent (–)
I read in phrases. score:	I read sentences in phrases.	I read some sentences in phrases.	I often read word by word.
I paused at middle punctuation and end punctuation. score:	I paused after end (period, question mark, exclamation point) and middle punctuation (comma, semicolon, colon).	I paused at most end punctuation, but not always for middle punctuation.	I often did not pause after punctuation.
My voice changed to show expression and match the meaning and emotions in the passage. score:	I changed my voice to show expression or different characters when needed.	I sometimes changed my voice to show expression or different characters when needed.	I often did not change my voice to show expression or different characters when needed.
I read smoothly. score:	My reading was smooth, with only a few short pauses if I needed to figure out words.	Sometimes my reading was smooth, and sometimes I needed to stop or reread more often.	My reading sounds choppy. I skipped words, stopped, or reread often.
I used strategies to correct my reading if it didn't make sense. score:	I was able to quickly correct my reading if it didn't make sense.	It took some time, but I used several strategies to correct my reading if it didn't make sense.	I did not or could not correct my reading if it didn't make sense.
I read at a conversational pace. score:	I read at a conversational pace.	Sometimes I read at a conversational pace, but other times I read too fast or too slow.	I read very slowly.
I can read most of the words. score:	I could read almost all of the words.	I could read most of the words.	I could not read many words.
I can retell what I read. score:	I can retell all of the important parts of the story or explain the main idea and major details in nonfiction.	I can retell most of the important parts of the story or explain the main idea and major details in nonfiction.	I cannot retell the important parts of the story or the main idea and major details in nonfiction.

Analysis:

GOOD READERS POSTER

Good Readers........

Look at the pictures and think about the story.

Say the beginning 3 sounds. blocks

Read on to collect clues.

Go back and read again.

Break words into parts. paint + er = painter

Try different sounds.   cane

Think:

    Does it make sense?

    Does it sound right?

    Does it look right?

Self-correct.

Summarize.

ORAL READING STRATEGY CHECKLIST FOR TEACHERS

Name: _____ Date: _____

Title/Author: _____ Level: _____ Genre: _____

Strategies: Place a tally mark each time a strategy is used by the student.

_____ Look at the pictures and think about the story.

_____ Say the beginning three sounds.

_____ Read on to collect clues.

_____ Go back and read again.

_____ Break words into parts.

_____ Try different sounds.

_____ Miscues have similar meanings.

_____ Miscues are visually similar.

_____ Miscues have similar syntax.

_____ Self-correct.

_____ Summarize.

Teacher Prompts: Place a tally mark for each prompt given.

_____ Provide wait time.

_____ Look at the pictures and think about the story.

_____ Say the beginning three sounds.

_____ Read on to collect clues.

_____ Go back and read again.

_____ Break words into parts.

_____ Try different sounds.

_____ Does that make sense?

_____ Does that look right?

_____ Does that sound right?

_____ Where is the tricky part?

_____ Are you right?

_____ How do you know?

_____ What else can you do?

_____ Try that again?

_____ Summarize

Observations:

ORAL READING STRATEGY CHECKLIST FOR PEERS

Name: _____ Date: _____

Reader's Name: _____ Title/Author: _____

Directions: Put a stamp each time the reader uses a strategy.

1. Look at the pictures and think about the story.

2. Say the beginning 3 sounds. **B** **L** **O** blocks

3. Read on to collect clues.

4. Go back and read again.

5. Break words into parts.   paint + er = painter

6. Try different sounds.   can   cane

7. Think:

     Does it make sense?

     Does it sound right?

     Does it look right?

8. Self-correct.

Strategy number that worked well ✚ _____, Strategy number that might help ✔ _____

Comments:

ORAL READING STRATEGY CHECKLIST FOR SELF

Name: _____ Date: _____

Title/Author: _____ Level: _____ Genre: _____

Directions: After reading or listening to a tape recording of your reading, put a stamp each time you use a strategy.

1. Look at the pictures and think about the story.

2. Say the beginning 3 sounds. **B** **L** **O** blocks

3. Read on to collect clues.

4. Go back and read again.

5. Break words into parts. paint + er = painter

6. Try different sounds. can cane

7. Think:

   Does it make sense?

   Does it sound right?

   Does it look right?

8. Self-correct.

9. Summarize.

Strategy number that worked well _____, Strategy number that might help _____

Comments:

READERS THEATRE RUBRIC ANALYSIS

Name: _____ Date: _____

Title/Author: _____ Grade: _____ Level: _____

Directions: Read the indicators for each element of the Readers Theatre Rubric Analysis and rate the student or have the student rate themselves on the basis of the student's performance. Write a plus sign (+) for excellent, a checkmark (✓) for satisfactory, and a minus sign (−) for needs work.

	Excellent +	Satisfactory ✓	Needs Work −	Score
Phrasing and punctuation	Read sentences in meaningful phrases or clauses and paused appropriately for punctuation	Read with some appropriate phrases and paused for punctuation	Read only one to two words at a time, rarely pausing for punctuation	
Expression	Changed expression, stress, intonation, and voice as appropriate for character or narrator	Some change in expression, stress, intonation, and voice as appropriate for character or narrator	Rarely used or changed expression	
Volume	Read at an appropriate volume and loud enough for the audience to hear	Usually read loud enough for audience to hear	Read too loud or too soft for audience to hear	
Clarity	Words are pronounced correctly and clearly	Most words are pronounced correctly and clearly	Many words are pronounced incorrectly or not clearly	
Pace	Read at a conversational pace	Often read at a conversational pace but may be inconsistent	The pace is either too fast or too slow	
Timing	Consistently took turns in a timely fashion	Took turns but not always in a timely fashion	Rarely took turns in a timely fashion; had to be prompted to read	
Facial and body language	Frequently used facial expressions and body language to communicate the story	Used some facial expressions and body language to communicate the story	Rarely used facial expressions and body language to communicate the story	
Interpretation	Correctly and imaginatively interpreted each scene	Most scenes were interpreted correctly	Most scenes were not correctly interpreted	
Staging	Stood and moved appropriately in relation to others	Sometimes stood and moved appropriately in relation to others	Rarely stood and moved appropriately in relation to others	
Cooperation	Consistently worked well with others	Sometimes worked well with others	Difficulty in working well with others	

Analysis:

COMPREHENSION ANALYSIS SUMMARY

Name: _____ Grade: _____ Date: _____

Title: _____ Word Count: _____ Level: _____

Text Type: Narrative, Descriptive, Expository, or Persuasive   Reading Method: Silent or Listening

COMPREHENSION ANALYSIS SUMMARY

Prior Knowledge (+, ✓, —)	
Prediction (+, ✓, —)	
Retelling (+, ✓, —) **Narrative** **Expository** Characters Main Idea Setting Details Plot Main Idea Resolution Details	

Comprehension Score	Without Look Backs	With Look Backs*
Explicit Questions: right there	____/ ____ = ____%	____/ ____ = ____%
Implicit Questions: inference	____/ ____ = ____%	____/ ____ = ____%
Total Correct	____/ ____ = ____%	____/ ____ = ____%
Critical Questions: evaluative*	____/ ____ = ____%	
Comprehension Functioning Level		

* Not used for determining level

Functioning Levels for Text Comprehension

	Independent	Instructional	Frustration
Comprehension	90–100%	70–89%	69% and below

Analysis:

NONFICTION LAYOUT AND TEXT FEATURES ASSESSMENT

Name: _____ Date: _____

Title/Author: _____ Level: _____

Directions: Select a text with as many of these concepts as possible. Predetermine words to complete the blanks.

Score: Mark a plus sign (+) if correct, a minus sign (–) if incorrect, and *N/A* if the feature is not in the book.

Questions	Response	Score
1. What is the title of the book?		
2. Who is the author of the book? 3. Who is the illustrator of the book? 4. Is there any information about the author or illustrator? If yes, write one fact.		
5. What is the copyright date? 6. Why is it important? 7. Who is the publisher?		
8. Where is the table of contents? 9. What information do you find there? 10. What page can you find _____ on?		
11. Where is the glossary? 12. What information do you find there? 13. What is the definition of _____?		
14. Where is the index? 15. What information do you find there? 16. What page is _____ on?		
17. Where is a heading? 18. What information does it tell you?		
19. Where are boldfaced or italicized words? 20. Why are they boldfaced or italicized in the text?		
21. Where is a caption? 22. What information does it tell you?		
23. Where is a photograph or illustration? 24. What information does it tell you?		
25. Where is a diagram or map? 26. What information does it tell you?		
27. Where is a table or chart? 28. What information does it tell you?		
29. Where can you go to get additional information on this topic?		
30. Looking through the book, what do you think it is going to be about?		
Total Correct:		

Analysis:

GUIDED READING CHECKLIST

Score

\+ ✓ −

Reading Silently

Stays on task ____

Chooses to read ____

Uses parts of the book such as the table of contents, glossary, and index to clarify information ____

Refers back to parts already read to clarify or extend new information ____

Reads for detail rather than always skimming ____

Participates actively in discussion of the text ____

Contributes to discussion and questioning that indicates an appropriate level of comprehension ____

Connects text to self, other texts, or to the world ____

Reading Orally

Accuracy

Uses a variety of strategies to problem-solve unknown words ____

Rereads if the reading doesn't make sense, look right, or sound right ____

Self-corrects miscues that affect the meaning of the text ____

Makes fewer than 5 miscues in 50 words ____

Uses resources to gain meaning of unknown words ____

Fluency

Reads in phrases ____

Pauses at punctuation ____

Changes expression and intonation according to the author's style ____

Generally reads smoothly and resolves any problems quickly ____

Adjusts pace according to material and purpose ____

Reads at a conversational pace ____

Comprehension

Predicts content based on cover page, table of contents, graphic information, headings, or reading the first paragraph ____

Identifies the genre and can explain how ____

Makes inferences and evaluates them during reading ____

Rereads to clarify meaning ____

Uses resources or asks questions to clarify meaning ____

Can identify and explain the narrative story elements in own words ____

Can identify and explain the main ideas and details of expository texts ____

Can identify and explain the expository text structures in own words ____

Can summarize the text in own words ____

Makes connections within the text, to other texts, to self, and to the world ____

Evaluates the text for author bias, content, and interest ____

ORAL OR WRITTEN STORY RETELLING ANALYSIS

Name: _____ Date: _____

Title/Author: _____ Genre: _____

Oral Retelling or Written Retelling (circle one)

Directions: Before and after the student reads a narrative story, say, "I want you to tell me (or write) everything you remember about the story, in order."

Scoring: Record the student's responses and mark each element with a plus sign (+) if the student provides a complete correct response, a checkmark (✓) if it is a partial or partially correct response, or a minus sign (−) if the response is incorrect or not given.

	+ ✓ − score
Introduction of Characters and Setting	
Begins retelling with an introduction	
Names the main character	
Describes the main character	
Names other characters (total number of other characters = _____)	
Describes other characters	
Describes the setting: Place(s) and time period	
Theme, Plot, and Events	
Describes the important message or lesson that the author was trying to convey	
Describes the main goal or problem to be solved	
Number of events recalled (total number of events = _____)	
Details of events recalled	
Resolution	
Describes the solution to the problem	
Describes the ending of the story	
Sequence	
Retells story in structural order: characters, setting, theme, events, resolution	

Analysis:

Adapted from Shearer-Mariotti, A.P., & Homan, S.P. (1997). *Linking reading assessment to instruction: An application worktext for elementary classroom teachers* (2nd ed.). Mahwah, NJ: Erlbaum; and Morrow, L. (2005). *Literacy development in the early years: Helping children read and write* (5th ed.). Boston: Allyn & Bacon.

EMERGENT WRITING STAGE ASSESSMENT

Name: _____ Grade: _____ Date: _____

Emergent Writing Stage:

Directions and Scoring: Observe and collect several writing samples from the student. Read each of the descriptors in the checklist and evaluate it using a plus sign (+) to indicate that the student exhibited the behavior frequently, a checkmark (✓) to indicate that the behavior was sometimes exhibited, or a minus sign (−) to indicate that the student rarely or never exhibited this behavior. N/A indicates not applicable. Afterwards identify the highest stage that the child had a majority of checks and/or pluses, with three or less minuses.

Score + ✓ −	Descriptor	Date observed Comments
Stage 1		
	CONTENT	
	Dictates words or phrases to be written down	
	Begins to differentiate between scribbled picture and scribble writing	
	HANDWRITING	
	Scribbles on page with no message intended	
	Scribbles include random, circular, vertical, and/or horizontal marks.	
	Uses a variety of writing utensils (crayon, pencil, markers, paintbrush)	
Stage 2		
	CONTENT	
	Dictates sentences to be written	
	"Reads" story with consistent oral text	
	Differentiates between picture and story	
	HANDWRITING	
	Symbols or scribbles represent letters, words or strings of words	
	Writes mock letters or real letters, but they have no phonetic representation	
	Begins to write alphabet letters	
Stage 3		
	CONTENT	
	Dictates more complete stories to be written	
	Completes sentence frames or patterned sentences	
	Draws recognizable pictures	
	Attempts to label pictures and writes letters for words	

(continued)

EMERGENT WRITING STAGE ASSESSMENT (continued)

Score + ✓ –	Descriptor	Date observed Comments
	SPELLING	
	Writes letters to represent a word or idea	
	Attempts inventive spelling of words with some correct sound/symbol association	
	Hears and writes letters for beginning consonant sounds	
	Hears and writes letters for ending consonant sounds	
	HANDWRITING	
	Awareness of letter and word spacing begins.	
	Awareness of left-to-right sequence of letters and words	
	Begins to copy words	
	Most letters are recognizable, may mix between capitals and lower case letters	
Stage 4		
	CONTENT	
	Writes on a self-selected topic	
	Writes on a teacher selected topic	
	Draws illustrations that match text	
	SENTENCE STRUCTURE	
	Writes one sentence with at least four words	
	CAPITALIZATION/PUNCTUATION	
	Uses of correct capitalization sometimes	
	Uses of correct end punctuation sometimes	
	SPELLING	
	Writes short sentences using inventive spelling	
	Writes name and some sight words correctly	
	Writes words with beginning and ending consonant sounds	
	Writes words with some vowel sounds	
	Begins to use written resources for spelling	
	HANDWRITING	
	All letters are recognizable	
	Uses lowercase letters, generally	
	Is beginning to write within lines	
	Writes from left to right	
	Is beginning appropriate spacing between words	

(continued)

EMERGENT WRITING STAGE ASSESSMENT (continued)

Score + ✓ −	Descriptor	Date observed Comments
Stage 5		
	CONTENT	
	Writes at least three sentences on one topic	
	Sequences ideas	
	Writes on different self-selected topics	
	Writes on different teacher-selected topics	
	Writes for functional purposes (notes, lists, share ideas)	
	Draws illustrations that are detailed and match text	
	SENTENCE STRUCTURE	
	Writes complete sentences	
	Often writes with correct subject-verb agreement	
	Writes using a variety of words	
	Writes using specific and interesting words for the content	
	Is beginning to write with adjectives	
	Is beginning to write with adverbs	
	Is beginning to write complex and compound sentences	
	CAPITALIZATION/PUNCTUATION	
	Uses capital letters at the start of a sentence	
	Capitalizes names of people and the pronoun *I*	
	Is beginning to capitalize other proper nouns correctly	
	Uses periods at the end of statements	
	Is beginning to use question marks correctly	
	Experiments with other punctuation marks	
	SPELLING	
	Is moving from transitional to conventional spelling	
	Spells several common words correctly	
	Uses inventive spelling with letters representing the consonant sounds and vowel sounds	
	Uses written resources for spelling	

(continued)

EMERGENT WRITING STAGE ASSESSMENT (continued)

Score + ✓ −	Descriptor	Date observed Comments
	HANDWRITING	
	Shows appropriate spacing between words	
	Shows appropriate text wrapping	
	Forms letters correctly (though may still have some reversals)	
	Writes the letters correctly between the lines	
	REVISING	
	Begins to make changes in selection of words	
	Begins to make changes in content, such as adding, deleting, or rearranging information	
	EDITING	
	Begins to make changes in grammar, capitalization, punctuation, spelling, and handwriting	

Analysis:

Adapted from Morrow, L. (2005). *Literacy development in the early years: Helping children read and write* (5th ed.). Boston: Allyn & Bacon; and Solley, B.A. (2000). *Writer's Workshop*. Boston: Allyn & Bacon.

HANDWRITING RUBRIC ASSESSMENT

Name: _____ Grade: _____ Date: _____

Directions: This rubric can be used with any writing assessment or writing sample to indicate the student's specific development in handwriting. Using the criteria listed under exceeds, meets, and does not meet, mark a plus sign (+), checkmark (✓) or minus sign (–) for each of the standards.

Note: Because the goal of writing is communication, emphasize legibility over exact handwriting style.

Standard	Score	Exceeds (+)	Meets (✓)	Does Not Meet (–)
Letters are easily recognizable.		Letters are always recognizable.	Letters are mostly recognizable.	Letters are rarely recognizable.
Letters are mostly formed correctly.		Letters are always formed correctly.	Letters are mostly formed correctly.	Letters are rarely formed correctly.
Letters start and end in the correct place.		Letters always start and end correctly.	Letters mostly start and end correctly.	Letters rarely start and end correctly.
Letters are mostly placed correctly within the lines.		Letters are always placed correctly within the lines.	Letters are mostly placed correctly within the lines.	Letters are rarely placed correctly within the lines.
Usually uses capital letters appropriately.		Always uses capital letters appropriately.	Usually uses capital letters appropriately.	Capital letters are rarely used appropriately.
Letters are usually spaced properly.		Letters are always spaced properly.	Letters are usually spaced properly.	Letters are rarely spaced properly.
Words are usually spaced properly.		Words are always spaced properly.	Words are usually spaced properly.	Words are rarely spaced properly.
Return sweep is used properly.		Return sweep is always used properly.	Return sweep is usually used properly.	Return sweep is rarely used properly.

WRITING COMPOSITION ASSESSMENT SUMMARY

Name: _____ Date: _____

Title: _____ Genre: _____

Directions: Select a genre and a writing prompt. Example prompts are below. Provide this form or the editing and revising checklist as a reference for revising and editing. Ask the student to do prewriting brainstorming or talk about their topic, write, reread, revise, and edit their own writing.

Scoring: For each writing element, put a plus sign (+) if it is excellent, a checkmark (✓) if it is satisfactory, or a minus sign (–) if it needs work or is incomplete in the left column and then write details for each in the right column. In the analysis, indicate areas of strength or need.

Prompt: (circle one)

Narrative—"Write about an important event in your life."

Descriptive—"Write a poem or song about something you like."

Expository—"Write about a specific topic or how to make something."

Persuasive—"Write about what you would like to change in your school."

Title or Topic: _____

Content

	Ideas and details
	Organization
	Voice
	Sentence fluency
	Word choice

Conventions

	Grammar
	Punctuation
	Capitalization
	Spelling

Analysis of content and conventions:

Length: Number of sentences ___   Number of paragraphs ___

Average number of words per sentence ___   Appropriate length for topic: (yes or no)

Evidence of prewriting:

Evidence of revision and editing:

WRITING COMPOSITION RUBRIC
FOR WRITER AND TEACHER

Name: _____ Date: _____

Title: _____ Genre: _____

Directions and Scoring: Circle either Student or Teacher in the score column. After the reading the entire composition, read each of the descriptors in the rubric and evaluate each element with a plus sign (+) for excellent, a checkmark (✓) for satisfactory, or a minus sign (–) for needs improvement. Underline any descriptive words that seem appropriate. Then analyze with specific examples from the composition.

	Excellent (+)	Satisfactory (✓)	Needs Work (–)	Student/ Teacher Score
Content				
Ideas/details	Interesting. Well focused. Accurate. Specific details and description. Shows insight, originality, and careful thought. No irrelevant details.	Clear, but has limited details. Not very specific. Some ideas important while others are not. Parts lack specific details or description.	Seems to lack purpose or focus. Limited or unclear information. Doesn't seem meaningful or real. Lacks specific details or description.	
Organization	Inviting introduction. The order makes sense and is easy to follow. Ideas are connected with smooth transitions. Details fit. Strong conclusion adds impact. Follows structure for genre.	The reader can follow what is being said but lacks focus and impact. The introduction or conclusion can be found but seems weak or forced. Limited transactions. Some details seem confusing.	Almost no identifiable introduction or conclusion. Details strung together without logical order. No transition. Gaps in information.	
Voice	Appropriate tone and mood for purpose and audience. Shows unique personality and feelings of writer.	Some evidence of writer's personality in writing, but parts lack personal feeling.	Almost no evidence of the writer's personality in writing.	
Sentence fluency	Complete. Clear meaning. Varied sentence structure and length. Easy to read. Flowing, interesting word patterns. Natural dialogue. Paragraphs as needed.	Some sentences seem awkward. Most follow a single pattern. Sentences seem somewhat isolated and forced.	Difficult to understand. Choppy. Simplistic word patterns. Unnatural. Disjointed. Monotonous.	
Word choice	Interesting. Precise and natural. Words are specific and accurate. Strong images and verbs. Description of multiple senses.	Words are ordinary but convey message. Meaning comes through but lacks precision. Some language seems overused.	Limited, vague, or abstract words. Repetitious, monotonous words and stale expressions. Few images. Weak verbs.	

Analysis:

(continued)

WRITING COMPOSITION RUBRIC
FOR WRITER AND TEACHER (continued)

	Excellent (+)	Satisfactory (✓)	Needs Work (–)	Student/ Teacher Score
Conventions				
Grammar	Correct grammar and word forms.	A few grammatical errors.	Several grammatical errors making it hard to read.	
Punctuation	Correct punctuation.	Ending punctuation correct with minor other punctuation errors.	Several punctuation errors making it hard to read.	
Capitalization	Correct capitalization.	Correct capitalization at beginning of sentences with minor mistakes on proper nouns.	Several capitalization errors.	
Spelling	Correct spelling.	Spelling correct on common words and decodable on others.	Spelling makes the writing hard to read.	

Analysis:

WRITING PROCESS RUBRIC FOR WRITER AND TEACHER

Name: _____ Date: _____

Title: _____ Genre: _____

Directions and Scoring: For each step of the writing process, the student and/or the teacher evaluates the student's performance; circle either Student or Teacher in the score column. Read each of the descriptors in the rubric and evaluate each element with a plus sign (+) for excellent, a checkmark (✓) for satisfactory, or a minus sign (–) for needs improvement. Underline any descriptive words that seem appropriate. Then analyze with specific examples from observations and anecdotal notes on the writing process.

	Excellent	Satisfactory	Needs Work	Student/ Teacher Score
Content				
Prewriting	Prewriting plan.	Limited prewriting plan found.	No evidence of prewriting plan.	
Drafting	Two or more rough drafts each showing significant work. Final draft shows careful editing.	One or more rough drafts showing minor work. Some editing on final draft but more needed.	One draft only. No significant changes or corrections.	
Conferring	Conference form completed. Significant evidence of revising and editing if needed. Partner's signature.	Conference form mostly completed. Some evidence of revising and editing. Partner's signature.	Conference form incomplete. Little evidence of revising and editing. No signature	
Revising	Several meaningful notes on draft for ideas, organization, word choice, and sentence fluency. Several significant changes made to final draft.	A few meaningful notes on draft for ideas, organization, word choice, and sentence fluency. A few significant changes made to final draft.	Limited notes and changes to content.	
Editing	Almost no errors found on final draft. Final draft is in attractive, legible form.	Final draft with four or fewer errors. Final draft shows some corrections. It could be more legible or attractive.	Final draft shows five or more errors. Editing is hard to see.	
Publishing/ sharing	The piece was shared or published appropriately and with pride.	The piece was shared or published appropriately.	The piece was not appropriately shared or published.	

Analysis:

PRIMARY NARRATIVE REVISING AND EDITING CHECKLIST

Name: _____ Date: _____

Title: _____ Genre: _____

Directions: Reread your story and put a checkmark for each item you have completed.

Content

____ I reread it.

____ The story makes sense.

____ The story has a clear beginning that describes the characters, place, and time (setting).

____ The story has a clear middle that describes the events (plot).

____ The story has a clear ending (resolution).

____ Each sentence is a complete idea.

____ I used interesting and descriptive words in each sentence.

____ I wrote a catchy title.

Conventions

____ Each sentence begins with an uppercase letter.

____ *I* is always capitalized.

____ Each sentence ends with the correct punctuation.

____ The names of people and important places are capitalized.

____ Quotation marks are used to show when someone is talking.

____ Each new paragraph is indented.

____ I circled the words I did not know how to spell.

____ I used writing resources to correct the spelling of the words.

____ My handwriting is clear and legible.

Analysis:

Adapted from Solley, B.A. (2000). *Writer's workshop: Reflections of elementary and middle school teachers.* Boston: Allyn & Bacon.

ADVANCED REVISING AND EDITING CHECKLIST

Name: _____ Date: _____

Title/Author: _____ Genre: _____

Title

_____ I wrote a catchy title and capitalized the appropriate words.

Ideas and Details

_____ My topic is narrowed and appropriate.
_____ My ideas and details are clearly stated, make sense, and are accurate.
_____ My details are focused and related to the main idea.
_____ My main idea is easy to see. It jumps right out at you.
_____ I used evidence and examples to support every point. There are no gaps.
_____ I have plenty of information from experience or research.
_____ I chose information I knew would answer the readers' questions.
_____ My ideas are interesting.

Organization

_____ My ideas follow a sequence that makes sense.
_____ The format goes with the purpose or style of writing: narrative, expository, persuasive, and descriptive.
_____ My lead gets your attention and lets you know where I'm headed.
_____ My conclusion reinforces, supports, or restates my main point.
_____ For stories, I had a clear beginning (characters and setting), middle (plot), and end (resolution).
_____ For reports, I used a title and subtitles and bullets or numbers to help make the information easy to find.
_____ My pictures and graphics are linked to the ideas in the writing.

Sentence Fluency

_____ My sentences begin in a variety of ways.
_____ My sentences are concise.
_____ I use linking words such as *also* and *in addition*.
_____ I use transitions to connect ideas.

Word Choice

_____ The meaning of every word is clear. Any confusing words are defined or examples are given for them.
_____ I avoid vague language such as *stuff* or *things* that may confuse the reader.
_____ The words I chose are "right" for my audience.
_____ I used vocabulary words specific to the content.
_____ I used a variety of strong verbs.
_____ I used descriptive adjectives.

Conventions

_____ Every sentence in my paper is grammatically correct.
_____ The verb tense is consistent throughout each paragraph.
_____ I edited my paper for capitalization.
_____ I edited my paper for punctuation.
_____ I edited my paper for spelling.

Analysis:

EDITING AND REVISING BOOKMARKS

My Writing Bookmark

___ I reread.

___ It makes sense.

___ It sounds right.

___ It looks right.

___ I used uppercase letters. T, I

___ I used end punctuation. . ? !

___ I used resources for spelling.

___ My pictures match the story.

Narrative/Descriptive Writing

___ I reread my writing.

I described the...

___ characters

___ places

___ time of day, season, and year

___ plot with the events in sequence

___ end or resolution

___ point of view of the storyteller

I checked for...

___ complete interesting sentences

___ capitalization

___ punctuation

___ spelling and resources used

Expository/Persuasive Writing

___ I reread my writing.

___ I wrote an interesting opening statement or question.

___ I defined my topic or main idea.

___ I explained my essay organization.

___ I supported my ideas with specific details and examples.

___ I used resources to verify the information.

___ I used transitions to mark sequences or connections of the information.

___ I wrote a concluding sentence that summarizes my main idea.

___ I checked for correct grammar, capitalization, punctuation, and spelling.

ANECDOTAL RECORD FORM

Name: _____ Date: _____

Directions: Write anecdotal comments on the form for students' thinking or writing processes.

Topic of Writing or Assignment: _____

Thinking/Writing Process	Comments
Cognitive (thinking, reasoning, problem solving)	
Knowledge of writing style	
Communication (use of written language)	
Affective (expression of feelings, ability to handle constructive criticism)	
Social interaction (seeking help from peers, conference skills, responses)	
Creativity (use of imagination, description, detail)	

PEER CONFERENCE SUMMARY FORM

Writer's name: _____ Date: _____

Partner's name: _____ Project title: _____

Questions to ask conference partners	Answers
What is my story/project about?	
What do I like best about it?	
Did I say anything confusing? What?	
Do I need to add more details? Where?	
Did I have a clear beginning, middle, and end?	
Did my writing catch your attention? How?	
How can it be summarized?	

PERSONAL NARRATIVE ACTION RUBRIC

Name: _____ Date: _____

Title of Writing: _____

Directions: Write an example of a problem that you have had. Show the students the rubric and help them to identify the problem, rising action, and ending action in your writing. Then have the students write a personal narrative about a problem that they had, the events leading up to the solution, and then explain how the problem was solved.

Scoring: Using the Narrative Action Rubric score each element 1–4, with 4 being the highest.

Beginning Action					
Story problem is clear.	4	3	2	1	Story problem is unclear.
Rising Action					
The events leading up to the solution are clear.	4	3	2	1	The events leading up to the solution are not clear.
Ending Action					
Solution to the problem is clear and logically follows from the previous events.	4	3	2	1	Solution to the problem is not clear and does not logically follow from the previous events.
Voice					
The events are described with feeling and emotion.	4	3	2	1	The events are listed but not described with feeling or emotion.
Conventions					
Grammar, capitalization, punctuation, spelling, and legibility promote understanding of the story.	4	3	2	1	Grammar, capitalization, punctuation, spelling, and legibility interfere with the understanding of the story.

Analysis:

REPORT WRITING CHECKLIST

Name: _____ Date: _____

Reviewer: _____ Title: _____

Ideas/Details

_____ I used brainstorming and a concept map or outline to create and organize ideas.

_____ I generated questions or identified problems related to my topic.

_____ I gathered information from a variety of sources and cited them correctly.

_____ I write showing a clear understanding of my topic.

_____ Ideas are written in my own words.

_____ My report is clear and focused; I stay on topic.

_____ My ideas are logically related to one another.

_____ All major points are supported with specific details or examples.

_____ My details give the reader important information.

Organization

_____ My introduction is clear and inviting.

_____ My report is sequenced in a logical order.

_____ I maintain my focus or logic throughout my paper.

_____ Each of my paragraphs has one main idea with related details and examples.

_____ My ideas flow well and are clearly connected to one another.

_____ I have an effective conclusion that summarizes or restates main idea.

Sentence Fluency

_____ My sentences build upon the ones before.

_____ My sentences begin in different ways.

_____ My sentences are of different lengths.

_____ The meaning of each of my sentences is clear.

_____ My sentences flow from one to another.

_____ There are no run-on sentences.

_____ There are no sentence fragments.

Voice and Word Choice

_____ Voice is formal and appropriate for topic, purpose, and audience.

_____ Every word shows the exact meaning I want to communicate.

_____ I used specific and technical words related to my topic.

_____ I used several descriptive words (adjectives and adverbs).

_____ My words paint pictures in the reader's mind.

_____ I used strong verbs.

_____ I used synonyms to add variety.

(continued)

REPORT WRITING CHECKLIST (continued)

Conventions

_____ I used correct grammar.

_____ I used commas, periods, question marks, and exclamation points correctly.

_____ I used quotation marks around dialogue.

_____ I used apostrophes correctly in contractions and possessives.

_____ I have capitalized the first word of each sentence and the pronoun _I_.

_____ I have capitalized proper nouns (people, places, dates, and titles).

_____ My handwriting is legible.

_____ The final report has no errors in conventions or format.

Presentation

_____ The cover of the report is neatly designed with title, author, and graphics or illustrations related to the topic.

_____ Illustrations, diagrams, maps, charts, and/or graphs are added to clarify or enhance information in the text.

_____ A table of contents is included with all of the major headings in the report.

_____ A glossary is included with definitions of important words.

_____ The bibliography is included with all of the references written in APA or MLA format.

INTEREST AND ACTIVITIES INVENTORY

Name: _____ Grade: _____ Date: _____

Names of family members in order from oldest to youngest:

Types and names of pets:

Favorites

Food: _____   Game: _____

Friend: _____   Color: _____

Sport: _____   Music: _____

Book: _____   Magazine: _____

TV show: _____   Movie: _____

Activities

Activities in school:

Activities out of school:

Hobbies or collections:

Things I like to do:

Things that make me laugh:

Places I like to visit:

People I like to visit:

What I want to be when I get older:

If I had a million dollars I would:

Reading and Writing Time

Outside of school I read this much per week (circle one)

up to 30 minutes   up to 1 hour   up to 1½ hrs.   up to 2 hours   up to 3 hours   over 3 hours

Examples include books, magazines, Internet articles

Outside of school I write this much per week (circle one)

up to 30 minutes   up to 1 hour   up to 1½ hrs.   up to 2 hours   up to 3 hours   over 3 hours

Examples include journals, letters, poetry, instant messages

SCHOOL ATTITUDE INVENTORY

Name: _____ Grade: _____ Date: _____

How do you feel about going to school?

What do you like about school?

What are your concerns about school?

What do you do well in school?

What is something you would like to do better in school?

Tell me about reading in school.

Tell me about writing in school.

Tell me about a teacher you remember.

READING INTEREST INVENTORY: ELEMENTARY

Name: _____ Grade: _____ Date: _____

	Yes ☺	No ☹
I like to read or listen to...		
stories about kids my age		
stories about animals		
funny stories or jokes		
picture books		
folk tales or fairy tales		
books about the future		
books about the past		
comics		
poetry		
books about important people		
stories about sports and athletes		
books about discoveries		
stories about things that couldn't possibly happen		
mysteries		
adventure stories		
books about different people and places		
books about space		
books about science		
books about how things work or how to make things		
books about my hobbies or collections		

	Yes ☺	No ☹
Interest in Reading		
I like to get new books or borrow books from the library.		
I read to learn new things.		
I read for fun in my free time.		
I read some books more than once.		
I like to have books read to me.		
I like to share books with a friend.		
I like to read at home.		
I like to read chapter books.		
I like to read magazines.		
I like to play computer games that include reading.		
I like to look up information on the computer.		
I like to read in school.		

READING INTEREST INVENTORY: MIDDLE LEVEL AND SECONDARY

Name: _____ Grade: _____ Date: _____

	Yes ☺	No ☹
I like to read the following types of literature:		
FICTION		
Modern realistic fiction		
Historical fiction		
Fantasy		
Comics		
Outdoor adventures		
Science fiction and space fantasy		
Modern or traditional folk tales		
Westerns		
Romance		
Horror and thrillers		
Mysteries		
Poetry		
NONFICTION		
Biographies and autobiographies		
Documentaries		
Modern people and culture		
Occupations		
Historical people and culture		
Political science: Government, citizenship		
Religion		
Fine and applied arts, music, and theater		
Sports		
Geography and travel		
Geology and meteorology: Rocks, minerals, weather, and natural disasters		
Astronomy and space science		
Prehistoric earth, plants, and animals		
Environmental science		
Biology: Animals, plants		
Human body: Physical, mental, and emotional development and understanding		
Language development and communication		
Physical science and technology: How things work, what things are made of		
Mathematical concepts and problem solving		
Hobbies and collections		

LITERACY PROCESS INTERVIEW

Name: _____ Grade: _____ Date: _____

Directions: Say to the student, "I am going to ask you some questions about what you do when you read and write. I am going to write down what you say."

Reading Questions

1. When you are reading and you come to a word you do not know, what do you do? Do you do anything else?

2. When you are reading and you do not understand something, what do you do? Do you do anything else?

3. How would you help someone who is having trouble reading?

4. During reading, at what do you think you do well? Why?

5. What would you like to change about your reading? Why?

Writing Questions

1. When you are writing and you come to a difficult part, what do you do? Do you do anything else?

2. If you are given a writing assignment, what would you do first? Next? Then what? Last?

3. How would you help someone who is having trouble writing?

4. During writing, at what do you think you do well? Why?

5. What would you like to change about your writing? Why?

Analysis:

Adapted from Goodman, Y., Watson, D.J., & Burke, C. (2005). *Reading miscue inventory: From evaluation to instruction* (2nd ed.). Katonah, NY: Richard C. Owen.

TEXT SELECTION BOOKMARKS

## Read to me!	## Read with me!	## I can read this on my own!

Before Reading:

Talk about the front cover and pictures.

During Reading:

Briefly talk about what the book is about and the meaning of new words.

After Reading:

Talk about what you learned and liked.

Before Reading:

Talk about the front cover and pictures.

During Reading:

Take turns reading and briefly talk about what the book is about and the meaning of new words and ideas.

After Reading:

Talk about what you learned and liked.

Before Reading:

Look through the book and think about what it will be about and what you already know.

During Reading:

Think about what the book is about and try to figure out the meaning of new words.

After Reading:

Think about what you learned and liked. If possible share this.

AT-HOME READING LOG

Name: _____

Directions: Listen to the child read, talk about the story, sign this form, and mark a plus sign (+) if it was read very well with almost no help, a checkmark (✓) if it was read pretty well with some help, and a minus sign (–) if it was read with difficulty and needed a lot of help. Then return the log and book to school the next day.

Date	**Title and Level** Reading Recovery Level = RR Guided Reading Level = GR Grade Level = GL	**Signature and Evaluation** + ✓ –

REFERENCES

Abromeit, J. (2001). Assessment essentials: Definitions of terms. Retrieved March 26, 2008, from Alverno College website: depts. alverno.edu/saal/terms.html

Adams, M.J. (1990). *Beginning to read: Thinking and learning about print.* Cambridge, MA: MIT Press.

Advanced Learning Technologies. (2006). *Project based learning writing checklists grades 5–8.* Retrieved May 15, 2008, from pblchecklist.4teachers.org

Allen, K.E., & Marotz, L. (1994). *Developmental profiles: Pre-birth through eight* (2nd ed.). Albany, NY: Delmar.

Allington, R.L., & Cunningham, P.M. (2002). *Schools that work: Where all children read and write.* Boston: Allyn & Bacon.

Anderson, L.W., & Krathwohl, D.R. (Eds.). (2001). *A taxonomy for learning, teaching, and assessing: A revision of Bloom's taxonomy of educational objectives* (Complete ed.). New York: Longman.

Anderson, R.C. (2004). Role of reader's schema in comprehension, learning, and memory. In R. Ruddell & N. Unrau (Eds.), *Theoretical models and processes of reading* (5th ed., pp. 594–606). Newark, DE: International Reading Association.

Applegate, M.D., Quinn, K.B., & Applegate, A.J. (2002). Levels of thinking required by comprehension questions in informal reading inventories. *The Reading Teacher, 56*(2), 174–180.

Atwell, N. (1987). *In the middle: Writing, reading, and learning with adolescents.* Portsmouth, NH: Heinemann.

Auman, M. (2005). *Step up to writing.* Frederick, CO: Sopris West.

Baker, L., & Brown, A.L. (1984). Metacognitive skills and reading. In P.D. Pearson, R. Barr, M.L. Kamil, & P.B. Mosenthal (Eds.), *Handbook of reading research* (pp. 353–394). New York: Longman.

Bandura, A. (1994). Self-efficacy. In V.S. Ramachaudran (Ed.), *Encyclopedia of human behavior* (Vol. 4, pp. 71–81). New York: Academic.

Barchers, S. (1993). *Readers Theatre for beginning readers.* Englewood, CO: Teacher Ideas.

Baron, G. (1969). The study of educational administration studies in England. In G. Baron & W. Taylor (Eds.), *Educational administration and the social sciences.* London: Athlone.

Barr, R., Blachowicz, C., Buhle, R., Chaney, J., Ivy, C.A., Uchtman, A., et al. (2004). Illinois snapshot of early literacy (ISEL). Springfield, IL: State Board of Education.

Bean, R.M. (2004). *The reading specialist: Leadership for the classroom, school, and community.* New York: Guilford.

Bear, D., Invernizzi, M., Templeton, S., & Johnston, F. (2000). *Words their way: Word study for phonics, vocabulary, and spelling instruction* (2nd ed.). Upper Saddle River, NJ: Merrill.

Beaty, J. (1994). *Observing development of the young child* (3rd ed.). Englewood Cliffs, NJ: Merrill.

Beaver, J. (2001). *Developmental reading assessment.* Parsippany, NJ: Celebration Press.

Beck, I.L., & McKeown, M.G. (1981). Developing questions that promote comprehension: The story map. *Language Arts, 58*(8), 913–918.

Beck, I.L., McKeown, M.G., Hamilton, R., & Kucan, L. (1997). *Questioning the author: An approach for enhancing student engagement with text.* Newark: DE: International Reading Association.

Betts, E.A. (1946). *Foundations of reading instruction.* New York: American Book.

Blachowicz, C.L.Z., & Fisher, P. (1996). *Teaching vocabulary in all classrooms.* Englewood Cliffs, NJ: Merrill.

Blachowicz, C.L.Z., & Fisher, P. (2006). *Teaching vocabulary in all classrooms* (3rd ed.). Upper Saddle River, NJ: Pearson.

Black, P.J., & Wiliam, D. (1998). *Inside the black box: Raising standards through classroom assessment.* London: King's College.

Bloom, B.S. (1956). *Taxonomy of educational objectives: The classification of educational goals: Book 1 Cognitive domain.* New York: David McKay.

Bloom, L., & Lahey, M. (1978). *Language development and disorders.* New York: Wiley.

Bos, C.S., & Anders, P.L. (1990). Effects of interactive vocabulary instruction on the vocabulary learning and reading comprehension of junior-high learning disabled students. *Learning Disability Quarterly, 13*(1), 31–42.

Braun, W., & Braun, C. (1996). *A readers theatre treasury of stories.* Calgary, AB: Braun & Braun Educational Enterprises.

Brown, R. (1973). *A first language: The early stages*. Cambridge, MA: Harvard University Press.

Buss, K., & Karnowski, L. (2000). *Reading and writing literary genres*. Newark, DE: International Reading Association.

Calkins, L. (1983). *Lessons from a child: On the teaching and learning of writing*. Portsmouth, NH: Heinemann.

Cambourne, B. (1988). *The whole story: Natural learning and the acquisition of literacy in the classroom*. New York: Scholastic.

Camp, D. (2000). It takes two: Teaching with twin texts of fact and fiction. *The Reading Teacher*, *53*(5), 400–408.

Carbo, M. (1978). Teaching reading with talking books. *The Reading Teacher*, *32*(3), 267–273.

Carr, E., & Ogle, D.M. (1987). K-W-L Plus: A strategy for comprehension and summarization. *Journal of Reading*, *30*(7), 626–631.

Carrell, P.L. (1983). Some issues in studying the role of schemata, or background knowledge, in second language comprehension. *Reading in a Foreign Language*, *1*(2), 81–92.

Carlisle, J.F., & Stone, C.A. (2005). Exploring the role of morphemes in word reading. *Reading Research Quarterly*, *40*(4), 428–449.

Caswell, L.J., & Duke, N. (1998). Non-narrative as a catalyst for literacy development. *Language Arts*, *75*(2), 108–117.

Clay, M.M. (1991). *Becoming literate: The construction of inner control*. Portsmouth, NH: Heinemann.

Clay, M.M. (1993a). *An observation survey of early literacy achievement*. Portsmouth, NH: Heinemann.

Clay, M.M. (1993b). *Reading recovery: A guidebook for teachers in training*. Portsmouth, NH: Heinemann.

Collier, V.P. (1995). *Promoting academic success for ESL students*. Elizabeth, NJ: NJTESOL-BE.

Commeyras, M. (1993). Promoting critical thinking through dialogical-thinking reading lessons. *The Reading Teacher*, *46*(6), 486–494.

Cooper, D. (2006). *Talk about assessment: Strategies and tools to improve learning*. Toronto, ON: Thomson Nelson.

Crank, J.N., & Bulgren, J.A. (1993). Visual depictions as information organizers for enhancing achievement of students with learning disabilities. *Learning Disabilities Research & Practice*, *8*(3), 140–147.

Crystal, D. (1987).*The Cambridge encyclopedia of language*. Cambridge, England: Cambridge University.

Cunningham, J.W. (1982). Generating interactions between schemata and text. In J.A. Niles & L.A. Harris (Eds.), *New inquiries in reading research and instruction* (31st yearbook of the National Reading Conference, pp. 42–47). Chicago: National Reading Conference.

Cunningham, P.M. (1995). *Phonics they use: Words for reading and writing* (2nd ed.). New York: HarperCollins.

Cunningham, P.M., & Allington, R.L. (2003). *Classrooms that work: They can all read and write* (3rd ed.). Boston: Allyn & Bacon.

Cunningham, P.M., Hall, D., & Sigmon, C. (1999). *The teacher's guide to the four blocks: A multimethod, multilevel framework for grades 1–3*. Greensboro, NC: Carson-Dellosa.

Dickinson, O.K., & Tabors, P.O. (Eds.). (2001). *Beginning literacy with language: Young children learning at home and school*. Baltimore: Paul H. Brookes.

Doiron, R. (1994). Using nonfiction in a read-aloud program: Letting the facts speak for themselves. *The Reading Teacher*, *47*(8), 616–624.

Donovan, C.A., & Smolkin, L.B. (2001). Genre and other factors influencing teachers' book selections for science instruction. *Reading Research Quarterly*, *36*(4), 412–440.

Dowhower, S.L. (1999). Supporting a strategic stance in the classroom: A comprehension framework for helping teachers help students to be strategic. *The Reading Teacher*, *52*(7), 672–689.

Duke, N.K. (2000). 3.6 minutes per day: The scarcity of informational texts in first grade. *Reading Research Quarterly*, *35*(2), 202–224.

Duke, N.K., & Kays, J. (1998). "Can I say 'Once upon a time'?" Kindergarten children developing knowledge of information book language. *Early Childhood Research Quarterly*, *13*(2), 295–318.

Ehri, L.C., Nunes, S.R., Willows, D.M., Schuster, B.V., Yaghoub-Zadeh, Z., & Shanahan, T. (2001). Phonemic awareness instruction helps children learn to read: Evidence from the National Reading Panel's meta-analysis. *Reading Research Quarterly*, *36*(3), 250–287.

Elkonin, D.B. (1973). U.S.S.R. In I. Downing (Ed.), *Comparative reading* (pp. 551–580). New York: Macmillan.

Emig, J. (1971). *The composing process of twelfth graders*. Urbana, IL: National Council of Teachers of English.

Fey, M. (1986). *Language intervention with young children*. San Diego, CA: College-Hill Press.

Fielding, L.G., & Pearson, P.D. (1994). Reading comprehension: What works. *Educational Leadership*, *51*(5), 62–68.

Farris, P.J., Fuhler, C.J., & Walther, M.P. (2004). *Teaching reading: A balanced approach for today's classrooms*. Boston: McGraw-Hill.

Fisher, D. (2007). *Instructional design—The taxonomy table.* Corvallis, OR: Oregon State University Extended Campus. Retrieved March 17, 2007, from oregonstate.edu/instruct/coursedev/models/id/taxonomy/#table

Fitzpatrick, J. (1999). *Teaching beginning writing.* Huntington Beach, CA: Creative Teaching.

Flower, L., & Hayes, J. (1981). A cognitive process theory of writing. *College Composition and Communication, 32*(4), 365–387.

Forehand, M. (2005). Bloom's taxonomy: Original and revised. In M. Orey (Ed.), *Emerging perspectives on learning, teaching, and technology.* Bloomington, IN: Association for Educational Communications and Technology. Retrieved February 27, 2008, from coe.uga.edu/epltt/bloom.htm

Fountas, I.C., & Pinnell, G.S. (1996). *Guided reading: Good first teaching for all children.* Portsmouth, NH: Heinemann.

Fountas, I.C., & Pinnell, G.S. (1999). *Matching books to readers: Using leveled books in guided reading, K–3.* Portsmouth, NH: Heinemann.

Fountas, I.C., & Pinnell, G.S. (2001). *Guiding readers and writers (grades 3–6): Teaching comprehension, genre, and content literacy.* Portsmouth, NH: Heinemann.

Freeman, J. (1990). Nonfiction 71 top books of the century [Book review]. *Instructor, 110*(6), 20–23.

Fry, E.B. (1977). Fry's Readability Graph: Clarifications, validity, and extension to Level 17. *Journal of Reading, 21*(3), 242–252.

Fry, E.B., Kress, J.E., & Fountoukidis, D.L. (1993). *The reading teacher's book of lists* (3rd ed.). Upper Saddle River, NJ: Prentice Hall.

Gillet, J.W., & Temple, C. (1994). *Understanding reading problems: Assessment and instruction* (4th ed.). New York: HarperCollins.

Goodman, K. (1965). A linguistic study of cues and miscues in reading. *Elementary English, 42*(6), 639–643.

Goodman, K. (1968).The psycholinguistic nature of the reading process. Detroit, MI: Wayne State University Press.

Goodman, K. (1987). Language and thinking in school. New York: Richard C. Owen.

Goodman, K. (1996). *On reading: A common-sense look at the nature of language and the science of reading.* Portsmouth, NH: Heinemann.

Goodman, Y.M., & Marek, A. (1996). Retrospective miscue analysis in the classroom. Katonah, NY: Richard C. Owen.

Goodman, Y.M., Watson, D.J., & Burke, C.L. (1987). *Reading miscue inventory: Alternative procedures.* Katonah, NY: Richard C. Owen.

Goodman, Y.M., Watson, D.J., & Burke, C.L. (2005). *Reading miscue inventory: From evaluation to instruction* (2nd ed.). Katonah, NY: Richard C. Owen.

Gould, J. S., & Gould, E. J. (1999). *Four square writing method: A unique approach to teaching basic writing skills, grades 1–3.* Carthage, IL: Teaching & Learning.

Graves, D.H. (1983). *Writing: Teachers and children at work.* Portsmouth, NH: Heinemann.

Graves, M.F., & Graves, B.B. (1994). *Scaffolding reading experiences: Designs for student success.* Norwood, MA: Christopher-Gordon.

Greene, F.P. (1979). Radio reading. In C. Pennock (Ed.), *Reading comprehension at four linguistic levels* (pp. 104–107). Newark, DE: International Reading Association.

Griffiths, R., & Clyne, M. (1991). *Books you can count on: Linking mathematics and literature.* Portsmouth, NH: Heinemann.

Gunning, T.G. (2000). *Best books for building literacy for elementary school children.* Boston: Allyn & Bacon.

Gunning, T.G. (2004). *Creating literacy instruction for all students in grades 4–8.* Boston: Allyn & Bacon.

Gunning, T.G. (2007). *Creating literacy instruction for all students* (6th ed.). Boston: Allyn & Bacon.

Gutkoska, J.P. (1982). *Gutkoska synonym and antonym test.* Unpublished manuscript, University of Maryland.

Halliday, M.A.K. (1975). *Learning how to mean: Explorations in the development of language.* New York: Elsevier.

Harris, T.L., & Hodges, R.E. (1995). *The literacy dictionary: The vocabulary of reading and writing.* Newark, DE: International Reading Association.

Harste, J., Woodward, V., & Burke, C. (1984). Examining our assumptions: A transactional view of literacy and learning. *Research in the Teaching of English, 18*(1), 84–108.

Harvey, S. (1998). *Nonfiction matters: Reading, writing, and research in grades 3–8.* York, ME: Stenhouse.

Harvey, S. (2002). Nonfiction inquiry: Using real reading and writing to explore the world. *Language Arts, 80*(1), 12–22.

Harvey, S., & Goudvis, A. (2007). *Strategies that work: Teaching comprehension to enhance understanding* (2nd ed.). York, ME: Stenhouse.

Headley, K.N., & Dunston, P.J. (2000). Teachers' choices books and comprehension strategies as transaction tools. *The Reading Teacher, 54*(3), 260–268.

Herber, H. (1978). *Teaching reading in content areas.* Englewood Cliffs, NJ: Prentice Hall.

Hiebert, E.H., Valencia, S.W., & Afflerbach, P.P. (1994). Definitions and perspectives. In S.W. Valencia, E.H. Hiebert, & P.P. Afflerbach (Eds.), *Authentic reading assessment: Practices and possibilities* (pp. 6–25). Newark, DE: International Reading Association.

Illinois Board of Education. (2000). *ISBE monograph: Using informational texts in the classroom.* Springfield: Illinois Board of Education.

Institute for Propaganda Analysis. (1938). *Propaganda analysis.* New York: Columbia University. Retrieved May 12, 2008, from www.propagandacritic.com

International Phonetic Association. (2005). *The international phonetic alphabet* (Revised). Retrieved March 26, 2008, from www.arts.gla.ac.uk/ipa/ipachart.html

International Reading Association & National Council of Teachers of English. (1996). *Standards for the English language arts.* Newark, DE; Urbana, IL: Authors.

International Reading Association. (2000). *Teaching all children to read: The roles of the reading specialist* (Position statement). Newark, DE: Author.

International Reading Association, Professional Standards and Ethics Committee. (2003). *Standards for reading professionals–Revised 2003.* Newark, DE: Author.

Jensen, J. (Ed.). (1984). Composing and comprehending. Urbana, IL: National Conference on Research in English.

Johnson, D.D. (2001). *Vocabulary in the elementary and middle school.* Boston: Allyn & Bacon.

Johnson, D.D., & Pearson, P.D. (1984). *Teaching reading vocabulary* (2nd ed.). New York: Holt, Rinehart and Winston.

Johnson, K.L., & Roseman, B.A. (2003). *The source for phonological awareness.* East Moline, IL: LinguiSystems.

Kamil, M., & Lane, D. (1997, March). *A classroom study of the efficacy of using informational text for first grade reading instruction.* Paper presented at the meeting of the American Educational Research Association, San Diego, CA.

Kear, D.J., Coffman, G.A., McKenna, M.G., & Ambrosia, A.L. (2000). Measuring attitude toward writing: A new tool for teachers. *The Reading Teacher, 54*(1), 10–23.

Keene, E.O., & Zimmermann, S. (1997). *Mosaic of thought: Teaching reading comprehension in a reader's workshop.* Portsmouth, NH: Heinemann.

Keene, E.O., & Zimmermann, S. (2007). *Mosaic of thought.* Portsmouth, NH: Heinemann.

Kletzien, S.B., & Dreher, M.J. (2004). *Informational text in K–3 classrooms: Helping children read and write.* Newark, DE: International Reading Association.

Kobrin, B. (1995). *Eyeopeners II: Children's books to answer children's questions about the world around them.* New York: Scholastic.

Lahey, M., & Bloom, L. (1988). *Language disorders and language development.* New York: Macmillan.

Langer, J.A. (1981). From theory to practice: A prereading plan. *Journal of Reading, 25*(2), 152–156.

Laster, B., & McAndrews, S. (2004, December). *Using vocabulary assessments to guide text selection in the QRI-3.* Paper presented at the 54th National Reading Conference, San Antonio, TX.

Leslie, L., & Caldwell, J. (2006). *Qualitative reading inventory-4* (4th ed.). Boston: Pearson.

Lipson, M.Y., & Wixson, K.K. (2003). *Assessment and instruction of reading disability: An interactive approach* (3rd ed.). Boston: Allyn & Bacon.

Loban, W. (1961). *Language ability in the middle grades of the elementary school.* Berkeley: University of California Press.

Lyons, C.A., Pinnell, G.S., & DeFord, D.E. (1993). *Partners in learning: Teachers and children in reading recovery.* New York: Teachers College Press.

Manz, S.L. (2002). A strategy for previewing textbooks: Teaching readers to become THIEVES. *The Reading Teacher, 55*(5), 434–435.

Manzo, A.V. (1969). ReQuest: A method for improving reading comprehension through reciprocal questioning. *Journal of Reading, 13*(2), 123–126.

Marzano, R.J. (1992). *A different kind of classroom: Teaching with dimensions of learning.* Alexandria, VA: Association for Supervision and Curriculum Development.

Marzano, R.J., Brandt, R.S., Hughes, C.S., Jones B.F., Presseisen, B.Z., Rankin, S.C., et al. (1988). *Dimensions of thinking: A framework for curriculum and instruction.* Alexandria, VA: Association for Supervision and Curriculum Development.

McAndrews, C.L. (2004). *Creating hope through reading: African literacy project.* Unpublished manuscript, Southern Illinois University Edwardsville.

McAndrews, S.L. (1999). *Reading discovery: The development of an early literacy program through reflective practice and analysis.* Ann Arbor, MI: UMI Company.

McAndrews, S.L. (2002). Enhancing reading strategies through teacher, peer and self assessment. *Illinois Reading Council Journal, 30*(3), 32–41.

McAndrews, S.L. (2004). Word work with meaning: Assessment and instructional strategies. *Missouri Reader, 29*(1), 9–22.

McAndrews, S.L. (2006). Auditory processing disorders: Linking literacy with instructional strategies. In T.K. Parthasarathy (Ed.), *An introduction to auditory processing in children.* (pp. 109–143). Mahwah, NJ: Erlbaum.

McGinley, W.J., & Denner, P.R. (1987). Story impressions: A prereading/writing activity. *Journal of Reading, 31*(3), 248–253.

McKenna, M.G., & Kear, D.J. (1990). Measuring attitude toward reading: A new tool for teachers. *The Reading Teacher, 43*(9), 626–639.

Morrow, L. (2005). *Literacy development in the early years: Helping children read and write* (5th ed.). Boston: Allyn & Bacon.

Moss, B. (2004). Teaching expository text structures through information trade book retellings. *The Reading Teacher, 57*(8), 710–718.

Moss, B., Leone, S., & Dipillo, M. (1997). Exploring the literature of fact: Linking reading and writing through information trade books. *Language Arts, 74*(6), 418–429.

Nagy, W.E. (1988). *Teaching vocabulary to improve reading comprehension.* Newark, DE: International Reading Association.

National Dissemination Center for Children With Disabilities. (2004). *Reading and learning disabilities.* Washington, DC: Author. Retrieved March 3, 2008, from nichcy.org/pubs/factshe/fs17txt.htm

National Institute of Child Health and Human Development. (2000). *Report of the National Reading Panel. Teaching children to read: An evidence-based assessment of the scientific research literature on reading and its implications for reading instruction Reports of the subgroups* (NIH Publication No. 00–4769). Washington, DC: U.S. Government Printing Office.

Newingham, B. (2008). *Adding strong voice to your writing.* New York: Scholastic. Retrieved April 1, 2008, from teacher.scholastic.com

Nilsen, A.P., & Nilsen, D.L.F. (2004). *Vocabulary plus high school and up: A source-based approach.* Boston: Allyn & Bacon.

Norris, B., & Brock, D. (2001). *WebQuest: The power of persuasive writing.* Retrieved December 15, 2007, from volweb.utk.edu/Schools/bedford/harrisms/teahpage.htm

Norton, D. (1995). *Through the eyes of a child: An introduction to children's literature* (4th ed.). Englewood Cliffs, NJ: Prentice Hall.

Nunes, T, Bryant, P., & Bindman, M. (1997). Morphological spelling strategies: Developmental stages and processes. *Developmental Psychology, 33*(4), 637–649.

Ogle, D.M. (1986). K-W-L: A teaching model that develops active reading of expository text. *The Reading Teacher, 39*(6), 564–570.

Ogle, D.M., & Correa, A. (2007, May). Motivating and scaffolding middle school English language learners: Focus on content and collaboration. Symposium conducted at the annual convention of the International Reading Association, Toronto, Canada.

Opitz, M.F., & Rasinski, T.V. (1998). *Good-bye round robin: 25 effective oral reading strategies.* Portsmouth, NH: Heinemann.

Palincsar, A.S., & Brown, A.L. (1986). Interactive teaching to promote independent learning from text. *The Reading Teacher, 39*(8), 771–777.

Panman, S., & Panman, R. (2006). *Writing essentials.* New Paltz, NY: Active Learning Corporation.

Paris, S.G., Calfee, R.C., Filby, N., Hiebert, E.H., Pearson, P.D., Valencia, S.W., et al. (1992). A framework for authentic literacy assessment. *The Reading Teacher, 46*(2), 88–98.

Peterson, B. (1988). *Characteristics of texts that support beginning readers.* Unpublished doctoral dissertation, The Ohio State University, Columbus.

Pikulski, J.J. (1997). *Teaching word identification skills and strategies: A balanced approach.* Boston: Houghton Mifflin. Retrieved November 30, 2003, from www.eduplace.com/rdg/res/teach/index.html

Rand McNally. (1994). *Discovery atlas of Native Americans.* Skokie, IL: Author.

Raphael, T.E. (1982). QARs: Question-answering strategies for children. *The Reading Teacher, 36*(2), 186–190.

Raphael, T.E., Pardo, L.S., & Highfield, K. (2002). *Book club: A literature-based curriculum* (2nd ed.). Lawrence, MA: Small Planet Communications.

Robb, L. (2001). *35 must-have assessment & record-keeping forms for reading.* New York: Scholastic.

Rog, L.J. (2003). *Guided reading basics: Organizing, managing, and implementing a balanced literacy program in K–3.* Portland, ME: Stenhouse.

Ross, S. (1998). Self-assessment in second language testing: A meta-analysis and analysis of experiential factors. *Language Testing, 15*(1), 1–20.

Routman, R. (1992). Teach skills with a strategy. *Instructor, 109*(9), 34–37.

Routman, R. (2005). *Writing essentials: Raising expectations and results while simplifying teaching.* Portsmouth, NH: Heinemann.

Rubin, H., Patterson, P.A., & Kantor, M. (1991). Morphological development and writing ability in children and adults. *Language, Speech, and Hearing Services in Schools, 22*(4), 228–235.

Rumelhart, D.E. (1994). Toward an interactive model of reading. In R.B. Ruddell, M.R. Ruddell, & H. Singer (Eds.), *Theoretical models and processes of reading* (4th ed., pp. 864–894). Newark, DE: International Reading Association.

Schumaker, J.B., Denton, P., & Deshler, D.D. (1984). *The paraphrasing strategy.* Lawrence: University of Kansas Press.

Schwartz, R.M., & Raphael, T.E. (1985). Concept of definition: A key to improving students' vocabulary. *The Reading Teacher, 39*(2), 198–205.

Shearer-Mariotti, A.P., & Homan, S.P. (1997). *Linking reading assessment to instruction: An application worktext for elementary classroom teachers* (2nd ed.). Mahwah, NJ: Erlbaum.

Short, K., Harste, J., & Burke, C. (1996). *Creating classrooms for authors and inquirers.* Portsmouth, NH: Heinemann.

Singer, H., & Ruddell, R.B. (1985). *Theoretical models and processes of reading* (3rd ed.). Newark, DE: International Reading Association.

Smith, C.C., & Bean, T.W. (1980). The guided writing procedure: Integrating content reading and writing improvement. *Reading World, 19*(3), 290–294.

Solley, B.A. (2000). *Writer's workshop: Reflections of elementary and middle school teachers.* Boston: Allyn & Bacon.

Spandel, V. (2004). *Creating young writers: Using the six traits to enrich writing process in primary classrooms.* Boston: Allyn & Bacon.

Stauffer, R.G. (1969). *Directing reading maturity as a cognitive process.* New York: Harper & Row.

Steward, F., & Borgia, L. (2004, March). Radio reading: Broadcasting and higher order thinking questions. Paper presented at the Illinois Reading Council Conference, Springfield, IL.

Sulzby, E., & Teale, W. (1991). Emergent literacy. In R. Barr, M.L. Kamil, P.B. Mosenthal, & P.D. Pearson (Eds.), *Handbook of reading research* (Vol. 2). White Plains, NY: Longman.

Taba, H. (1967). *Teacher handbook for elementary social studies.* Palo Alto, CA: Addison-Wesley.

Taberski, S. (2001). Fact and fiction: Read aloud. *Instructor, 110*(6), 24–26.

Taylor, W.L. (1953). Cloze procedure: A new tool for measuring readability. *Journalism Quarterly, 30*, 415–433.

Teacher Created Materials. (n.d.). *Celebrate literature and critical thinking notebook.* Westminster, CA: Author.

Tierney, R.J., & Pearson, P.D. (1984). Toward a composing model of reading. In J.M. Jensen (Ed.), *Composing and comprehending* (pp. 33–45). Urbana, IL: National Council of Teachers of English.

Tierney, R.J., & Readence, J.E. (2000). *Reading strategies and practices: A compendium* (5th ed.). Boston: Allyn & Bacon.

Tierney, R.J., & Readence, J.E. (2005). *Reading strategies and practices: A compendium* (6th ed.). Boston: Allyn & Bacon.

Tompkins, G.E. (2002). *Language arts: Content and teaching strategies* (5th ed.). Upper Saddle River, NJ: Pearson.

Treiman, R., & Cassar, M. (1996). Effects of morphology on children's spelling of final consonant clusters. *Journal of Experimental Child Psychology, 63*(1), 141–170.

Vacca, J.L., Vacca, R.T., Gove, M.K., Burkey, L.C., Lenhart, L.A., & McKeon, C.A. (2006). *Reading and learning to read* (6th ed.). Boston: Allyn & Bacon.

Vygotsky, L.S. (1978). *Mind in society: The development of higher psychological processes* (M. Cole, V. John-Steiner, S. Scribner, & E. Souberman, Eds. & Trans.). Cambridge, MA: Harvard University Press.

Walker, B. (2004). *Diagnostic teaching of reading: Techniques for instruction and assessment* (5th ed.). Upper Saddle River, NJ: Prentice Hall.

Wepman, J. (1958). *Auditory discrimination test*. Chicago: Language Research Associates.

Wilhelm, J.D., Baker, T.N., & Dube, J. (2001). *Strategic reading: Guiding students to lifelong literacy, 6–12*. Westport, CT: Heinemann.

Williams, K.T., & Wang, J.-J. (1997). *Technical references to the Peabody Picture Vocabulary Test (PPVT-III)*. Circle Pines, MN: American Guidance.

Winograd, P., & Niquette, C. (1988). Assessing learned helplessness in poor readers. *Topics in Language Disorders, 8*(3), 38–55.

Wood, D.J., Bruner, J.S., & Ross, G. (1976). The role of tutoring in problem-solving. *Journal of Student Psychology and Psychiatry, 17*(2), 89–100.

Yopp, H.K. (1992). Developing phonemic awareness in young children. *The Reading Teacher, 45*(9), 696–703.

Yopp, H.K. (1995). A test for assessing phonemic awareness in young children. *The Reading Teacher, 49*(1), 20–29.

Yopp, R.H., & Yopp, H.K. (2000a). Sharing informational text with young children. *The Reading Teacher, 53*(5), 410–423.

Yopp, H.K., & Yopp, R.H. (2000b). Supporting phonemic awareness development in the classroom. *The Reading Teacher, 54*(2), 130–143.

Young, T.L., & Hadaway, N.L. (Eds.). (2006). *Supporting the literacy development of English learners: Increasing success in all classrooms*. Newark, DE: International Reading Association.

Zimmerman, B.J. (2000). Attaining self-regulation: A social cognitive perspective. In M. Boekaerts, P.R. Pintrich, & M. Zeidner (Eds.), *Handbook of self-regulation* (pp. 13–39). San Diego, CA: Academic.

Zimmerman, B.J., Bandura, A., & Martinez-Pons, M. (1992). Self-motivation for academic attainment: The role of self-efficacy beliefs and personal goal setting. *American Educational Research Journal, 29*(3), 663–676.

Zutell, J., & Rasinski, T.V. (1991). Training teachers to attend to their students' oral reading fluency. *Theory Into Practice, 30*(3), 211–217.

Literature Cited

Avi. (2002). *Crispin*. New York: Hyperion Books for Children.

Bingham, C., Morgan, B., & Robertson, M. (2007). *Buzz*. New York: Dorling Kindersley.

Bolden, T. (1998). *And not afraid to dare: The stories of ten African-American women*. New York: Scholastic.

Brett, J. (1985). *Annie and the wild animals*. New York: Scholastic.

Brett, J. (1989). *The mitten*. New York: Scholastic.

Brown, M. (1990). *Arthur's pet business*. New York: Little, Brown.

Byars, B.C. (1991). *Wanted...mud blossom*. New York: Delacorte.

Cannon, J. (2005). *Crickwing*. New York: Voyager.

Carle, E. (1987). *The very hungry caterpillar*. New York: Scholastic.

Challoner, J. (2004). *Hurricane and tornado: Eyewitness books*. New York: Dorling Kindersley.

Ching, P. (2002). *The tale of Rabbit Island*. Waipahu, HI: Island Heritage Publishing.

Clark, B. (2000). *Amphibian: Eyewitness books*. New York: Dorling Kindersley.

French, J. (2003). *Hitler's daughter*. New York: HarperCollins.

George, J.C. (1990). *On the far side of the mountain*. New York: Dutton.

Giff, P.R. (1990). *Ronald Morgan goes to bat*. New York: Puffin.

Goldish, M. (2000). *The river road*. Northborough, MA: Newbridge Educational Publishing.

Goodrich, F., & Hackett, A. (1996). *The diary of Anne Frank*. Evanston, IL: McDougal Littell.

Harness, C. (2003). *Rabble rousers*. New York: Dutton.

Housel. (2005). *Time for kids: Mammals*. New York: HarperTrophy.

Jeunesse, G. (1992). *The river: A first discovery book*. New York: Scholastic.

Lobel, A. (1979). *Days with Frog and Toad*. New York: Scholastic.

Lowell, S. (1992). *The three little javelinas*. Flagstaff, AZ: Rising Moon.

MacLachlan, P. (1985). *Sarah, plain and tall*. New York: Joanna Cotler.

Martin, B., Jr. (1967). *Brown bear, brown bear, what do you see?* New York: Henry Holt.

McKissack, P., & Pinkney, J. (2001). *Goin' someplace special*. New York: Scholastic.

Parish, P. (1963). *Amelia Bedelia helps out*. New York: HarperCollins.

Paulsen, G. (1987). *Hatchet*. New York: Simon & Schuster.

Raffi. (1989). *Five little ducks*. New York: Crown.

Ricciuti, E.R. (1994). *What on earth is a chuckwalla?* Woodbridge, CT: Blackbirch.

Romero, L. (2005). *Habitats: Tropical rain forests*. Carlsbad, CA: Dominie.

Sachar, L. (1998). *Holes*. New York: Dell Yearling.

Schotter, R. (2000). *F is for freedom*. London: Dorling Kindersley Children.

Sendak, M. (1963). *Where the wild things are*. New York: Scholastic.

Seuss, Dr. (1960). *Green eggs and ham*. New York: Random House.

Wildsmith, B. (1982). *Cat on the mat*. Oxford, England: Oxford University Press.

INDEX

Note. Page numbers followed by *f* or *t* indicate figures or tables, respectively.